THE NATIONAL UNDERWR

2014 Healthcare Reform Facts
By Alson R. Martin, J.D., LL.M.

Authoritative and easy to use, *2014 Healthcare Reform Facts* is the single source for updated answers to Healthcare Reform questions arising out of the Patient Protection and Affordable Care Act (PPACA).

Organized in a convenient Q&A format to speed you to the information you need, *2014 Healthcare Reform Facts* provides you with hundreds of the most frequently asked questions and answers on the tax implications, compliance, and implementation of the new rules.

Authored by Alson R. Martin, Esq., a Partner of Lathrop & Gage, widely published author, and nationally recognized authority on healthcare reform, *2014 Healthcare Reform Facts* is the time-saving, reader-friendly, go-to-resource that helps you confidently navigate healthcare reform rules, regulations, as well as scores of requirements.

These are just some of the many vital questions answered in *Healthcare Reform Facts*:

- What are the effective dates of various requirements and penalties, and how are the fines levied?

- What are the special tax incentives that apply to small businesses?

- What are the revised W-2 reporting requirements for health benefits and who is exempt?

- What types of health insurance are not affected by healthcare reform?

- What are the reasons employers should or should not continue to offer health insurance in 2014? Why will different employers reach different decisions?

- What must be considered in changing employer or individual health insurance plans?

- How will the new health insurance exchanges (marketplaces) work and who can obtain a tax subsidy for buying a policy? What are the options for those in states without their own exchanges?

- What are the tax and other benefits of a grandfathered plan?

Highlights of the 2014 Edition

- Details on the employer mandate penalties and the impact of implementation delays. Most of the 2014 deadlines are not delayed.

- How to minimize the impact of the employer mandate.

- New guidance on and provisions of the updated SBC (HHS prescribed summary of benefits and coverage) template.

- The 90-day waiting period limit rule effective in 2014.

- State Insurance Exchanges (Marketplaces).

- Explanation of various requirements that have been eliminated or revised, such as W-2 Reporting and contraceptive care for religion-affiliated institutions.

- Information on the Exchange Notice required for most employers by October 1, 2013.

- Information on the unintended impact of the law on certain employer fringe benefits.

- Analysis of the federal SHOP Exchanges for small employers and their potential impact.

- Detailed information on the PCORI (Patient Centered Outcome Research Institute) fees and remittance requirements.

- Complete information on the Department of Labor Self-Help Healthcare Reform Grandfathered Plan Checklist.

- Details on health insurance purchased on the Exchanges.

To place additional orders for *2014 Healthcare Reform Facts* or any of our products, or for additional information, contact Customer Service at **1-800-543-0874**.

Keep Up with Critical Healthcare Reform Changes

Critical legislative changes that affect the subject matter in these books will be posted at **http://pro.nuco.com/booksupplements/healthcarereform**. Bookmark the site so that you can easily access new critical information that affects our clients and your business.

2014 HEALTHCARE REFORM FACTS

Employer & Individual Provisions • Financial & Tax Decisions • Grandfathered Health Plans • Implementation Timeline • Individual & Employer Mandates • Required Disclosure & Information Reporting • Revenue Raising Provisions • State & Federally Facilitated Exchanges

Alson R. Martin, J.D., LL. M.

ISBN 978-1-939829-53-5

Circular 230 Notice – The content in this publication is not intended or written to be used, and it cannot be used, for the purposes of avoiding U.S. tax penalties.

THE NATIONAL UNDERWRITER COMPANY

Copyright © 2013, 2014

The National Underwriter Company
5081 Olympic Blvd.
Erlanger, KY 41018

Printed in the United States of America

ABOUT SUMMIT BUSINESS MEDIA

Summit Business Media is the leading B2B media and information company serving the insurance, financial, legal and investment advisory markets. Summit strives to be "The Next Generation of Business Information" for executives and practitioners by providing breaking news and analysis, in-depth practice management strategies, business-building techniques and actionable data. Summit services the information needs of its customers through numerous channels, including digital, print, and live events. Summit publishes 16 magazines and 150 reference titles, operates 20 websites and hosts a dozen conferences, including the world's largest mining investment conference held each year in South Africa. Summit's Marketing Data division provides detailed information on millions of benefits plans, agents and advisors in the U.S.

Summit employs more than 300 employees in ten offices across the United States. For more information, please visit www.summitbusinessmedia.com.

ABOUT THE NATIONAL UNDERWRITER COMPANY

For over 110 years, The National Underwriter Company has been the first in line with the targeted tax, insurance, and financial planning information you need to make critical business decisions. Boasting nearly a century of expert experience, our reputable Editors are dedicated to putting accurate and relevant information right at your fingertips. With Tax Facts, Tools & Techniques, National Underwriter Advanced Markets, Field Guide, FC&S®, FC&S Legal® and other resources available in print, eBook, CD, and online, you can be assured that as the industry evolves National Underwriter will be at the forefront with the thorough and easy-to-use resources you rely on for success.

The National Underwriter Company
Update Service Notification

This National Underwriter Company publication is regularly updated to include coverage of developments and changes that affect the content. If you did not purchase this publication directly from The National Underwriter Company and you want to receive these important updates sent on a 30-day review basis and billed separately, please contact us at (800) 543-0874. Or you can mail your request with your name, company, address, and the title of the book to:

> The National Underwriter Company
> 5081 Olympic Boulevard
> Erlanger, KY 41018

If you purchased this publication from The National Underwriter Company directly, you have already been registered for the update service.

National Underwriter Company Contact Information

To order any National Underwriter Company title, please

- call 1-800-543-0874, 8-6 ET Monday – Thursday and 8 to 5 ET Friday

- online bookstore at www.nationalunderwriter.com, or

- mail to The National Underwriter Company, Orders Department, 5081 Olympic Blvd, Erlanger, KY 41018

PREFACE

2014 Healthcare Reform Facts is written for employers and their advisors. This edition of the book substantially updates the first edition to reflect the many recent developments. This book contains a thorough yet I hope practical discussion of the tax and non-tax rules relating to United States healthcare reform, as enacted in March 2010 by the Patient Protection and Affordable Care Act, and the volumes of regulations interpreting the law issued by the Internal Revenue Service and the Departments of Labor and Health and Human Services. This book incorporates not only the provisions of the original healthcare reform law but also recent developments concerning healthcare reform in terms of changes in the law, regulations, and other regulatory pronouncements.

2014 Healthcare Reform Facts is intended to help employers and their advisors understand, plan for, and comply with the many rules and requirements of our federal healthcare reform. To assist readers, important statutes, cases, and regulations are cited throughout the book. I also discuss the federal law's objectives and discuss the factors that will influence whether the law will work as intended. I also discuss some of the loopholes and unintended consequences of the law. The book also discusses several provisions of the original law that have already been discarded and will not go into effect.

As the reader is no doubt aware, the comprehensive federal changes concerning healthcare require that employers rethink past practices and choices about whether and how to offer healthcare benefits to employees. Forms and sample required notices are provided along with a detailed timeline of when each important provision of the rules goes into effect. I hope that you will find this book useful, both as a resource with answers for your questions as well as a starting point for some of the required notices documentation. Of course, this book does not provide legal advice for specific situations, which should be sought from a competent professional.

Alson R. Martin
September 2013

ABOUT THE AUTHOR

Alson R. Martin, J.D., LL.M is a Partner of Lathrop & Gage LLP in Overland Park, Kansas. The firm also has offices in Los Angeles, California; Denver and Boulder, Colorado; Washington, D.C.; Chicago, Illinois; Kansas City, St. Louis, Jefferson City, Springfield & Columbia, Missouri; Boston, Massachusetts; and New York, New York.

Al is a Fellow of the American College of Tax Counsel and American College of Employee Benefits Counsel, as well as a charter Life Member of the American Tax Policy Institute. He is listed in the book The Best Lawyers in America (from inception in three categories), Outstanding Lawyers of America, Missouri-Kansas Super Lawyers, Ingram's Best Lawyers in Kansas City (three categories), American Lawyer Media and Martindale-Hubbell™ Top Rated Lawyers in Health Care, and Guide to Leading U.S. Tax Lawyers. He was selected by Best Lawyers as the 2010 Kansas City, Kansas, Corporate Lawyer of the Year and 2013 Tax Lawyer of the Year.

Al is the author of *Healthcare Reform Facts* (2012), *Limited Liability Companies and Partnerships* (3rd edition, 2011), and coauthor of *Kansas Corporation Law & Practice (Including Tax Aspects)* (5th edition, 2011), and has written many articles in various publications. He was also Technical Editor of Panel Publication's monthly newsletter *The 401k Advisor* from 1990- 2012. . He has published numerous articles and made hundreds of speeches. Mr. Martin was for many years cochair and speaker at the Annual Advanced Course of Study Professional Service Organizations, a faculty member for the ALI-ABA Courses Estate Planning for the Family Business Owner and Sophisticated Estate Planning Techniques, as well as a speaker at many national meetings of the American Bar Association Tax Section, ESOP Association Annual Convention, Mountain States Pension Conference, Southern Federal Tax Conference, Notre Dame Estate Planning Symposium, and the Ohio Pension Conference, as well as the Alabama, Georgia Federal, Kansas, Missouri, and Tennessee Tax conferences.

He is President and Director of the Small Business Council of America, and he was a delegate to the 1995 White House Conference on Small Business and the 2006 Savers' Summit, Washington, D.C. Mr. Martin has testified in Congress.

Al graduated with Highest Distinction from Kansas University and was a Phi Beta Kappa, Summerfield Scholar, and Student Body President. He received his J.D., *cum laude*, and LL.M. in taxation from New York University School of Law, where he was a Root-Tilden Scholar and Note & Comment Editor, *New York University Law Review*.

ABOUT THE EDITORIAL DIRECTOR

Diana B. Reitz, CPCU, AAI, is the editorial director of the Professional Publishing Division of The National Underwriter Company. As such she is responsible for the overall integrity of all division publications. She previously was the Director of the Property & Casualty Publishing Department of the Reference Division.

Ms. Reitz has been with The National Underwriter Company since 1998, when she was named editor of the *Risk Financing and Self-Insurance* manuals and associate editor of the *FC&S Bulletins*®. She also is coauthor of the National Underwriter publication, *Workers Compensation Coverage Guide, 1st Edition*, and has edited and contributed to numerous other books and publications, including *The Tools & Techniques of Risk Management and Insurance, Claims* magazine, and *National Underwriter Property & Casualty* magazine.

Prior to joining The National Underwriter she was with a regional insurance broker, concentrating on commercial insurance. She is a graduate of the University of Maryland and St. Francis College.

EDITORIAL SERVICES

Connie L. Jump, Supervisor, Electronic Publication Production
Patti O'Leary, Editorial Assistant

TABLE OF CONTENTS

APPENDICES

Keep Up with Critical Healthcare Reform Changes

Critical legislative changes that affect the subject matter in these books will be posted at http://pro.nuco.com/booksupplements/healthcarereform. Bookmark the site so that you can easily access new critical information that affects our clients and your business.

TABLE OF CONTENTS

APPENDICES

Keep Up with Critical Healthcare Reform Changes

Critical legislative changes that affect the subject matter in these books will be posted at http://pro.nuco.com/booksupplements/healthcarereform. Bookmark the site so that you can easily access new critical information that affects our clients and your business.

HEALTHCARE REFORM FACTS
COMPLETE LIST OF QUESTIONS
PART I: GOALS AND MAJOR COMPONENTS OF HEALTHCARE REFORM
Overview

1. What is healthcare reform?

2. What terms and acronyms will be used repeatedly in this book?

3. What does health reform do?

4. Will healthcare reform work to reduce costs?

5. What is the focus of this book?

6. What benefits are regulated by health reform?

7. What health benefits are not affected by health reform?

8. Do the provisions of healthcare reform only apply to businesses and residents in the United States?

9. Where are the provisions of the health reform law found?

10. How does healthcare reform provide for expanded coverage?

11. Has healthcare reform been revised since it was enacted?

Health Coverage Not Affected by Healthcare Reform: "Excepted Benefits" and Retiree-Only Plans

12. What benefits are not governed by PPACA, the 2010 health reform law?

13. What are the "excepted benefits" that are not covered by the health reform law?

14. What are the retiree-only health plans that are not governed by PPACA?

15. Is the retiree-only exemption available for self-funded and insured plans?

16. From which PPACA mandates are retiree-only plans exempt?

17. Does the 2018 "Cadillac Tax" apply to retiree-only health plans?

18. Who are current employees for purposes of the retiree-only exemption?

Employer and Individual Mandates
See Part XI for a Complete Discussion of the Employer Mandate Provisions and Appendix B Copies of Several Mandatory Notices

55. How can employers use the Code section 36B in its health-insurance planning?

56. May an employer establish an employee contribution schedule and allow employees to be eligible for reduced contributions if they provide evidence that their required contributions would otherwise be in excess of the affordability limits?

57. Can applicable large employers with 50 or more full-time equivalent employees avoid the employer mandate penalty by offering an actuarially equivalent contribution to an HSA or FSA so that employees can buy health care coverage on the exchange or in the private non-group market?

58. What is minimum essential coverage?

59. What individuals are not subject to the individual mandate?

60. Could you provide more detail on persons who are not subject to the individual mandate because they are not "applicable individuals"?

61. How is the individual mandate tax penalty enforced?

Health Plan and Insurance Changes: Coverage Mandates

62. What are the ten essential health benefits (EHBs) required by the 2010 federal health reform? How do state health insurance mandates relate to them?

63. How will the essential health benefits mandate be implemented?

64. What is required to become a state selected EHB-benchmark plan?

65. What new requirements are there for grandfathered health plans?

66. What new requirements are there for new and non-grandfathered health plans?

State Health Insurance Exchanges

67. What are the state health insurance exchanges?

68. How do employers use exchanges?

69. Are there any issues with state exchanges?

70. How do individuals apply for health insurance from an Exchange?

71. What is a loophole in the law as to exchange purchased insurance and its impact on insureds and providers?

72. Were there any operating state exchanges prior to 2014?

73. What are the functions of the state health insurance exchanges?

Health Reform's Medicaid Expansion

91. What is the Medicaid expansion in the 2010 health reform law?

92. Can a state later change its 2014 decision as to whether to participate in the Medicaid expansion?

PART II: IMPACT OF HEALTHCARE REFORM ON EMPLOYER FRINGE BENEFITS

Fringe Benefit Tax Planning

Retaining a Grandfathered Plan; Benefits of a SIMPLE Cafeteria Plan, and 2013 Limits on Health FSAs

93. Why should employers verify whether they have a grandfathered health plan?

94. Why should an eligible employer consider a SIMPLE cafeteria plan?

95. What are the limits on health FSAs in cafeteria plans (also called flex plans)?

96. Is FSA, HSA, MERP, or HRA subject to the PHSA §2711 prohibition on annual and lifetime dollar limits?

97. Can 2013 fiscal year cafeteria plan elections to purchase health insurance be changed mid-year to purchase insurance on an exchange or in the employer-offered plan for plan years beginning in 2013?

PART III: TIMELINE FOR IMPLEMENTATION OF PROVISIONS: WHAT NEEDS TO BE DONE AND WHEN

98. What are the major components of healthcare reform and when are they effective?

PART IV: HEALTH REFORM PROVISIONS THAT HAVE BEEN REPEALED, EXPIRED, OR NOT IMPLEMENTED

Free Choice Vouchers – Repealed

99. What were free choice vouchers and what were they intended to do?

100. When was the provision for free choice vouchers repealed?

101. What is the impact of the repeal of free choice vouchers?

Expanded 1099 Requirements – Repealed

102. What were the repealed 1099 requirements?

103. When and how were the expanded 1099 requirements repealed?

104. Did the repeal of the expanded 1099 reporting repeal the penalties for 1099 failures that were increased in 2010?

105. Why were the expanded 1099 requirements repealed?

Early Retiree Reinsurance Program (ERRP) – Expired

106. How was the Early Retiree Reinsurance Program (ERRP) intended to work?

Federal Long-Term Care Benefit – Not Implemented

107. What was the federal long-term care benefit for which employees could have elected to pay?

108. Why was the federal long-term care program cancelled by HHS?

PART V: SMALL BUSINESS PROVISIONS

Employer Income Tax Credit for Health Insurance

109. Which employers are eligible for the tax credit for the purchase of health insurance available in 2010 and thereafter?

110. Can more than one employer be treated as a single employer for determining the credit available, the number of employers, and the average compensation?

111. How is the employer 50 percent payment requirement applied?

112. Which persons are not counted in determining the number of employees or their average compensation?

113. How much is the employer tax credit for employer purchase of health insurance?

114. How is the employer tax credit calculated?

115. How is the average annual wage calculated?

116. How does the employer health insurance tax credit change in 2014?

Simple Cafeteria Plan

No Employer Mandate

Automatic Enrollment Exclusion

W-2 Reporting Exemption

PART VI: GRANDFATHERED HEALTH PLANS

PART VII: PHSA COVERAGE MANDATES AND ENFORCEMENT

Coverage Mandates and Enforcement

Annual Limits on Essential Health Benefits Limited, Then Eliminated

Lifetime Limits on Essential Health Benefits Eliminated

Dependent Coverage Extended to Children until Age Twenty-six

Wellness Program Rules

227. What are wellness programs?

228. How are stand-alone wellness programs treated?

229. How are wellness programs that relate to group health plans regulated?

Bringing Down the Cost of Coverage
Medical Loss Ratio (MLR) Rules; PHSA, ERISA and Tax Ramifications

230. What are the health reform provisions relating to reducing the cost of health insurance?

231. When were the final MLR regulations issued?

232. How may the insurance company rebates be paid to persons ("enrollees") purchasing individual policies in the individual market?

233. How are insurers to pay rebates in connection with employer health insurance plans?

234. What if the plan has been terminated when the rebate is due?

235. What if the MLR limits on insurers cause financial problems for insurers?

236. Do the MLR rules limit commissions paid to brokers and agents?

237. How is the MLR computed?

238. What if an insurer has several entities licensed in a state?

239. What are the rules for MLR rebates for state and local government (non-federal) group health plans?

240. What are the rules for group insured health plans sponsored by employers and subject to ERISA?

241. How does an employer comply with the three-month rule?

242. How does an employer decide whether an MLR belongs to the employer or the employees when the health plan is not funded through a trust?

243. How does an employer decide how amounts belonging to employees are used?

244. What are the special considerations when an employer has a plan with several insurance options?

245. What are the special issues if insurance is paid in part by employee pre-tax cafeteria plan payments?

Exchange Notice Required

HIPAA Electronic Transactions and Operating Rules

Automatic Enrollment

New Health Insurance Nondiscrimination Provisions

285. Who is liable to pay the excise tax?

286. How is the liability for the excise tax reported?

287. What is the penalty if an insured plan incorrectly believes that it is grandfathered, but it is not?

288. What if the failure to meet the nondiscrimination rules is due to reasonable cause and not willful neglect?

Waiting Period Limits and Eligibility Requirements

289. What is a waiting period?

290. What is the maximum waiting period for essential health benefits in 2014?

291. When does a waiting period begin?

292. Is the ninety-day limit extended if employees take additional time to elect coverage?

293. What other eligibility requirements can an employer have?

294. What other prohibitions apply to the eligibility requirements?

295. How are permissible eligibility requirements applied to part-time and variable hour employees?

Guaranteed Coverage
No Preexisting Conditions or Health Status Discrimination for Essential Health Benefits

296. How does health reform affect the ability of a health insurance policy or plan covering essential health conditions not to deny coverage or reimbursement for preexisting conditions (PCEs)?

297. What is a preexisting condition (PCE)?

298. Are certificates of creditable coverage still required?

Cost-Sharing Limits

299. What are the cost-sharing limits on out-of-pocket expenses and annual deductibles?

300. What are the 2014 limits for annual deductibles?

Clinical Trials and Coverage

301. What patient protections does the law create for persons participating in clinical trials?

Fair Insurance Premiums
Health Insurance Rating Rules

No Discrimination against Providers

PART VIII: REQUIRED DISCLOSURES AND INFORMATION REPORTING

W-2 Reporting Beginning 2013

Annual Fee on Manufacturers and Importers of Branded Drugs

369. What is the annual fee on manufacturers and importers of branded drugs?

370. When is this new tax effective?

Repeal of Employer-Paid Retiree Prescription Drug Rebate Income Tax Exclusion

371. What was the employer-paid retiree prescription drug rebate income tax exclusion?

Tax on Sale of Medical Devices

372. What is the new tax on the sale of taxable medical devices?

373. What is a taxable medical device?

Expanded Medicare Tax on Wages

374. What is the expanded Medicare tax on wages that goes into effect January 1, 2013?

New 3.8 Percent Medicare Tax on Investment Income

375. What is the new 3.8 percent Medicare tax on investment income, effective in 2013?

376. Does this new Medicare tax on investment income apply to estates and trusts also?

377. How does this new Medicare tax on investment income apply to S corporation electing small business trusts?

378. What is "net investment income?"

379. How does the Medicare tax on investment income apply to pass-through entities?

380. What items are not subject to the Medicare tax on net investment income?

Cafeteria Plan Changes
$2,500 Cap on Employee FSA Contributions

381. What are the cafeteria plan changes enacted in health reform?

382. To what does the new $2,500 FSA limit apply?

383. What clarifications has the IRS made regarding issues relating to the $2,500 health FSA employee deferral limit?

384. What is the deadline to amend a cafeteria plan to limit employee deferrals into health FSAs?

Two Alternate Employer Mandate Penalties

439. In general, what are the two alternative employer mandate penalties?

440. What is an employer offer of health coverage?

441. How does the 4980H(a) penalty work?

442. How does the 4980H(b) alternative penalty work?

443. What does "affordable value" for a plan mean?

444. When does an employer health plan provide minimum value?

445. When is employer coverage unaffordable?

446. What safe harbors are available for an employer to determine if its health coverage is affordable?

HRA Reimbursement Arrangements and the Employer Penalty

447. Can an employer health reimbursement account (HRA) that pays or reimburses employees for exchange purchased health insurance qualify as employer-provided minimum essential coverage to avoid the 4980H(a) penalty?

Separate Assessment of Shared Responsibility Penalties within Controlled Group

448. Where there is an applicable large employer comprised of related employers, how is the employer mandate penalty, if applicable, calculated?

449. Will the insured plan nondiscrimination requirements, when effective, impact health insurance offered by related employers?

Determining Applicable Large Employer Status

450. How are those "applicable large employers" potentially subject to the employer mandate penalty determined?

451. What if payroll periods begin after the calendar year starts or end after the calendar year ends?

452. What if the employer only has fifty or more full time and full-time equivalent employees for four or fewer months?

Counting U.S. Employees
Full-time and Part-time

453. How are employees' U.S. hours of service counted and determined?

454. How are hours of service counted for hourly workers?

477. What happens after variable-hour and seasonal employees have been employed for at least one standard measurement period?

478. Can you provide examples of how these rules work?

Anti-abuse Rules and Staffing (Employee Leasing or Professional Employment Organization) Firms

479. Are any anti-abuse rules contemplated for employers who shift employees to staffing companies?

Planning to Minimize Impact of Employer Mandate Penalties

480. Since the employer mandate penalty is calculated solely based on full-time (thirty hours of service per week) employees, can an employer reduce or eliminate the mandate's impact by reducing hours of service to less than thirty hours per week?

481. Is outsourcing work a solution to reduce the employee count?

482. How can an applicable large employer offer low cost health benefits and still avoid or reduce the impact of the employer mandate penalty?

483. How does an employer avoid the 4980H(a) employer mandate penalty?

484. How does an employer avoid or reduce the 4980H(b) employer mandate penalty?

485. How does an applicable large employer utilize the 95 percent rule in planning for the employer mandate penalties?

PART I: GOALS AND MAJOR COMPONENTS OF HEALTHCARE REFORM

Overview

1. What is healthcare reform?

The term "healthcare reform" refers to the healthcare law passed in March 2010, known as the Affordable Care Act ("ACA") or the Patient Protection and Affordable Care Act (PPACA),[1] including regulations and other guidance implementing that law. The effective date of the law is March 23, 2010, although various provisions have their own effective dates from January 1, 2010, (the small business income tax credit) through 2018.

2. What terms and acronyms will be used repeatedly in this book?

The following are the most common terms and acronyms that will be used throughout this book.

- **Applicable Large Employer.** An employer with fifty or more full-time employees.

- **Code.** Internal Revenue Code, as amended.

- **Employer Mandate.** A tax penalty on certain employers not offering a group health plan or offering one that does not meet specified requirements.

- **ERISA.** The Employee Retirement Income Security Act of 1974, as amended, which governs employer-sponsored, qualified retirement plans and welfare benefit plans, including group health plans.

- **Essential Health Benefits.** The benefits that must be offered in nongrandfathered plans sold in the small group market on or outside of an exchange beginning in 2015. Grandfathered plans, self-insured group health plans, and health insurance coverage offered in the large group market are not required to offer essential health benefits. *Minimum essential coverage* is a separate concept. It is the term used to describe the coverage required to fulfill the individual mandate and coverage that employers must offer to avoid the employer mandate tax.

- **Exchange, State Exchange," or Health Insurance Exchange.** State or multi-state exchanges where health insurance options may be compared and purchased.

---

1. See H.R. 3590, the Patient Protection and Affordable Care Act, Pub. L. No. 111-148 (PPACA), signed on March 23, 2010; and H.R. 4872, the Health Care and Education Reconciliation Act of 2010, Pub. L. No. 111-152 (HCERA), signed on March 30, 2010.

- **Grandfathered Health Plan.** A group health plan in existence on March 23, 2010, that meets specified requirements and is exempt from certain health reform requirements.

- **Group Health Plans.** Plans provided by employers or employee organizations (unions) providing comprehensive health benefits. The term does not include "excepted benefits" or retiree-only plans.

- **Healthcare Reform.** Health reform under the Patient Protection and Affordable Care Act of 2010.

- **Health FSA.** Flexible savings accounts (FSAs), often found in cafeteria plans (sometimes called "flex plans"), for health care, but not dependent care.

- **Health Reform.** The 2010 federal law known as the Affordable Care Act (ACA) or the Patient Protection and Affordable Care Act (PPACA), including regulations and other guidance implementing that law. Health reform amended the Code, ERISA, and the Public Health Service Act (PHSA).

- **HHS.** The U.S. Department of Health and Human Services.

- **HIPAA.** The Health Insurance Portability and Accountability Act of 1996.

- **Individual Mandate.** The tax penalty imposed on individuals (unless they are exempt) who do not have health coverage from an employer or individual health insurance.

- **MEC.** Minimum essential coverage.

- **MLR.** Medical Loss Ratio, a concept limiting how much insurers can pay for administrative expense for health insurance governed by health reform.

- **PHSA or PHS Act.** Public Health Service Act.

- **QHP.** A qualified health plan offered on a state health insurance exchange.

- **SBC.** A summary of benefits and coverage summarizing health plan or health insurance benefits that must meet specified requirements.

3. What does health reform do?

The 2010 law has and will materially change healthcare law in the United States. Healthcare reform included an array of new requirements for individuals, employers, health plans, and healthcare providers. The purpose of this law is to:[1]

- make insurance companies more accountable,

- lower healthcare costs,

- guarantee more choice of providers and plans,

- make health care more available (including but not limited to eliminating exclusions for pre-existing conditions as well as Medicare and Medicaid expansions),

- expand preventive services, and

- promote the use of health information technology through electronic medical records, and generally to enhance the quality, safety, and coordination of health care.

4. Will healthcare reform work to reduce costs?

The healthcare reform law has a carrot and stick approach. One big carrot is the subsidies individuals can receive for purchasing insurance on an exchange if their income is less than 400 percent of federal poverty level. Two of the sticks are the employer mandate and the individual mandate penalties.

There are low participation rates in company-sponsored health insurance, even in many companies that offer health coverage and especially those with lower wage workers. One CEO has asked employees why they do not participate in the employer provided coverage.[2] The answers he received are typical:

- Younger workers were unconcerned about illness or injury.

- Others already had insurance through a spouse or parent.

- A significant number said they declined coverage because they could get medical treatment "for free at the emergency room." This fact remains true in and after 2014 as the federal law known as EMTALA requires hospitals to provide emergency services, even to those who cannot pay.

---

1. See http://xnet.kp.org/reform/guiding_principles.htm; John K. Iglehart, "Implementing Health Care Reform — An Interview with HHS Secretary Kathleen Sebelius" 364 N Engl. J. Med. pp. 297-99 (Jan. 27, 2011).
2. CEO's-Eye View of ObamaCare, Wall Street Journal p. A-17 (July 22, 2013), available at http://online.wsj.com/article/SB100014241278873 23309404578613653344566068.html?mod=hp_opinion.

- Among those who had signed up, many said it was because they were concerned about developing a medical condition and then being unable to get affordable coverage due to this preexisting condition. Significantly, in 2014, these people will be able to obtain health insurance on exchanges despite any preexisting conditions, which will further disincentivize enrollment in both employer and exchange offered health insurance.

This reality leads to the idea that healthcare reform may be proven to be more expensive and not work as hoped. The law's success depends on young, healthy people who are lower risk signing up for health insurance to offset the costs of insuring individuals with preexisting conditions, many who in the past have been unable to purchase insurance and who are at higher risk for the need for expensive medical care. If predominantly high-risk individuals sign up on the state exchanges, that health insurance will be expensive. Nevertheless, people will still be able to get medical care at the emergency room. Further, the law in 2014 prohibits insurers from denying coverage because of preexisting conditions. Therefore, individuals have even less incentive to purchase health insurance as they will no longer have much incentive to get health insurance as a hedge against the possibility of developing a medical condition when they are presently healthy.

One of the law's answers to these issues is the individual mandate penalty tax on uninsured individuals that goes into effect in 2014. The penalty in 2014 is $95 or 1 percent of household income, whichever is greater. It increases in 2016 to $695 or 2.5 percent of household income, whichever is greater. The individual mandate is not sufficient to change the behavior of many persons who are not otherwise inclined to buy health insurance. A person making $50,000 per year with no health coverage will be subject to an initial individual mandate penalty of $500 and a maximum penalty of $1,250 in 2016. The typical share of employee cost for company sponsored health coverage will often exceed this amount, often by a significant amount. Low paid employees who earn, for example, $11,500 per year would be subject to an initial penalty of $115 in 2014 and a maximum penalty of $695 in 2016. Such workers' share of health insurance premiums, even if there is an exchange insurance subsidy, will again often be much more than any potential penalty.

5. What is the focus of this book?

This book will focus on the health reform requirements for employers and individuals. It does not discuss in any detail the rules that relate to healthcare providers, such as physicians, hospitals, or accountable care organizations, etc., except in their capacity as employers. For this book, health reform primarily relates to the requirements for major medical coverage offered by employers, both insured and self-insured, and purchased by individuals from insurance companies.

The book is written in several parts, and each part covers specific provisions of healthcare reform as it pertains to employers and individuals.

Many healthcare reform provisions (such as the individual and employer mandates, healthcare exchanges, and the ban on preexisting conditions) go into effect in 2014 or 2015. However, many of the group health plan and individual health insurance requirements for content, design, and administration are effective sooner, and many are now in effect. Part III of this book contains a timeline as to when the various requirements become effective. Part IV discusses financial and tax decisions that should be made by the end of 2012, although some can be made later as well.

6. What benefits are regulated by health reform?

The 2010 health reform law imposes many new requirements on individual health insurance policies and group health plans, both insured and self-insured. The new requirements on group health plans are in addition to those previously imposed by HIPAA in 1996.

A group health plan is defined as an insured or self-insured plan of, or contributed to by, an employer (including a self-employed person) or employee organization to provide health care (directly or otherwise) to the employees, former employees, the employer, others associated or formerly associated with the employer in a business relationship, or their families.[1] The definition of a group health plan does not include any group health plan that has fewer than two participants who are current employees—one subset of which is retiree-only plans.[2] While this is an important exclusion, there are a number of open issues regarding the scope of retiree-only plans. In addition, a group health plan does not include a plan offering "excepted benefits."[3]

The Health Insurance Portability and Accountability Act of 1996 (HIPAA) imposed several new requirements for group health coverage that are designed to provide protection to health plan participants. These protections include:

- limitations on exclusions from coverage based on pre-existing conditions;

- the prohibition of discrimination on the basis of health status;[4]

- guaranteed renewability in multiemployer plans and certain employer welfare arrangements;[5]

- standards relating to benefits for mothers and newborns;[6]

- mental health benefits parity;[7] and

---

1. IRC Secs. 9832(a) and 5000(b)(1).
2. ERISA Sec. 701(a); IRC Sec. 9801(a).
3. See Preamble to Grandfathered Health Plan Regulations, 75 Fed. Reg. 34537, 34539 (June 17, 2010) (confirming that the exceptions in the IRC and ERISA still exist, and announcing an HHS nonenforcement policy with respect to the PHSA provisions).
4. ERISA Sec. 702 and IRC Sec. 9802.
5. ERISA Sec. 703; IRC Sec. 9803(a).
6. ERISA Sec. 711 and IRC Sec. 9811.
7. ERISA Sec. 712 and IRC Sec. 9812.

- coverage of dependent students on medically necessary leaves of absence.[1] [These requirements are located in HIPAA Chapter 100 of Subtitle K, Group Health Plan requirements.

For plan years beginning on or after May 21, 2009, Code Section 9834 made it explicit that the tax imposed by Code Section 4980D applies to any failure to satisfy the requirements of Code Sections 9801 through 9812. The excise tax is $100 for each day in the noncompliance period with respect to each individual to whom such failure relates. Civil suits may be brought for violation of certain HIPAA requirements under ERISA Section 701.[2]

7. What health benefits are not affected by health reform?

Health reform does not change the rules for "excepted benefits" or retiree-only plans. These items will be discussed below, at Q 12 through Q 22.

8. Do the provisions of healthcare reform only apply to businesses and residents in the United States?

No. HHS has issued a letter to the Governors of the U.S. territories describing the applicability of the healthcare reform Exchange requirements and the employer and individual mandates, as well as the premium tax credits, to their governments and residents.[3] U.S. territories are American Samoa, Guam, Northern Mariana Islands, Puerto Rico, and the U.S. Virgin Islands.[4] The letter states that territories have until October 1, 2013, to notify HHS if they have elected to establish an Exchange, and states that HHS will not operate federally facilitated Exchanges in the territories. Territories electing not to establish an Exchange will instead receive increased federal Medicaid funding.

The letter also addresses three Exchange-related tax provisions as they apply to the territories: the individual mandate penalty,[5] the premium tax credit,[6] and the employer shared responsibility (employer mandate or play or pay) penalty.[7] HHS offers general observations based on its consultation with the Treasury. First, residents of territories are not subject to the individual penalty due to statutory exemption.[8] HHS states that the applicability of the individual premium tax credit depends on whether a territory's tax laws mirror the federal tax Code. In mirror territories that establish an Exchange, residents would be eligible for the premium tax credit, whereas that would not be the case in a non-mirror territory, although a separate financial assistance mechanism may be established.

---

1. ERISA Sec. 714 and IRC Sec. 9813.
2. ERISA Sec. 502. Group health plans of governmental employers and churches that are exempt from ERISA by virtue of ERISA Sec. 4(b) are not subject to ERISA Sec. 701. Instead, plans of nonconforming, nonfederal governmental employers and church plans generally are subject to the parallel provisions under the PHSA.
3. Information for the Territories Regarding the Affordable Care Act (Dec. 10, 2012) at http://cciio.cms.gov/resources/files/gov-letter-territories-12-10-2012.pdf.
4. IRC Sec. 937(a).
5. IRC Sec. 5000A.
6. IRC Sec. 36B.
7. IRC Sec. 4980H.
8. IRC Sec. 5000A(f)(4)(B).

The employer shared responsibility penalty under Code section 4980H does not apply in mirror or non-mirror territories. Mirror territories are not obligated to mirror excise tax provisions, and this penalty is an excise tax. Non-mirror territories have their own tax codes and, thus, are not subject to Code section 4980H. However, a territory could adopt a comparable provision.

9. Where are the provisions of the health reform law found?

PPACA, the health reform law, is contained in three places:

- the Internal Revenue Code,

- the Employee Retirement Income Security Act (ERISA), and

- the Public Health Service Act (PHS Act or PHSA).

For health reform, the IRS, Department of Labor (DOL), and Department of Health and Human Services (HHS) respectively administer the laws. Many of the regulations are co-authored by all three federal agencies. The states have the primary authority to enforce the PHSA provisions with respect to group and individual market health insurance issuers, and HHS will only step in to the extent HHS believes the state has failed to substantially enforce these provisions. HHS, IRS and DOL have already issued several PPACA regulations, some interim, and some final and more regulations are expected. In many cases, the law is vague, and regulations are needed to know what it means in practice.

10. How does healthcare reform provide for expanded coverage?

The law does this in several ways. Healthcare reform provides incentives for (1) individuals without health coverage to buy insurance and (2) employers to provide group health benefits. It also requires employer-provided group health plans and insurers to meet certain standards, with some exceptions for plans and coverage existing on March 23, 2010, referred to as "grandfathered health plans." New rules contain requirements for health plans and health insurance, including coverage requirements and administration. Provisions exist, for example, for eliminating preexisting condition exclusions, limiting waiting periods, eliminating annual and lifetime limits, expanded adult child coverage, and claims appeals.

Expanded health coverage is encouraged with a carrot-and-stick approach. The carrots include mechanisms to expand coverage through state health insurance exchanges and tax subsidies for specified individuals and small employers. The sticks include a tax penalty for individuals, with several exceptions, who do not have health insurance (called the individual mandate), as well as penalties for certain employers with fifty or more full-time equivalent employees who provide:

(1)   no healthcare benefits or

(2)   coverage that does not meet several tests, including affordability, minimum essential health benefits, and a minimum employer contribution.

The penalties are known as the employer mandate.

11. Has healthcare reform been revised since it was enacted?

Yes. Part II of this book discusses the provisions that have already expired, been repealed, or will not be implemented. Part III provides a timeline of implementation dates, many of which have been revised since 2010.

Health Coverage Not Affected by Healthcare Reform: "Excepted Benefits" and Retiree-Only Plans

12. What benefits are not governed by PPACA, the 2010 health reform law?

The law does not apply to "excepted benefits" and retiree-only health plans.

13. What are the "excepted benefits" that are not covered by the health reform law?

The IRS, Labor Department and Public Health Service Act regulations identically define excepted benefits.[1]

Excepted benefits are:

(1)   Accident, or disability income insurance, or any combination thereof; a supplement to liability insurance; liability insurance, including general liability insurance and automobile liability insurance; workers' compensation or similar insurance; automobile medical payment insurance; credit-only insurance; coverage for on-site medical clinics; or other similar insurance coverage, specified in regulations;[2]

(2)   Benefits not subject to requirements if offered separately and not part of a health plan:

   ○   limited scope dental or vision benefits;

   ○   long-term care, nursing home care, home healthcare, community-based care, or any combination thereof; and

   ○   similar benefits specified in regulations;[3]

(3)   Benefits not subject to requirements if offered as independent, noncoordinated benefits. (Coverage only for a specified disease or illness; or hospital indemnity or other fixed indemnity insurance;[4]

---

1. Treas. Reg. 26 CFR §54.9831–1(c), Labor Reg. 29 CFR §2590.732(c), PHSA Reg. 45 CFR §146.145(c).
2. IRC Sec. 9832(c)(1).
3. IRC Sec. 9832(c)(2).
4. IRC Sec. 9832(c)(3).

(4)   Medicare supplemental health insurance (so-called "Medigap insurance") offered by a separate policy.[1]

PPACA inadvertently removed the exemption for retiree-only plans and "excepted benefits" from the PHS Act, but left those exemptions intact in the Internal Revenue Code and ERISA. The preamble to the interim final grandfathered plan regulations clarifies the issue by stating that the exemption for retiree-only plans and excepted benefit plans still applies for those plans subject to the Code and ERISA. Thus, with respect to retiree-only and excepted benefits, the regulators have decided that they will read the PHS Act as if an exemption for retiree-only and excepted benefit plans is still in effect, and they have encouraged state insurance regulators to do the same.

14. What are the retiree-only health plans that are not governed by PPACA?

A retiree-only plan that is exempt from PPACA's mandates for a particular plan year is defined as any group health plan (and group health insurance coverage offered in connection with a group health plan) with less than two participants who are current employees. Exempt retiree plans covering dependents need not follow the adult child to age twenty-six rule but they must follow any applicable state rule unless the plan is self-insured, in which case state insurance law does not apply.

15. Is the retiree-only exemption available for self-funded and insured plans?

Yes, the retiree-only exemption applies to both self-funded and insured plans. PPACA technically eliminates the exemption in the Public Health Services Act for "plans with less than two participants who are current employees" but preserves the exemption under the parallel provisions in ERISA and the Internal Revenue Code.

The PHSA is applicable to governmental plans and to issuers of insured plans. The preamble to the PPACA grandfathering Interim Final Regulation, however, confirms that the retiree-only plan exemption under ERISA and the Code has been preserved, and also provides that, even though the exemption was technically eliminated from the PHSA:[2]

- HHS will not enforce the requirements of HIPAA or PPACA with regard to non-federal governmental retiree-only plans, and

- states are encouraged not to apply the provisions of PPACA to issuers of retiree-only plans (i.e., insured plans).

---

1. IRC Sec. 9832(c)(4).
2. 75 Fed. Reg. 34538, 34540.

16. From which PPACA mandates are retiree-only plans exempt?

Retiree-only plans are exempt from the PPACA-mandated "insurance market reforms" listed below (referring to PPACA sections):

- Section 2711 – No lifetime or annual limits

- Section 2712 – Prohibition on rescission

- Section 2713 – Coverage of preventive health services

- Section 2714 – Extension of dependent coverage

- Section 2715 – Development and utilization of uniform explanation of coverage documents and standardized definitions

- Section 2715A – Provision of additional information

- Section 2716 – Prohibition on discrimination in favor of highly compensated individuals for insured plans

- Section 2717 – Ensuring the quality of care reporting

- Section 2718 – Medical loss ratio restrictions

- Section 2719 – Required appeals process

- Section 2719A – Patient protections (selecting providers and emergency room services)

- Section 2794 – Rate review

- Section 2704 – Prohibition of preexisting condition exclusions or other discrimination based on health status

- Section 2701 – Restrictions on what criteria can be used in rating and rate band limits

- Section 2702 – Guaranteed issue

- Section 2703 – Guaranteed renewability

- Section 2705 – Prohibiting discrimination against individual participants and beneficiaries based on health status

- Section 2706 — Non-discrimination towards healthcare providers

- Section 2707 — Cost-sharing requirements and essential benefit requirements

- Section 2708 — Prohibition on waiting periods of more than ninety days

- Section 2709 — Coverage for individuals participating in approved clinical trials

17. Does the 2018 "Cadillac Tax" apply to retiree-only health plans?

It is unclear to what extent other PPACA provisions apply to retiree-only plans. For example, the excise tax on high-cost employer-sponsored health coverage[1] applies to "qualified retirees." The Cadillac Tax is discussed in more detail in Part VIII of this book.

18. Who are current employees for purposes of the retiree-only exemption?

The HIPAA regulations do not provide any guidance defining who is a current employee for purposes of the retiree-only plan exemption. However, a retiree who is rehired as an employee (and receives either a W-2 or 1099 for the year) should be treated as a current (i.e., active) employee that counts against retiree-only plan status and should be covered under the ERISA plan maintained for purposes of current employees immediately upon rehire.

HHS issued an FAQ indicating that the retiree-only exemption may be available for plans that cover both retirees and persons on long-term disability. Until further guidance is issued, HHS will treat such plans as satisfying the retiree-only exemption. To the extent future guidance on this issue is more restrictive with respect to the availability of the retiree-only exemption; the guidance will be prospective, applying to plan years that begin sometime after its issuance.

19. What should plan sponsors do in order to demonstrate that they have established a retiree-only plan that satisfies the exemption?

For ERISA welfare plans, the plan sponsor should maintain a separate plan document and summary plan description (SPD) and file a separate Form 5500 (if it has more than 100 participants at the beginning of the plan year). Plan sponsors that do not currently maintain a separate retiree-only plan but intend to establish one on a prospective basis for the following plan year should also follow these steps.

For non-ERISA retiree-only plans (for example, government plans), the plan should be a separate document and cover fewer than two current employees, other than dependents, who are beneficiaries for this purpose. Because non-ERISA plans do not file a Form 5500 or maintain SPDs as required by ERISA, as part of the certification process some insurance companies will require formal documentation describing the plan's eligibility rules.

---

1. PPACA §9001; new IRC Sec. 4980I.

20. What will happen if a plan sponsor does not amend its group health plan to carve out retirees into a separate retiree-only ERISA plan?

If a plan sponsor continues covering current employees and retirees under the same ERISA plan, the retiree-only plan exemption will most likely not be met. This means that PPACA's requirements will apply. Plans that are not exempt from PPACA still may be "grandfathered" if they were in effect on March 23, 2010, and meet the criteria in PPACA for grandfathered status. Grandfathered plans are subject to some but not all of the PPACA mandates.

21. Can a plan sponsor amend its plan to carve out retirees into a retiree-only plan and preserve the grandfather status of the plan for current (i.e., active) employees?

Yes. Regulators have informally confirmed that amending a plan to carve out retirees into a separate retiree-only plan will not impact the grandfathered status of the plan for current employees under the following conditions:

- No changes may be made to the benefits or cost sharing for current employees, and

- The new separate retiree-only plan must be created as the new plan in the sequence.

The grandfathered plan Interim Final Regulations contain complex anti-abuse rules for changes in plan eligibility, but these rules apply only when the individuals transferred into another plan are employees, not retirees.[1]

22. How does the retiree-only exemption relate to the Retiree Drug Subsidy Program (RDS) and Early Retiree Reinsurance Program (ERRP)?

A plan may receive reimbursements under the ERRP or subsidies under the RDS regardless of whether it meets the retiree-only plan exemption for HIPAA (and PPACA) purposes.[2]

Employer and Individual Mandates

See Part XI for a Complete Discussion of the Employer Mandate Provisions and Appendix B Copies of Several Mandatory Notices

23. What mandates were delayed by the IRS in July 2015?

IRS Notice 2013-45 provided a one-year delay to three requirements under the healthcare reform law:

- The annual obligation under Section 6055 of the Internal Revenue Code (Code) for insurers, self-insuring employers and other parties that provide "minimum essential coverage" to provide certain information to the IRS.

---

1. 45 CFR §147.140(b)(2)(ii).
2. See HHS questions and answers at http://www.errp.gov/faq_eligible.shtml.

- The annual obligation under Code Section 6056 for applicable large employers to report to the IRS and to the employer's full-time employees as to whether and what healthcare coverage is offered to such employees.

- The requirement under Code Section 4980H for applicable large employers to offer healthcare coverage to full-time employees or pay penalties, commonly known as the "play-or-pay" penalties (POP).

The Notice postpones compliance with only these three requirements until 2015. Other aspects of PPACA that were scheduled to become effective in 2014 will go into effect in 2014.

24. What else does Notice 2013-45 specify?

The Notice advises that the IRS will in the summer of 2013 propose regulations for the two information-reporting provisions now effective in 2015. The IRS encourages employers, insurers and other reporting entities to voluntarily comply with the proposed rules for information reporting for 2014, but no penalties for failure to comply with these reporting provisions now exist for 2014.

The Notice makes clear that the 2014 transition relief is limited solely to these three items and has no effect on the effective date or application of other provisions under the Act, many of which go into effect in 2014. For example, the transition relief has no effect on the provisions taking effect in 2014 as to premium tax credits for those purchasing subsidized health insurance on an exchange marketplace or the individual mandate requirements under Code section 5000A for individuals to maintain healthcare coverage for themselves or pay penalties.

25. What is the employer mandate that begins in 2015?

Health reform and its "employer mandate" do not require employers to provide health coverage for their employees. However, beginning in 2015, any applicable large employer (one with fifty or more full-time employees) can be liable for a substantial "assessable payment"[1] if it "fails to offer its full-time employees (and their dependents) the opportunity to enroll in minimum essential coverage under an eligible employer-sponsored plan."[2]

There are two alternative penalties. The annual amounts are $2,000 or $3,000, but the actual amount is calculated monthly. Both the $2,000 and $3,000 penalty amounts will be adjusted for inflation.[3] Neither penalty is triggered unless an employee receives a tax credit for the purchase of health insurance on a state exchange.

Generally, if an employee is offered affordable minimum essential coverage (MEC) under an employer-sponsored plan, then the individual is ineligible for a premium tax credit and cost-sharing reductions for health insurance purchased through a state exchange. However, an employee may be offered minimum essential coverage by the employer that is either

---

1. In contrast, the amount that individuals are required to pay for failure to comply with the Individual Mandate is called a "penalty."
2. IRC Sec. 4980H(a)(1), (2).
3. IRC Sec. 4980H(c)(5).

"unaffordable" or that consists of a plan under which the plan's share of the total allowed cost of benefits is less than 60 percent. In that situation, the employee is eligible for a premium tax credit and cost-sharing reductions if the employee declines to enroll in the coverage and purchases coverage through an exchange.

"Unaffordable" is defined by PPACA as coverage with a premium required to be paid by the employee that is more than 9.5 percent of the employee's household income (as defined for purposes of the premium tax credit[1] for individuals, discussed in Question 29). This percentage of the employee's income is indexed to the per capita growth in premiums for the insured market as determined by the Secretary of Health and Human Services. The employee must seek an affordability waiver from the state exchange and provide information as to family income and the lowest cost employer option offered to the employee. The state exchange then provides the waiver to the employee. The employer penalty generally applies for employees receiving an affordability waiver.

For purposes of determining whether coverage is unaffordable, required salary reduction contributions are treated as payments required to be made by the employee. However, if an employee is reimbursed by the employer for any portion of the premium for health insurance coverage purchased through the exchange, including any reimbursement through salary reduction contributions under a cafeteria plan, the coverage is employer-provided and the employee is not eligible for premium tax credits or cost-sharing reductions. Thus, an individual is not permitted to purchase coverage through the exchange, apply for the premium tax credit, and pay for the individual's portion of the premium using salary reduction contributions under the cafeteria plan of the individual's employer.[2]

26. How does the state insurance exchange obtain information on the affordability to an individual?

The Tax Code[3] permits the disclosure of taxpayer return information to assist exchanges and state agencies, but not employers, in performing certain functions for which income verification is required. Under proposed regulations, the IRS would be permitted to disclose income and other specified information about an individual taxpayer to HHS for purposes of making eligibility determinations for advance payments of the premium tax credit or the cost-sharing reductions.[4] HHS could then disclose the information to the Exchange or the state agency processing the individual's application. As a condition for receiving return information, each receiving entity (i.e., HHS, the Exchanges, and state agencies as well as their respective contractors) is required to adhere to the privacy safeguards established under Code Section 6103(p)(4).

---

1. IRC Sec. 36B, as discussed in more detail hereafter.
2. Joint Comm. Staff, Tech Explanation of the Revenue Provisions of the Reconciliation Act of 2010, as amended, in combination with the Patient Protection and Affordable Care Act (JCX-18-10), 3/21/2010, p.37.
3. IRC Sec. 6103(l)(21).
4. 77 Fed. Reg. 25378 (Apr. 30, 2012).

27. How do the two employer mandate penalties work?

Employers can be penalized for not providing minimum essential coverage or for having an inadequate health plan.

No Minimum Essential Coverage – $2000 Per Full Time Employee Less 30 Penalty. Employers with at least fifty full-time equivalent employees and with at least thirty-one full-time employees must offer minimum essential health coverage meeting specified requirements. If the employers offer no health plan, they must pay a $2,000 per full-time employee penalty if any of the full-time employees receive a federal premium subsidy through a health care exchange.

The calculation of "a large employer" includes part-time workers. However, the $2,000 per Full-Time Employee Less 30 Penalty is only calculated based on full-time workers therefore, not all large employers who have a full-time employee receiving a credit would actually pay a penalty. This could occur because the first thirty workers are not counted.

For example, an employer with 100 part-time workers (fifteen hours per week) and thirty full-time workers (thirty-plus hours per week) would be considered a large employer with eighty full-time equivalent workers. Even if one or more workers received a premium credit, the penalty would only be assessed against the number of full-time workers: (30-30) × $2,000 = 0. Thus, read literally, if only one employee purchases insurance on an exchange and receives a premium tax credit, the penalty applies to all full-time employees less thirty full-time employees times $2,000.

The IRS has indicated that "it is contemplated that the proposed regulations will make clear that an employer offering [minimum essential] coverage to all, or substantially all, of its full-time employees would not be subject to the 4980H(a) 'all-full time employees minus 30' assessable payment provisions."[1]

To avoid the $2,000 penalty, the employer must offer "minimum essential coverage" to its full-time employees and their dependents.[2] Dependents can include not only children, but also parents, siblings, uncles, aunts, nieces, nephews, grandchildren, and various in-laws.[3] Any person who has the same principal place of abode and is a member of the same household as the taxpayer is eligible to become a dependent.[4]

The minimum essential coverage that an employer must offer in order to avoid the "all full-time employees minus 30" penalty calculation is defined in the statutory provisions imposing the individual mandate. It includes only:

---

1. IRS Notice 2011-36.
2. IRC Sec. 4980H(a)(1), (b)(1)(A); IRC Sec. 5000A(b)(3)(A). Several comments submitted in response to Notice 2011-36 argue that employers should not be obligated to provide coverage to dependents of full-time employees. These comments contend that employers should not be mandated to provide family or other types of coverage beyond self-only coverage and that such dependents will often either have minimum essential coverage available elsewhere or will not be required to carry minimum essential coverage under the exceptions contained in Code Section 5000A . *See, e.g.,* Business Round Table Comments on IRS Notice 2011-36 (submitted June 17, 2011); Society for Human Resource Management Comments on IRS Notice 2011-36 (submitted June 17, 2011); American Benefits Council Comments on IRS Notice 2011-36 (submitted June 15, 2011).
3. IRC Secs. 152(d)(2)(A)–(C), (E)–(G).
4. IRC Sec. 152(d)(2).

- government-sponsored programs (such as Medicare, etc.),

- eligible employer-sponsored plans,

- plans offered in the "individual market,"

- grandfathered health plans, and

- other coverage that "the Secretary of Health and Human Services, in coordination with the Secretary [of the Treasury], recognizes" for purposes of this determination.[1]

There are some fundamental unresolved issues with respect to this definition. First, an "eligible employer-sponsored plan" is defined as a "group health plan or group health insurance coverage" that is either a governmental plan or another "plan or coverage offered in the small or large group market within a State."[2] Even though the language of that definition specifically seems to contemplate a "group health plan," as opposed to "group health insurance coverage," there was a question as to whether a private self-insured plan would qualify as "any other plan or coverage offered in the small or large group market within a State." However, the IRS has indicated that self-insured plans qualify.[3]

Second, the grandfathered health plan exception may not be applicable because of the ease with which a plan can lose grandfathered status. The actions that can destroy grandfathered status include:

- the elimination of all or substantially all benefits to diagnose or treat a particular condition,

- any increase in a percentage cost-sharing requirement,

- a decrease in the employer contribution rate by more than 5 percent, and

- certain changes to annual limits on benefits.[4]

---

1. IRC Sec. 5000A(f)(1).
2. IRC Sec. 5000A(f)(2).
3. *See* IRC §5000A(f)(5); 42 U.S.C. §18024(a)(1) (PPACA §1304(a)(1)) (defining "group market" as "the health insurance market under which individuals obtain health insurance coverage (directly or through any arrangement) on behalf of themselves (and their dependents) through a group health plan maintained by an employer" (emphasis added)). However, the preamble to the proposed regulations under Code Section 36B, states that regulations under Code Section 5000A will "provide that an employer-sponsored plan will not fail to be minimum essential coverage solely because it is a plan to reimburse employees for medical care for which reimbursement is not provided under a policy of accident and health insurance (a self-insured plan)."
4. Treas. Reg. §54.9815-1251T(g)(1)(i), (ii), (v). When the interim final regulations were first issued, an employer's entrance into a new policy, certificate or contract of insurance after March 23, 2010 (*e.g.*, because the previous policy, certificate or contract was not being renewed), would trigger loss of grandfathered status. Treas. Reg. §54.9815-1251T(a)(1)(ii). However, this was subsequently changed in Treasury Decision 9506. This decision amended the interim final regulations to allow employers to change insurance providers, so long as the new policy, certificate or contract did not otherwise make changes triggering loss of grandfathered status under the regulations. It should be noted that this amendment does not apply retroactively; therefore, plans undergoing carrier changes prior to November 17, 2010 still lost grandfathered status (subject to a special exception for collectively bargained plans). T.D. 9506 (amending Treas. Reg. §54.9815-1251T(a)(1)).

In addition, it seems that failure annually to give plan participants a notice that the plan is grandfathered causes a loss of grandfathered status.[1]

Third, minimum essential coverage is treated as being provided only if "the plan's share of the total allowed costs of benefits provided under the plan is at least 60 percent of such costs."[2] However, if the employee nevertheless participates in the plan, this rule does not apply.[3] Determining whether this requirement is satisfied is easy only for fully insured plans with no deductibles, co-pays or coinsurance. When the employer pays 60 percent or more of the premium, such a plan would be treated as providing "minimum essential coverage."

How deductibles, co-pays, and coinsurance should be handled is not clear. The plan's 60 percent share is measured against "the total allowed costs of benefits provided under the plan." To the extent that an employee pays deductibles, co-pays, and coinsurance, those benefits are not provided under the plan. If deductibles, co-pays, and coinsurance are to be counted, then, application of the 60 percent test is much more difficult.

Inadequate Health Plan – $3000 Per Full-Time Employee Penalty. A different penalty applies for employers of at least fifty full-time equivalent employees that offer minimum essential coverage that does not meet the federal requirements. Employers that offer health coverage will not meet the requirements if:

- at least one full-time employee obtains a premium credit in an exchange plan, and

- the plan does not provide:

  ○ minimum essential benefits,

  ○ the employee's required contribution for self-only coverage exceeds 9.5% of the employee's household income, or

  ○ the employer pays for less than 60 percent of the benefits.

In 2015, the monthly penalty assessed to the employer for each full-time employee who receives a premium credit will be one-twelfth of $3,000 for any applicable month. However, the total penalty is limited to the total number of the firm's full-time employees minus thirty, multiplied by one-twelfth of $2,000 for any applicable month. After 2015, the penalty amounts will be indexed by the premium adjustment percentage for the calendar year.

This penalty is imposed for any month in which "at least one full-time employee of the applicable large employer has been certified to the employer under Section 1411 of the Patient Protection and Affordable Care Act as having enrolled for such month in a qualified health

---

1. This issue is discussed in more detail later in this book.
2. IRC Sec. 36B(c)(2)(C)(ii). This special rule does not apply if the employee, or dependent, does in fact procure coverage under the eligible employer-sponsored plan or grandfathered health plan. IRC Sec. 36B(c)(2)(C)(iii).
3. IRC Sec. 36B(c)(2)(C)(iii).

plan through a state health insurance exchange for which a tax credit is allowed or paid."[1] As explained in Question 29, this individual tax credit is available to most low- and middle-income individuals that are not offered affordable, minimum essential coverage by their employers and are not covered by Medicaid.[2]

28. Is the employer mandate excise tax deductible?

The employer mandate excise tax is not deductible. The IRS is establishing a vast information-gathering process through which it will calculate and assess the tax proactively without self-reporting by employers. To avoid the tax, proper health coverage must be offered to at least 95 percent of an employer's employees. Independent contractors who should be treated as full-time employees under the common law standards must be taken into account in the 95 percent threshold test.

29. How is the 95 percent of the employer's employees calculated?

The 95 percent threshold must be calculated monthly, because the excise tax is assessed monthly, at a rate of $166.67 ($2,000/12). Therefore, each month, an employer must identify its full-time employees based on weekly average hours of service during the month and determine whether they have been offered coverage for the month. For hourly employees, actual hours must be counted. For salaried employees, actual hours may be counted or hours-equivalency rules may be used to eliminate the administrative burden of counting actual hours.

To make the full-time employee determination more predictable, an employer can take advantage of rules that allow an employee's status as a full-time employee in future periods to be based on hours of service in prior periods. While these rules are helpful, they, too, are complex and have exacting standards.

30. Does the employer have to offer coverage for all days of the month in order to avoid the penalty?

Yes. If an employer fails to offer coverage to a full-time employee for any day of the month, the employee is treated as not having been offered coverage for the entire month.

31. How are full-time and full-time-equivalent employees calculated?

A large employer potentially subject to the employer mandate penalty is an employer with more than fifty full-time-equivalent employees during the preceding calendar year. Additionally, an employer who is part of a group of employers treated as a single employer under Code Section 414 (b), (c), (m), or (o) (including employees of a controlled group of corporations, employees of partnerships, proprietorships, etc., which are under common control, and employees of an affiliated service group) is treated as a single employer.[3] When a mandate penalty applies, it is to be paid ratably by members of the group.[4] For employers not

---

1. IRC Sec. 4980H(a)(2).
2. IRC Sec. 36B(c)(1), (2)(C); 42 USC §18071(b) (PPACA §1402(b)).
3. IRC Sec. 4980H(c)(2)(C)(i).
4. IRC Sec. 4980H(c)(2)(D)(ii).

in existence throughout the preceding calendar year, the determination of large employer is based on the average number of employees a firm is reasonably expected to employ on business days in the current calendar year.[1] Any reference to an employer includes a reference to any predecessor of that employer.[2]

The statutes use the term "full-time employee" in the definition of large employer, but then expand on the definition to include both full- and part-time workers.[3] Full-time employees are those working thirty or more hours per week.[4] The number of full-time employees excludes any full-time seasonal employees[5] who work for less than 120 days during the year.[6] The hours worked by part-time employees (i.e., those working less than 30 hours per week) are included in the calculation of a large employer, on a monthly basis, by taking their total number of monthly hours worked divided by 120.[7] In addition, an employer will not be considered a large employer if its number of full-time-equivalent employees exceeded 50 for 120 days or less or the employees in excess of 50 employed during the 120-day period were seasonal workers.[8]

> *Example:* A firm has 35 full-time employees who work 30 or more hours per week. In addition, the firm has 20 part-time employees who all work 24 hours per week (96 hours per month). These part-time employees' hours would be treated as equivalent to 16 full-time employees, based on the following calculation:
>
> $$20 \text{ employees} \times 96 \text{ hours} = 1920$$
>
> $$1920 / 120 = 16$$

32. Can you provide examples of the employer mandate tax penalties?

> *Example A:* The large employer does not offer coverage, but no full-time employees receive credits for exchange coverage. No penalty would be assessed.
>
> *Example B:* The large employer offers coverage and no full-time employees receive credits for exchange coverage. No penalty would be assessed.
>
> *Example C:* The large employer does not offer coverage, and one or more full-time employees receive credits for exchange coverage. The annual penalty calculation is the number of full-time employees minus 30, times $2,000. The penalty does not vary if only one employee or all fifty employees received the credit; the employer's annual penalty in 2015 would be $40,000 calculated as follows:

---

1. IRC Sec. 4980H(c)(2)(C)(ii).
2. IRC Sec. 4980H(c)(2)(C)(iii).
3. IRC Sec. 4980H(c)(2).
4. IRC Sec. 4980H(c)(4).
5. The term "seasonal worker" means a worker who performs labor or services on a seasonal basis as defined by the Secretary of Labor, including workers covered by Section 500.20(s)(1) of title 29, Code of Federal Regulations and retail workers employed exclusively during holiday seasons. IRC Sec. 4980H(c)(2)(B)(ii).
6. IRC Sec. 4980H(c)(2)(B).
7. IRC Sec. 4980H(c)(2)(E).
8. IRC Sec. 4980H(c)(2)(B).

$$50 - 30 = 20$$

$$20 \times \$2,000 = \$40,000.$$

Example D: The employer offers health plan coverage, but one or more full-time employees receive credits for exchange coverage. The number of full-time employees receiving the credit is used in the penalty calculation for an employer that offers coverage. The annual penalty is the *lesser of* the following:

- o   The number of full-time employees minus 30, multiplied by $2,000, or $40,000 for the employer with fifty full-time employees, as shown in Example C, or

- o   The number of full-time employees who receive credits for exchange coverage, multiplied by $3,000.

Thus, for an employer that hires only full-time employees, hiring that fiftieth employee could trigger a penalty of $40,000 if the employer does not offer health coverage to its employees. This will likely affect hiring for small employers close to the "applicable large employer" fifty full-time-equivalent employee limit.

Although the penalties are assessed on a monthly basis (with the dollar amounts above then divided by 12), this example uses annual amounts, assuming the number of affected employees is the same throughout the year.

Example E: If the employer with fifty full-time employees had ten full-time employees who received premium credits, then the potential annual penalty on the employer for those individuals would be $30,000. Because this is less than the overall limitation for this employer of $40,000, the employer penalty in this example would be $30,000.

However, if the employer with fifty full-time employees had thirty full-time employees who received premium credits, then the potential annual penalty on the employer for those individuals would be $90,000. Because $90,000 exceeds this employer's overall limitation of $40,000, the employer penalty in this example would be limited to $40,000.

33. What reporting is required by employers, other than the W-2 requirements?

Beginning in 2015[1], large employers with fifty or more full-time-equivalent employees and "offering employers"[2] will have certain reporting requirements with respect to their full-time employees.[3] Employers will have to file a return including:

---

1. IRS Notice 2013-45
2. An offering employer is one that offers minimum essential coverage through an employer plan and pays for some of the costs. Reporting requirements apply to these employers, regardless of size, only if the required contribution for self-only coverage by any employee exceeds 8 percent of wages. This is required because individuals whose household income exceeds 8 percent of wages are exempt from the individual mandate and may be eligible for free-choice vouchers. However, an employer would only have knowledge of the individual's wages, not his or her household income. Because this reporting requirement is linked to wages (and not household income), it is a first step in determining whether an individual is exempt from the individual mandate.
3. PPACA §1502.

- The employer's name, address, and employer identification number;

- A certification as to whether the employer offers its full-time employees (and dependents) the opportunity to enroll in minimum essential overage under an eligible employer-sponsored plan;

- The length of any waiting period;

- The months that coverage was available;

- Monthly premiums for the lowest-cost option;

- The employer plan's share of covered healthcare expenses;

- The number of full-time employees; and

- The name, address, and tax identification number of each full-time employee.

Additionally, an offering employer will have to provide information about the plan for which the employer pays the largest portion of the costs (and the amount for each enrollment category).

Insurers must also report certain information to the IRS[1] as discussed subsequently in this book.

Additionally, the employer must also provide each full-time employee with a written statement showing contact information for the person preparing the required return, and the specific information included in the return, for that individual employee. An employer may enter into an agreement with a health insurance issuer to provide necessary returns and statements.

34. How do the information reporting requirements and the employer mandate penalties interact?

The information reporting required by Code Sections 6055 and 6056 must occur for the IRS to enforce and administer the employer mandate requirements under Code Section 4980H. The employer mandate penalties are triggered if one or more of an applicable large employer's full-time employees are entitled to premium tax credits for the purchase of insurance on a state exchange marketplace under Code section 36B and (1) the employer fails to offered 95 percent of full-time employees and their dependents the opportunity to enroll in minimum essential coverage or (2) the employer offers full-time employees and dependents the opportunity to enroll in minimum essential coverage but the coverage is not affordable or does not provide minimum value. The second penalty can never exceed the first penalty.

An employer typically will not know whether a full-time employee has received such a tax credit, and the employer will not have all the information needed to determine whether it owes an employer mandate penalty. Therefore, IRS Notice 2013-45 provides that applicable

---

1. PPACA §1501, 1502, and 10106 adding IRC Secs. 5000A and 6055.

large employers do not have to calculate employer mandate penalties or file returns submitting payment for such penalties. Instead, the IRS, after receiving the information returns filed by applicable large employers under Code Section 6056 and the information about employees claiming the premium tax credit for any given calendar year, will determine whether any of the employer's full-time employees received the premium tax credit and, if so, whether any employer mandate penalty is due. The IRS will thus contact any applicable large employer if the employer owes a penalty, and the employer will have an opportunity to respond to the information provided by IRS before any penalty is assessed.

35. Can employees still receive premium tax credits in 2014?

Yes. The Notice states that the transition relief does not affect an individual's eligibility for a premium tax credit if he or she purchases health insurance through one of the health insurance exchange marketplaces established under the Act. Participants in the exchanges will continue to qualify for premium tax credits if their household income is within the specified range and they are not eligible for other minimum essential coverage. Such other minimum essential coverage includes eligible employer-sponsored group health plans that are affordable and provide minimum value.

36. Does a state health insurance exchange notify the employer if an individual is determined to be eligible for the income tax credit?

HHS regulations require the Exchange to notify the employer and identify the employee when the Exchange determines an applicant is eligible to receive advance payments of the premium tax credit or cost-sharing reductions based in part on a finding that his or her employer does not provide minimum essential coverage, or provides coverage that is not affordable, or does not meet the minimum value standard.[1] The notice includes the employee's identity, that the employee has been determined eligible for advance payments of the premium tax credit, that the employer may be liable for a shared responsibility payment, and that there is an opportunity to appeal.[2] The details such as the employee's tax return information or the exact reason the employee is eligible for assistance are not included.[3]

37. Under what circumstances may employers otherwise subject to the tax qualify for exemption?

Employers otherwise subject to the tax are exempt if (1) no full-time employee decides to purchase health insurance through a state or federal exchange or (2) no full-time employee's household income is low enough to qualify for a premium tax credit or subsidy. Income below these levels below qualifies for the subsidy. The premium credits will be provided as advanceable, refundable federal tax credits ultimately calculated through individual tax returns (although the credit payments will go directly to insurers). The credits can only be obtained by qualifying individuals (among others, lawful state residents) who file tax returns and are not eligible for

---

1. 45 CFR §155.310(h).

2. 45 CFR §155.310(h).

3. PPACA; Establishment of Exchanges and Qualified Health Plans; Exchange Standards for Employers, 77 Fed. Reg. 18310, 18357 (Mar. 27, 2012).

other acceptable minimum essential coverage, such as an employer plan (that is affordable [IRS and HHS will issue guidance and provide an on-line calculator for this] and pays for at least 60 percent of projected health costs), Medicare, Medicaid, the Children's Health Insurance Program (CHIP), coverage related to military service, a grandfathered plan.

# of individuals	Household income[1] (four times federal poverty level in 2013)
1	$45,960
2	$62,040
3	$78,120
4	$94,200
5	$110,280
6	$126,360
7	$142,440
8	$158,520

38. What effect will a state's decision whether to expand Medicaid under the ACA have on the employer mandate penalty?

If a state elects to expand Medicaid under healthcare reform, a person earning less than 138 percent[2] of the Federal Poverty Level or FPL ($15,857 for an individual in 2014) can qualify even if not a parent or not disabled. If a state does not elect the healthcare reform Medicaid expansion, additional penalty exposure is created for employees whose household income is between 100 percent and 138 percent of FPL because they could be eligible for exchange purchased health insurance premium subsidies.

39. How does an employer appeal the tax penalties?

Employers will have an appeals mechanism to contest a determination that it is liable for the new employer mandate penalties imposed under Code Section 4980H because:

- The employee was not eligible for an individual tax credit due to the employee's household income or

- The employer had provided minimum essential coverage that was affordable.

As part of the appeals process, the employer will "have access to the data used to make the determination to the extent allowable by law," but it is still subject to the nondisclosure provision.[3] This appeals mechanism would be in addition to the employer's appeals rights under the Internal Revenue Code.[4]

---

1. This is Modified Adjusted Gross Income for federal purposes. These threshold amounts apply to the 48 contiguous states and the District of Columbia. The amounts are 25 percent higher for Alaska and 15 percent higher for Hawaii. They are adjusted annually to reflect changes in the cost of living.
2. In fact, eligibility is not 133 percent but is 138 percent of FPL because §1004(e) of P.L. 111-152 requires income equivalent to 5 percent FPL to be disregarded.
3. 42 USC §18081(f)(2) (PPACA §1411(f)(2)).
4. Id.

This process raises several questions – with no clear answers – regarding the extent to which, if at all, an employer may contest an employee's income taxes. For instance, if an employee claims numerous dependents (which could significantly reduce household income) would an employer be able to investigate whether the employee provided more than 50 percent of the support for those claimed dependents? Could an employer seek to challenge above-the-line business deductions claimed by an employee?

40. What other issues must be considered by employers in planning for the employer mandate tax penalties?

Applicable large employers (those with 50 or more full time equivalent employees) that may be subject to an employer mandate penalty will need to consider taking action, if possible, (1) to avoid the employer mandate versus (2) minimizing its effect or (3) embracing it strategically. Certain industries and business sectors will be hit hard while others will gain relief. In addition, the competitive balance regarding costs will be impacted. For example, consider regional and national restaurants operating as one employer versus franchised operations where the small franchisees will not be subject to the employer mandate tax penalty. Issues to be considered include workforce size and composition.

- Workforce size determines whether the mandate applies and potential cost/penalty exposure.

- Workforce composition will trigger other issues, such as

    o   Part-Time vs. Full-Time Employees.

    o   Independent Contractors and/or Leased Employees.

    o   Lower-Income vs. Higher-Income.

    o   Bargaining-Unit Employees.

Risk of Independent Contractor Reclassification. An employer may have one or more independent contractors that are reclassified as employees. As a result, that employer with fewer than fifty full-time employees could find itself with fifty or more after the reclassification. Additionally, such persons could trigger one of the employer mandate penalties if they receive a tax credit for purchasing health insurance on an exchange.

Changing Status of Full-Time Employees. Employers with group health plans that consider converting full-time employees to part-time status or independent contractors, or terminating employees to avoid the employer mandate penalties, could face ERISA claims by these employees.

A group health plan is an employee welfare plan governed by ERISA. Under ERISA Section 510, it is unlawful to hire, suspend, fine, discipline, expel, or discriminate against a participant or beneficiary for the purpose of interfering with the attainment of any right to which such a participant may become entitled under the plan or ERISA. A plaintiff in such a case typically has the burden of proving there was an adverse action against the participant or beneficiary for the purpose of interfering with the attainment of an ERISA benefit. However, employers should be cautious as to the reasons and documentation for any such employee changes.

Employers Slightly Below 50 Full-Time Equivalent Employee Limit. Thus, for an employer that hires only full-time employees, hiring that fiftieth employee could trigger a penalty of $40,000 if the employer does not offer health coverage to its employees. This will likely affect hiring for small employers close to the "applicable large employer" fifty full-time-equivalent employee limit.

41. What is the individual mandate that is effective in 2014?

The U.S. Supreme Court ruled that the individual mandate is constitutional.[1] Beginning January 1, 2014, health reform requires most individuals to have some form of health coverage. If an applicable individual does not have minimum essential coverage, for that individual or his or her dependents who also meet the definition of applicable individual, a tax "penalty" will be imposed on the individual.[2] The penalty is equal to the greater of:

(i)   the "applicable dollar amount" for the individual and all such dependents (up to a maximum of three applicable dollar amounts), or

(ii)   a specified percentage of the applicable individual's household income.

In no event will the penalty be more than "the national average premium for qualified health plans which have a bronze level of coverage with coverage for the applicable family size involved, that are offered through exchanges."[3]

The minimum penalty ranges from $95 in calendar year 2014 up to $695 in calendar year 2016, and is inflation-adjusted thereafter.[4] Moreover, the applicable percentage of income increases from 1 percent in calendar year 2014, to 2 percent in calendar year 2015 and to 2.5 percent for calendar year 2016 and thereafter.[5] For low-income employees, the minimum penalty is small in comparison to the actual cost of coverage, thereby increasing the likelihood that an individual without minimum essential coverage will not purchase health insurance, although the tax credit subsidies will make the insurance less expensive.

---

1. *NFIB v. Sebelius* (June 28, 2012).
2. IRC Sec. 5000A(f).
3. IRC Secs. 5000A(b)(1), (c)(1), (2). Use of the national average for bronze coverage means that calculation might not bear much relationship to the actual cost of coverage available in a specific location. However, the premium amounts likely will not be lower than the penalty.
4. IRC Secs. 5000A(c)(3)(A), (B), (D).
5. IRC Sec. 5000A(c)(2)(B). The net effect of these percentage increases for taxpayers who do not procure minimum essential coverage and whose income is sufficient to be above the minimum penalty is an increase in their marginal tax rate by 1 percent in calendar year 2014 rising to a 2.5 percent marginal tax rate increase for subsequent years.

42. Will the individual mandate work to induce individuals to purchase health insurance?

There are low participation rates in health insurance, even in many companies that offer health coverage. One CEO has asked employees why they do not participate in the employer provided coverage.[1] The answers he received are typical:

- Younger workers were unconcerned about illness or injury.

- Others already had insurance through a spouse or parent.

- A significant number said they declined coverage because they could get medical treatment "for free at the emergency room." This fact remains true in and after 2014, as the federal law known as EMTALA requires hospitals to provide emergency services, even to those who cannot pay.

- Among those who had signed up, many said it was because they were concerned about developing a medical condition and then being unable to get affordable coverage due to this preexisting condition. Significantly, in 2014, these people will be able to obtain health insurance on exchanges despite any preexisting conditions, which will further disincentivize enrollment in both employer and exchange offered health insurance.

This reality may mean that healthcare reform may be more expensive and not work as hoped. The law's success depends on young, healthy people who are lower risk signing up for health insurance to offset the costs of insuring individuals with preexisting conditions, many who in the past have been unable to purchase insurance, and who are at higher risk for the need for expensive medical care. If predominantly high-risk individuals sign up on the state exchanges, that health insurance will be expensive. Nevertheless, people will still be able to get medical care at the emergency room. Further, the law in 2014 prohibits insurers from denying coverage because of preexisting conditions. Therefore, individuals have even less incentive to purchase health insurance as they will no longer have much incentive to get health insurance as a hedge against the possibility of developing a medical condition when they are presently healthy.

One of the law's answers to these issues is the individual mandate penalty tax on uninsured individuals that goes into effect in 2014. The penalty in 2014 is $95 or 1 percent of household income, whichever is greater. It increases in 2016 to $695 or 2.5 percent of household income, whichever is greater. The individual mandate is not sufficient to change the behavior of many persons who are not otherwise inclined to buy health insurance. A person making $50,000 per year with no health coverage will be subject to an initial individual mandate penalty of $500 and a maximum penalty of $1,250 in 2016. The typical share of

---

1. A CEO's-Eye View of ObamaCare, Wall Street Journal p. A-17 (July 22, 2013), available at: http://online.wsj.com/article/SB100014241278 873233309404578613653344566068.html?mod=hp_opinion.

employee cost for company sponsored health coverage will often exceed this amount, often by a significant amount. Low paid employees who earn, for example, $11,500 per year, would be subject to an initial penalty of $115 in 2014 and a maximum penalty of $695 in 2016. Such workers' share of health insurance premiums will again often be more than any potential penalty.

Thus, the individual mandate will likely neither raise as much money as projected nor induce as many uninsured to purchase insurance as hoped. In addition, if more individuals move from employer to subsidized state exchange provided insurance than projected, this too will make healthcare reform much more expensive than projected.

Controlled Group and Affiliated Service Group Issues

43. Are there special issues for controlled groups and affiliated service groups?

If there is more than one such business involved, the thirty-employee base amount must be allocated among all such businesses "ratably" on the basis of the number of full-time employees in each business. However, there are still some unanswered questions, for example:

- What if one employer within a controlled group of corporations provides coverage for all of its employees? Will it be exempt from the penalties, even though another employer within the same controlled group is not?

- Will the exempt employer's employees serve to increase the penalty on a related taxable employer?

Example: A married couple owns two businesses: a financial planning business (with fourteen full-time (FT) employees and six part-time employees), plus a franchise (with eighteen FT employees and fifty part-time employees). The businesses are treated as a single employer because they are commonly owned (80 percent or more by same five or fewer people) by the husband and wife. Assuming the part-time employees each work an average of eighty hours per month, they collectively count as thirty-seven full-time-equivalent employees.

FTE status is calculated by taking the average number of hours worked per month times the number of part-time employees [those regularly scheduled to work less than 30 hours per week] divided by 120, rounded down to the whole number). Thus, the combined business will be subject to the employer mandate once it takes effect in 2015 (because 32 FT employees and 37 FTEs is a total of 69 FTEs).

First, if the businesses do not provide all of the full-time employees of both businesses with coverage that meets the new standards, the combined businesses will be subject to a $4,000 per year nondeductible excise tax. While the businesses are subject to the employer mandate, the penalty is calculated on the basis of full-time employees only (a total of thirty-two) and there is an exemption for the first thirty full-time employees.

$$32 - 30 = 2$$

$$2 \times \$2,000 = \$4,000.$$

Second, even if the businesses do not provide affordable minimum essential coverage, the penalty will not exceed $4,000 per year even if one or more full-time employees:

- Opt out of the coverage,

- Purchase their own coverage on an exchange, and

- Qualify for taxpayer-subsidized coverage (because their family incomes fall below the applicable federal thresholds).

The overall penalty is limited to what it would be if the employers provided no coverage at all.

44. Will applicable employers terminate their health plans so that employees must purchase health insurance on a state exchange because the penalties are much less than the costs of a group health plan?

Whether employers subject to the employer mandate will decide to cease offering health coverage in 2015 or thereafter and elect to pay the $2,000 "all-full time employees minus 30" penalty is likely to substantially affect the ultimate impact of health reform.[1] An employer's annual healthcare costs will be much greater than the penalty. Even though the penalty is nondeductible and amounts paid for employee healthcare coverage should continue to be deductible, some – and perhaps many – employers will consider ceasing to offer a group health plan in 2015 or thereafter, especially those with low-paid workforces whose employees will receive income tax subsidies for health insurance purchased on a state exchange. The tax credit discussed in Q 49 for low- and middle-income persons (with incomes below 400 percent of the federal poverty level) buying insurance through the exchanges will be substantial. Therefore, as described in more detail in Q 49 although health coverage is an important part of many employers' benefit packages, discontinuing such coverage would allow some employers with lower wage employees, as well as the employees themselves, to both come out ahead economically. For example, the employer could terminates health coverage and pass some of the net savings (after taking the penalty into account) on to its employees in the form of additional cash compensation.

---

1. One study concludes that 30 percent of employers will definitely or probably stop offering traditional employer-sponsored coverage after 2014; the study found that the percentage increases to 50 percent among employers with a high awareness of the healthcare bills' contents. *See* Shubham Singhal *et al.*, *How US Health Care Reform Will Affect Employee Benefits*, mckinsey quarterly 2 (June 2011).

However, it could be more expensive for many employers to discontinue coverage and increase employee compensation up to the amount saved in health costs less the penalty paid. Depending on workforce demographics, offering coverage may save money.

Exchanges and Individual Tax Subsidies Change Calculations[1]

Today about 163 million workers and their families receive health insurance coverage from their employers. Proponents of PPACA insisted that a key tenet was to build on this system of employer-sponsored coverage. Importantly President Obama himself repeatedly promised that individuals would get to keep their own health insurance if they liked it.

Roughly half of the $900 billion of spending in PPACA is devoted to subsidies for individuals who do not receive health insurance from their employers. These subsidies are remarkably generous, even for those with relatively high incomes. For example, in 2014:

- A family earning about $59,000 a year would receive a premium subsidy of about $7,200.

- A family earning about $71,000 would receive a premium subsidy of about $5,200

- A family earning about $95,000 would receive a premium subsidy of almost $3,000.

By 2018, subsidy amounts and the income levels to qualify for those subsidies would grow substantially:

- A family earning about $64,000 would receive a subsidy of m $10,000,

- A family earning $77,000 would receive a subsidy of $7,800, and

- Families earning $102,000 would receive a subsidy of almost $5,000.

An obvious question is how employers will react to the presence of an alternative – a subsidized source of insurance for their workers – that can be accessed if companies drop coverage for their employees. The most simple calculation focuses on the tradeoff between employer savings and the $2,000 penalty (per employee) imposed by the PPACA on employers whose employees move to an exchange for subsidized health insurance.

The following chart shows situations in which the purely economic decision of an employer would be to drop or keep its health plan. The answer frequently depends on the size of the federal tax credit subsidy. The first row of the table below shows a worker at 133 percent of the Federal Poverty Level (FPL) or $31,521 in 2014. This worker is expected to be in the 15 percent federal tax bracket, which means that $100 of wages (which yields $85) is needed to offset the loss of $85 dollars of untaxed employer-provided health insurance. Consider now a health insurance policy worth $15,921, of which the employer pays 75 percent of the cost.

---

1. See Douglas Holtz-Eakin, President & Cameron Smith, Labor Markets and Health Care Reform: New Results (May 2010), at http://ameri-canactionforum.org/files/LaborMktsHCRAAF5-27-10.pdf.

The employer's contribution to health insurance of $11,941 is the equivalent of a wage increase of $14,048, ignoring any state income taxes.

Healthcare Reform and Employer-Sponsored Insurance in 2014
Employer Health Plan Cost of $11,941[1]

Percent of Federal Poverty Level	Income[2]	Tax Bracket[3]	Wage Equivalent[4]	Federal Subsidy	Pay Raise[5]	Employer Cash Flow[6]	Decision[7]
133%	$31,521	15%	$14,048	$14,176	-$128	$9,941	Drop
150%	$35,550	15%	$14,048	$13,385	$663	$9,941	Drop
200%	$47,400	25%	$15,921	$10,985	$4,936	$9,941	Drop
250%	$59,250	25%	$15,921	$7,530	$8,391	$9,941	Drop
300%	$71,100	25%	$15,921	$5,187	$10,734	$9,941	Keep
400%	$94,800	28%	$16,585	$2,935	$13,650	$9,941	Keep

The Congressional Budget Office (CBO) estimated that only nineteen million residents would receive subsidies, at a cost of about $450 billion over the first ten years. This analysis suggests that the number could easily triple (nineteen million plus an additional thirty-eight million in 2014). The gross price tag would be roughly $1.4 trillion, which would be partially offset by employer mandate tax penalties.[8]

PEO (Staffing Industry) Compliance with Employer Mandate

45. Will the employee mandate and related penalties apply to professional employer organizations (PEO), also known as the staffing industry?

The healthcare reform employer mandate tax penalty (also called Play or Pay or Shared Responsibility) rules apply to "applicable large employers," which include employers with fifty or more full-time and full-time equivalent employees. Many if not most Professional Employer Organizations (PEOs), also known as staffing firms and employee leasing companies, are applicable large employers.

---

1. Id. Health plan costs $14,048 and employer pays 75 percent.
2. Income calculated based on 2009 FPL for a family of four of $22,050 (HHS), indexed to CPI projections (CBO).
3. 2010 tax brackets, indexed to CPI projections (CBO).
4. Wage equivalent value of employer health plan; CBO estimate of Silver Plan in 2016, indexed to 2014 ($11,941),and divided by Tax Rate)..
5. Wage equivalent minus subsidies.
6. Value of insurance plan minus $2,000 penalty.
7. Employer decision to keep or drop health plan; drop if pay raise greater than free cash flow.
8. See Douglas Holtz-Eakin, President & Cameron Smith, Labor Markets and Health Care Reform: New Results (May 2010), at http://ameri-canactionforum.org/files/LaborMktsHCRAAF5-27-10.pdf.

There is no one right answer for how employers will comply with the employer mandate penalty. Some will continue to offer health insurance or not offer it if they do not now. Others may adopt a different program or cease to offer health coverage.

See Q 23 through Q 40 for information on the employer mandate and the employer mandate penalty. See also Part XI for a detailed discussion of the employer mandate penalties.

46. How does the nature of a PEO's clients affect how the PEO may handle the employer mandate?

The complexity in complying with the employer mandate rules differs based on the nature of the recipient, i.e., the client of the PEO. Industries with large, stable workforces consisting mostly of full-time employees who are provided with major medical benefits will likely continue these benefits and will be able to comply with the employer mandate rules without significant difficulty. However, businesses that rely on variable hour, contingent, or low paid workers will face difficulties. Many PEOs, along with hospitality, retail, and restaurant businesses, are in this latter group and face significant issues in dealing with the employer mandate rules.

PEOs specializing in IT or professional employees routinely offer comprehensive health care coverage to employees placed on long assignments. PEO firms often provide several services and benefits, including permanent placement, temp-to-permanent, and payroll for the recipient employer in addition to the placement of temporary workers on short-term assignments to supplement a client company's core workforce.

47. What specific issues will PEOs likely need to consider in regard to the employer mandate?

Issues for PEOs from Employer Mandate

Most PEOs employ internal staff who run the company and recruit the temporary employees and workers to perform temporary work for the PEO firms' clients (recipients). The latter often consist of lower-wage employees, sometimes with high rates of turnover.

Temporary employees have, at least in the past, shown little interest in obtaining health insurance coverage. Thus, many PEO firms have not provided health benefits to those workers. They are more likely to have arrangements under which the internal employees are provided major medical benefits, and the temporary employees are offered no plan or perhaps a limited benefit plan. The employer mandate rules encourage broad-based offers of major medical health coverage to all full-time employees and dependents. Thus, many PEO firms that do not offer affordable minimum value coverage to at least 95 percent of their full-time employees will be subject to an annual nondeductible employer mandate penalty of $2,000 multiplied by the number of all full-time employees, including full-time temporary employees, less thirty.

Additionally, nondiscrimination rules, presently delayed, will apply to health insurance plans. Those rules are to be based on IRS regulations, not yet issued, modeled on the nondiscrimination rules that apply to self-insured plans. There are exclusions in the self-insured nondiscrimination rules that allow exclusion of high-turnover employers or part-time employees.

Employer Mandate and PEO Employees Working for Recipient Employers

For the employer mandate, employee status is determined under the common law standard. A worker is a common law employee if the employer has the right to control and direct the individual who performs the services, not only as to the result to be accomplished by the work but also as to the details and means by which that result is accomplished. It is not necessary that the employer actually direct or control the manner in which the services are performed; it is sufficient if the employer has the right to do so.

Historically, many temporary employees assigned by PEO firms to client firms have been treated as common law employees of the PEO firm. There is no reason to believe this will change, at least with respect to traditional temporary PEO services. PEO employees performing services for many clients, such as payroll services, likely will continue to be PEO employees unless the PEO leases back employees performing payroll solely for one recipient employer. However, where the PEO employee is assigned to one recipient employer, it is likely that the worker will be the common law employee of the recipient if the recipient determines the services to be performed and has a right to determine the details and means used by the employee to perform those services.

Additionally, the employer mandate proposed regulations preamble states that if the primary purpose of the PEO arrangement is to avoid the employer mandate provisions of the Act, the client may be the responsible employer.

Obtaining Minimum Value Coverage to Satisfy Employer Mandate

Healthcare reform's insurance market reforms require that insurers guarantee the availability and renewability of health insurance products in the individual and group markets with no exclusions for preexisting health problems. Thus, PEO firms that want to offer coverage in 2015 and beyond should be able to obtain coverage that provides 60 percent of minimum value, the required minimum threshold for adequate coverage. Prior to 2014, health insurers have often required employers to meet minimum participation requirements to meet their underwriting requirements and avoid adverse selection. This practice will no longer be permitted in 2014 and thereafter. In the past, many health plans also imposed annual and lifetime payment limits to contain health care coverage costs. Beginning in 2014, this practice is no longer allowed. The Act also imposes maximum limits on out-of-pocket costs. Large PEO firms may also elect to self-insure their own health plan, administered by an insurance company or a third-party administrator.

The requirement of guaranteed availability means that carriers cannot apply traditional underwriting practices. This could result in adverse selection with greater numbers of people needing health care to elect it, which would increase the cost of health coverage. Final HHS regulations acknowledge that adverse selection may present a significant economic exposure to insurance companies. As a result HHS allows insurance companies to limit open enrollment periods in the individual and small group markets to once a year to reduce the risk that those needing health care would wait to purchase it when they needed the coverage.

However, HHS did not extend that provision to the large group market. Despite measures to limit adverse selection, insurance costs could still increase substantially due to these insurance reform rules, thereby making affordable, minimum value coverage impracticable for many PEOs. However, nonminimum value health plans may provide a solution, as discussed hereafter.

PEOs and Other Employers May Offer Nonminimum Value Group Health Plans

Penalties under the Code section 4980H(b) apply where an employer offers health coverage that is not affordable or does not provide minimum essential coverage. The term "minimum essential coverage" refers to the source and not the scope of the coverage. Medicare, Medicaid, and VA health benefits provide minimum essential coverage, as does coverage under an eligible employer-sponsored health plan. An "eligible employer-sponsored plan" means a "group health plan" that provides for medical care other than just a HIPAA excepted benefit (e.g., stand-alone vision and/or dental, fixed indemnity, and single disease plans).[1]

Code section 5000A, the individual mandate, requires U.S. citizens and green card holders to maintain minimum essential coverage for themselves and any nonexempt family members or pay a penalty with their federal income tax return. Employer-sponsored minimum essential coverage need not provide for essential health benefits. Nevertheless, it avoids the employee mandate penalty if it is affordable, in which the cost does not exceed 8 percent of the individual's household income for self-only Bronze coverage or individual and family Bronze coverage where the individual has nonexempt family members. Essential health benefits are ten types of health coverage[2] that must be included in fully-insured products sold in the individual and small group markets as part of an "essential health benefits package." These rules don't apply, however, to large group and self-funded plans.

Minimum essential coverage need not offer minimum value, which requires that the coverage pay for sixty percent or more of expected health costs. As discussed, if an employer plan does not provide minimum value coverage, an employee may apply for subsidized coverage through a public exchange, which could trigger a $3,000 employer penalty per full-time employee per year. If an employer is not concerned with meeting the minimum value standard, it may sponsor a group plan that covers "medical care" and that complies with the Act's insurance market reforms. Thus, a plan that covers only preventative care and clinical trials covers medical care and qualifies as an eligible employer-sponsored plan. Indeed, excepted benefits included dental or vision insurance offered under a separate policy, certificate, or contract of insurance, so theoretically it is possible that a self-insured vision plan could be minimum essential coverage.

---

1. Medical care is amounts paid for the diagnosis, cure, mitigation, treatment, or prevention of disease, or amounts paid for the purpose of affecting any structure or function of the body; it includes amounts paid for transportation primarily for and essential to such care, as well as amounts paid for insurance covering such care.
2. Essential health benefits are ambulatory patient services, emergency services, hospitalization, maternity and newborn care, mental health and substance use disorder services (including behavioral health treatment), prescription drugs, rehabilitative and habilitative services and devices, laboratory services, preventive and wellness services and chronic disease management, and pediatric services, including oral and vision care.

Nonminimum value plans will generally be much less expensive and may not require underwriting. Such plans allow the employer to satisfy the coverage option and avoid the $2,000 per full-times employee less thirty no-coverage penalty. Admittedly, the employer can be liable for the 4980H(b) penalty. In many cases, however, the plan's cost plus any penalty will be much lower than the cost of providing affordable coverage that provides minimum value.

Plans that fail to provide minimum value means that low-income employees in firms sponsoring such plans can still obtain subsidized coverage under a plan that provides an essential health benefits package from a public exchange, and the applicable large employer can be subject to the employer mandate penalties. Moreover, for low-income employees, the cost of subsidized coverage will in most cases be less than 9.5 percent of household income, which is what an "affordable" employer plan would cost. If the employee decides to forgo exchange coverage and buys the employer's nonminimum value product, he or she will not be subject to the individual tax penalty for failing to have minimum essential coverage, and the employer will not be subject to the employer mandate for such employees.

Impact of Individual Mandate on Employer Decision Making

48. What is the expected impact of the individual mandate on employer decision making?

To the extent that the individual mandate achieves its purpose of inducing individuals to purchase health insurance coverage, it may have an impact on employer compensation practices. If employees believe that they must purchase health insurance, their favorable perception of the value of employer-provided coverage should increase. This could result in employers providing health insurance coverage in lieu of cash compensation, which has additional employment and income tax advantages for the employer and employee.

However, this would not be the case for employees subject to and paid at the lowest permissible minimum wage. For minimum wage employees, employers have an incentive to keep their hours below thirty per week as a result of the $2,000 employer mandate penalty. Thus, to the extent employees perceive health insurance coverage as being relatively more valuable, vis-à-vis cash compensation, employers should be relatively more likely to provide it.

Example: ABC Corp has 100 full-time employees earning an average of $50,000 per year. ABC Corp's family coverage costs $15,000 per year, of which employees pay $3,000 per year. Most of ABC Corp's employees enroll in family coverage. Mike Smith, a full-time employee has a spouse, Melinda, who also earns $50,000, and Mike has family coverage through ABC Corp's plan.

Mike and Melinda do not qualify for a tax subsidy from the state exchange. If ABC Corp drops its plan altogether, Mike will be required to get coverage through the exchange or pay a penalty. Family coverage for a similar plan in the state exchange costs $15,000.

Mike would need a raise to pay for coverage through the exchange. Since it would be taxable (paid with extra taxable income), to "break even" he would need approximately $14,500 ($12,000 + tax of $1,500). ABC Corp would also have to pay payroll taxes of $1,109 on this amount. In addition, ABC Corp would have to pay the $2,000 penalty. While the coverage now costs ABC Corp $12,000, which is completely deductible, the increased compensation of $14,500, payroll taxes of $1,109, and nondeductible penalty total $17,609 – a net loss to the employer.

For employers that fail to meet the "minimum essential coverage" test, the penalty is based on an annualized amount of $2,000 per year times the number of full-time employees in excess of thirty.[1] There are issues as to how the triggering language for this penalty – whether an employer fails to "offer to its full-time employees (and their dependents)" – will be interpreted. For example, does this penalty apply even to an employer who employs hundreds of full-time employees and provides most, but not all, of them with "minimum essential coverage?" If this is the rule, what happens if an employer does offer such coverage to all of its full-time employees, but incorrectly characterizes another full-time worker as an independent contractor and fails to provide that individual with such coverage? Could that employer potentially be subject to a $2,000 penalty with respect to all of its employees in excess of 30 as a consequence of that single failure to provide coverage?[2]

The IRS has indicated that "it is contemplated that the proposed regulations will make clear that an employer offering [minimum essential] coverage to all, or substantially all, of its full-time employees would not be subject to the 4980H(a) 'all-full time employees minus 30' assessable payment provisions."[3]

Individual Health Insurance
Premium Tax Credits

49. Who is entitled to a subsidy in the form of a tax credit for purchasing health insurance from a state exchange?

The premium tax credit (cost-sharing reduction) for individuals who purchase in insurance on a state exchange is what triggers both the $2,000 all-full time employees minus 30 and $3,000 per-employee penalties for violating the employer mandate, employee eligibility for either of these subsidies is likely to be a matter of significant concern for many employers. Both subsidies are available to lower and middle income taxpayers with "household incomes" up to 400% of the "poverty level."[4] The following chart reflects the federal poverty level and multiples of income.

---

1. IRC Sec. 4980H(c)(2)(D).
2. *See* technical explanation, at 39-40
3. IRS Notice 2011-36.
4. 42 USC §18071(b) (PPACA §1402(b)); IRC Secs. 36B(b)(2)(B)(ii), (3)(A).

2013 Federal Poverty Level Percentage of Gross Yearly Income

Family Size	100%	133%	150%	200%	250%	300%	400%
1	$11,490	$15,282	$17,235	$22,980	$28,725	$34,470	$45,960
2	$15,510	$20,628	$23,265	$31,020	$38,775	$46,530	$62,040
3	$19,530	$25,975	$29,295	$39,060	$48,825	$58,590	$78,120
4	$23,550	$31,322	$35,325	$47,100	$58,875	$70,650	$94,200
5	$27,570	$36,668	$41,355	$55,140	$68,925	$82,710	$110,280
6	$31,590	$42,015	$47,385	$63,180	$78,975	$94,770	$126,360
7	$35,610	$47,361	$53,415	$71,220	$89,025	$106,830	$142,440
8	$39,630	$52,708	$59,445	$79,260	$99,075	$118,890	$158,520
For each additional person, add	$4,020	$5,347	$6,030	$8,040	$9,907	$12,060	$16,080

Source: The information is compiled from the 2013 HHS Poverty Guidelines, U.S. Dept. of Health and Human Services at http://aspe.hhs.gov/poverty/13poverty.cfm.

Under the current poverty-line income levels and the household income multiples thereof triggering eligibility for the premium tax credit and cost-sharing, a large part of the population will be eligible for these subsidies.[1] As the chart above shows, an individual with annual income below $45,960 and a family of four with a household income of $94,200 would qualify for the tax credit based on 400 percent of the calendar year 2013 poverty-level numbers, which are adjusted each year for inflation. The median household income in the United States was $49,445 in 2010.[2] Note that these 2013 numbers are for illustration purposes and the actual numbers will be based on the 2014 federal poverty level numbers.

The applicable poverty level for any given employee is dependent upon the number of dependents for which he or she is entitled to personal exemption deductions. Generally, employers typically do not have this information, even though they may be obligated to provide coverage for all such dependents.

A large number of Americans purchasing insurance on a state exchange will be eligible for the individual premium subsidies and cost-sharing reductions. The following chart shows the percent of household income that an individual is required to spend on his insurance premiums. The federal government will provide the rest of the health insurance premium cost with a tax subsidy.

---

1. There is a single uniform poverty line for the 48 contiguous states and the District of Columbia, and separate ones for Alaska and Hawaii, respectively. The Secretary of HHS is to conduct a study to determine the feasibility and implications of adjusting the poverty line for different geographic locations. PPACA §1416, as added by PPACA §10105.
2. DeNavas-Walt, Carmen *et al.*, Income, Poverty & Health Insurance Coverage in the United States: 2010, U.S. Census Bureau, (Sept. 2011), http://www.census.gov/prod/2011 pubs/p60-239.pdf. This is the last year for which such statistics are currently available.

Income Level*	Premium/Percent of Income
• 100-133% of FPL	2% of income
• 133-150% of FPL	3-4% of income
• 150-200% of FPL	4-6.3% of income
• 200-250% of FPL	6.3-8.05% of income
• 250-300% of FPL	8.05-9.5% of income
• 300-400% of FPL	9.5% of income

*Note: In 2013, 100% of FPL for a family of 4 is $23,550; 400% is $94,200. The actual numbers that will apply will be based on the 2014 federal poverty level tables.

**Household Income Defined**. Household income is defined as the modified adjusted gross income of the taxpayer and all other individuals for whom the taxpayer is allowed a dependency exemption.[1] Moreover, proposed regulations would limit this to include only dependents who actually file their own income tax returns.[2] Modified adjusted gross income is adjusted gross income increased by the foreign earned income exclusion, tax-exempt interest, and the tax-exempt portion of Social Security benefits.[3]

Knowing employees' household income is important to an employer for several reasons. First, the employee will only be entitled to a premium tax credit or cost-sharing reduction if his or her household income is below 400 percent of the poverty level.[4] The required contribution for the employer mandate affordability test is based on the cost of self-only coverage to the employee. Employer-sponsored coverage is affordable for an employee (and his or her dependents) if the cost of employer-sponsored self-only coverage is less than 9.5 percent of household income, even if the employee selects employer-sponsored family coverage at a cost greater than 9.5 percent of household income.[5]

Second, even if an employer offers minimum essential coverage, an employee is eligible for the premium tax credit or cost-sharing reduction if that employee's required contribution to obtain employer coverage exceeds 9.5 percent [6] of "household income."[7] An employee who is offered such affordable minimum essential coverage by the employer cannot claim the premium tax credit or cost-sharing reduction, even though he or she would otherwise be eligible.[8]

The determination of affordability is made at the time that the employee enrolls in the exchange, and the determination lasts the entire plan year.[9] Thus, if the exchange initially

---

1. IRC Secs. 36B(d)(1), (2)(A).
2. Prop. Treas. Reg. §1.36B-1(e).
3. IRC Sec. 36B(d)(2)(B) (as amended by the Three Percent Withholding Repeal and Job Creation Act, Pub. L. No. 112-56, §401). This is in contrast to the definition of "modified adjusted gross income" for purposes of the new Medicare tax on "net investment income", which does not adjust for tax-exempt interest.
4. IRC Sec. 36B(c)(1)(A); 42 USC §18071(b) (PPACA §1402(b)).
5. See Prop. Treas. Reg. §1.36B-2(c)(3)(v)(A)(l) and preamble thereto.
6. This 9.5% cap may be adjusted for the excess of premium growth inflation over income growth and/or the consumer price index. See IRC Sec. 36B(c)(2)(C)(iv), (b)(3)(A)(ii).
7. IRC Sec. 36B(c)(2)(C); 42 USC §18071(f)(2) (PPACA §1402(f)(2)).
8. IRC Sec. 36B(c)(2)(C).
9. Prop. Treas. Reg. §1.36B-2(c)(3)(v).

determined that the employer-sponsored plan was not affordable, then it is treated as such, regardless of whether the employee's household income ultimately proves high enough to make it affordable in hindsight. On the other hand, the employer will not be responsible for the penalty if the exchange determines that the coverage is not affordable but in fact it is.

W-2 Safe Harbor. The regulations will provide an affordability safe harbor for employers. An employer that meets certain requirements, including offering its full-time employees (and their dependents) the opportunity to enroll in eligible employer-sponsored coverage, will not be subject to an assessable payment under Section 4980H(b) (the $3,000 "per-employee" penalty) with respect to an employee who receives a premium tax credit or cost-sharing reduction for a taxable year if the employee portion of the self-only premium for the employer's lowest cost plan that provides minimum value does not in fact exceed 9.5 percent of the employee's current wages from the employer, as shown in Box 1 of Form W-2.[1]

For employers who are interested in providing coverage only to the extent necessary to avoid penalties, these household income and poverty level tests are problematic. It will be difficult, if not impossible, for an employer to reliably know what an employee's household income is.[2] Even if the employer pays an employee compensation in excess of 400 percent of the poverty level, it is still possible for the employee or his or her spouse to have a net loss from partnership, S corporation, or even sole proprietorship activities that will bring their joint household income down below that level.

Employees eligible for Medicaid are treated as being "eligible for minimum essential coverage other than eligibility for coverage described in Section 5000A(f)(1)(C) (relating to coverage in the individual market)," and therefore not eligible for the premium tax credit or cost sharing reduction.[3] Such eligibility is typically based, at least in part, on an individual's income in relation to the poverty level or a related statistic.

Additionally, it could be difficult or impossible for an employer to procure such household income information for an employee and his or her dependents. The employee can refuse to provide it. Section 1411(f)(2)(B) of PPACA provides as follows:

Notwithstanding any provision of this title (or the amendments made by this title) or Section 6103 of the Internal Revenue Code of 1986, an employer shall not be entitled to any taxpayer return information with respect to an employee for purposes of determining whether the employer is subject to the penalty under Section 4980H of such Code with respect to the employee, except that —

---

1. See IRS Notice 2011-73, which states that it believes this would be a "workable and predictable method" based on information that "employers know." The Notice states that employers may be able to use the safe harbor prospectively to structure its plan and operations to set the employee contribution at a level so that the employee contribution for each employee would not exceed 9.5% of that employee's W-2 wages for the upcoming year.
2. The safe harbor noted above based on an employee's actual W-2 wages from the employer would apply only for purposes of the affordability test.
3. IRC Secs. 36B(c)(2)(B)(i); 5000A(f)(1)(A)(ii); Prop. Treas. Reg. §1.36B-2(c)(2).

(i) the employer may be notified as to the name of an employee and whether or not the employee's income is above or below the threshold by which the affordability of an employer's health insurance coverage is measured; and

(ii) this subparagraph shall not apply to an employee who provides a waiver (at such time and in such manner as the Secretary may prescribe) authorizing an employer to have access to the employee's taxpayer return information.

There is a question as to whether this provision only restricts the federal government from disclosing this information, or whether it precludes an employer from asking the employee for such information. To avoid penalties, an employer potentially subject to the penalty may have to provide minimum essential coverage to each of its employees if it does not know whether their respective household incomes are or were above or below 400 percent of the poverty level (or low enough to trigger Medicaid). Under the above provision, the employer would only be entitled to know "whether or not the employee's income is above or below the threshold by which the affordability of an employee's health insurance coverage is measured."[1] Presumably, the employer would have to inform the Secretary of HHS of what the actual employee contribution was and then the Secretary would be able to tell the employer whether the employee is eligible for reduced cost-sharing or the premium tax credit (and the employer was therefore subject to the penalty). It could be too late for the employer to avoid substantial penalty(ies) for prior years.

50. Who is entitled to a subsidy in the form of a tax credit for purchasing health insurance from a state exchange?

The affordability tests are for employee-only coverage. It must cost no more than the household income or one of several safe harbors, such as the employee's current Box 1, W-2 income: 9.5 percent of the employee's rate of pay, or 9.5 percent of the FPL for a single person. The insurance offered in 2015 must be for employees and dependents (including children under 26 but not their spouses), but only the employee coverage needs to meet the affordability test. Uninsured spouses are eligible for exchange subsidies if they qualify, based on household income being under 400 percent of FPL and dependents (where employer dependent coverage is offered but not selected) may be eligible for coverage in a state sponsored plan.

51. Who are qualified individuals for purposes of the final regulation for the Code section 36B credit?

T.D. 9611, 01/30/2013, Reg. §1.36B explains the Code section 36B health insurance premium tax credit enacted by healthcare reform. The regulation applies to tax years ending after Dec. 31, 2013, and provides guidance to individuals related to employees who may enroll in eligible employer-sponsored coverage and who wish to enroll in qualified health plans through Affordable Insurance Exchanges and claim the premium tax credit. The regulations extend

---

1. 42 USC §18081(f)(2)(B) (PPACA §1411(f)(2)(B)). Presumably, this language is intended to allow the employer to find out whether its required employee contribution is above or below the 9.5 percent household income affordability threshold for the employee in question, although the language is not clear.

these tax credits and subsidies to the purchase of health insurance on state created exchanges and federal exchanges created in states without exchanges of their own.

52. What is the purpose of the Code section 36B credit regulation?

The Code section 36B credit is designed to make health insurance affordable to individuals with modest incomes (i.e., between 100 percent and 400 percent of the federal poverty level, or FPL) who are not eligible for other qualifying coverage, such as Medicare, or "affordable" employer-sponsored health insurance plans. Eligibility for other coverage is determined on a month-by-month basis. The credit applies beginning in 2014.

Code section 5000A(e) provides an employer-sponsored plan is not affordable if the employee's required contribution for single (self-only) coverage exceeds 9.5 percent of household income for the tax year. The percentage may be adjusted after 2014. The employee's cost for self-only coverage is used even if the employee has family coverage, which is more expensive. For an individual other than an employee who is eligible to enroll in the plan because of a relationship the individual bears to the employee, affordability is also measured by the employee's cost of self-only coverage.

Thus, the statutory language specifies that for both employees and others (such as spouses or dependents) who are eligible to enroll in employer-sponsored coverage because of their relationship to an employee (related individuals), the coverage is unaffordable only if the required contribution for "self-only" coverage exceeds 9.5 percent of household income.

In May of 2012, final Code section 36B regulations were issued. However, Reg. §1.36B-2(c) (3)(v)(A)(2) reserved the question of determining affordability of employer-sponsored coverage for related individuals. Consistent with these statutory provisions, the proposed regulation would provide that an employer-sponsored plan also is affordable for a related individual if the employee's required contribution for self-only coverage under the plan does not exceed 9.5 percent of the applicable taxpayer's household income for the tax year, even if the taxpayer's required contribution for the family coverage exceeds 9.5 percent of household income for the year.

53. How can a qualified individual receive a Code section 36B credit?

The eligible individual purchases affordable coverage through "Affordable Insurance Exchanges" that will make qualified health insurance plans available to individuals as well as small businesses.

The Exchange makes subsidy payments to the qualified health plan on behalf of the individual. The subsidy payments take the form of an advance credit payment ("monthly premium assistance amount") under Code section 36B. Using information available at the time of enrollment, the Exchange determines (1) whether the individual meets the income and other requirements for advance credit payments, and (2) the amount of the advance payments. Advance payments are made monthly to the issuer of the qualified health plan in which the individual enrolls. The monthly premium assistance amount is the lesser of the premium for the qualified health plan in which a taxpayer or family member enrolls, or the excess of the premium for the benchmark plan (the second-lowest "silver plan") over the applicable percentage of the taxpayer's household income. The applicable percentage of the premium assistance increases as the percentage of the FPL for the taxpayer's family size increases.

The eligible individual reconciles the actual credit for the tax year computed on the taxpayer's tax return for the prior year with the amount of advance payments paid on the taxpayer's behalf. If a taxpayer's credit amount exceeds the amount of advance payments paid on the taxpayer's behalf for the tax year, the taxpayer may receive the excess as an income tax refund. If advance payments made on the taxpayer's behalf exceed the taxpayer's credit amount, the taxpayer owes the excess as an additional income tax liability. However, Code section 36B(f)(2)(B) caps the additional tax liability for taxpayers with household income under 400 percent of the FPL. The repayment limitation amounts range from $600 to $2,500 (one half that amount for single taxpayers) depending on FPL, and will be adjusted to reflect changes in the cost of living beginning in 2015.

For tax years beginning before Jan. 1, 2015, an eligible employer-sponsored plan is affordable for related individuals if the portion of the annual premium the employee must pay (the employee's required contribution percentage) for self-only coverage does not exceed 9.5 percent of the taxpayer's household income.[1]

54. How does the Code section 36B credit work for related individuals?

The final regulation provides guidance to individuals related to employees who may enroll in eligible employer-sponsored coverage and who wish to enroll in qualified health plans through Affordable Insurance Exchanges and claim the premium tax credit.

Example: H is married to W and Employer X's plan requires H to contribute $5,300 for coverage for H and W for 2014, which reflects 11.3 percent of H's household income. However, the contribution attributable to self-only coverage of $3,450 does not exceed 9.5 percent of household income as required by Reg. §1.36B-2(c)(3)(v)(A)(2). Therefore, X's plan is affordable for both H and W. Reg. §1.36B-2(c)(3)(v)(D), Example 2.

By contrast, Code section 5000A, which establishes the shared responsibility payment applicable to individuals (the individual mandate) for failure to maintain minimum essential coverage addresses affordability for employees in Code section 5000A(e)(1)(B) and for related individuals in Code section 5000A(e)(1)(H). The proposed regulations under Code section 5000A provide that, for purposes of applying the affordability exemption from the shared responsibility payment in the case of related individuals, the required contribution is based on the premium the employee would pay for employer-sponsored family coverage.[2]

---

1. Reg. §1.36B-2(c)(3)(v)(A)(2).
2. See T.D. 9611, 01/30/2013.

55. How can employers use the Code section 36B in its health-insurance planning?

If an employer limits every employee's premium for self-only coverage at 9.45 percent of pay, it will never pay the $3,000 employer mandate penalty for failure to provide affordable coverage. It is perfectly legal to set lower premium for lower-paid employees. An employer can set the employee's premium for family coverage as high as it wishes.

56. May an employer establish an employee contribution schedule and allow employees to be eligible for reduced contributions if they provide evidence that their required contributions would otherwise be in excess of the affordability limits?

An employee's information for as many as three taxable years could be relevant in making all of these various determinations. First, eligibility for the premium tax credit is dependent upon an employee's household income for the current taxable year.[1] Second, the determination as to whether an employee is eligible for reduced cost-sharing is apparently going to be based on the employee's income for the preceding taxable year.[2] Third, any advance payment of the credit or cost-reduction, which can also trigger an employer penalty, must be made "on the basis of the individual's household income for the most recent taxable year for which the Secretary of HHS, after consultation with the Secretary of the Treasury, determines information is available," which could easily be the employee's second preceding taxable year.[3]

57. Can applicable large employers with 50 or more full-time equivalent employees avoid the employer mandate penalty by offering an actuarially equivalent contribution to an HSA or FSA so that employees can buy health care coverage on the exchange or in the private non-group market?

To avoid the employer penalties, coverage must be minimum essential coverage. Health savings accounts (HSAs) are not minimum essential coverage because they are not group health plans under ERISA.[4] For health flexible spending accounts (FSAs), the answer is not clear but likely no. It is possible that FSAs could be minimum essential coverage if they are the only coverage offered by the employer and the employer contribution is greater than two times the employee contribution, or $500 over the employee contribution.

Additional guidance is needed to clarify if such FSAs are minimum essential coverage. If so, then perhaps an FSA contribution could avoid the employer mandate penalty. However, FSAs cannot be used to pay premiums for other coverage (other than COBRA coverage, if the plan allows). Accordingly, this rule would need to be changed in order for individuals to use FSA money to purchase exchange coverage. The way employee contributions are used to purchase

---

1. IRC Sec. 36B(b)(2)(B)(ii).
2. 42 USC §18071(f)(3); 18082(b)(1)(B) (PPACA §§1402(f)(3); 1412(b)(1)(B)).
3. IRC Sec. 4980H(c)(3)(C); 42 USC §18082(b)(1)(B) (PPACA §1412(b)(1)(B)).
4. DOL FAB 2004-1.

insurance in a cafeteria plan is through premium conversion so that the employee election is specifically and solely for employer sponsored health insurance.

58. What is minimum essential coverage?

The individual mandate requires individuals to be responsible for ensuring that they, and any of their dependents, are covered under minimum essential coverage. Minimum essential coverage includes:

- Government sponsored programs including: Medicare, Medicaid, Children's Health Insurance Program coverage (CHIP), TRICARE, coverage through Veterans Affairs, and Health Care for Peace Corps volunteers;

- Employer-sponsored plans including governmental plans, grandfathered plans, and other plans offered in the small or large group market;

- Individual market plans, including grandfathered plans; and

- Other coverage designated as minimum essential coverage by HHS and/or the Dept. of the Treasury.[1] There is more detail on this in the following section.

59. What individuals are not subject to the individual mandate?

Beginning January 1, 2014, all U.S. residents are required to maintain minimum essential coverage unless the individual falls into one of the following exceptions:

- individuals with a religious conscience exemption (applies only to certain faiths);

- incarcerated individuals;

- undocumented aliens;

- individuals who cannot afford coverage (i.e. required contribution exceeds 8 percent of household income);

- individuals with a coverage gap of less than three months;

- individuals in a hardship situation (as defined by HHS);

- individuals with income below the tax filing threshold; and

- members of Indian tribes.[2]

---

1. PPACA §1501, adding IRC Sec. 5000A(f).
2. PPACA §1501 and 10106 adding IRC Sec. 5000A(d) and (e).

60. Could you provide more detail on persons who are not subject to the individual mandate because they are not "applicable individuals"?

Applicable Individual. The individual mandate tax penalty applies only to applicable individuals, and the definition of that term excludes designated categories of individuals. These excluded categories include members of certain religious faiths already exempt from self-employment tax, members of healthcare-sharing ministries which, among other things, share medical expenses among members and have been in continuous existence since December 31, 1999, illegal aliens, and incarcerated individuals after they have been convicted.[1]

There are also exemptions for members of Indian tribes, short-term coverage gaps of one or two months, hardships (as determined by the Secretary of HHS) and persons residing outside of the United States or within U.S. possessions.[2] There are no corresponding exceptions for employers under the employer mandate. Thus, it appears that both the "all full-time employees minus 30" and per-employee penalties under the employer mandate would take such employees into account.[3]

Affordability. Another major exemption is the one for applicable individuals whose "required contribution (determined on an annual basis) for coverage for the month exceeds 8 percent of such individual's household income for the taxable year."[4] For this exemption, the required contribution for an individual eligible to participate in an employer-sponsored plan is equal to "the portion of the annual premium which would be paid by the individual (without regard to whether paid through salary reduction or otherwise) for self-only coverage."[5] For individuals whose sole option is to purchase insurance through an exchange, the required contribution is equal to the annual premium for the lowest cost bronze plan available in the individual market through the exchange in the state in the rating area in which the individual resides reduced by the amount of the credit allowable under Section 36B for the taxable year (determined as if the individual was covered by a qualified plan offered through the exchange for the entire taxable year).[6] The tax code provision does not define required contribution for other types of plans. For example, the Medicare Part A premium should be the required contribution for individuals over sixty-five who are not eligible to participate in employer-sponsored plans.

While an individual's current "required contribution" is "determined on an annual basis," the 8 percent affordability amount is determined "on the basis of the individual's household income for the most recent taxable year for which the Secretary of Health and Human Services, after consultation with the Secretary of the Treasury, determines information is available."[7] Thus, the household income for affordability is likely to be determined on the basis of the income tax return filed for the preceding, and possibly the second preceding, taxable year of the applicable

---

1. IRC Sec. 5000A(d)(2), (3), (4).
2. IRC Sec. 5000A(e)(3), (4), (5), (f)(4).
3. *See generally* IRC Sec. 4980H(c).
4. IRC Sec. 5000A(e)(1)(A). It is not clear why the affordability test for employers is 9.5 percent whereas this individual "affordability test" is 8 percent.
5. IRC Sec. 5000A(e)(1)(B)(i). This affordability test based on the premium for self-only coverage will be integrated into the penalty calculation under which an individual may also be responsible for providing coverage for a spouse and/or dependents. *See* Preamble to Proposed Regulations for Code Section 36B.
6. IRC Sec. 5000A(e)(1)(B)(ii).
7. IRC Sec. 5000A(e)(1)(A); 42 USC §18082(b)(1)(B) (PPACA §1412(b)(1)(B)).

individual. Finally, the 8 percent affordability factor is to be adjusted to reflect "the excess of the rate of premium growth between the preceding calendar year and 2013 over the rate of income growth for such period."[1]

Income Below Filing Threshold. Taxpayers whose household income for a taxable year is less than the gross income necessary to trigger an income tax return filing requirement[2] are not applicable individuals and are not subject to the employee mandate. These gross income levels are unlikely to exempt many applicable individuals who are not already exempt under the 8 percent affordability exemption discussed above. However, many such individuals are also likely to be eligible for Medicaid and thus exempt from the penalty as long as they apply to procure such coverage.

Dependents. The individual mandate Code provisions' use of the dependency deduction for triggering and calculating the penalty creates conflicting planning considerations for individuals who may be subject to the penalty. Claiming someone as a dependent is favorable under the Code. For example, in addition to the dependency exemption itself and possible qualification for head-of-household tax rates,[3] there is the benefit of having a higher applicable poverty-level threshold for purposes of the premium tax credit discussed above. On the other hand, the $95/$325/$695 (inflation adjusted) 2014/2015/2016 minimum penalty is increased with each additional dependent, although at a rate of only one-half of the applicable dollar amount for children under the age of 18.[4] Thus, a parent getting divorced may be less willing to be allocated the dependency deduction for children of the marriage if it means being obligated to procure health coverage for such children.[5] Parents will be less inclined to provide over one-half of the individual's support for the calendar year (the requirement to be a dependent) if it means that the taxpayer will end up owing a penalty for failure to procure health coverage for such individual.[6]

It seems that the household income of a young child with no income would be zero, and therefore such a child would not trigger additional penalty obligations for his or her parents under the individual mandate provisions as a result of the affordability and filing threshold exemptions.

Spouses. The individual mandate creates issues for certain spouses. Both spouses are jointly liable for whatever penalty is due on a joint return.[7] However, the individual mandate only requires that an applicable individual ensure that minimum essential coverage is procured both for the individual and any dependent of the individual who is an applicable individual.[8] Additionally, the definition of "family-size" for determining household income is "the number of individuals for whom the taxpayer is allowed a deduction under Section 151."[9] Neither spouse is a dependent of the other. Rather, they are each entitled to the deduction on a joint return.[10]

---

1. IRC Sec. 5000A(e)(1)(D).
2. IRC Sec. 5000A(e)(2).
3. IRC Sec. 2(b)(1)(A)(i) (being entitled to the dependency exemption for a child is a precondition to qualifying for head of household status).
4. IRC Sec. 5000A(c)(3)(C).
5. *See* IRC Sec. 152(e).
6. *See* IRC Sec. 152(b)(1)(C).
7. IRC Sec. 5000A(b)(3)(B).
8. IRC Sec. 5000A(a).
9. IRC Sec. 5000A(c)(4)(A).
10. *See* IRC Sec. 151, 152.

There is a provision that entitles a taxpayer to take an additional exemption for his or her spouse when the spouse has no gross income and is not a dependent of another taxpayer. However, this provision only applies when a joint return is *not* filed.[1]

As for dependents, there is an issue of how the penalty is calculated for a non-earning spouse. Such spouse should be entitled to an exemption based on the 8 percent affordability test or the low-income filing threshold test. Both are based on household income, but, again, that in turn is defined by reference to the modified adjusted gross income of the taxpayer and all other "individuals for whom the taxpayer is allowed a deduction under section 151 (relating to allowance of deduction for personal exemptions)."[2] Thus, it seems that the income of the earning spouse and dependent should not be included in a non-earning spouse's household income. Therefore, a non-earning spouse might not be taken into account in calculating the penalty for the earning spouse because the Code provides that "[n]o penalty shall be imposed ... with respect to" exempted individuals. Although there is no penalty with respect to a non-earning spouse, that spouse is still jointly and severally liable for the individual mandate penalty with respect to his or her spouse and the dependents of his or her spouse. The non-earning spouse could refuse to sign a joint return. However, in addition to the tax bracket, deduction, and other ramifications of that decision, the earning spouse would also then not be eligible for the premium tax credit.[3]

61. How is the individual mandate tax penalty enforced?

The law limits the IRS ability to collect this tax penalty from individuals. Although the individual mandate tax penalty is supposed to be assessed and collected in the same manner as other penalties assessable under the Code, there can be no criminal prosecution or penalty for failure to pay the penalty,[4] though presumably civil penalties could be applicable. Moreover, the Service "shall not ... file notice of lien with respect to any property of a taxpayer by reason of any failure to pay the [Individual Mandate] penalty ... or levy on any such property with respect to such failure."[5]

Thus, the IRS's collection tools are limited, although it could send a notice of demand and/or offset refunds as to the applicable individual who fails to pay the assessed penalty.

Health Plan and Insurance Changes: Coverage Mandates

62. What are the ten essential health benefits (EHBs) required by the 2010 federal health reform? How do state health insurance mandates relate to them?

The 2010 Patient Protection and Affordable Care Act[6] requires the Secretary of HHS to define the EHBs through regulation. It also requires that at least some items and services

---

1. *See* IRC Sec. 151(b).
2. IRC Sec. 5000A(e)(1), (2), (c)(4)(b), (a).
3. IRC Sec. 36B(c)(1)(C).
4. IRC Sec. 5000A(g)(2)(A). This leaves open the question of whether or not there could be a criminal penalty, for example under Section 7203 of the Code, with respect to the failure "to make a return, keep any records or supply any information" as required by the Code for purposes of calculating and imposing the penalty.
5. IRC Sec. 5000A(g)(2)(B).
6. PPACA §1302(b).

within specific categories of benefits be included in the definition. The term "essential health benefits" means the benefits that non-grandfathered plans sold in the small group market on or outside of a state exchange must have, beginning in 2014. Grandfathered plans, self-insured group health plans, and health insurance coverage offered in the large group market are not required to offer essential health benefits. Minimum essential coverage is a separate concept and the phrase used to describe the coverage required to fulfill the individual and employer mandates.

The ten EHB categories are:

- Ambulatory patient services;

- Emergency services;

- Hospitalization;

- Maternity and newborn care;

- Mental health and substance use disorder services, including behavioral health treatment;[1]

- Prescription drugs;

- Rehabilitative and habilitative services and devices;

- Laboratory services;

- Preventive and wellness services and chronic disease management; and

- Pediatric services, including oral and vision care.

The scope of essential health benefits is intended to equal the scope of benefits provided under a "typical employer plan" and establish an appropriate balance among the ten benefit categories.[2] Each state's essential health benefits are based on that state's base-benchmark plan.[3] After the application of any adjustments, the plan is known as the "EHB-benchmark plan."[4] The EHB-benchmark plan contains the scope of services and limits offered by a typical employer plan in that state. This EHB benchmark plan process applies for at least the 2014 and 2015 benefit years.[5]

HHS is required to take into account:

---

1. In general, the plans and products studied cover inpatient and outpatient mental health and substance use disorder services; however, coverage in the small group market often has limits. ASPE Research Brief, "Actuarial Value and Employer Sponsored Insurance," November 2011. Available at: http://aspe.hhs.gov/health/reports/2011/AV-ESI/rb.pdf.
2. PPACA §1302(b).
3. 45 CFR §156.100.
4. 45 CFR §156.20.
5. PPACA; Standards Related to Essential Health Benefits, Actuarial Value, and Accreditation; 45 Parts 147, 155, and 156, 78 Fed. Reg. 12841 (Feb. 25, 2013).

- The need for balance between the ten federal EHB categories;

- The needs of diverse segments of the population; and

- The need to not discriminate against individuals because of age, disability, or expected length of life.

EHB Requirements by Market Segment[1]

Market Segment	Subject to EHB Requirement	Not Subject to EHB Requirement
Large Group Market	Effective 2017, states may allow large group purchasing through the exchange, which would subject large group plans and policies to EHB requirements[2]	**Outside the Exchange:** • State regulated plans and policies
Small Group Market	**Outside the Exchange:** • State regulated plans and policies **Inside the Exchange:** • QHPs and CO OP plans[3] • Multistate Plans offered by the federal Office of Personnel Management (OPM)[4]	**Outside the Exchange:** • Grandfathered plans • Grandfathered policies

Individual Market	**Outside the Exchange:**
	• State regulated plans and policies
	
	Inside the Exchange:
	• State regulated QHPs, including:
	  – Catastrophic plans[5]
	  – CO-OP plans[6]
	  – Interstate healthcare choice compacts
	• Multistate Plans, offered by the federal Office of Personnel Management (OPM)
		Outside the Exchange:
		• Grandfathered plans
		• Grandfathered policies

63. How will the essential health benefits mandate be implemented?

Federal health reform requires coverage of essential health benefits (EHBs) for most major medical health plans and policies sold in the individual and small group markets, both inside and outside the state's health insurance exchange. Broadly, inside the state's health insurance exchange, qualified health plans (QHPs) will be subject to state and federal mandates. See Q 76. Self-insured group health plans, health insurance offered

---

1. There are other sources of health insurance, including self-insured plans, the Veterans Administration, and Medicare, that are not addressed in this table. These coverages are not subject to the EHB coverage requirements.
2. PPACA §1312(f)(2)(B).
3. PPACA §1322 provides for nonprofit, member-run health insurance issuers offering qualified health plans (QHPs) in the individual and small group markets.
4. PPACA §1334 directs OPM to offer at least two multistate qualified health plans in each state exchange.
5. PPACA §1302(e).
6. PPACA §1322 provides for nonprofit, member-run health insurance issuers offering qualified health plans in the individual and small group markets.

in the large group market (generally companies with more than 100 employees), and grandfathered health plans are not required to cover essential health benefits or provide minimum essential coverage. Additionally, outside of a state's health insurance exchange, non-grandfathered plans and policies in the individual and small group markets will be required to cover essential health benefits. Effective in 2017, states may allow large group purchasing through the exchange, which would subject large group plans and policies to the EHB requirements.[1]

Federal health reform requires that certain items and services within ten specific categories of benefits must be included in the essential health benefits, which must be defined by HHS through regulation.[2] The law distinguishes between a plan's covered services and the plan's cost-sharing features, such as deductibles, copayments, and coinsurance. The cost-sharing features will determine the level of actuarial value of the plan, expressed as a "metal level" as specified in the statute:

- Bronze at 60 percent of actuarial value,

- Silver at 70 percent of actuarial value,

- Gold at 80 percent of actuarial value, and

- Platinum at 90 of percent actuarial value.

In December 2011, HHS released initial guidance on essential health benefits. HHS's approach to defining the essential health benefits allows states to select a benchmark plan from four options that reflect the scope of services offered by a "typical employer plan."[3] The general categories to be considered in defining a typical employer plan (which is undefined by the statute or regulations) include large employer, small employer, and government health plans.

HHS states that the following four benchmark plan types for 2014 and 2015 best reflect the statutory standards for EHB in the Affordable Care Act:[4]

A state may select its base-benchmark plan from four types of health plans:

- one of the three largest by enrollment small group plans in the state;

- one of the three largest by enrollment state employee health plans;

- one of the three largest by enrollment federal employee health plan options; or

---

1. PPACA §1312(f)(2)(B).
2. PPACA §1302(b).
3. CCIIO, Essential Health Benefits Bulletin (December 16, 2011). Available at http://cciio.cms.gov/resources/files/Files2/12162011/essential_health_benefits_bulletin.pdf.
4. CCIIO, Essential Health Benefits Bulletin (December 16, 2011). Available at cciio.cms.gov/resources/files/Files2/.../essential_health_benefits_bulletin.pdf.

- the largest by enrollment insured commercial HMO operating in the state.[1]

A plan's enrollment is determined from that of the first quarter two years prior to the coverage year.[2] If a state fails to select, the benchmark plan will be the largest plan by enrollment in the largest product in the state's small group market.[3]

64. What is required to become a state selected EHB-benchmark plan?

In order to become a state selected EHB-benchmark plan, a base-benchmark plan must include coverage of the ten categories listed previously.[4] A state's benchmark selection in 2012 is applicable for the 2014 and 2015 benefit years, and be based on plan benefits offered by the selected benchmark at the time of selection, including any applicable state-required benefits enacted prior to December 21, 2011.[5]

The state's EHB-benchmark plan standard covers the benefits, limits on coverage (including limits on the amount, duration, and scope of covered benefits), and prescription drug benefits.[6] Mental health and substance use disorder services must be provided in a manner that complies with the parity standards under the Mental Health Parity and Addiction Equity Act of 2008.[7] Insurers may substitute benefits, or sets of benefits, that are actuarially equivalent to the benefits in the state's EHB benchmark plan within each of the ten categories[8] but not between different benefit categories.[9] Additionally, benefit substitution cannot occur for prescription drug benefits.[10] For prescription drug benefits, a plan must cover at least the *greater of* one drug in every category or class; or the same number of drugs in each category and class as the EHB-benchmark plan.[11] Thus, if the EHB benchmark plan's drug list offers more than one drug in a category or class, then plans covering essential health benefits must offer at least the number of drugs in the EHB-benchmark plan for that class.

The benefits and services included in the benchmark plan option selected by the state would be considered the essential health benefits. State benefit mandates that fall within the benchmark plan selected by the state would be included in the defined essential health benefits for 2014. A requirement in the law that states must defray the costs of state benefit mandates that fall outside the essential health benefits would be waived. However, for any mandates that fall outside the selected benchmark plan, the state would be required to cover the cost of those mandates.

1. 45 CFR §156.100(a).
2. PPACA; Standards Related to Essential Health Benefits, Actuarial Value, and Accreditation; 45 Parts 147, 155, and 156, 78 Fed. Reg. 12841 (Feb. 25, 2013).
3. 45 CFR §156.100(c).
4. 45 CFR §156.100(a); PPACA; Standards Related to Essential Health Benefits, Actuarial Value, and Accreditation; 45 Parts 147, 155, and 156, 78 Fed. Reg. 12841 (Feb. 25, 2013).
5. PPACA; Standards Related to Essential Health Benefits, Actuarial Value, and Accreditation; 45 Parts 147, 155, and 156, 78 Fed. Reg. 12841 (Feb. 25, 2013).
6. 45 CFR §156.115(a)(1).
7. 45 CFR §156.115(a)(2).
8. 45 CFR §156.115(b)(1)(i).
9. 45 CFR §156.115(b)(1)(ii).
10. 45 CFR §156.115(b)(1)(iii).
11. 45 CFR §156.120(a)(1).

Whether the coverage for an existing state benefit mandate will be included in the essential health benefits will depend on the benchmark plan the state selects. State laws regarding required coverage of benefits vary widely in number, scope, and topic, so that generalizing about mandates and their impact on typical employer plans is difficult. All states have adopted at least one health insurance mandate, and there are more than 1,600 specific service and provider coverage requirements across the fifty states and the District of Columbia.[1] Each of the benchmark plan options will include a differing set of state benefit mandates. For example, one of the four benchmark plan options, the Federal Employee Health Benefits Plan, will not include any state benefit mandates as these plans are not subject to state benefit mandates. However, if the state selects the small-group insurance product benchmark plan option, some subset of state benefit mandates would be included in the benchmark plan that would define the essential health benefits. Given the potential for additional marginal costs to the state of benefit mandates above the essential health benefits, there seems to be an incentive for states to select a benchmark plan that includes state benefit mandates.

Because of the complexity of identifying the differing benchmark plan options – and thus identifying the possible essential health benefits for a state – it remains to be seen which state benefit mandates would be included for each of the benchmark options. Under HHS's regulatory approach for defining essential health benefits, until a state selects a benchmark plan, which state benefit mandates, if any, will be included in the essential health benefits for 2014 is unknown, as is the potential cost to the state of benefit mandates outside the essential health benefits.

65. What new requirements are there for grandfathered health plans?

Grandfathered health plans are those continuously in existence since March 23, 2010, and with no prohibited changes subsequently described in this book. Grandfathered health plans are subject to certain health reform requirements, as follows:

- Prohibition of annual and lifetime benefit limits (except that provisions annual limit prohibitions not applicable for individual health insurance coverage but not group coverage).[2]

- No rescission except for fraud or intentional misrepresentation.[3]

- For plan years beginning before January 1, 2014, children who are not eligible for employer-sponsored coverage must be covered up to age twenty-six on an employee's family policy.[4]

---

1. California Health Benefits Review Program, Interaction between California State Benefit Mandates and the Affordable Care Act's "Essential Health Benefits" (March 2012).
2. PHSA §2711.
3. PHSA §2703.
4. PHSA §2714.

- Preexisting condition exclusions for covered individuals younger than age nineteen are prohibited.[1]

- Preexisting condition exclusions prohibited for all persons in 2014.[2]

- Plans may not require a waiting period of more than ninety days.[3]

- Plans must provide a Summary of Benefits and Coverage (SBC).[4]

- Medical Loss Ratio provisions.[5]

66. What new requirements are there for new and non-grandfathered health plans?

New and non-grandfathered plans are subject to the requirements for grandfathered plans (described in Q 65) plus the following requirements:

- The plan must guarantee that coverage is renewable regardless of health status, utilization of health services, or any other related factor. Coverage can only be cancelled under specific, enumerated circumstances.[6]

- The plan may not require cost-sharing for preventive services, immunizations, and screenings.[7]

- Discrimination based on salary is prohibited (the effective date has been postponed until regulations are issued).[8]

- Children must be covered up to age twenty-six on a family policy, regardless of whether they are eligible for coverage with their employer.[9]

- The plan must provide internal appeal and external review processes to ensure independent review.[10]

- Emergency services must be available at the in-network cost-sharing level with no prior authorization.[11]

---

1. PHSA §2704.
2. PHSA §2704.
3. PHSA §2708.
4. PHSA §2709.
5. PHSA §2718.
6. PHSA §2703.
7. PHSA §2713.
8. See IRC Sec. 9815, incorporating by reference Public Health Service Act §2716, which in turn incorporates by reference the principles of IRC Sec. 105(h).
9. PHSA §2714.
10. PHSA §2719.
11. PHSA §2719A.

- Parents must be allowed to select a pediatrician as a primary care physician for children and women must be allowed to select an OB-GYN as their primary care physician.[1]

- Health insurance issuers may not charge discriminatory premium rates. The rate may vary only by whether such plan or coverage covers an individual or family, the rating area, the actuarial value of the plan, the age of the plan participant, and tobacco use.[2]

- Health insurance companies in the small group and individual markets (and large group markets to the extent of purchasing insurance through state exchanges) must include coverage that incorporates defined essential benefits, provides a specified actuarial value, and requires all group health plans to comply with limitations on allowable cost sharing.[3]

- Health insurance issuers are prohibited from dropping coverage because an individual (who requires treatment for cancer or another life-threatening condition) chooses to participate in a clinical trial. Issuers also may not deny coverage for routine care that they would otherwise provide because an individual is enrolled in a clinical trial.[4]

- HIPAA nondiscrimination requirements are continued and no discrimination due to health status is permitted for wellness programs and individual insurance.[5]

- Group health plans and health insurance issuers offering group or individual health insurance coverage must disclose certain enrollee information, such as claims payment policies and practices and enrollee rights, to the federal government and the state insurance commissioner. Such plans and issuers also must provide information to enrollees on the amount of cost-sharing for a specific item or service.[6]

- Health insurance issuers must report information on initiatives and programs that improve health outcomes. A wellness program may not require the disclosure or collection of any information relating to the presence or storage of a lawfully possessed firearm or ammunition in the residence or the lawful use, possession, or storage of a firearm or ammunition by an individual.[7]

---

1. PHSA §2719A.
2. PHSA §2701.
3. PHSA §2707.
4. PHSA §2709.
5. PHSA §2705.
6. PHSA §2715A.
7. PHSA §2717.

State Health Insurance Exchanges[1]

67. What are the state health insurance exchanges?

The law refers to state health insurance exchanges, a major component of the federal health reform, as "American Health Benefit Exchanges."[2] The rules for the state exchanges or marketplaces are discussed in detail in Part X of this book. In theory, insurance companies will compete for business on a transparent, level playing field, which should reduce costs and give individuals and small businesses the purchasing power enjoyed by big businesses. However, health reform does many things to increase costs by covering those who are now uninsurable and by increasing mandated benefits. Many predict these factors will far outweigh any efficiencies created by the exchanges and that health insurance prices will increase. If exchanges succeed, they will create the first viable alternative to the group markets for the younger than age sixty-five population.

Beginning in 2014:

- Each state is required to create an exchange (a governmental agency or nonprofit organization, established by the state[3]) to facilitate the sale of qualified health plans (QHPs), including federally administered multistate plans and nonprofit cooperative plans.[4] The law requires HHS to create an exchange in states that do not set up their own exchanges. However, the health reform law does not provide the federal government with adequate funding to set up or operate federal health insurance exchanges.

  o States can create either one exchange to serve both small group and individual markets[5] or separate exchanges for these pools.

  o One goal is to facilitate a comparison of available health insurance options by purchasers.

- Standards for qualified coverage must include:

  o Mandated essential coverage

  o Cost-sharing requirements (deductibles, copayments, and coinsurance)

    — Out-of-pocket limitations

---

1. For more detailed information see Part X of this publication, which discusses state health insurance exchanges (marketplaces) in detail.
2. PPACA §1311(b).
3. PPACA §1311(d)(1).
4. PPACA §1311(f).
5. PPACA §1311(b)(1)(C).

      –   Minimum actuarial value of 60 percent, which means that the policy, on average, pays 60 percent of the costs for essential health benefits and the insured pays the remaining 40 percent. [The coverage levels are Bronze (60 percent), Silver (70 percent), Gold (80 percent), and Platinum (90 percent).]

    ○   Catastrophic coverage for purchasers aged thirty and younger in the individual market.

    ○   States must also create Small Business Health Option Programs, or "SHOP Exchanges,"1 for small employers to purchase coverage. See Q 77. The states can expand the programs to include large employers beginning in 2017.

States can offer employers certain options:

- Employers can choose any QHP offered in the SHOP in any tier;

- Employers can select specific tiers from which an employee may choose a QHP;

- Employers can select specific QHPs from different tiers of coverage from which an employee may choose a QHP; or

- Employers can select a single QHP to offer employees.

68. How do employers use exchanges?

There is rolling enrollment for employers, but, upon enrollment, the employer is locked into the plan for one-year periods. The plan premiums are also locked in for the same amount of time. Once the employer enrolls in a state exchange:

- The employer must offer Exchange coverage to all employees.

- The Exchange must provide an aggregate bill to the employer for all employees.

- Employers must notify the Exchange about any employee change of status, for example, adding dependents or terminating employment.

- Employers with multiple worksites can offer access to a single Exchange or to state Exchanges where employees are located.

69. Are there any issues with state exchanges?

There are several issues that may affect a state's exchange. For example, states do not have full authority over their own exchanges. HHS has final approval authority for each exchange.

---

1. PPACA §1311(b)(1)(B).

Another issue is the interaction with cafeteria plans regulated by Code Section 125. Coverage offered through an exchange is not a permitted benefit under Code Section 125 and cannot be offered under a cafeteria plan[1] unless the employer offers its employees the opportunity to enroll through an exchange in a group market.[2]

Although the law does not provide the federal government with adequate funding to set up or operate federal health insurance exchanges, exchange costs must be funded by HHS until January 1, 2015. Thereafter, all exchanges must be self-funded.

70. How do individuals apply for health insurance from an Exchange?

HHS has posted a package of draft applications[3] that will be used by individuals seeking to enroll in health insurance coverage through an Exchange, via an online application, for 2014. Exchanges are to begin taking applications for coverage when open enrollment begins on October 1, 2013. The applications will collect information to determine whether the applicant (1) is eligible to purchase a qualified health plan through an Exchange and (2) qualifies for any affordability programs, such as advance payment of premium tax credits, cost-sharing reductions, or Medicaid.

One basic application is eight pages, and a second is twenty-one pages. Appendix A, which lists all possible questions an individual may be asked, is sixty pages long. Items will be displayed on the online application depending on applicants' household and income situations, so applicants will not be required to complete the entire list of items if they apply online. The information that is available from other federal sources, such as taxable income from the prior year from the IRS, are automatically shown on the on-line application. The completed application can be printed out for the applicant's records. The completed form will list the programs for which the individual qualifies, including advance application of the premium tax credit, which can also be applied for online. Additionally, a person can apply for Exchange provided health insurance using a paper form, over the phone, and in person. There is a video[4] walking through the application process for a single person and another for a family of three.

71. What is a loophole in the law as to exchange purchased insurance and its impact on insureds and providers?

Doctors and hospitals who contract with insurers selling policies on state health insurance exchanges in 2014 and thereafter may find themselves liable for treatment costs due to the healthcare reform law. Under the ACA,[5] families who obtain subsidized health plan coverage through an exchange and who fail pay their premiums have a three-month grace period for premium payment[6] before the policy is cancelled.[7]

---

1. PPACA §1515(a); IRC 125(f)(3)(A).

2. PPACA §1515(a); IRC 125(f)(3)(B).

3. See http://cms.gov/Regulations-and-Guidance/Legislation/PaperworkReductionActof1995/PRA-Listing-Items/CMS-10440.html.

4. See http://www.youtube.com/cmshhsgov.

5. PPACA §1412(c)(2)(B)(iv)(II).

6. 45 CFR §§155.430(b)(2)(ii)(A) and (B) and 156.270(d).

7. 76 Fed. Reg. 41866; 45 CFR §§155.430 & 156.270 available at https://www.federalregister.gov/articles/2012/03/27/2012-6125/patient-protection-and-affordable-care-act-establishment-of-exchanges-and-qualified-health-plans#h-165.

However, insurers are responsible only for paying claims during the first month of this three-month grace period. During months two and three, families are asked to pay their hospital and doctor's bills or their insurance premium if they seek health care services. However, if they do not pay either bill, providers will not be paid for the cost of the treatment. Such families would face a tax penalty for the advance payment of the premium tax credit paid on their behalf when the initial coverage was purchased, but they would not receive a fine, a premium rate increase, or a repayment order. They could also purchase another subsidized exchange policy the next year.

The three-month grace period was meant to ensure continuity of care for low-income families who might be between jobs and cannot afford to pay their premiums for a few weeks. However, it is not the provider's job to manage this risk.

Health plans are supposed to give providers fifteen days' notice of the termination of payment by the policy, in which case providers might be unable to avoid treating exchange patients. However, contracts by providers with large health insurers often include an "all-products" clause, which requires that doctors treat any patients covered under the health plan. Additionally, doctors have legal and ethical obligations not to abandon their patients during course of treatment. A round of chemotherapy can cost tens of thousands of dollars or more.

In a notice published in the Federal Register,[1] HHS acknowledged that nonpayment of premiums for subsidized exchange policies would "increase uncertainty for providers and increase the burden of uncompensated care." HHS officials said that the agency will "monitor this issue moving forward and will continue to work on the development of policies to prevent misuse of the grace period."

Here is how this three-month grace period works per examples in the regulations:

Example 1: Individual misses $50 payment that is due February 28 for March coverage and misses $50 payment that is due March 31st for April coverage. Individual Pays $150 on April 30 for March, April, and May coverage.

- ○ Issuer adjudicates claims for March

- ○ Coverage continues for April and May (2nd and 3rd months of the grace period), but:

  (1) Providers are notified of the potential for a denied claim.

  (2) Issuer pends claims for services performed in April and May until individual pays outstanding premiums.

  (3) Individual has paid full premium for March, April, and May and is eligible for premium tax credit for March, April, and May.

---

1. Id.

Example 2: Same facts as Example #1 except that the individual does not pay enrollee's share of premium for March, April, or May.

- ○ Coverage terminated retroactively to March 31.

- ○ Issuer can deny claims for services rendered during April and May. Provider could then seek payment directly from the individual for any services provided during that time.

- ○ Individual may have additional tax liability attributable to the $450 for the advance payment of the premium tax credit paid on his or her behalf for March's coverage. The exact amount of additional tax liability would be determined in accordance with the rules for tax credit reconciliation under section 36B of the Code.

72. Were there any operating state exchanges prior to 2014?

Massachusetts and Utah have operating exchanges, but neither one has produced lower costs. Massachusetts has some of highest insurance rates in the United States,[1] and Utah's exchange rates are higher than purchasing outside the exchange.[2]

One study, conducted for the Ohio Department of Insurance,[3] has predicted that the likely cost increases for health insurance in Ohio will be a total of 55 percent to 85 percent for several reasons, including:

- The law's requirements for commercial, employer-sponsored, small group, and individual health insurance markets, both inside and outside the exchanges, including guaranteed issue of insurance coverage regardless of preexisting medical conditions or health status,

- Adjusted community rating with premium rate variations only for benefit plan design, geographic location, age rating (limited to ratio of 3:1), family status, and tobacco usage (limited to ratio of 1.5:1),

- Premium rate consistency inside and outside the exchanges, and

- Requirements for essential health benefits.

In addition, the study noted that:

---

1. Additionally, Massachusetts spent more than $29.4 million in 2009 on the Commonwealth Connector, not including the high administrative costs. "State Insurance Exchanges: The Case Against Implementation." The Heartland Institute at http://heartland.org/policy-documents/state-insurance-exchanges-caseagainst-Implementation.
2. Lessons From Utah Health Insurance Exchange," Low Cost Health Insurance, at www.californiahealthplans.com/blog/2010/10/lessons-from-the-utah-health-insuance-exchange.
3. Milliman Study for Ohio Department of Insurance (August 31, 2011).

- Although the percentage of Ohio residents with coverage could rise by about 7.9 percent, the price of individual health insurance coverage might rise by about 55 percent to 85 percent, excluding the impact of medical inflation, Milliman predicts. These increases will be 8 percent to 12 percent higher than adjusted small group rates. This is primarily driven by the estimated health status of the new individual health insurance market and the expansion of covered benefits.

- The small group market (from 2 to 100 individuals) is expected to see increases of 5 percent to 15 percent.

- Due to community ratings, some groups could see an increase of 150 percent while others could receive a decrease of up to 38 percent.

- Employers with age fifty-five and older dominant demographics are likely to see the decreases.

- The highest rate increases are expected in companies with two to nine employees.

- Large groups are expected to see an increase of 0 percent to 5 percent.

- None of these increases take into account the increase in medical inflation, which for 2012 is estimated to be 7 percent to 8 percent.

- One important factor for cost increases in group plans is the pass-through fees resulting from increased taxes on insurance companies and medical manufacturers.

73. What are the functions of the state health insurance exchanges?

The exchange functions and responsibilities[1] include the following:

- Certification, recertification, and decertification of health insurance options as qualified,

- Operation of a toll-free hotline,

- Maintenance of a website for providing information on plans to current and prospective enrollees,

- Assignment of a price and quality rating to plans,

- Presentation of plan benefit options in a standardized format,

- Provision of information on Medicaid and CHIP eligibility and determination of eligibility for individuals in these programs, as well as eligibility for the refundable income tax credit,[2]

---

1. PPACA §1311(d)(4)(A)-(K).
2. 45 CFR §155.300.

- Provision of an electronic calculator to determine the actual cost of coverage, taking into account eligibility for premium tax credits and cost sharing reductions,

- Certification of individuals exempt from the individual responsibility requirement,

- Provision of information on certain individuals and to employers, and

- Establishment of a "navigator" program that provides grants to entities assisting consumers.

74. What are the areas over which HHS has responsibility for the state health insurance exchanges?

HHS is responsible for regulatory standards in five areas that insurers must meet in order to be certified as qualified health plans (QHPs) by an exchange:

- marketing,

- network adequacy,

- accreditation for performance measures,

- quality improvement and reporting, and

- uniform enrollment procedures.[1]

75. What are the primary federal requirements for state exchanges?

Only lawful U.S. residents may obtain coverage in an exchange.[2] Exchanges must comply with federal regulatory standards in the following areas:

- Information on the availability of in-network and out-of-network providers, including provider directories and availability of essential community providers;

- Consideration of plan patterns and practices with respect to past premium increases and a submission of the plan justifications for current premium increases;

- Public disclosure of specific plan data, including claims-handling policies, financial disclosures, enrollment and disenrollment data, claims denials, rating practices, cost sharing for out-of-network coverage, and other information identified by HHS;

- Timely information for consumers requesting their amount of cost sharing for specific services from specified providers;

---

1. PPACA §1311(c).
2. PPACA §1312(f).

- Establishment of "navigators" to assist consumers in selecting their health insurance;[1]

- Information for participants in group health plans;

- Information on plan quality-improvement activities;

- Presentation of enrollee satisfaction-survey results; and

- Publication of data on the Exchange's administrative costs.[2]

Additionally, exchanges must meet detailed requirements for call centers and an Internet web site.[3]

76. What is a Qualified Health Plan (QHP)?

A qualified health plan (QHP) is health insurance certified by a state Exchange that offers "essential health benefits."[4] A QHP must be offered by an insurer that:

(1)   Is licensed and in good standing to offer health insurance coverage in each state in which it offers health coverage;

(2)   Agrees to offer at least one QHP in the silver level and at least one QHP in the gold level in each Exchange;

(3)   Agrees to charge the same premium rate for each QHP, whether offered through an Exchange or offered directly from the insurer or through an agent; and

(4)   Complies with regulations to be issued by HHS and any requirements established by an applicable Exchange.[5]

However, a QHP may vary premiums by rating area.[6]

For QHP purposes, the term health plan includes "health insurance coverage" and a "group health plan."[7] Health insurance coverage means benefits consisting of medical care (provided directly, through insurance or reimbursement, or otherwise, and including items and services paid for as medical care) under any hospital or medical service policy or certificate, hospital or medical service plan contract, or health maintenance organization contract offered by a health insurer.[8]

A "group health plan" is an ERISA welfare benefit plan that provides medical care.[9] Health plans must be subject to state regulation; therefore, the term "health plan" does not include

---

1. 45 CFR §155.210.
2. PPACA §1311.
3. 45 CFR §155.205.
4. PPACA §1301(a).
5. PPACA §1301(a)(1).
6. PPACA §1301(a)(4).
7. PPACA §1301(b)(1(A)).
8. PPACA §1301(b)(2); PHSA §2791(b)(1).
9. PPACA §1301(b)(3); PHSA §2791(a)(1).

a group health plan or multiple employer welfare arrangement (MEWA) not subject to state insurance regulation under ERISA Section 514. Thus, self-insured group health plans cannot qualify as QHPs.[1]

Health insurance plans must:

- Meet certain marketing requirements;

- Ensure a sufficient provider choice and include, where available, providers that serve low-income and medically underserved individuals;

- Be accredited (see Q 23) for clinical quality, patient experience, consumer access, and quality assurances, and implement a quality improvement strategy;

- Use a uniform enrollment form and a standard format for presenting plan options; and

- Provide information on quality standards used to measure plan performance.[2]

The U.S. Office of Personnel Management (OPM) must enter into contracts with health insurers to offer at least two multistate QHPs through each Exchange in each state.[3]

77. How are state health insurance exchanges regulated?

The Patient Protection and Affordable Care Act includes two federal requirements for state health insurance exchanges:[4]

- Minimum functions that Exchanges must perform directly or by contract, and

- Oversight responsibilities Exchanges must exercise in certifying and monitoring the performance of Health Plans.[5]

Plans participating in the exchanges also must comply with state insurance laws and federal requirements in the Public Health Service Act.

The final regulations set "standards for establishing exchanges, setting up a Small Business Health Options Program (SHOP), performing the basic functions of an exchange, certifying health plans for participation in the exchange," and establishing "a streamlined, web-based system for consumers to apply for and enroll in qualified health plans and insurance affordability programs." HHS has also issued questions and answers on federally facilitated

---

1. PPACA §1301(b)(1)(B).
2. PPACA §1311(c).
3. PPACA §1334(a).
4. PPACA §1311.
5. PPACA §1301.

Exchanges, including for instance, how the Exchanges will interact with state departments of insurance.[1]

State exchanges are to be operational in 2014. A change in the final rule gives more flexibility to states that are not able to show "complete readiness" to operate an exchange on January 1, 2013. HHS may conditionally approve a state-based exchange upon demonstration that it is likely to be fully operationally ready by October 1, 2013. Applications of a state's Exchange Blueprint must be submitted thirty 30 business days before January 1, 2013, or by November 16, 2012.

Individuals and small businesses will be able to purchase private health insurance via these exchanges. Starting in 2014, exchanges are intended to:

- Facilitate the comparison by individuals and small businesses of health plans,

- Provide answers to questions,

- Determine eligibility for tax credits for private insurance or health programs like the Children's Health Insurance Program (CHIP), and

- Allow enrollment by individuals and small employers in a Qualified Health Plan (QHP).

78. How should states set up health insurance exchanges?

The U.S. Department of Health and Human Services (HHS) issued final regulations[2] that provide a framework to assist states in building health insurance exchanges, state-based competitive marketplaces authorized by the 2010 federal health care reform law.[3] These rules set minimum standards for exchanges and give states some flexibility to design the exchanges to fit their insurance markets, subject to HHS approval. The regulations propose rules and guidance on how to structure the exchanges in two areas:

- Setting standards for establishing exchanges, setting up a Small Business Health Options Program (SHOP), performing the basic functions of an exchange, and certifying health plans for participation in an exchange; and

- Ensuring premium stability for the exchanges, especially in the first three years.

According to HHS, forty-eight states and the District of Columbia have been awarded grants to help plan and operate exchanges.[4] By mid-June 2013, seventeen states and the District of

---

1. See State Exchange Implementation Questions and Answers (Nov. 29, 2011), at http://cciio.cms.gov/resources/files/Files2/11282011/exchange_q_and_a.pdf.pdf (as visited June 11, 2012).
2. Federal Register Volume 77, Number 59 (March 27, 2012), 45 CFR Parts 155 and 157 (March 27, 2012) (superseding two sets of proposed regulations, namely, Establishment of Exchanges and Qualified Health Plans, 45 CFR Parts 155 and 156, 76 Fed. Reg. 41866 (July 15, 2011); PPACA; Standards Related to Reinsurance, Risk Corridors, and Risk Adjustment, 45 CFR Part 153, 76 Fed. Reg. 41930 (July 15, 2011)).
3. Federal Register Volume 77, Number 59 (March 27, 2012), 45 CFR Parts 155 and 157 (March 27, 2012).
4. http://www.hhs.gov/ociio/regulations/guidance_to_states_on_exchanges.html. Kansas governor Sam Brownback returned the state's $30 million grant as did Alaska.

Columbia were pursuing state-based exchanges, six were pursuing state partnership exchanges, and twenty-eight declined to establish a state-based exchange and will default to a federally facility exchange. All of the twenty-four states working toward state-based or state partnership exchanges have been conditionally approved by HHS.[1]

The rules allow states to decide:

- Whether their exchanges should be local, regional, or operated by a nonprofit organization,

- How to select plans to participate, and

- Whether to collaborate with HHS for the work.

However, HHS must approve each exchange and the criteria for its insurance policies.

In 2014, exchanges will initially be available only to individuals and small employers, but states may expand them in 2017 to be available to large employers as well.

Using the standards and processes in the regulations to approve exchanges, HHS must determine by January 1, 2013, whether an exchange will be operational by 2014, which means it must begin open enrollment on October 1, 2013. In states that do not obtain this HHS approval (or decide not to establish an Exchange), a federally facilitated exchange would be implemented for 2014.

Initial Open Enrollment. The initial open-enrollment period is proposed to extend from October 1, 2013, through March 31 2014.[2] Only those enrolling in a qualified health plan (QHP) on or before December 22, 2013, would be ensured coverage effective January 1, 2014. Special enrollment periods are also provided in the regulations.[3] The annual enrollment period for 2015 and subsequent years will begin on October 15 and end after December 7.[4]

Eligibility and Consumer Assistance. Exchanges would make eligibility determinations and provide consumer assistance tools, including a toll-free call center, a website with comparative information about available qualified health plans (QHPs), and a "navigator" program that facilitates enrollment and provides other information and services. Navigators cannot be insurers but can be agents or brokers. They cannot receive direct or indirect compensation from an insurer for enrolling eligible individuals, employers, or employees in a QHP.

Each exchange must provide the following:

- A toll-free call center to address the needs of those seeking assistance;

---

1. www.cbpp.org. Center on Budget and Policy Priorities, Status of State Health Insurance Exchange Implementation.
2. 45 CFR §155.410(b.
3. PPACA §1311(c)(6) (2010). Special enrollment periods include those specified in Code Section 9801, other special enrollments under circumstances similar to such periods under part D of title XVIII of the Social Security Act, and special monthly enrollment periods for Indians pursuant to section 4 of the Indian Health Care Improvement Act).
4. 45 CFR §155.410(e).

- An Internet website providing a variety of features, including comparative information on available QHPs, certain financial information, and information about the Navigator and call center;

- An Exchange calculator to facilitate comparisons of QHPs that takes into consideration the premium tax credit and any cost-sharing reductions;

- A consumer-assistance function, including the Navigator program discussed below; and

- Outreach and education activities.[1]

Small Business Health Options Program (SHOP). Each state will establish insurance options for qualifying small businesses through a SHOP, and participation by small employers will be voluntary. SHOP is intended to give small employers the same purchasing power that large employers have and to allow them to offer employees a choice of plans for a single monthly payment. For 2014 through 2016, only employers with fewer than 100 employees or fewer than fifty employees (states have the option of choosing either) will be granted access to the SHOP exchange. As discussed in Q 23, certain small employers will be eligible to receive a small business tax credit for up to 50 percent of the contributions they make toward employees' premiums for two consecutive years if certain tax rules are met. See Q 79 for additional information on SHOPs.

QHP Certification. Exchanges must establish procedures, which must be approved by HHS, for certification, recertification, and decertification of qualified health plans (QHPs). The regulations do not require exchanges to accept all eligible QHPs, although that is allowed. Alternatively, exchanges could limit QHP participation to those plans that meet the state's selection criteria. The regulations include minimum standards for QHPs and QHP issuers. States may impose additional requirements, if approved by HHS.

An Exchange is required to allow the insurer of a plan that provides certain limited-scope dental benefits to offer the plan through the Exchange (either separately or in conjunction with a QHP) if the plan provides pediatric dental benefits.[2]

Reinsurance, 3-Year Risk Corridor Program, and Risk Adjustment. The HHS regulations outline standards for various programs required by healthcare reform that are intended, beginning in 2014, to mitigate the impact of adverse selection and stabilize premiums in the individual and small group markets. Standards are established for the transitional reinsurance program, which is a required state-based program that reduces uncertainty for insurers during the first three years the exchange is in operation by making payments for high-cost cases. A temporary risk corridor program from 2014 through 2016 will protect against uncertainty in setting rates within the exchanges by limiting the extent of insurer losses and gains.

---

1. 45 CFR §155.205.
2. PPACA §1311(d)(2) (2010). The limited-scope dental benefits must meet the requirements of IRC Sec. 9832(c)(2)(A). The pediatric dental benefits must meet the requirements of PPACA §1302(b)(1)(J).

The proposed regulations also include standards for a risk adjustment program, which is an optional program that a state may establish inside or outside of an exchange, after 2014. The program is intended to provide stability in the individual and small group markets by transferring funds from insurers of lower-risk enrollees to insurers of higher-risk enrollees.

79. What is the status of federal SHOP exchanges in 2014 for small employers?

Each state Exchange is required to create a Small Business Health Options Program (SHOP).[1] HHS has also provided for a federally facilitated SHOP (FF-SHOP) in states that do not establish a state-based Exchange.[2] Participation in a SHOP is strictly voluntary for small employers.

Beginning in 2014, however, purchasing employer-provided health coverage for employees through a SHOP is the only way for qualified employers to obtain a small business health care tax credit.[3] Both state operated SHOPs and federally facilitated SHOPs (FFSHOPs) are to allow employees to have a choice among all QHPs at the metal level chosen by the employer (bronze, silver, gold, or platinum). However, SHOP regulations delay the effective date for this "employee-choice" model for FFSHOPS until 2015, so that, for plan years beginning before January 1, 2015, FFSHOPS will only offer one option and state-operated SHOPs may choose but are not be required to offer an employee choice option.[4]

This will allow employers who prefer to offer employees a single Qualified Health Plan (QHP) to participate in an FFSHOP and retain potential eligibility for the small business tax credit, which, beginning in 2014, is only available through a SHOP Exchange.

For SHOP eligibility, a "small employer" is an employer that employed an average of at least one but not more than 100 employees on business days during the preceding calendar year and that employs at least one employee on the first day of the plan year.[5] A qualified employee is an individual employed by a qualified employer who has been offered health insurance coverage by such qualified employer through the SHOP.[6]

For counting employees to determine whether an employer is a small employer that is SHOP eligible, the regulations use the Code section 4980H(c)(2) employer mandate counting method, which counts not only full-time employees, i.e., those averaging 30 hours of service per week, but also part-time employees as full-time equivalents under Code section 4980H(c)(4)). However, a transitional rule allows state-operated SHOPS to rely on state counting methods, which in some states may not include part-time employees, for determining group size and status

1. PPACA §1311(b)(1)(B).
2. General Guidance on Federally-facilitated Exchanges (May 16, 2012); Fact Sheet: Affordable Insurance Exchanges (May 16, 2012) at http://cciio.cms.gov/resources/files/FFE_Guidance_FINAL_VERSION_051612.pdf.
3. 45 CFR §§155.705(b)(2) and (3).
4. Patient Protection and Affordable Care Act; Establishment of Exchanges and Qualified Health Plans; Small Business Health Options Program, 45 CFR Parts 155 and 156, 78 Fed. Reg. 15553 (Mar. 11, 2013).
5. PPACA §§1304(b), 1312(f); HHS Reg. §155.20.
6. 45 CFR §155.20.

as a full-time employee until 2016.[1] A qualified employer participating in a SHOP must provide information to its employees about the methods for selecting and enrolling in a QHP through the SHOP.[2] This requirement is in addition to the Notice of Exchange.

80. What is the Employer Exchange Notice requirement?

The 2010 health reform law amends the Fair Labor Standards Act (FLSA)[3] to require that employers provide all new hires and current employees with a written notice (Employer Exchange Notice) about the exchange and some of the consequences if an employee decides to purchase a qualified health plan through the exchange in lieu of employer-sponsored coverage.[4] Regulations implementing the Employer Exchange Notice requirement will be issued and enforced by the Department of Labor.[5]

The Employer Exchange Notice requirement is effective on March 1, 2013. Employees hired on or after the effective date must be provided with the notice when they are hired. All employees already employed on the effective date must be provided with the notice no later than the effective date (i.e., no later than March 1, 2013).[6]

The Employer Exchange Notice rule applies to employers that are subject to the FLSA. The FLSA's minimum wage and maximum hour provisions apply to entities that are engaged in interstate commerce and have a gross annual volume of sales that is not less than $500,000 (enterprises engaged in commerce or in the production of goods for commerce).[7] However, the Employer Exchange Notice requirement does not have the same limitation. As a result, it seemingly applies to "any person acting directly or indirectly in the interest of an employer in relation to an employee."[8]

The Employer Exchange Notice must include the following information:[9]

- Employees must be informed of the existence of an Exchange, given a description of the services provided by the Exchange, and told how to contact the Exchange to request assistance.

- Employees must be informed that they may be eligible for a premium tax credit (under Code Section 36B) or a cost-sharing reduction (under PPACA Section 1402) through the Exchange if the employer's plan share of the total cost of benefits under the plan is less than 60 percent.

---

1. 45 CFR §155.20.
2. 45 CFR §157.205(c).
3. 29 U.S.C. §201 et seq.
4. FLSA §18B.
5. DOL delegated responsibility for regulations under FLSA §18B, to its Employee Benefits Security Administration (EBSA). See FAQs About the Affordable Care Act Implementation Part V, Q/A-2, at http://www.dol.gov/ebsa/faqs/faq-aca5.html.
6. FLSA §18B.
7. 29 U.S.C. §§206 and 207.
8. 29 U.S.C. §203(d).
9. FLSA §18B.

- Employees must be informed that:

  o   If they purchase a qualified health plan through the Exchange, they may lose any employer contribution toward the cost of employer-provided coverage; and

  o   All or a portion of the employer's contributions to employer-provided coverage may be excludable for federal income tax purposes.

81. What is the role of health insurance brokers or agents in the state health insurance exchanges?

The final regulation contains welcome news for agents and brokers of health insurance.[1] HHS, in the final regulation, permits states to allow an agent or broker to enroll individuals, employers or employees in qualified health plans (QHPs), in a manner that constitutes "enrollment through the exchange," on their own Web site. It is up to each state to determine whether its exchange can list approved insurance agents and brokers.[2] [However, navigators need not be agents or brokers.[3]] An individual can be enrolled in a QHP through an exchange with the assistance of an agent or broker only if the agent or broker ensures that the individual receives an eligibility determination through the state's Exchange Web site.[4]

If the consumer would be eligible for a refundable federal income tax credit (See Q 49) for a QHP purchased on the exchange's Web site, the consumer may access the tax credit for purchases through the broker or agent's private Web portal.

The regulation sets out a series of requirements brokers or agents must meet in order for their clients to be able to access the tax credits for purchases through their Web sites. For consumers to do this, brokers and agents must be registered with the Exchange. This means that the state (or the federal government in the case of a federally facilitated exchange (FFE)), controls whether their exchange remains the exclusive market for the tax credit or whether brokers and agents can assist eligible individuals and families in obtaining the subsidies.

Additionally, all QHPs must be available for purchase through the Web site, and the agents and brokers assisting the customer must be trained on all QHP options. Thus, a single-carrier exchange will not meet the qualifications for a purchaser to access the tax credit. The private websites must present all QHPs and all QHP data in a manner that meets HHS standards and must not use financial incentives, such as rebates or free prizes, to lure customers to one QHP instead of another. Consumers may withdraw from this process at any time and use the exchange website. Any private web portal must be compliant with exchange privacy and security standards. Of course, state laws related to the qualifications and conduct of agents and brokers continue to apply.

---

1. 45 CFR §155.220(a)(3).
2. 45 CFR §155.205(b)(3).
3. 45 CFR §155.210(c)(2).
4. 45 CFR §155.220(c)(1).

Interestingly, the private web portals, unlike the state or federally facilitated exchanges, do not have restrictions on selling products other than QHPs. Thus, brokers and agents can use their existing web portals to sell other products as well as QHPs, as long as the requirements noted previously in this section are met.

Thus, if permitted to use an agent or broker, consumers never have to go to the state exchange website to buy a product and access the refundable tax credit. All of the information transfers between the private broker site, the exchange, and the insurance carriers can be invisible to the consumer.

This aspect of the final regulation indicates that HHS believes that private distribution of exchange health insurance will help to stimulate the use of exchanges. For agents, brokers, and private exchanges, the shift presents a new opportunity to access the exchange population. For consumers, it is likely that more will look into whether or not they qualify for a tax credit while shopping for insurance, which could increase QHP sales.

Employer Funds for Insurance Purchased on State Exchange and ERISA

82. Are individual health or other policies purchased in whole or part with employer funds an ERISA plan and subject to COBRA?

This will be an important issue if employers provide funds for employees to purchase policies at a state health insurance exchange beginning in 2014. While the policies purchased by individual employees are not necessarily ERISA plans, a program where the employer systematically pays all or a portion of the premium may become an ERISA plan. Consider whether an HRA or cafeteria plan funded at least in part by the employer that allows reimbursement for individual health insurance purchased by employees creates an ERISA plan for the policies themselves. Clearly, there is a plan as to the HRA or cafeteria plan.

As discussed in this section, there are several court decisions finding that where an employer pays for or contributes to an individual policy for one or more employees, there is an ERISA plan. There are also cases to the contrary. The employer's payment of all or part of the premiums on behalf of the employee is an important factor when courts determine whether an individual policy is part of an ERISA welfare plan.

83. How does ERISA define a group health plan?

ERISA defines a group health plan as one "established or maintained by an employer" (rather than "of, or contributed to by, an employer").[1] Seemingly, while the HRA or 125 plan with employer funding is an ERISA plan, the individual policies purchased by employees with no employer involvement in their selection may mean that the policies themselves are not part of an ERISA plan. See *Waks v. Empire Blue Cross/Blue Shield*, 263 F3d 872 (9th Cir. 2001) where the issue arose as to whether an individual policy arising out of a conversion from a group health

---

1. 29 U.S.C. §1002(1).

plan is covered by ERISA preemption. There, the Ninth Circuit ruled no, that the conversion policy was not an ERISA plan, and stated:

> We conclude that claims arising under a converted individual policy are not "related to" an ERISA plan for purposes of ERISA preemption. This conclusion is consistent not only with the words but also the purposes of the statute. A converted policy is created when an ERISA plan participant leaves the plan and obtains a new, separate, individual policy based on conversion rights contained in the ERISA plan. The contract under the converted policy is directly between the insurer and insured. It is independent of the ERISA plan and does not place any burdens on the plan administrator or the plan. There are also no relevant administrative actions by the employer.

Arguably, the same analysis applies and the fact that the employer funds are in an ERISA plan does not mean that the policies purchased with those funds by employees without any employer involvement in the purchase are part of an ERISA plan. However, the conclusion is not clear. Additionally, *Brooks v. Blue Cross & Blue Shield of Florida,* 116 F.3d 1364 (11th Cir. 1997) held that individual health insurance policies purchased through payroll deduction do not constitute a group health plan for purposes of the Medicare Secondary Payor rule, despite the fact that Medicare regulations include an "employee-pay-all plan." See Q 172 for additional information on ERISA and the ACA requirements.

84. What is the DOL safe harbor on ERISA plan status?

DOL regulations establish a safe harbor that provides no ERISA plan exists where several conditions are met: (1) the employer does not contribute any funds; (2) employee participation is voluntary; (3) the employer does not endorse the arrangement (interpreted from employee's point of view, not that of insurance company); (4) the employer does nothing more than allow uninsured to publicize the arrangement to employees and to collect premiums through payroll deductions; and (5) the employer receives no consideration beyond reasonable compensation for administrative services.[1] In addition, ERISA does not apply to government and church plans.[2]

85. What is the three-part test to determine whether an ERISA plan exists?

Determining whether an ERISA plan exists involves a three-part test, which was established in *Thompson v. American Home Assurance Co.*, 95 F.3d 429, 434-35 (6th Cir. 1996). This case provides for a detailed analysis of whether a plan is an ERISA plan. The existence of an ERISA plan is a question of fact, to be answered in light of all the surrounding circumstances and facts from the point of view of a reasonable person.[3]

---

1. 29 C.F.R. §2510.3-1(j). See *New England Mut. Life Ins. Co. v. Baig,* 166 F.3d 1 (1st Cir. 1999); *O'Brien v. Mutual of Omaha Ins. Co.,* 99 F.Supp. 2d 744 (E.D. La. 1999).
2. See ERISA §§4(b)(1), (3) and (32) and 4(b)(2) and 3(33), respectively.
3. See *Credit Managers Ass'n of So. Calif. v. Kennesaw Life and Acc. Ins. Co.,* 809 F.2d 617, 625 (9th Cir.1987), citing *Donovan v. Dillingham,* 688 F.2d 1367, 1373 (11th Cir.1982) (en banc). Accord *Gahn v. Allstate Life Ins. Co.,* 926 F.2d 1449, 1451 (5th Cir.1991); *Wickman v. Northwestern Nat'l Ins. Co.,* 908 F.2d 1077, 1082 (1st Cir.), *cert. denied,* 498 U.S. 1013 (1990).

First, the court must apply the so-called "safe harbor" regulations established by the Department of Labor to determine whether the program was exempt from ERISA.[1] See Q 84.

Second, the court must look to see if there was a "plan" by inquiring whether "from the surrounding circumstances a reasonable person [could] ascertain the intended benefits, the class of beneficiaries, the source of financing, and procedures for receiving benefits."[2] Finally, the court must ask whether the employer "established or maintained" the plan with the intent of providing benefits to its employees.[3]

Some courts collapse the first and third prongs of this analysis by interpreting the Department of Labor regulations as the indicia for determining whether a plan is established and maintained by the employer.[4] However, those courts agree that even if a plan is not within the safe harbor, there must be an additional finding that the employer intended to establish or maintain a plan in order to find that an ERISA plan exists.

A policy will be exempted under ERISA only if all the "safe harbor" criteria of 29 CFR 2510.3-1(j) are satisfied.[5]

Often, the third part of the test, whether the employer "endorsed the policy," is argued by insurers to establish ERISA preemption. In *Thompson*, the Sixth Circuit adopted the test set out previously by the First Circuit in *Johnson v. Watts Regulator Co.*[6] In *Johnson*, the First Circuit clarified the standards that govern a finding of endorsement, including its belief that "endorsement of a program requires more than merely recommending it."[7] According to the *Johnson* court, "[a]s long as the employer merely advises employees of the availability of group insurance, accepts payroll deductions, passes them on to the insurer, and performs other ministerial tasks that assist the insurer in publicizing the program, it will not be deemed to have endorsed the program under 29 CFR 2510.3-1(j) It is only when an employer purposes to do more, and takes substantial steps in that direction, that it offends the ideal of employer neutrality and brings ERISA into the picture."[8] The First Circuit further found that, while the *Hansen* court had relied on the employer's intent in determining endorsement, the proper focus was on whether employees could reasonably conclude that the employer had endorsed the policy based on their observation of the employer's activities in connection with the plan.[9]

---

1. *Fugarino v. Hartford Life and Accident Ins. Co.*, 969 F.2d 178, 183 (6th Cir. 1992) (abrogated on other grounds in *Yates v. Hendon*, 541 U.S. 1 (2004)).

2. *Int'l Resources, Inc. v. New York Life Ins. Co.*, 950 F.2d 294, 297 (6th Cir.1991) (citing *Donovan*, 688 F.2d at 1373), *cert. denied*, 504 U.S. 973 (1992).

3. See *McDonald v. Provident Indem. Life Ins. Co.*, 60 F.3d 234, 236 (5th Cir.1995), *cert. denied*, 516 U.S. 1174 (1996); *Hansen v. Continental Ins. Co.*, 940 F.2d 971, 977 (5th Cir.1991).

4. See, e.g., *Gahn*, 926 F.2d at 1451.

5. *Fugarino*, 969 F.2d at 184, citing *Hansen*, 940 F.2d at 977. Accord *Grimo*, 34 F.3d at 150; *Gahn*, 926 F.2d at 1451; *Kanne v. Connecticut General Life Ins. Co.*, 867 F.2d 489, 492 (9th Cir.1988) (per curiam), *cert. denied*, 492 U.S. 906 (1989).

6. *63 F.3d 1129 (1st Cir.1995)*.

7. 63 F.3d at 1136.

8. *Id.* at 1133.

9. 63 F.3d at 1134 and 1137 n. 6.

The Sixth Circuit ruled that the First Circuit's approach in *Johnson* was consistent with Congress' intent in enacting ERISA. According to the Department of Labor, "employer neutrality is the key to the rationale for not treating such a program as an employee benefit plan".[1] As Johnson noted, therefore, where the employer "offends the ideal of employer neutrality" because of its level of involvement, ERISA is properly invoked.[2] "Where, however, the employer separates itself from the program, making it reasonably clear that the program is a third party's offering, not subject to the employer's control, then the safe harbor may be accessible."[3]

Thus, the Sixth Circuit explained that the key element whether an employer endorsed a plan, is whether the employer acted neutrally. A finding of endorsement is appropriate if, upon examining all the relevant circumstances, there is some factual showing on the record of substantial employer involvement in the creation or administration of the plan.[4] For example, where the employer plays an active role in either determining which employees will be eligible for coverage or in negotiating the terms of the policy or the benefits provided thereunder, the extent of employer involvement is inconsistent with "employer neutrality" and a finding of endorsement may be appropriate.[5] Similarly, where the employer is named as the plan administrator, a finding of endorsement may be appropriate.[6]

The test of whether the employer "endorsed" the plan is not measured from the point of view of the insurance company, but from the point of view of the employee viewing the conduct of the employer.[7] In *Thompson,* the Court found that the employer did not endorse the plan. While the insurance policy here included an introductory letter encouraging employees to obtain accident insurance, that letter was not printed on Burns' letterhead, nor did it refer to the accident insurance policy as Burns' plan. Further, while Burns' name was featured on the cover of the policy description, this fact may be as consistent with identification as endorsement, depending on what the evidence on remand shows concerning the circumstances of its placement. The policy documentation nowhere mentions that the policy is subject to ERISA, nor does it set out a description of an employee's rights under ERISA. It is unclear from the record whether Burns acts as an administrator, nor is it clear whether Burns participated in either devising the terms of the policy or in processing claims, although the record does indicate that Thompson submitted her claim directly to American Home. The court finds that such evidence presents a material question of fact as to whether Burns endorsed the policy under the DOL regulation.[8] ("The question of endorsement vel non is a mixed question of fact and law. In some cases, the evidence will point unerringly in one direction so that a rational

---

1. 40 Fed. Reg. 34,526 (1975).
2. 63 F.3d at 1133.
3. *Id.* at 1137.
4. See *Hansen,* 940 F.2d at 977 (requiring "some meaningful degree of participation by the employer in the creation or administration of the plan").
5. See, e.g., *Custer v. Pan American Life Ins. Co.,* 12 F.3d 410, 417 (4th Cir.1993) (considering, inter alia, employer's role in negotiating terms and benefits of the policy in determining whether a plan should fall out of the safe harbor); *Wickman,* 908 F.2d at 1083 (considering, inter alia, employer's role in devising eligibility requirements when determining the applicability of the safe harbor regulations).
6. See, e.g., *Kanne,* 867 F.2d at 493; *Shiffler v. Equitable Life Assur. Soc. of U.S.,* 838 F.2d 78, 82 n. 4 (3d Cir.1988) (both considering, inter alia, the employer's role in administering the plan when determining whether to allow the policy to come under the safe harbor provision of the DOL regulation).
7. *Johnson,* 63 F.3d at 1134 & 1137 n. 6; *Thompson,* 95 F.3d at 436-7.
8. See *Johnson,* 63 F.3d at 1135 n. 3.

fact finder can reach but one conclusion. In those cases, endorsement is a question of law In other cases, the legal significance of the facts is less certain, and the outcome will depend on inferences that the fact finder chooses to draw In those cases, endorsement becomes a question of fact. This case is of the latter type.").[1]

In remanding the claim, the Sixth Circuit gave specific instructions as to what factors a trial court should consider:

The district court's further consideration of this issue, whether in the context of a renewed summary judgment motion based on a more complete factual record or at trial, should take into account, but is not limited to, Burns's role in administering benefits under the plan, whether the policy language itself contemplates the application of ERISA, and Burns's role in determining eligibility and coverage. The crucial question is whether Burns was substantially involved in the creation and administration of the plan to such an extent that employees could reasonably conclude that Burns had endorsed the plan. Further, if the district court determines that the policy is not excluded from ERISA coverage under the safe harbor regulations, the court on remand must also determine that a "plan" exists under the standards set forth in *Int'l Resources, Inc.*[2] Furthermore, the district court must conclude that Burns "established or maintained" the plan with an intent to provide benefits to its employees.[3] ("In addition to some meaningful degree of participation by the employer in the creation or administration of the plan, the statute requires that the employer have had a purpose to provide health insurance, accident insurance or other specified types of benefits to its employees.[4] Thus, the evidence must show that the employer had an intent to provide its employees with a welfare benefit program through the purchase and maintenance of [the] group insurance policy.") Only upon completing a three-step factual inquiry can a district court ascertain that an ERISA plan exists, thus requiring the application of the federal common law of ERISA to the underlying insurance claim.[5]

86. What other factors have been used to determine whether a plan does fall under ERISA?

ERISA applies if the employer intends to establish or maintain a plan to provide benefits as part of the employment relationship, regardless of whether the employer intended the plan to be governed by ERISA.[6] However, as noted in the following, if there is a plan document and it says it is governed by ERISA, that is a factor counting toward ERISA plan status in some court decisions.

In determining whether an ERISA "plan, fund or program" exists when individual policies are purchased, courts must "determine whether from the surrounding circumstances a reasonable person could ascertain the intended benefits, beneficiaries, source of financing, and procedures

---

1. See 95 F.3d at 437.
2. *950 F.2d at 297 (a "plan" exists if "from the surrounding circumstances a reasonable person [could] ascertain the intended benefits, the class of beneficiaries, the source of financing, and procedures for receiving benefits"). See also Dist. of Columbia v. Greater Wash. Bd. of Trade, 506 U.S. 125, 131 n. 2 (1992); Fort Halifax Packing Co. v. Coyne, 482 U.S. 1, 12, (1987); Belanger v. Wyman-Gordon Co., 71 F.3d 451, 454 (1st Cir.1995) (all defining "plan").*
3. See *McDonald*, 60 F.3d at 236; Hansen, 940 F.2d at 977.
4. 29 U.S.C. 1002(1).
5. 95 F.3d at 437-8.
6. *Anderson v. Unum Provident Corporation,* 369 F.3d 1257, 1262 (11th Cir. 2004).

for receiving benefits." *Donovan v. Dillingham*,[1] is the seminal case followed in all circuits and holds that the purchase of a group policy or multiple individual policies covering a class of employees was substantial evidence that a plan, fund, or program had been established under ERISA if a reasonable person could ascertain the intended benefits, a class of beneficiaries, the source of financing, and procedures for receiving benefits.

The courts have gone both ways on the issue of whether individual policies can constitute an ERISA plan.

87. Which courts have ruled that plans are not employee welfare benefits plans under ERISA despite employee contributions to them?

In *McCall v. Focus Worldwide Television Network Inc.*, 2009 WL 1046791 (E.D. La. 2009) the court ruled that an employer's employment contract agreement to pay premiums for an employee's life insurance policy of $10,000 per year "funded in her name and on her behalf" was not an employee welfare benefit plan under ERISA. In *New Eng. Mut. Life Ins. Co., Inc. v. Baig*,[2] the court stated that no ERISA plan had been established from an employer's reimbursement of premiums paid directly by an employee. The policy was not initially established by a contractual arrangement between Cardiology Associates and New England Mutual, and Baig made the initial purchase and paid the premiums directly.

88. What are examples of cases with rulings that plans with employer financial involvement do fall under ERISA?

In *O'Leary v. Provident Life and Accident Ins. Co.*[3] the court reasoned that an ERISA plan existed where an employer agreed to provide disability insurance to one employee, when the employee applied for the individual policy and the employer paid the premiums. *O'Leary* noted that, while an ERISA plan can be established through the purchase of insurance, the purchase of insurance does not mean that an ERISA plan always exists. *O'Leary* stated that to prove an ERISA plan, the employer must have paid the premiums and intended to provide benefits on a regular and long-term basis.

Another example is *Pierson v. Cont'l Cas. Co.*[4] In this case, an ERISA plan existed where the employee was insured under two individual income protection policies issued by CNA that were individual policies not issued pursuant to a master policy and the employee paid 100 percent of the premiums for the policy. In *Peterson v. American Life & Health Ins. Co.*,[5] the court held that an individual insurance policy was part of an ERISA plan where the employer "not only paid its partners" and employees' insurance premiums but also played an active role in the administration of the coverage, including choosing the insurance, adding and deleting employees and partners from various policies, contacting insurance companies for employees and partners, and distributing information relevant to the coverage.

---

1. 688 F.2d 1367 (11th Cir. 1982).
2. *166 F.3d 1 (1st Cir. 1999).*
3. *456 F. Supp. 2d 285 (D. Mass. 2006).*
4. 2000 U.S. Dist. LEXIS 21380, 4-5 (C.D. Cal. Nov. 22, 2000).
5. 48 F.3d 404 (9th Cir. 1995).

Other examples are:

Heidelberg v. National Foundation Life Ins. Co.,[1] in which the court held that the employer's purchase of two individual health insurance policies constituted an ERISA plan where there was evidence of employer intent to provide health insurance coverage for its white-collar employees and there was testimony that, had it been economically feasible, the employer would have purchased a group policy rather than two individual policies).

Burrill v. Leco Corp.,[2] a case in which the court ruled that several individual insurance policies purchased by the employer constituted a group health plan for COBRA purposes where such plans were "an integral part of a broader scheme to provide health coverage to LECO employees".

Strange v. Plaza Excavating, Inc.,[3] where individual health policies were provided to provide benefits on a regular and long term basis and COBRA applied.

Madonia v. Blue Cross & Blue Shield,[4] which involved an individual health insurance policy of sole shareholder who is thus not an "'employee" but nevertheless was part of an ERISA plan. The court reasoned that payment of premiums on behalf of employees is substantial evidence that a plan, fund, or program was established.

Other Examples

When the employer selects the insurance and pays the premiums, an ERISA plan almost universally is found. This is shown in *Fugarino v. Hartford Life and Acc. Ins. Co.*[5] and *Randol v. Mid-West Nat. Life Ins. Co. of Tennessee.*[6]

The court ruled in *Heral v. Unum Life Ins. Co. of Am.*[7] that individual disability policies purchased by the employer for two or more employees was an ERISA plan, but a separate policy that the employer purchased for an owner from another insurer was not a plan. That program did not cover at least one employee.

In *Burrill v. Leco Corp.*[8] the court held that a short-term individual health insurance policy purchased by the employer for employees before they became eligible for the employer's group health plan is an ERISA employee welfare benefit plan.

The court, in *Nicholas v. Standard Ins. Co.*,[9] ruled that ERISA applied where the insurance agent who sold the policy testified that he helped procure employee benefits for the employer, the employer was named as the plan administrator, and the documents specifically referred to ERISA.

---

1. 2000 WL 1693635 (E.D. La. 2000).
2. 1998 WL 34078144 (W.D. Mich. 1998).
3. 2001 WL 114407 (N.D. Ill. 2001).
4. 11 F.3d 444(4th Cir. 1993).
5. 969 F.2d 178, 183 (6th Cir. 1992) (abrogated on other grounds in *Yates v. Hendon*, 541 U.S. 1 (2004)).
6. 987 F.2d 1547, 1551-2 (11th Cir. 1993).
7. 2008 U.S. Dist. LEXIS 94418, 6-8 (E.D. Ark. Nov. 18, 2008).
8. 1998 U.S. Dist. LEXIS 8178 (W.D. Mich. May 11, 1998).
9. 48 Fed.Appx. 557, 564 (6th Cir., 2002).

The court, in *Libbey-Owens Ford v. Blue Cross & Blue Shield*,[1] reasoned that an employer may establish an ERISA plan very easily, through the mere purchase of a group health insurance policy – even though it does not retain control, administrative power, or responsibility for benefits. Likewise, in *Int'l Resources v. New York Life Ins. Co.*,[2] the court held that, where the employer obtained insurance coverage for employees and paid the premiums, an ERISA plan was established.

The 2012 U.S. Supreme Court Decision on Health Reform

89. What is the impact of the 2012 U.S. Supreme Court decision on the constitutionality of the health reform law?

The U.S. Supreme Court in *NFIB v. Sebelius* (June 28, 2012)[3] upheld the health reform law (PPACA), except for the federal government's power to terminate existing federal Medicaid funds for states not agreeing to participate in the law's Medicaid expansion that begins in 2014. Several decisions were five to four, with different combinations of justices for different issues. Chief Justice Roberts proved to be the critical swing vote.

The threshold issue was whether the Supreme Court could rule on the constitutionality of the individual mandate, which is effective in 2014, before any taxpayer is required to pay the tax. Beginning in 2014, individuals who fail to have minimum essential coverage will be subject to a penalty,[4] which is known as the individual mandate. The Anti-Injunction Act applies to suits "for the purpose of restraining the assessment or collection of any tax."[5] Under the Anti-Injunction Act, a court cannot rule on the validity of a tax until it has been assessed by the IRS on a taxpayer. The Supreme Court, by a vote of nine justices to none, stated that its decision on the validity of the individual mandate was not precluded by the Anti-Injunction Act, because the law calls the mandate a penalty, not a tax.

The Court ruled, in a five to four decision, that the individual mandate is not authorized by the Constitution's Commerce Clause or the Necessary and Proper Clause, but it is valid because the federal taxing power allows it. For purposes of determining its constitutionality, the Court ruled that the individual mandate is a tax on individuals (despite being a penalty for purposes of the Anti-Injunction Act):

> Our precedent demonstrates that Congress had the power to impose the exaction in Section 5000A under the taxing power, and that Section 5000A need not be read to do more than impose a tax. This is sufficient to sustain it.

The only effect of not complying with the mandate is that one must pay the tax.

---

1. 982 F.2d 1031, 1034 (6th Cir. 1993).
2. 950 F.2d 294, 297-98 (6th Cir. 1991), cert. denied, 504 U.S. 973, 119 L. Ed. 2d 565, 112 S. Ct. 2941 (1992).
3. *National Federation of Independent Business v. Sebelius*, 567 U.S. ___, 132 S. Ct. 2566, 183 L. Ed. 2d 450, 2012 U.S. LEXIS 4876, 2012 WL 2427810, 80 U.S.L.W. 4579; 2012-2 U.S. Tax Cas. (CCH) P50,423; 109 A.F.T.R.2d (RIA) 2563; 53 Employee Benefits Cas. (BNA) 1513.
4. IRC Sec. 5000A.
5. IRC Sec. 7421(a).

Why did the Supreme Court rule that the individual mandate penalty is really a tax for this purpose? There were four reasons:

- A person who is subject to the "tax" has not violated the law.

- The "tax" is low enough so that a person can make a "reasonable financial decision" to pay the tax instead of doing whatever is being taxed. The tax is not at a "prohibitory" level.

- The "tax" is collected by the Internal Revenue Service in the same manner as other taxes.

- The individual mandate has no intent requirement. Intent ("scienter") is required for crimes or other unlawful acts.

The third issue before the Court of whether the entire law is invalid if the individual mandate is invalid became moot when the individual mandate was upheld.

Finally, while the law's Medicaid expansion was ruled constitutional by a seven to two vote, seven justices agreed that the law's sanction[1] for not participating in the Medicaid expansion is unconstitutional. The Court held that it is unconstitutional for the federal government to withhold existing Medicaid funds for noncompliance with the Medicaid expansion provisions.[2]

90. Under the health reform law, in 2014 individuals are eligible for Medicaid if their income is less than 133 percent of the federal poverty level. What are the implications of the Supreme Court's decision?

Medicaid Expansion not Fully Implemented. Some, perhaps many, states may decide not to participate in the Medicaid expansion due to political opposition to the federal health reform law or because the new federal funds are 10 percent less than the extra costs to the state (which will be the case in 2020 and thereafter). In that situation, the burden for the care of those persons who would have been covered by Medicaid will be shifted from federal and state governments to free care provided by hospitals and physicians, as is now the case.

Health Reform May Still Be in Jeopardy. It is possible that health reform could be undone if the Republicans win the House, Senate, and presidency in November 2012. If President Obama is re-elected, any repeal legislation would require a two-thirds majority vote in the House and in the Senate to override the expected presidential veto. If there is a Republican sweep of the

---

1. 42 USC §1396c.
2. Chief Justice Roberts' opinion, joined by Justices Breyer and Kagan, contains the narrowest rationale and is controlling. [When Congress threatens to terminate other grants as a means of pressuring the States to accept a Spending Clause program, the legislation runs counter to this Nation's system of federalism.] Justice Ginsburg, joined by Justice Sotomayor, upheld the expansion on a broader ground. [Construing the Commerce Clause to permit Congress to regulate individuals precisely because they are doing nothing would open a new and potentially vast domain to congressional authority.]

House, Senate, and presidency, bear in mind that the Senate traditionally requires sixty votes to avoid a filibuster by the other side.

Even if health reform is implemented, it may perform poorly and be more expensive than predicted, leading to calls for change. The mandate system was the second choice of many Democrats. It was an alternative to a "public option." The idea for a public option to be added to existing options could be adopted. If passed, the public option could force private insurance to be priced out of business, perhaps then leading to a federal government single-payor plan.

Health Reform's Medicaid Expansion

91. What is the Medicaid expansion in the 2010 health reform law?

Medicaid provides healthcare and long-term care services for lower-income individuals. It is administered by the states and jointly funded by state and federal governments. The current Medicaid program offers federal funding to states to pay for healthcare for pregnant women, children, needy families, the blind, the elderly, and the disabled.[1] Many states now cover adults with children but only if their income is considerably lower than 133 percent of the federal poverty level (FPL) and they meet certain asset tests. Most states do not cover childless adults at all.

Beginning in 2014, health reform would make everyone whose income is at or below 133 percent of the federal poverty level (FPL eligible for Medicaid.[2] If all states participated, this would add about fifteen million individuals to the Medicaid program in 2014 and nearly twenty-six million by 2020.[3] For the first three years of the expansion (2014 through 2016), the federal government will pay the entire extra cost of a state participating in the expansion.

If some (perhaps many) states do not accept this Medicaid expansion due to political opposition to the federal health reform law or because the new federal funds for the expansion will be 10 percent less than the extra cost to the state in 2020 and thereafter, the Supreme Court decision, by making participation in the Medicaid expansion optional for each state, will remove part of the law's safety net for people in states who decide not to participate in Medicaid expansion. However, many individuals, as they do now, likely will be able to get free care from hospitals and physicians.

Other reasons that a state may not, at least initially, participate in the Medicaid expansion include:

- Operational challenges that could affect their ability to meet Medicaid expansion and system development deadlines, such as time-consuming state procurement processes;

---

1. 42 U. S. C. §1396d(a).
2. PPACA §2001(a)(1).
3. Office of the Actuary, Centers for Medicare and Medicaid Services, U.S. Department of Health and Human Services: 2011 Actuarial Report on the Financial Outlook for Medicaid (Mar. 16, 2012).

- The need to modify existing systems or develop new systems;

- Coordination of multiple programs and systems, and

- Resource limitations.

State eligibility determination systems must interface with a Federal Data Services Hub—an electronic service states will use to verify certain information with other federal agencies, such as an applicant's citizenship, immigration status, and income data.[1]

Despite the initial funding of the extra benefits at the rate of 100 percent by the federal government, participating states' costs could be increased by three aspects of Medicaid expansion:

- The administration for managing Medicaid enrollment,

- The acquisition or modification of information technology systems to support Medicaid (although federal assistance is available), and

- Enrolling previously eligible but not enrolled individuals in Medicaid.

Another complicating factor for those in states not participating in the expansion is that most individuals with incomes less than 100 percent of the federal poverty level will not eligible in 2014 for income tax subsidies to purchase insurance at the state insurance exchanges.[2] These individuals still may end up without affordable access to insurance.

For states participating in the Medicaid expansion, states with low coverage levels and high uninsured rates will see the largest increases in coverage and federal funding. Higher levels of coverage will allow states to reduce the payments they make to support uncompensated care costs.[3]

The state exchanges will determine eligibility for Medicaid. HHS regulations implement rules on Medicaid and Children's Health Insurance Program (CHIP) eligibility, enrollment simplification, and coordination by the state exchange.[4]

92. Can a state later change its 2014 decision as to whether to participate in the Medicaid expansion?

There is no clear answer to this question in the law.

The GAO has stated that in "the Supreme Court's June 28, 2012, decision that states can make their own decisions about whether to expand Medicaid", HHS reiterated that:

---

1. GAO letter to Sen. Charles Grassley (Aug. 1, 2012) at http://gao.gov/assets/600/593210.pdf.
2. IRC Sec. 36B(c)(1)(A).
3. Kaiser, Medicaid and the Uninsured, at http://www.kff.org/healthreform/upload/medicaid-coverage-and-spending-in-health-reform-national-and-state-by-state-results-for-adults-at-or-below-133-fpl.pdf.
4. Medicaid Program; Eligibility Changes Under the Affordable Care Act of 2010, 77 Fed. Reg. 17144 (Mar. 23, 2012).

(1)   There is no deadline for a state to decide to undertake the expansion;

(2)   A state can receive an enhanced administrative federal match for information technology costs, even if it has not yet decided whether to expand Medicaid, as long as it is modernizing its eligibility systems; and

(3)   A state will not have to pay back the extra funding if it ultimately decides not to expand Medicaid."[1]

---

1. GAO letter to Sen. Charles Grassley (Aug. 1, 2012) at http://gao.gov/assets/600/593210.pdf.

PART II: IMPACT OF HEALTHCARE REFORM ON EMPLOYER FRINGE BENEFITS

Fringe Benefit Tax Planning

Retaining a Grandfathered Plan; Benefits of a SIMPLE Cafeteria Plan, and 2013 Limits on Health FSAs

93. Why should employers verify whether they have a grandfathered health plan?

Grandfathered health plans are discussed in detail in Part VI of this book. They offer a way to avoid the health insurance nondiscrimination rules. An employer is eligible to implement a simple cafeteria plan if, during either of the preceding two years, the business employed 100 or fewer employees on average (based on business days). For a new business, eligibility is based on the number of employees the business is reasonably expected to employ on average (based on business days). Businesses maintaining a simple cafeteria plan that grow beyond 100 employees can maintain the simple arrangement until they have exceeded an average of 200 or more employees during a preceding year.

For many employers, the most important benefit is that an employer's grandfathered health insurance plan will not be subject to the new health insurance nondiscrimination rules, discussed in detail in Part VII of this book. When those rules go into effect, if an insured plan discriminates in favor of the top 25 percent of highly compensated employees (HCEs), for example, by paying more of the premiums, then there will be a $100 per day per employee penalty for the employer based on the number of non-highly compensated employees (NHCEs). For an employer with twenty-eight employees, violation of the nondiscrimination rules could result in a penalty of $766,500!

Example: The employer's grandfathered plan is in effect for the entire year, and twenty-one participants are not highly compensated employees.

21 NHCEs × $100 = $2,100 penalty per day

$2,100 × 365 days = $766,500

Thus, for employers that have had their plan since March 23, 2010, have made few if any changes, and provide better benefits or pay more for HCEs, a careful review of the grandfathered plan requirements should be done before any changes are made to the plan.

94. Why should an eligible employer consider a SIMPLE cafeteria plan?

The SIMPLE cafeteria plan is discussed in detail in Part V of this book. The 2010 health reform law includes a provision creating "simple cafeteria plans" for small businesses, effective for years beginning in 2011. Simple cafeteria plans will be treated as meeting nondiscrimination requirements applicable to cafeteria plans if they meet minimum eligibility, participation, and contribution requirements. This safe harbor covers the regular cafeteria plan nondiscrimination requirement of Code Section 125(b) (the provision that limits benefits to key employees to 25 percent of the plan's benefits) and also the nondiscrimination requirements of Code Sections 79(d), 105(h), and 129(d), which are applicable to group term life insurance, a self-insured health or medical reimbursement plan, and dependent care assistance benefits (child care), respectively.

One of the changes proposed in the original legislation drafted by the Small Business Council of America was not adopted. When a business wants to avoid the 25 percent concentration test and contribute for owner-employees, only a regular C corporation can do so. The provisions for simple cafeteria plans apply to "employees," but the term excludes proprietors, partners, LLC members in LLCs taxed as partnerships, and more than 2 percent shareholders in S corporations, all of whom are self-employed individuals and not employees for income tax purposes.

Simple cafeteria plans, available for plan years beginning in 2011, offer a work-around to the new health insurance nondiscrimination rules applicable to all employer-sponsored plans other than grandfathered plans. In addition, these plans allow shareholder-employees and other key employees to benefit under the plan and be exempt from the regular cafeteria plan rule that limits benefits for such individuals to 25 percent of the total nontaxable plan benefits (the so-called concentration test). Additionally, a simple cafeteria may allow key employees to have greater dependent care reimbursement than otherwise available in a regular cafeteria plan.

It would seem safe for the employer to proceed on the basis that the health insurance nondiscrimination rules are met when the plan provides the same eligibility and offers the same benefit options for all participants. Even if all HCEs take family coverage (and it was available on an equal basis and equal contribution level for NHCEs) and all NHCEs took single or none, then the employer should still pass.

95. What are the limits on health FSAs in cafeteria plans (also called flex plans)?

A health FSA is a flexible spending account (FSA), typically part of a cafeteria plan, that reimburses participants from their pre-tax salary deferrals for medical and dental expenses. The deferrals are not reported as taxable income and the reimbursement is not taxable. In effect, the expenses are paid with pre-tax dollars. Prior to 2013, there was no limit on such accounts except those the employer imposed on the plan. It has not been unusual for such health FSAs to be available in amounts of $5,000, $10,000, and sometimes more. The health reform law limits the annual reimbursement from health FSAs to $2,500 per year, as a revenue raiser to help pay for the law's new costs. The details of this rule are discussed in Part VIII of this book.

Plans must be amended to provide for this new limit. The $2,500 limit does not apply to dependent care (child care) FSAs, adoption assistance FSAs, or health insurance premium conversion plan elections, where salary deferrals can be used to pay an employee's share of health insurance with pre-tax dollars.

96. Is FSA, HSA, MERP, or HRA subject to the PHSA §2711 prohibition on annual and lifetime dollar limits?

PHSA §2711, effective in 2014 and discussed in Part VII, prohibits annual and lifetime dollar limits by group health plans on essential health benefits by group health plans and individual insurance policies, including grandfathered plans and policies.[1] Annual or lifetime dollar limits can be imposed on benefits that are not essential health benefits.[2] Healthcare reform also adds new ERISA §715 and new Code §9815, which impose the PHSA mandates not only on group health plans but also on health insurance issuers. The penalty for violating PHSA §2711 is an excise tax under IRC §4980D of $100 per day ($36,500 per year) per affected individual (per participant) for violating the Chapter 100 requirements, including IRC §9815, which incorporates the PHSA mandates.

Group Health Plan. ERISA and the PHSA define "group health plan" in virtually identical language, providing that the term means an employee welfare benefit plan to the extent that the plan provides medical care (including items and services paid for as medical care) to employees or their dependents directly or through insurance, reimbursement, or otherwise.[3]

HRA/MERP. IRS guidance specifically confirms that, generally, health reimbursement accounts (HRAs) and their close cousin, medical expense reimbursement accounts (MERPs), both of which are funded with employer contributions, are generally group health plans.[4] Group health plans generally are subject to the PHSA §2711 prohibition on annual/lifetime dollar limits in 2014 and thereafter. However, four types of HRAs are exempt from PHSA and can continue in 2014 and thereafter:

- A stand-alone HRA that is limited to one employee or retirees is not subject to the PHSA §2711 annual/lifetime dollar limit restrictions.[5] Such HRAs are not group health plans under ERISA §607(1) because they are not employee welfare benefit plans.

- A plan is not an ERISA welfare benefit plan if it covers only individuals who own, or whose spouses own, an interest in an unincorporated business (as partner or proprietor). It is not a plan subject to federal regulation, but ERISA does apply if one or more common law employees is a participant.[6] If a corporation is wholly owned by an individual (or by an individual and his or her spouse), a plan that does not cover any other employee is also exempt from ERISA.[7] Accordingly, the incorporation of a sole proprietorship does not affect ERISA's coverage, but the

1. PHSA §2711(a)(1).
2. PHSA §2711(b).
3. ERISA §733(a)(1); PHSA §2791(a)(1). Under ERISA, group health plans are welfare benefit plans.
4. Rev. Rul. 2002-41; IRS Notice 2002-45.
5. Preamble to TD 9491, 6/22/2010.
6. 29 CFR §2510.3-3(b), (c) (1997). To trigger ERISA the program must cover a common law employee who is not an owner's spouse.
7. Id. This rule applies even if the shareholder or spouse is also a common law employee of the corporation. It does not extend to cases where the corporation is closely held but not wholly owned by an individual or a married couple.

incorporation of a partnership usually does because there will be shareholders who are not spouses of one another.

- HRAs that are or provide for excepted benefits (vision and dental coverage) should also be exempt from the annual/lifetime dollar limit prohibition.[1] The regulators have confirmed that the HIPAA excepted benefits provisions apply for the PHSA mandates, including those in the PHSA itself (applicable to insurers and governmental employers) and as incorporated into ERISA and the Code.[2]

- Finally, HRAs that are integrated with other major medical coverage as part of a group health plan will not violate the annual limit rules so long as the other coverage on its own would comply "because the combined benefit satisfies the requirements."[3] While there is no clear definition of "integration" for this purpose, all individuals covered under the HRA must also be covered by the major medical coverage to be integrated.[4]

Stand-alone HRAs/MERPs that do not satisfy the definition of "integrated" cannot continue beyond 2014 unless they are limited to excepted benefits, have no annual or lifetime dollar limit (which could expose an employer to substantial, perhaps devastating, liability), or are otherwise exempt from the PHSA mandates. The agencies have provided limited transition relief for HRAs in existence prior to January 1, 2013, for amounts accrued prior to January 1, 2014. To qualify for the transition relief, the accrued amounts must be made pursuant to a formula established prior to January 1, 2013, or, if there is no formula, must be less than the amounts accrued in 2012.[5]

There is very little guidance on what "integrated" means. "The Departments intend to issue guidance under PHS Act section 2711 providing that an employer-sponsored HRA may be treated as integrated with other coverage only if the employee receiving the HRA is actually enrolled in that coverage."[6] It is clear that employees must be participants in both plans for the plans to be integrated. However, it is not clear whether an HRA or MERP could cover additional benefits not covered by the employer's group health plan, such as vision or dental benefits when those

---

1. To be excepted benefits, limited-scope dental or vision benefits must be provided either under a separate policy, certificate, or contract of insurance, a condition generally not met by an HRA or must satisfy the conditions necessary for the benefits to be considered "not an integral part" of the employer's other group health plan(s).
2. Preamble to Grandfathered Health Plan Regulations, 75 Fed. Reg. 34537, 34539 (June 17, 2010) (confirming that the exceptions in the Code and ERISA still exist, and announcing an HHS nonenforcement policy with respect to the PHSA provisions); FAQs About the Affordable Care Act Implementation Part II, Q/A-6.
3. Preamble to Interim Final Rules Relating to Preexisting Condition Exclusions, Lifetime and Annual Limits, Rescissions, and Patient Protections Under PPACA, 75 Fed. Reg. 37188, 37190 (June 28, 2010).
4. Fees on Health Insurance Policies and Self-Insured Plans for the Patient-Centered Outcomes Research Trust Fund, 26 CFR Parts 40, 46, and 602, 77 Fed. Reg. 72721, 72725 (Dec. 6, 2012) (addressing an HRA combined with "a separate applicable self-insured health plan" or a separate fully insured plan, in context of determining amount of PCORI fee); and FAQs About the Affordable Care Act Implementation Part XI, Q/A-3 at http://www.dol.gov/ebsa/faqs/faq-aca11.html, stating: "Any HRA that credits additional amounts to an individual when the individual is not enrolled in primary coverage meeting the requirements of PHS Act section 2711 provided by the employer will fail to comply with PHS Act section 2711."
5. See FAQs About the Affordable Care Act Implementation Part XI, Q/A-3.
6. DOL FAQ Part IX, Q&A-3.

are not covered by the employer's main major medical plan. It seems likely that guidance will limit the reimbursement to the types of coverage provided by the major medical plan but which is not paid due to coinsurance, copay, or deductible provisions.

HSAs/FSAs. Neither health savings accounts (HSAs) nor most health flexible spending accounts (health FSAs), which cover medical reimbursement as part of a cafeteria or flex plan, are subject to the PHSA rule prohibiting annual and lifetime dollar limits.

A health savings account (HSA) is a tax-favored individual account vehicle for paying medical expenses.[1] An HSA may be used only in conjunction with a high-deductible health plan (HDHP). An HSA may be established by an employee (with or without employer involvement), and contributions may be made by the employee, the employer, or both. The DOL has stated that HSAs are not ERISA employee welfare benefit plans even if funded by the employer.[2] Similarly, the preamble to the DOL/HHS/IRS) HIPAA portability regulations notes that "the HIPAA portability requirements generally are not relevant for purposes of HSAs."[3] Therefore, HSAs will not be group health plans for the PHSA mandate.

Health FSAs meeting two conditions, which most of them meet, are excepted benefits and thus not required to comply with the PHSA mandates.[4] First, the maximum benefit payable under the health FSA to any participant in the class for a year cannot exceed two times the participant's salary reduction election under the health FSA for the year (or, if greater, the amount of the participant's salary reduction election for the health FSA for the year, plus $500).[5] Thus, the maximum health FSA annual benefit where the participant makes the maximum annual $2,500 salary reduction contribution means that the employer can contribute up to $500 per year to the health FSA.[6] IRS officials have informally indicated that for purposes of the maximum benefit condition, benefits provided during a grace period from the prior year's contributions are attributed to the prior year. Second, other nonexcepted group health plan coverage (major medical coverage) must be made available for the year to the class of participants by reason of their employment.[7] Finally, interim final regulations jointly issued by the IRS, DOL, and HHS on the annual and lifetime limits (the "joint regulations") appear to go further, exempting any plan that is a health FSA within the meaning of Code §106(c)(2), even if it does not satisfy the two additional conditions for the HIPAA exception, so long as the amount of available reimbursement is less than 500% of the value of such coverage.[8]

---

1. IRC §213(d).
2. DOL Field Assistance Bulletins 2004-1 and 2006-02. however, too much employer control over AN HSA could make the HSA subject to ERISA. Id.
3. 69 Fed. Reg. 78719, 78734 (Dec. 30, 2004).
4. Treas. Reg. §54.9831-1(c)(3)(v); DOL Reg. §2590.732(c)(3)(v); HHS Reg. §146.145(c)(3)(v).
5. Treas. Reg. §54.9831-1(c)(3)(v)(B); DOL Reg. §2590.732(c)(3)(v)(B); HHS Reg. §146.145(c)(3)(v)(B).
6. Other examples of health FSA funding that meet the maximum benefit condition are:
   • Any one-for-one employer match (employer $600, employee $600).
   • Any employer contribution of $500 or less (employer $500, employee $200).
7. Treas. Reg. §54.9831-1(c)(3)(v)(A); DOL Reg. §2590.732(c)(3)(v)(A); HHS Reg. §146.145(c)(3)(v)(A).
8. Treas. Reg. §54.9815-2711T(a)(2)(ii); DOL Reg. §2590.715-2711(a)(2)(ii); HHS Reg. §147.126(a)(2)(ii). Code §106(c)(2) defines the term "flexible spending arrangement" as a benefit program providing coverage under two conditions, one of which is that "the maximum amount of reimbursement which is reasonably available to a participant for such coverage is less than 500 percent of the value of such coverage."

97. Can 2013 fiscal year cafeteria plan elections to purchase health insurance be changed midyear to purchase insurance on an exchange or in the employer-offered plan for plan years beginning in 2013?

Yes, if the plan is amended, despite the fact that this is not a change in status, which is a normal prerequisite to change a cafeteria plan election.

Employees may want to terminate their election to purchase health insurance through the employer's cafeteria plan and go to the exchange if they are eligible for health insurance exchange tax credits. Other employees may want to elect to purchase health insurance from the employer plan effective Jan. 1, 2014, to avoid the individual mandate penalty. If the cafeteria plan year is a fiscal year, employees wanting exchange insurance on Jan. 1, 2014, would have to terminate or change their elections midyear. However, under current cafeteria plan regulations, these two elections are not a change in status allowing an election change midyear. The proposed regulations allow an applicable large employer with a fiscal year cafeteria plan, at its election, to amend the plan any time during the year on a retroactive basis (by Dec. 31, 2014, retroactive to beginning of 2013 plan year) to permit either or both of the following changes in salary reduction elections:[1]

(1)   An employee who elected to salary reduce through the fiscal year cafeteria plan for accident and health plan coverage beginning in 2013 is allowed to prospectively revoke or change his or her election with respect to the accident and health plan once, during that plan year, without regard to whether the employee experienced a change in status event described in Reg. §1.125-4; and

(2)   An employee who failed to make a salary reduction election through his or her employer's fiscal year cafeteria plan beginning in 2013 for accident and health plan coverage before the deadline in proposed §1.125-2 is allowed to make a prospective salary reduction election for accident and health coverage on or after the first day of the 2013 plan year of the cafeteria plan without regard to whether the employee experienced a change in status event as described in Reg. §1.125-4.

Some provisions of the transition relief refer to "applicable large employer members" (i.e., employers that are subject to healthcare reform's employer mandate), raising questions as to whether the relief is available for all non-calendar-year cafeteria plans or only those that are sponsored by applicable large employer members.

---

1. Preamble to Proposed Rules on Shared Responsibility for Employers Regarding Health Coverage, 78 Fed. Reg. 217, 237 (Jan. 2, 2013).

PART III: TIMELINE FOR IMPLEMENTATION OF PROVISIONS: WHAT NEEDS TO BE DONE AND WHEN

98. What are the major components of healthcare reform and when are they effective?

2010

- January 1, 2010

  ➤ Tax Credit. Beginning in 2010, small employers with low-paid employees are eligible for a tax credit for purchasing health care for their employees. The full credit applies to a business with no more than ten full-time equivalent (FTE) employees who have average wages not exceeding $25,000. The credit is phased out entirely if the business has twenty-five or more FTE employees or if the average wages of its employees is $50,000 or more. For 2010 through 2013, the credit is 35 percent (25 percent for tax-exempt employers) of the employer's non-elective premium for qualified health insurance policies. Starting in 2014, the credit increases to 50 percent (35 percent for tax-exempt employers) but it is available only if the health insurance policy is purchased on a state health insurance exchange. Related employers are treated as a single employer.

  ➤ ERRP (Early Retiree Reinsurance Program.) Temporary large claim reinsurance assistance is available for employers providing early retirement benefits to retirees ages fifty-five to sixty-four under a retiree group health plan. The reinsurance reimbursement, up to a $60,000 annual maximum per eligible retiree, is 80 percent of the costs incurred by the plan for eligible retirees (and their dependents) in excess of the first $15,000 of such costs. The costs that may be reimbursed include the portion paid by the retiree for deductibles, copayments, and coinsurance. Medical expenses incurred after June 1, 2010, were eligible for reimbursement under this program. Up to $5 billion was allocated for the program, but the money was spent quickly, and HHS stopped taking claims on Dec. 31, 2011.[1]

- March 23, 2010

  ➤ Grandfather Provision. Group plans in existence and with actual membership on and after March 23, 2010, have the right to maintain their existing coverage, except as otherwise provided.[2] Family members of individuals enrolled in grandfathered plans and new employees can enroll in the plan if its provisions allow such enrollment without jeopardizing the plan's "grandfathered" status.[3]

---

1. PPACA §§1102, 10102.
2. PPACA §1251.
3. PPACA §1251(b) & (c).

➤ Reasonable Break Time for Nursing Mothers. Employers must provide reasonable break times to allow nursing mothers to express breast milk for a child up to age one.[1]

➤ Nondiscrimination Rules for Health Program or Activity. An individual generally cannot be excluded from participation in, denied benefits of, or subjected to discrimination due to race, color, national origin, sex, age, or disability under any health program or activity that is receiving federal financial assistance on a ground that is prohibited under the following laws:

   ○ Title VI of the Civil Rights Act of 1964;

   ○ Education Amendments of 1972;

   ○ Age Discrimination Act of 1975; or

   ○ Section 504 of the Rehabilitation Act of 1973.[2]

➤ Employee Whistleblower Protections. PPACA added the FLSA "Protections for Employees", which prohibits employers from taking adverse action against any employee because the employee:

   ○ received a premium tax credit or subsidy for a health plan;

   ○ provided information to the employer or the federal or state government concerning a violation, act or omission the employee reasonably believes to be a violation relating to Title I of the Act. (Title I of the Act, among other things, provides rules for the establishment and operation of the Exchange and imposes certain mandates on employers, including the provision of certain standards of benefits for health coverage, the automatic enrollment requirements described above and the elimination of certain restrictions in health coverage, such as pre-existing condition exclusions and lifetime and annual dollar limitations in coverage);

   ○ testified or is about to testify in a proceeding concerning such violation;

   ○ assisted or participated, or is about to assist or participate, in such a proceeding; or

   ○ objected to, or refused to perform, any activity or assigned task the employee reasonably believes to be such a violation.[3]

The procedures for handling retaliation complaints are at 29 CFR 1984.102 et seq.

---

1. PPACA §4207; FLSA §(r).
2. PPACA §1557.
3. PPACA §1558; FLSA §18C.

- June 21, 2010

  ➤ Temporary High-Risk Health Insurance Pool. Adults with pre-existing conditions can participate in a temporary high-risk pool, the Pre-Existing Condition Insurance Plan (PCIP) program. The program can be run by the states or by HHS, if a state elects. It will be superseded by the state healthcare exchanges in 2014. To qualify for coverage, applicants must have a pre-existing health condition and have been uninsured for at least the six months prior to enrolling in coverage. There is no age requirement to enroll. The program sets premiums as if for a standard population, and it allows premiums to vary by age, geographic area, and family composition. It also limits out-of-pocket spending to $5,950 for individuals and $11,900 for families, excluding premiums.[1]

- Plan Years Beginning on or after September 23, 2010

  ➤ Annual and Lifetime Limits. Use of lifetime dollar limits on health benefits is prohibited. A group health plan may impose lifetime limits on non-essential health benefits for beneficiaries, but not participants. This applies to grandfathered plans. Use of unreasonable annual dollar limits for "essential health benefits" is prohibited. Starting in 2014, all annual dollar limits for non-essential health benefits are prohibited. Grandfathered plans are exempt from this rule.

  ➤ Pre-Existing Condition Exclusion for Children under Age Nineteen. Any pre-existing condition exclusion for children less than nineteen years of age is prohibited. This provision also applies to grandfathered plans.[2]

  ➤ Adult Dependent Coverage. Group health plans that provide dependent coverage must provide coverage to their employees' adult children (including those who are married) until age twenty-six, provided that, with respect to grandfathered plans, the child is not otherwise eligible for coverage under another employer-sponsored health plan.[3]

  ➤ Preventive Care. Group health plans must provide first-dollar coverage for preventive care. Grandfathered plans are exempt from this requirement.[4]

  ➤ Primary Care Physicians for Children and Women. Group health plans that use primary care provider gatekeepers must give participants the right to select any available primary care provider, including pediatricians for children. Women must have the right to see any participating OB/GYN physician without a primary care provider referral.[5]

---

1. PPACA §1201: PHSA §2704.
2. PHSA §2704; PPACA §§1201 1255, 10103.
3. PHSA §2714.
4. PPACA §§1001, 10101; PHSA §2713.
5. PPACA §§1001, 10101; PHSA §2719A(c) & (d).

➤ Emergency Care. Group health plans must cover emergency care without a requirement for a primary care provider referral or imposition of any "out-of-network" penalty. Grandfathered plans are exempt.[1]

➤ Policy Rescission Limited. Group health plans and health insurance issuers may not rescind coverage for reasons other than fraud or material misrepresentation by the plan participant or beneficiary. This provision also applies to grandfathered plans.[2]

➤ Claims and Appeals Procedures. All plans, including grandfathered plans, must implement an "effective appeals process." Church and government plans without ERISA-compliant claims procedures are required to adopt such procedures. External review must be conducted by one of the approved independent review organizations (IROs) with which the plan has contracted. Nongrandfathered, self-insured plans had an enforcement safe harbor that allowed them to contract with as few as two IROs. As of July 1, 2012, that was increased to at least three IROs for the safe harbor to apply. A grace period extended some of these requirements to July 1, 2011. The Employee Benefits Security Administration (EBSA) Technical Release 2011-01 extended the grace period for some of these rules to plan years beginning on or after January 1, 2012.[3]

➤ Nondiscrimination Requirements for Employer Provided Insured Health Plans Postponed. Originally to be effective for plan years beginning on or after September 23, 2010, but postponed by IRS Notice 2011-1 until regulations are issued. These nondiscrimination rules do not apply to grandfathered insured plans.[4]

- January 1, 2011

  ➤ New SIMPLE Cafeteria Plan. For employers with 100 or fewer employees during either of the two prior years, and employers can increase the number of employees to 200. Simple cafeteria plans are exempt from the 25 percent concentration tests and deemed nondiscriminatory for purposes of the nondiscrimination requirements applicable to life insurance, dependent care plans, and other benefits if the employer provides:

    ○ at least a 2 percent of pay contribution for participants, or

    ○ a matching contribution for participants, which is the lesser of:

      • 6 percent of pay, or

      • two times each qualified employee's pretax contribution.

---

1. PPACA §§1001, 10101, PHSA §2719A.
2. PPACA §1001; PHSA §2712.
3. PPACA §10101; PHSA §2719.
4. PHSA §2716.

A "qualified employee" is any employee who is not an HCE (as defined in Code Section 414(q)) or a key employee (as defined in Code Section 415(i)). Simple cafeteria plans must still comply with Code Section 125 nondiscrimination requirements regarding eligibility and benefits. Simple Cafeteria Plans are discussed in more detail in Part V of this book.[1]

➤   Reimbursement for Over-the-Counter Drugs. Reimbursement under flexible spending accounts (FSAs), health saving accounts (HSAs), medical savings accounts (MSAs), and health reimbursement accounts (HRAs) for over-the-counter drugs (except insulin) is no longer allowed unless the patient has a prescription for the drug.[2]

➤   HSA/MSA Excise Tax. The excise tax for distributions from HSAs and MSAs for expenses that are not Code Section 213 medical expenses increased to 20 percent from the current 10 percent and 15 percent respectively.[3]

➤   Employer W-2 Reporting Postponed.

➤   Federal Long-Term Care. The Community Living Assistance Services and Support (CLASS) Act authorized a voluntary federal insurance program for employees to purchase long-term care insurance. Employers could elect to automatically enroll employees in the program, allowing employees to opt-out. The provision was intended to be effective January 1, 2011; however, HHS has announced that it will not implement this program because it could not function cost effectively.

➤   Medical Loss Ratio (MLR) Requirements. The required MLRs are 85 percent in the large group health insurance market and 80 percent in the small group and individual markets (or higher, based on state regulations). The remaining percentage of health insurance premiums can be spent by insurers on administrative costs. Insurers' reports to policy holders for calendar year due by June 1 of following year; rebates by August 1 of following year. Health insurance companies must comply with medical loss ratio standards and are required to submit reports to HHS for each plan year relating to an accounting for costs, and are also required to provide rebates to policyholders under certain circumstances. Although the obligations to calculate the MLR and make rebates fall on insurers, in many cases the rebates will be paid to group health plans, and the plans will be required to determine how to use the rebates or refund them to plan participants.[4]

---

1. IRC Sec. 125(j).
2. IRC Secs. 106(f), 223(d)(2), 220(d)(2).
3. IRC Secs. 223(f)(4)(A), 220(f)(4)(A).
4. PHSA §2718.

2012

- January 1, 2012

  ➤ Expanded 1099 Reporting. Repealed.

- March 23, 2012

  ➤ Quality of Care Reporting. Health care reform requires group health plans and health insurance issuers to submit an annual report to the Secretary of HHS addressing plan or coverage benefits and provider "reimbursement structures" that may affect the quality of care in certain specified ways. The reporting requirements are to be developed in consultation with health care quality experts and "stakeholders" (e.g., representatives of care providers, care recipients, insurers, and employers) and may be enforced by "appropriate penalties" developed by the Secretary. Copies of the report must be made available to enrollees during each open enrollment period. HHS was required to "develop" the reporting requirements no later than March 23, 2012, and to issue regulations that provide criteria for determining whether a "reimbursement structure" is subject to the reporting rule. HHS guidance under this provision remains outstanding.[1]

- August 1, 2012

  ➤ Medical Loss Ratio Reports and Rebates. Health plans must have procedures in place to handle any rebates received from the insurer in accordance with the rules for distribution, including the rules requiring ERISA plans to determine the extent to which rebates are plan assets. Rebates need to be apportioned if premiums are paid with both employer and employee contributions. (Effective Aug. 1, 2012.)[2]

  ➤ Preventive Health Services for Women. Nongrandfathered group health plans must provide recommended preventive health services without cost sharing and must adjust the services covered in accordance with changes to recommended preventive services guidelines.

- September 23, 2012

  ➤ SBC Disclosures. HHS prescribed uniform summary of benefits that a group health plan sponsor or insurance issuer will need to distribute to plan participants and potential enrollees. This disclosure is in addition to the ERISA summary plan description. If any material modification is made after such summary is provided, then a notice of material modifications must be provided to participants at least sixty

---

1. PPACA §1251, adopting PHSA §2717.
2. PHSA §2718.

days prior to the modification's (Effective date: Must be distributed during open enrollment periods for plan years beginning or after September 23, 2012, or, for other enrollments (such as new hires), beginning on the first day of the first plan year that begins on or after September 23, 2012. (Effective Sept. 23, 2012; originally to be effective March 23, 2012.)[1]

2013

- January 1, 2013

  ➤ W-2 Reporting. W-2s must be issued showing employer and employee payments for certain health care items in 2012. This does not change the employer's deduction or cause employees to be taxed. IRS announced an exemption for employers that did not file at least 250 W-2s in preceding year, but this exemption can be eliminated in the future by IRS notice.[2]

  ➤ Health FSAs. A $2,500 annual limit will be imposed on health FSA deferrals; currently there is no such limit. Dependent care and adoption FSAs will not be limited.[3]

  ➤ Individual Deduction Threshold Increased. The current 7.5 percent of adjusted gross income (AGI) floor on income-tax deductions for healthcare expenses is raised to 10 percent of AGI. ; However, the floor is waived during 2013, 2014, 2015, and 2016 for individuals who turn age sixty-five before the end of those years.[4]

  ➤ Employer Deduction for Government-Subsidized Employer Drug Benefits Eliminated. The employer deduction for the portion of healthcare expenses that are reimbursed to the employer through the Medicare Part D subsidy program is eliminated.

  ➤ Administrative Simplification. The health reform law will affect relationships between payers and providers (hospitals, physicians, and allied care practitioners), as well as claims clearinghouses and banks that perform intermediary functions. HHS prescribes new "operating rules" that will govern the exchange of health data transactions, including eligibility, claim status, electronic funds transfers, electronic remittance advices, and other transactions. Group health plans must comply with "administrative simplification" rules for electronic exchange health information and electronic fund transfers, and they also must file a certification with the federal government that the plans are in compliance. This provision also applies to grandfathered plans. Systems must be compliant, and employers must certify compliance by December 31, 2013.[5]

---

1. PHSA §2715.
2. IRC Sec. 6051(a).
3. IRC Sec. 125(i).
4. IRC Sec. 213(a).
5. PPACA §1104.

> Medicare Tax Increases. The FICA Medicare tax rate will be increased by 0.9 percent for wages/earnings over $200,000 for individuals ($250,000 for married couples filing jointly). This will result in a combined 2.35 percent on wages over $200,000 ($250,000 for joint filers). The employer is required to collect the employee's share in the case of wages. The employer's share of FICA Medicare tax remains 1.45 percent. A new Medicare tax on investment income of 3.8 percent will apply to individuals who earn more than $200,000 a year ($250,000 for married couples filing jointly). Effective for tax years beginning January 1, 2013.

- July 31, 2013

> Comparative Clinical Effectiveness Research Fee. First temporary fees imposed on self-insured health plan sponsors[1] and insurers for insured plans.[2] (Effective July 21, 2013, for plan years ending prior to that date.)

> Patient Centered Outcomes Research Institute (PCORI) Health Plan Fees. Health insurance issuers and self-funded health plans will be required to pay an annual fee of $2.00, ($1.00 during first year) indexed for inflation starting in 2014, times the average number of covered lives under the health insurance policy or self-insured health plan. (Effective for plan years ending after September 3, 2012; scheduled to end for plan years ending after September 3, 2019.) The first payments are required July 31, 2013, and each July 31 thereafter through 2020.[3] The tax and return is due July 31 following the calendar year in which the plan year ends. For calendar year plans, the first return is due July 31, 2013. For a PYE 3/31/13, the calendar year ends in 2013 and the tax and return would be due 7/31/14. (See Q 404 through Q 412.)

- October 1, 2013

> Employer Health Insurance Exchange Notice. Employers, regardless of size and whether or not they have a health plan, must provide notice to employees of the upcoming existence of state insurance exchanges, which are to be established by all the states in 2014 or by HHS if a state fails to do so. Notice must be in the form specified in DOL guidance. (Original effective date of March 1, 2013, delayed until October 1, 2013.)

- December 31, 2013

> Plan Communications with Providers. Health plans must certify and document compliance with HHS rules for electronic transactions between providers and health plans.

---

1. IRC Sec. 4376.
2. IRC Sec. 4375.
3. PPACA §6301; IRC Secs. 4375, 4376.

2014

- January 1, 2014

  ➢   Cafeteria Plans with Fiscal Plan Year Beginning in 2013 Can Be Amended to Allow Employees to Change Election to Purchase Health Insurance or to Terminate Election to Purchase Insurance. Employees may want to terminate their election to purchase health insurance through the employer's cafeteria plan and go to the exchange if they are eligible for health insurance exchange tax credits. Other employees may want to elect to purchase health insurance effective January 1, 2014, to avoid the individual mandate penalty. If the cafeteria plan year is a fiscal year, employees wanting exchange insurance on January 1, 2014, would have to terminate or change their elections midyear. However, under current cafeteria plan regulations, these two elections are not a change in status allowing an election change midyear. The proposed regulations allow an applicable large employer with a fiscal year cafeteria plan, at its election, to amend the plan any time during the year on a retroactive basis (by December 31, 2014, retroactive to beginning of 2013 plan year) to permit either or both of the following changes in salary reduction elections:[1]

  (1)   An employee who elected to salary reduce through the fiscal year cafeteria plan for accident and health plan coverage beginning in 2013 is allowed to prospectively revoke or change his or her election with respect to the accident and health plan once, during that plan year, without regard to whether the employee experienced a change in status event described in Reg. §1.125-4; and

  (2)   An employee who failed to make a salary reduction election through his or her employer's fiscal year cafeteria plan beginning in 2013 for accident and health plan coverage before the deadline in proposed §1.125-2 for making elections is allowed to make a prospective salary reduction election for accident and health coverage on or after the first day of the 2013 plan year of the cafeteria plan without regard to whether the employee experienced a change in status event described in Reg. §1.125-4.

  Some provisions of the transition relief refer to "applicable large employer members" (i.e., employers that are subject to healthcare reform's employer mandate), raising questions as to whether the relief is available for all non-calendar-year cafeteria plans or only those that are sponsored by applicable large employer members.

---

1. Preamble to Proposed Rules on Shared Responsibility for Employers Regarding Health Coverage, 78 Fed. Reg. 217, 237 (Jan. 2, 2013).

➤ <u>Health Insurance Nondiscrimination Requirements</u>. Code Section 105(h) currently taxes the benefits received by highly compensated employees (HCEs) under discriminatory self-funded health plans. PPACA has extended these nondiscrimination rules to insured plans. It is unclear whether this change imposes tax penalties or is a substantive requirement. Employers with discriminatory insured arrangements, however, will need to consider changing them. Grandfathered plans are exempt from this rule. (New nondiscrimination requirement for insured plans was postponed in 2010 until IRS publishes regulations, which have not yet been issued; originally to be effective for plan years beginning on or after September 23, 2010. May not be effective in 2014.)[1]

➤ <u>State Health Insurance Exchanges</u>. Each state must establish a health insurance exchange (or HHS will do so) for use by the uninsured and small employers with 100 or fewer employees (although states may set the cap at 50 employees). The exchanges will offer fully insured insurance contracts that provide essential health benefits at different levels of coverage (bronze, silver, gold, and platinum).[2] Employees of small employers who offer health insurance coverage through an exchange may pay their employee premiums for such coverage on a pre-tax basis through the employer's cafeteria plan.[3]

➤ <u>State Health Insurance Exchange Tax Subsidies</u>. Individuals who do not have affordable minimum essential coverage from their employer will be eligible for tax credit subsidies for their health insurance purchase on a state exchange if their income is below 400 percent of federal poverty level.

➤ <u>Individual Mandate Tax Penalty</u>. Individuals are required to obtain minimum essential health coverage for themselves and their dependents or pay a monthly penalty tax for each month without coverage. The monthly penalty tax is one-twelfth of the greater of the dollar penalty or gross income penalty amounts. The dollar penalty is an amount per individual of:

  ○ $95 for 2014 (capped at $285 per family),

  ○ $325 for 2015 (capped at $975 per family), and

  ○ $695 for 2016 (capped at $2085 per family).

  These dollar penalties will be indexed for inflation starting in 2017.

---

1. PPACA §1201; PHSA §2716.
2. See Q 63, Part 1, for more information about the levels.
3. PPACA §1557.

The gross income penalty is a percentage of household income in excess of a specified filing threshold of:

○   1 percent for 2014,

○   2 percent for 2015, and

○   2.5 percent for 2016 and later years.

In no event will the maximum penalty amount exceed the national average premium for bronze-level exchange plans for families of the same size.

Minimum essential coverage includes Medicare, Medicaid, CHIP, TRICARE, individual insurance, grandfathered plans, and eligible employer-sponsored plans. Workers compensation and limited-scope dental or vision benefits are not considered minimum essential health coverage.[1]

➢   Employer Free Choice Vouchers. Repealed.

➢   Automatic Enrollment. Employers with more than 200 employees who maintain one or more health plans must automatically enroll new full-time employees in a health plan. The employer must give affected employees notice of this automatic enrollment procedure and an opportunity to opt out. State wage withholding laws are preempted to the extent that they prevent an employer from instituting this automatic enrollment program. The final effective date was [will be?] established by DOL regulations.[2]

➢   Pre-Existing Condition Exclusion Practices Eliminated. Pre-existing condition exclusions no longer will be allowed in group health plans or individual insurance policies, not even the limited exclusions previously allowed under HIPAA. This also applies to grandfathered plans.[3] Effective for plan years beginning on or after January 1, 2014.

➢   Ninety-Day Maximum Waiting Period. Group health plans and health insurance issuers may not impose waiting periods of more than ninety days before coverage becomes effective. This also applies to grandfathered plans.[4]

➢   Cost-Sharing Limits. Group health plans, including grandfathered plans, may not impose cost-sharing amounts (i.e., copays or deductibles) that are more than the maximum allowed for high-deductible health plans (currently these limits are $5,000 for an individual and $10,000 for a family coverage). After 2014, these amounts will be adjusted for health insurance premium inflation.[5]

---

1. PPACA §§1501, 10106; IRC Sec. 5000A.
2. PPACA §1511; FLSA §18A.
3. PHSA §2704 & §2705.
4. PHSA §2708.
5. PPACA §1302(c); PHSA §2707(b).

➢ Annual or Lifetime Limits. Group health plans, including grandfathered plans, may no longer include more than restricted annual or any lifetime dollar limits on essential health benefits for participants. Limits may exist in and after 2014 for non-essential benefits.[1]

➢ Wellness Program Health Plan Discount. The maximum premium discount an employer can offer under its health plan for participation in a wellness program is 30 percent. This is an increase from the prior 20 percent maximum premium discount. Regulatory agencies can increase this maximum discount to 50 percent in the future.

➢ Coverage for Those in Clinical Trials. Insurers and health plans, unless grandfathered, may not discriminate against an individual for participating in a clinical trial. If a plan covers a qualified individual, it may not deny or impose additional conditions for participation in a clinical trial.[2]

➢ Medicaid Expansion. Supreme Court in effect ruled that the requirement for states to offer Medicaid benefits to all persons with incomes at or below 133 percent of federal poverty level is optional with each state. States that participate will receive full reimbursement of additional costs from federal government until 2017, at which point reimbursement will gradually decline to 90 percent of extra costs in 2020 and thereafter.

2015

➢ Employer Mandate (Play or Pay) Tax Penalties. Employers with fifty or more full-time equivalent (FTE) employees will be required to offer their full-time employees (FTEs) minimum essential health coverage or pay a fine of up to $2,000 per year for each FTE in excess of thirty FTEs if any employee receives a premium tax credit on a state health insurance exchange. If an employer provides minimum essential health coverage to its FTEs, but fails to pay at least 60 percent of its actuarial value or the coverage is considered unaffordable (costs more than 9.5 percent of household income), then the employer must pay a penalty of up to $3,000 per year for each FTE who receives the premium credit on an exchange, but not more than would be owed for the $2,000 per year penalty. An FTE is defined as an employee who is employed for thirty or more hours per week, calculated on a forty-hour work week. This provision also applies to grandfathered plans.[3] (Originally effective January 1, 2014, but delayed until January 1, 2015.)

---

1. PHSA §2711.
2. PHSA §2709.
3. IRC Sec. 4980H. See Q 26, Part 1, for an explanation of how the penalties are calculated.

➤ Employer Minimum Essential Coverage Reporting. All employers providing minimum essential coverage must file information with the IRS and plan participants.[1] (Effective for calendar years beginning on and after Jan. 1, 2015, after one-year delay.)

➤ Large Employer Health Information Reporting. Large employers and employers with at least fifty full-time equivalent employees must submit annual health insurance coverage returns to the FTEs and the IRS. The returns must certify whether the employer offers healthcare insurance to its employees and, if so, describe the details regarding plan participation, applicable waiting periods, coverage availability, the lowest cost premium option under the plan in each enrollment category, and other information.[2] (Effective January 1, 2015, after one-year delay.)

• December 31, 2015

➤ Group health plans must use electronic systems for processing health claims, enrollment, and premium payments and certify to the federal government that their systems comply. This also applies to grandfathered plans (plans must certify compliance by December 31, 2015).

2017

• January 1, 2017

➤ Employers Purchasing Insurance on Exchange Can Be Increased. States can allow larger employers (those with more than 100 employees) to purchase health insurance for their employees on the state health insurance exchanges.

➤ Medicaid Expansion. Federal reimbursement will be reduced from 100 percent of the cost of expansion gradually to 90 percent in 2020.

2018

• January 1, 2018

➤ Cadillac Health Plan Tax. An excise tax of 40 percent, called the "Cadillac health plan" tax, will be imposed on "coverage providers" (i.e., health insurer for fully insured plans, the employer with respect to HSA or MSA contributions, and in all other cases, the "person that administers the plan") that provide high-cost healthcare coverage to the employer's employees. The excise tax will be imposed on the "excess benefit" provided to the employees.[3]

---

1. PPACA §1502; IRC Sec. 6055.
2. PPACA §§1311(e)(3), 10104; PHSA §2715A; IRC Sec. 5056.
3. See Part VIII of this book for more information on Cadillac plans. IRC Sec. 4980I.

PART IV: HEALTH REFORM PROVISIONS THAT HAVE BEEN REPEALED, EXPIRED, OR NOT IMPLEMENTED

Free Choice Vouchers – Repealed

99. What were free choice vouchers and what were they intended to do?

As originally enacted in 2010, the health reform law required certain employers to provide free choice vouchers to qualified employees to allow those employees to purchase a health plan through a state health insurance exchange, beginning in 2014.[1] In the original law, employers offering health coverage and paying a portion of the costs of the plan were to provide vouchers to certain employees with a value equal to the contribution that the employer would have made to its own plan. If multiple plans were offered, the amount of the voucher would have been equal to the most generous employer contribution. The employer was to provide its share of self-only or dependent coverage at the worker's choice. Employers providing these vouchers would not have been subject to the employer mandate tax penalty as to such employees.

Originally, employers that offered minimum essential coverage were required to offer vouchers beginning in 2014 to certain employees whose cost of coverage was more than 8 percent but less than 9.8 percent of household income. Those lower-income workers could then opt out of their employer's health insurance and purchase more affordable coverage on the insurance exchange, where they would have received a premium subsidy through an income tax credit if their income was below 400 percent of the federal poverty level.

The voucher would have permitted the employee to take the employer's contribution toward health coverage and use it for a potentially cheaper exchange plan when the tax subsidy was taken into account. If the amount of the voucher exceeded the cost of the premium for the plan the worker bought through the exchange, the excess was to be paid to the employee. The money spent on health insurance would have been income-tax free, and any cash payment to the employee would have been taxed.

100. When was the provision for free choice vouchers repealed?

In 2011, appropriations legislation[2] repealed the free choice voucher provisions. It is not clear why, but the motive may have been, at least in part, to save money because some of the individuals who would have received vouchers were not eligible for the premium subsidy. Additionally, it has been reported that certain groups, such as employers and unions, did not want workers to be able to buy health insurance on their own.

---

1. PPACA §10108(a); IRC Sec. 4980H(b)(3).
2. Department of Defense and Full-Year Continuing Appropriations Act, 2011, Pub. L. No. 112-10 (2011).

101. What is the impact of the repeal of free choice vouchers?

With free choice vouchers, Americans whose income fell below 400 percent of the federal poverty level and whose employer-sponsored health insurance premiums were between 8 percent and 9.8 percent of their total income would have been allowed to access the state insurance exchange and qualify for government assistance to buy insurance.

In 2014, if employees' share of their employer-sponsored health insurance premiums rose to 9.9 percent of their total income, they would be allowed to shop for more affordable health insurance in the new health insurance exchanges, with a taxpayer-funded subsidy. But again, at 9.8 percent and below, their only options would be to pay for their employer-sponsored coverage or to go without health coverage.

Had Free Choice Vouchers survived, fewer Americans would have had to go without health insurance. Through the use of private subsidy dollars versus relying solely on taxpayer funded subsidies, arguably money would have been saved for taxpayers. If employer premiums continue to rise, more and more Americans would have become eligible for this option. More choice, and perhaps competition, would have been present in the health insurance market.

Some employers, especially small employers, had expressed interest in expanding the free choice voucher provision so that they would no longer need to pick their employees' health insurance. They liked the idea of giving their employees access to a health insurance system, much like the Federal Employee Health Benefits Plan, in which employers can essentially subsidize their employees' ability to shop on the new health insurance exchanges.

Vouchers would be good for employees because they would be able to pick the plan that works best for them versus the plan that works best for their employer. Additionally, vouchers would likely have resulted in more Americans using the exchanges' risk pools, holding down costs for everyone.

Expanded 1099 Requirements – Repealed

102. What were the repealed 1099 requirements?

Under current tax law, a business making payments to a service provider (the "payee"), other than a corporation, aggregating $600 or more for services in the course of a trade or business in a year is required to send an information return (Form 1099) to the IRS (and to the service provider-payee) setting forth the amount, as well as name and address of the recipient of the payment (generally on Form 1099).[1]

Expanded 1099 Requirements to Have Been Effective in 2012. The new law makes two changes to Code Section 6041. First, businesses must issue the Forms 1099 to all persons and businesses, including corporations, for which aggregate annual payments are $600 or more. Second, the forms must be issued for payments made to "property" providers as well as service

---

1. Congressional Research Service Report: http://www.pppnet.org/pdf/crs._1099.pdf (last accessed May 27, 2011).

providers. The new law adds the phrase "amounts in consideration of property" as payments made to a provider that must be reported, but the law does not define the term "property." Regulations will need to define this term, but it probably means all property, including the goods a business purchases for resale.[1]

Exceptions. The report of the Joint Committee on Taxation, beginning at page 113, provided for exceptions to the expanded 1099 requirement for a payee that is a tax-exempt corporation under Code Section 501 and other specific provisions in the Code that except certain payments from reporting, such as securities or broker transactions as defined under Code Section 6045(a). This includes items reported under Code Sections 6042(a)(1), 6044(a)(1), 6047(e), 6049(a), or 6050N(a), other than payments with respect to which a statement is required under the authority of Code Sections 6042(a)(2), 6044(a)(2), or 6045.[2]

103. When and how were the expanded 1099 requirements repealed?

The Comprehensive 1099 Taxpayer Protection and Repayment of Exchange Subsidy Overpayments Act of 2011[3] repealed both the expanded Form 1099 information reporting requirements mandated by the 2010 health reform law and also the new 1099 reporting requirements imposed on taxpayers with rental income enacted by the 2010 Small Business Jobs Act.[4]

The Small Business Jobs Act enacted a requirement that individuals who receive rental income issue Forms 1099 to service providers for payments of $600 or more. It did this by specifying that "a person receiving rental income from real estate shall be considered to be engaged in a trade or business of renting property." The 1099 Act strikes Code Section 6041(h), retroactively and effective for payments made after December 31, 2010, the original effective date of Code Section 6041(h).

As a result of the repeal, the 1099 reporting rules continue unchanged. "All persons engaged in a trade or business and making payment in the course of such trade or business to another person" of $600 or more must report the amount and the name and address of the recipient to the IRS and to the recipient.[5] The Code applies this requirement to payments of "rent, salaries, wages, premiums, annuities, compensations, remunerations, emoluments, or other fixed or determinable gains, profits, and income." Treasury regulations add "commissions, fees, and other forms of compensation for services rendered aggregating $600 or more," as well as interest (including original issue discount), royalties, and pensions.[6]

---

1. Congressional Research Service Report: http://www.pppnet.org/pdf/crs._1099.pdf (last accessed May 27, 2011).
2. PPACA §9006, amending IRC Sec. 6041(a) and adding IRC Secs. 6041(h) and (i).
3. P.L. 112-9.
4. P.L. 111-240.
5. IRC Sec. 6041(a).
6. Treas. Reg. §1.6041-1(a)(1)(i).

104. Did the repeal of the expanded 1099 reporting repeal the penalties for 1099 failures that were increased in 2010?

No. The 2011 repeal did not repeal the expanded penalties for 1099 reporting failures enacted by the 2010 Small Business Jobs Act. The first-tier penalty under Code Section 6721 for failure to timely file an information return was increased from $15 to $30, and the calendar-year maximum from $75,000 to $250,000. The second-tier penalty was increased from $30 to $60, and the calendar-year maximum from $150,000 to $500,000. The third-tier penalty was increased from $50 to $100, and the calendar-year maximum from $250,000 to $1,500,000. For small-business filers, the calendar-year maximum increased from $25,000 to $75,000 for the first-tier penalty; from $50,000 to $200,000 for the second-tier penalty; and from $100,000 to $500,000 for the third-tier penalty. The minimum penalty for each failure due to intentional disregard increased from $100 to $250.

105. Why were the expanded 1099 requirements repealed?

The expanded 1099 reporting requirements would have created significant burdens for businesses and many property owners by dramatically increasing the number of 1099 filings. Payments by any method were included, such as check, credit card, etc. Consider the airlines, hotels, rental cars, and restaurants that appear on a proprietor's or business credit card bill. Under the repealed law, 1099s would have been required if annual payments were more than $600. Additionally, any business that pays a person – for example, a plumber – more than $600 would be sending that person a Form 1099.

In addition, affected businesses and property owners would have been responsible for obtaining taxpayer identification numbers from every payee that required a Form 1099. If a business was unable to obtain this information, it would have been required to withhold federal income taxes from payments to that payee ("backup withholding") and forward them to the government.

Absent the repeal, a huge increase in the paperwork burden would have ensued. It was not simply a matter of completing the forms, but also the work and time involved in obtaining the proper tax identification numbers and dealing with backup withholding requirements. Businesses are on different tax years, and some use cash-basis tax reporting while others use accrual accounting. As a result, the IRS would not have been able to match 1099s and tax returns in any meaningful way. Congress understood this, and both the House and Senate passed the repeal by very small bipartisan margins. President Obama also supported the repeal.[1]

Early Retiree Reinsurance Program (ERRP) – Expired

106. How was the Early Retiree Reinsurance Program (ERRP) intended to work?

Health reform provided for the Early Retiree Reinsurance Program (ERRP).[2] The statute and regulations required that reimbursements be used to lower plan sponsor and employee costs

---

1. See The White House Blog at http://www.whitehouse.gov/blog/2011/04/14/repealing-1099-reporting-requirement-big-win-small-business.
2. PPACA §1102; 45 C.F.R. Part 149. See also 75 Fed. Reg. 24,450 (May 5, 2010).

for the medical plan in various ways. Plan sponsors, including employers, unions, and other organizations, participating in health reform's ERRP were required to explain how they would use funds received under the program. HHS has stated that this program will be a major audit target over the next six years. Thus, plan sponsors must decide on how the funds will be used and develop a sustainable plan. Plan sponsors that deviate from their stated use run the risk of having their funds reclaimed after an HHS audit.

ERRP was a temporary program for sponsors of employment-based health plans that provide retiree health benefits to retirees who are over age fifty-five and not yet eligible for the Medicare program. The program provides an 80 percent subsidy for retiree claims of between $15,000 and $90,000 for plan sponsors that applied to and were accepted by HHS. Congress appropriated $5 billion for the program, which was effective June 1, 2010. The subsidy was to be available through the earlier of Jan. 1, 2014, or the date when the funds were exhausted, which was at the end of 2011.[1] An HHS report stated that almost 5,500 plan sponsors have been approved to participate in the ERRP and that $535 million in ERRP reimbursement payments were made by December 31, 2010.[2] On December 9, 2011, the Centers for Medicare & Medicaid Services (CMS) and HHS announced that ERRP would not reimburse any claims incurred after December 31, 2011. As of December 2, 2011, HHS had reimbursed $4.5 billion of the program's total funds.

Funds Use Requirements. Plan sponsors had to explain how they would meet the two primary requirements and then follow-through and continue to use the funds in that prescribed fashion.

Reduce Overall Costs. Plan sponsors were required to use reimbursements to reduce overall costs to the Plan. This could include:

- Using the funds to pay any increases in health benefit (or health benefit premium) costs for the plan sponsor (i.e. to offset increases in those costs);

- Reducing individuals' premium contributions, copayments, deductibles, coinsurance, or other out-of-pocket costs (or some combination of these costs); or

- Providing a combination of these two options.

An "employment-based plan" qualifying for ERRP reimbursements also was required to implement programs and procedures to generate cost-savings with respect to participants with chronic and high-cost conditions. Health benefit claims that qualified for ERRP reimbursement

---

1. Employee Benefit Research Institute – see http://www.ebri.org/pdf/notespdf/EBRI_Notes_07-July10.Reins-Early.pdf.

2. HHS, "Report on Implementation and Operation of the Early Retiree Reinsurance Program During Calendar Year 2010" (Mar. 2, 2011), available at http://www.healthcare.gov/center/reports/retirement03022011a.pdf. The largest share of 2010 reimbursements went to state and local governments, including school districts and other local agencies, for their early retirees, but approved sponsors also included for-profit companies, unions, religious organizations, and other nonprofits.

were only those for medical services that would be covered by the Medicare program.[1] The HHS guidance also described specific items and services that would not be covered. HHS issued a document providing a list of Current Procedural Terminology (CPT) and Healthcare Common Procedure Coding System (HCPCS) codes excluded under Medicare; which could not be credited toward the ERRP cost threshold or reimbursed as part of the ERRP claims submission process.[2] Further, the HHS guidance stated that sponsors must comply with applicable state and federal requirements regarding benefits. Even though an item or service would not be reimbursed under the ERRP, a sponsor could cover the item or service in its health benefits plan.

Offset Future Increases. Plan sponsors that elected to use the reimbursements (or a portion of the reimbursements) to offset future increases to the plan sponsor would have to summarize how the reimbursements would relieve the organization of using its own funds to subsidize the increases and instead use its own funds to maintain current contributions. A plan sponsor had to explain how long it would continue to maintain its current level of financial support to the plan.

Federal Long-Term Care Benefit – Not Implemented

107. What was the federal long-term care benefit for which employees could have elected to pay?

The health reform law contained a provision whereby individuals could elect to purchase long-term care coverage from the federal government.[3] By January 1, 2012, the Department of Health and Human Services (HHS) was to determine eligibility requirements for a federal long-term care program. By October 1, 2012, plan design and development was to have been completed. However, HHS asked Congress to de-fund the program, although its provisions remain in the law. These provisions provide that employees of companies that choose to participate will be automatically enrolled in the long-term care program, and they may elect to opt out. This part of the health reform law was called the Community Living Assistance Services and Support (CLASS) Act. The employee, not the employer, who does not opt out would pay for this coverage through payroll deductions. Other workers and the self-employed would have been able to enroll on their own. Retirees were not eligible.

After paying premiums for five years, is the employee would be eligible for a cash benefit of about $50 per day if he or she would have been unable to perform two or three activities of daily living, such as walking, bathing or dressing, or if he or she would have been cognitively impaired. In order to qualify for benefits, the employee was required to work for three of the five years during which he or she paid the premiums.

1. This requirement is not specified in the law or regulations. See "Common Questions, Costs and Reimbursement," available at http://www.errp. gov/faq_costs.shtml. A question, originally posted on August 31, 2010, and updated on December 2, 2010, asked, "For what types of health benefit items and services can a sponsor receive reimbursement?" The answer states: "A sponsor can receive reimbursement for health benefit items and services for which Medicare would reimburse under Parts A, B, and D. For general reference as to what items and services are covered by Medicare Parts A and B, please refer to the Centers for Medicare & Medicaid Services' (CMS) Medicare & You 2010 and Your Medicare Benefits publications, which are available on the Medicare.gov website."

2. HHS, "Claims Ineligible for Reimbursement under the Early Retiree Reinsurance Program, Coding Details for Ineligible Services under Medicare which will apply to ERRP" (Oct. 18, 2010), available at http://www.errp.gov/download/cpt/ProcedureCodesIneligibleForReimbursement.pdf.

3. PPACA §8002.

Under the CLASS Act, a person could not have been rejected for coverage because of health problems. It would have helped people with medical conditions that do not qualify for private long-term-care insurance or are subject to very high rates for the coverage. Additionally, it would have covered services that are not eligible for benefits under some long-term-care plans, including homemaker services, home modifications, and transportation, which could help a person stay out of a nursing home.

108. Why was the federal long-term care program cancelled by HHS?

On September 21, 2011, the Senate Appropriations Committee deleted the $120 million that was earmarked for the annual design and marketing of CLASS policies from the 2012 HHS budget, and HHS disbanded the CLASS program. On October 14, 2011, HHS Secretary Kathleen Sebelius told Congress by letter[1] that HHS did not see a viable fiscal future for the CLASS program.[2] (Implementation of the program was contingent on HHS determining that the program was fiscally sustainable and on not using any other funds to pay benefits. The administration determined that the program would be too costly over the long run.

Certain Republicans and Democrats had claimed that the program would eventually become a source of federal deficits. The nonpartisan Congressional Budget Office found the long-term care program would generate tens of billions of dollars between 2012 and 2021, when it was taking in premiums and paying out little in claims. However, the federal actuary for Medicare and Medicaid warned that, in subsequent years, the program would pay out more than it received.

---

1. U.S. Department of Health and Human Services. Secretary Sebelius' Letter to Congress about CLASS. (October 14, 2011) at http://www.hhs.gov/secretary/letter10142011.html.
2. In September 2011, HHS foreshadowed the administration's decision by terminating the CLASS program's chief actuary and reassigning other staff.

PART V: SMALL BUSINESS PROVISIONS

Employer Income Tax Credit for Health Insurance

109. Which employers are eligible for the tax credit for the purchase of health insurance available in 2010 and thereafter?

The new health insurance tax credit[1] is designed to help small for-profit businesses and tax-exempt organizations (estimated to be four million in number) that primarily employ low- and moderate-income workers.[2] This credit is available to employers that:

- Have twenty-four or fewer eligible full-time equivalent (FTE) employees with wages averaging less than $50,000 per employee per year, and

- Pay at least 50 percent of health insurance costs.[3]

Eligible employees do not include seasonal workers who work for an employer 120 days a year or less,[4] owners, and owners' family members with average annual compensation of less than $50,000. Such employees are also not eligible if the business pays 50 percent or more of employee-only (single person) health insurance costs. Thus, compensation for seasonal workers, specified owners, and their family members and dependents is not counted in determining average compensation, nor is the health insurance cost for these people eligible for the health insurance tax credit.[5]

The credit is a general business credit and can be carried back for one year and forward for twenty years.[6] The credit, which can be applied to tax liability under the alternative minimum tax, is as follows:[7]

- 35 percent (25 percent for a tax-exempt employer) in 2010 to 2013, and

- 50 percent (35 percent for a tax-exempt employer) beginning in 2014.

A tax-exempt employer can use the credit against payroll taxes.

110. Can more than one employer be treated as a single employer for determining the credit available, the number of employers, and the average compensation?

Yes. All employers treated as a single employer under the controlled group rules or the affiliated service group rules are treated as a single employer for purposes of the tax credit.[8]

---

1. IRC Sec. 45R.
2. http://www.irs.gov/newsroom/article/0,,id=223666,00.html (last accessed May 25, 2011).
3. IRC Sec. 45R(d)(2).
4. IRC Sec. 45R(d)(5).
5. http://www.irs.gov/newsroom/article/0,,id=220839,00.html (last accessed May 25, 2011).
6. IRC Sec. 38(b) & 39(A).
7. IRC Sec. 38(c)(4)(B)(vi).
8. IRC Sec. 45R(e)(5), incorporating the controlled group rules of IRC Sec. 414(b) and (c), the affiliated service group rules of IRC Sec. 414(m), and the anti-abuse rules of IRC Sec. 414(o).

111. How is the employer 50 percent payment requirement applied?

In 2010, the employer may qualify if it pays at least 50 percent of the cost of employee-only coverage, regardless of actual coverage elected by an employee. For example, at Company A, where employee-only coverage costs $500 per month and family coverage costs $1,500 per month, the employer pays at least $250 per month (50 percent of employee-only coverage) per covered employee. Even if an employee selected family coverage, Company A would meet the contribution requirement to qualify for the tax credit in 2010.

Beginning in 2011, however, the percentage paid by the employer for each enrolled employee must be a uniform percentage for that coverage level. If the employee receives coverage that is more expensive than single coverage (such as family or self-plus-one coverage), the employer must pay at least 50 percent of the premium for each employee's coverage in 2011 and thereafter.

Thus, grandfathered health insurance plans that, for instance, provide for 100 percent of family coverage for executives and 100 percent of employee-only coverage for staff will qualify for the tax credit in 2010 but not in 2011 or beyond.[1]

112. Which persons are not counted in determining the number of employees or their average compensation?

Owners are all self-employed individuals (proprietors, partners, members of LLCs taxed as partnerships), (more than) 2 percent shareholders of an S corporation,[2] (more than) 5 percent or more owners of a small business,[3] and family members[4] and dependents of the self-employer, (more than) 2% S corporation shareholders, or (more than) 5 percent or more owners.[5] Leased employees are eligible employees for the credit.[6]

Leased employees are considered eligible employees for purposes of the credit.[7]

113. How much is the employer tax credit for employer purchase of health insurance?

The new tax credit applies to for-profit and nonprofit employers meeting certain requirements. From 2010 through 2013, the amount of the credit for for-profit employers is 35 percent, and 25 percent for non-profit employers, of qualifying health insurance costs. The credit is increased for any two consecutive years beginning in 2014 to 50 percent of a for-profit employer's qualifying expenses and 35 percent for nonprofit employers.[8]

---

1. *See* http://www.irs.gov/newsroom/article/0,,id=220839,00.html (last accessed May 25, 2011). See also, Part VI for more information on grand-fathered health plans.
2. IRC Sec. 1372(b).
3. Defined by IRC Sec. 416(i)(1)(B)(i), which contains the top-heavy retirement plan rules.
4. Any individual who bears any of the relationships described in IRC Sec. 152(d)(2)(A) through (G).
5. IRC Sec. 152(d)(2)(H).
6. IRC Sec. 45R(e).
7. IRC Sec. 45R(e).
8. See http://www.ncsl.org/documents/health/SBtaxCredits.pdf (last accessed February 27, 2012). See Q 114 for sample calculations.

114. How is the employer tax credit calculated?

The credit is largest if there are ten or fewer employees and their average wages do not exceed $25,000.[1] The amount of the credit is phased out for businesses with more than ten eligible employees and average compensation of more than $25,000 (but less than $50,000). The amount of an employer's premium payments that counts for purposes of the credit is capped by the average premium for the small group market in the employer's geographic location, as determined by HHS.[2]

The IRS released state rates for 2010.[3]

For nonprofit employers, the credit is taken against the employer's income tax and Medicare withholding obligations and the employer's Medicare payment obligation, but not against Social Security taxes.[4]

Tax Credit Calculations – 2010 and 2014	
Example: For-Profit Employer with Ten Employees	
Number of Employees:	10
Wages:	$250,000 total, or $25,000 per worker
Employee Health Care Costs:	$70,000
2010 Tax Credit:	35% × $70,000 = $24,500
2014 Tax Credit:	50% × $70,000 = $35,000
Example: For-Profit Employer with Forty Part-Time Employees	
Number of Employees:	40 half-time employees (the equivalent of 20 full-time workers)
Wages:	$500,000 total, or $25,000 per full-time equivalent worker
Employee Health Care Costs:	$240,000
2010 Tax Credit:	$28,000 (35% credit with phase-out)
2014 Tax Credit:	$40,000 (50% credit with phase-out)
Example: Nonprofit Employer with Nine Employees	
Employees:	9
Wages:	$198,000 total, or $22,000 per worker
Employee Health Care Costs:	$72,000
2010 Tax Credit:	25% × $72000 = $18,000
2014 Tax Credit:	35% × $72,000 = $25,200[5]

---

1. IRC Sec. 45R(c).
2. http://www.irs.gov/newsroom/article/0,,id=220839,00.html (last accessed May 25, 2011).
3. Rev. Rul. 2010-13.
4. IRC Sec. 45R(f)(1)(B).
5. For additional guidance, see IRS Notices 2010-44 and 2010-82.

Tax Credit Calculations – 2011	
Example: For-Profit Employer with Nine Employees	
Employees:	9
Wages:	$216,000 total, or $24,000 per worker
Employee Health Care Costs:	$75,000
2011 Tax Credit:	35% × $75000 = $26,250

115. How is the average annual wage calculated?

Average annual wages are calculated by dividing the aggregate amount of wages paid by the employer by the number of full-time-equivalent (FTE) employees, for the taxable year.[1] Full-time employees would be calculated by dividing the total hours worked by all employees during the tax year by 2,080 (with a maximum of 2,080 hours for any one employee). Seasonal workers are disregarded.[2] Average annual wages would be determined by dividing the aggregate amount of wages paid by the employer by the number of FTE employees, for the taxable year.[3]

The average wage threshold for determining the phase-out of credits will be adjusted for inflation after 2013.

116. How does the employer health insurance tax credit change in 2014?

In 2014, the amount of the credit increases to 50 percent (35 percent in the case of a tax-exempt eligible small employer) of the lesser of:

- The aggregate amount of employer contributions for premiums for qualified health plans offered by the employer (nonelective contributions excluding employee compensation deferrals) to its employees through an exchange, or

- The average employer contributions (nonelective contributions excluding employee compensation deferrals) which the employer would have made to a qualified health plan for the small group market in the rating area in which the employee enrolls for coverage.[4]

Firms can claim the credit for 2010 through 2013 and for any two consecutive years after that.[5] [This includes regulations to prevent avoiding the 2-year limit on the credit period through the use of successor or multiple entities.][6]

---

1. IRC Sec. 45R(c) and (d).
2. IRC Sec. 45R(d)(5).
3. IRC Sec. 45R(c) and (d).
4. IRC Sec. 45R(e).
5. IRC Sec. 45R(e)(2).
6. IRC Sec. 45R(i).

The self-employed are eligible for individual premium assistance (the individual tax credit) for health insurance purchased through an exchange available in 2014 if they meet the income requirements (less than 400 percent of the federal poverty level).

To continue receiving a tax credit in 2014, a small employer must drop its existing coverage and purchase group coverage in the newly created exchanges.[1]

The average annual wage thresholds are indexed for inflation.[2]

Simple Cafeteria Plan

117. How do existing cafeteria plans work?

In general, employer and employee contributions to any cafeteria plan are deductible to the employer, not subject to Social Security tax, and not taxable income to the participant. Thus, available benefits, which can be purchased with "pre-tax dollars," include:

- health and dental insurance,

- accidental death and dismemberment policies,

- reimbursement for health and dental expenses not covered by insurance,

- dependent care,

- adoption assistance,[3]

- group term life insurance,

- Health Savings Accounts,

- 401(k) deferrals,

- adoption assistance, and

- disability insurance.

Benefits not available through cafeteria plans are:

- Archer Medical Savings Accounts (MSAs),

---

1. IRC Sec. 45R(e)(2).
2. IRC Sec. 45R(d)(3).
3. See Notice 97–9 Sec. II; Reg. §601.601(d)(2)(ii)(b); 2007 Prop. Reg. §1.125-5(h) (adding adoption assistance as a permissible FSA benefit to health and dependent care FSAs.

- scholarships,

- educational assistance,

- Section 132 fringe benefits[1]

- long-term care insurance and LTC services,[2] (though may be paid from an HSA funded through a cafeteria plan),

- health insurance purchased on an exchange that is not purchased pursuant to an employer's exchange-purchased group health insurance plan,[3]

- group term insurance for a spouse or dependent, and

- 403(b) elective deferrals.

A plan offering any nonqualified benefit is not a cafeteria plan.[4] If a cafeteria plan fails to operate in compliance with Code Section 125 or fails to satisfy any of the written plan requirements for health FSAs, the plan is not considered a Code Section 125 cafeteria plan, and employees' election of nontaxable benefits results in gross income to all employees.[5]

118. What is the new simple cafeteria plan that is available in 2011?

The 2010 health reform law included a provision creating "simple cafeteria plans" for small (average employment of 100 or fewer employees in either of the two preceding years) businesses, effective for years beginning in 2011.[6] The concept is similar to 401(k) retirement plan safe harbors, SIMPLE 401(k)s, and SIMPLE-IRAs, whereby most nondiscrimination requirements can be met by plan design and the use of either nonelective employer contributions for all eligible employees or employer-matching contributions for participating employees making salary reduction contributions.

Simple cafeteria plans will be of interest to eligible employers that might otherwise have difficulty passing one or more of the applicable income tax nondiscrimination tests. For example, small employers may have difficulty passing the 25 percent key employee concentration test[7] for cafeteria plans or the 55 percent average benefits test for dependent care.[8] In the past, these employers might have decided not to sponsor a cafeteria plan or designed their plans to exclude highly compensated employees (HCEs).

---

1. IRC Sec. 125(f)(1).
2. IRC Sec. 125(f)(2).
3. IRC Sec. 125(f)(3).
4. IRC Sec. 125(d)(1)(B); Prop. Treas. Reg. §1.125-1(q).
5. Prop. Treas. Reg. §1.125-1(c)(1), (c)(6) and (c)(7). However, benefits that fail discrimination tests under the various IRC sections do not fail to be qualified benefits. Rather, the discriminatory amounts are included in gross income, not the entire amount of the benefit(s).
6. See IRC Sec. 125(j).
7. IRC Sec. 125(b).
8. IRC Sec. 129(d).

119. Are simple cafeteria plans subject to any of the regular cafeteria plan tax rules?

Yes. A simple cafeteria plan is a cafeteria plan adopted by an eligible employer that meets specified contribution, eligibility, and participation requirements.[1] Except for the special rules that apply to the simple cafeteria plan, the plan also must meet the other cafeteria plan rules.[2] Thus, it must be a written plan[3] administered in accordance with the written plan terms. The cafeteria plan must, among other things:

- Be maintained by an employer for employees, and

- Operate in compliance with the Code and regulation requirements as well as the requirements of other applicable laws.

In part, the written plan requirements include the following:

- Describe all benefits.

- Provide rules for eligibility to participate.

- Indicate how employer and employer contributions are made under the plan.

- State the maximum amount of employer and employee elective contributions.

- Describe the procedure for making elections.

- Provide that all elections are irrevocable (except to the extent that the plan includes the "change in status" rules).

- List additional requirements if one of the offerings is a health, dependent care, or adoption assistance FSA.

- State the plan year.

- Provide rules for substantiation of expenses.

- If the plan provides a grace period, it must include required language applicable to the two-and-a-half-month grace period.

- Describe the regulations' "use it or lose it" rule.

---

1. IRC Sec. 125(j)(2).
2. IRC Sec. 125(j)(2), stating that a "simple cafeteria plan" means a **cafeteria plan** …. [Emphasis added.]
3. IRC Sec. 125(d)(1).

An employer maintaining a cafeteria plan in which any highly compensated employee participates must make sure that both the cafeteria plan and each qualified benefit satisfies the cafeteria plan and benefit-specific nondiscrimination requirements. A failure to satisfy the nondiscrimination rules results in additional taxable income to all employees.

120. What is the benefit of the simple cafeteria plan?

Simple cafeteria plans automatically meet all "applicable nondiscrimination requirements,"[1] which are the nondiscrimination requirements of Code Section 125(b) (the 25 percent concentration test) and the nondiscrimination requirements of Code Sections 79(d), 105(h), and 129(d) applicable to group term life insurance, self-insured health benefits (medical expense reimbursement), and dependent care assistance benefits (child care), respectively.

Through an apparent oversight, Code Section 125(j) does not provide an express exception for the health law reform's health insurance nondiscrimination rules of new Code Section 9815. However, it is likely that if the same insurance options are available to all participants, regardless of their use, the health insurance nondiscrimination rules will be met.[2] The health insurance nondiscrimination regulations, when they are issued, will provide the definitive answer.

Certain benefit-specific nondiscrimination rules continue to apply, such as those for adoption assistance plans because Code Section 137 is not listed in the exemption from the nondiscrimination rules.

121. What are the special rules for premium conversion plans?

A premium conversion cafeteria plan (POP) – but not a health FSA – is one that offers an election between cash and payment of the employee share of the premium for employer-provided health insurance. Health insurance premium conversion cafeteria plans meet the regular cafeteria plan eligibility nondiscrimination rules if they meet a safe harbor test[3] and pass a safe harbor/ unsafe harbor facts-and-circumstances test.[4] Examples of situations that meet or fail this test include the following:[5]

Example (1). Same qualified benefit for same salary reduction amount. Employer A has one employer-provided accident and health insurance plan. The cost to participants electing the accident and health plan is $10,000 per year for single coverage. All employees have the same opportunity to purchase the plan and reduce their salaries by $10,000. The cafeteria plan satisfies the eligibility test.

Example (2). Same qualified benefit for unequal salary reduction amounts. Same facts as Example 1 except the cafeteria plan offers nonhighly compensated employees (NHCEs)

---

1. IRC Sec. 125(j)(6).
2. Kevin Knopf, Attorney-Advisor, Office of Tax Policy of the Treasury Department, ECFC Annual Symposium (Aug. 6, 2010) stated that the safe harbor for simple cafeteria plans does extend to the nondiscrimination requirements of IRC Sec. 9815 that apply to employer-provided health insurance plans.
3. Prop. Reg. §1.125-7.
4. Prop. Reg. §1.125-7(b)(3).
5. Prop. Reg. §1.125-7(b)(3)(iv).

the election to reduce their salaries by $10,000 to pay premiums for single coverage. The cafeteria plan provides an $8,000 employer flex-credit to highly compensated employees (HCEs) to pay a portion of the premium, and it provides an election to reduce their salaries by $2,000 to pay the balance of the premium. The cafeteria plan fails the eligibility test because the employer contribution – the flex credit – is given solely to HCEs.

Example (3). Accident and health plans of unequal value. Employer B's cafeteria plan offers two employer-provided accident and health insurance plans: Plan X, available only to HCEs, is a low-deductible plan. Plan Y, available only to NHCEs, is a high-deductible plan (as defined in Code Section 223(c)(2)). The annual premium for single coverage under Plan X is $15,000 per year, and it is $8,000 per year for Plan Y. Employer B's cafeteria plan provides that HCEs may elect salary reduction of $15,000 for coverage under Plan X, and that NHCEs may elect salary reduction of $8,000 for coverage under Plan Y. The cafeteria plan fails the eligibility test.

Example (4). Accident and health plans of unequal value for unequal salary reduction amounts. Same facts as Example 3, except that the amount of salary reduction for HCEs to elect Plan X is $8,000. The cafeteria plan also fails the eligibility test.

122. Can business owners participate in a simple cafeteria plan?

When a business wants to avoid the 25 percent concentration test and contribute for owner-employees, it is likely that only a regular C corporation can do so because only these shareholder-employees are "employees" for income tax purposes. Sole proprietors, more-than-2-percent S corporation shareholders, and partners (including members of LLCs taxed as partnerships) are not employees for income tax purposes. Rather, they are "self-employed" individuals.

123. Which employers can sponsor a simple cafeteria plan?

In order to establish and maintain a simple cafeteria plan, an employer must qualify as an eligible employer. An "eligible employer" is one that employed an average of 100 or fewer employees on business days during either of the two preceding years. For this purpose, a year may only be taken into account if the employer was in existence throughout that year.[1] The Code's simple cafeteria plan provisions do not define the term "year" for the eligible employer definition. Pending IRS guidance, it seems reasonable to use the plan year selected by the employer as the plan's measuring period. If an employer was not in existence throughout the preceding year, the eligible employer determination is based on the average number of employees that it is reasonably expected such employer will employ on business days in the current year.[2]

If an eligible employer's workforce continues to grow, it can remain eligible in subsequent years until the employer employs an average of 200 or more employees on business days during any year preceding any such subsequent year.[3]

---

1. IRC Secs. 125(j)(5)(A) and (B).
2. IRC Sec. 125(j)(5)(B).
3. IRC Sec. 125(j)(5)(C)(ii).

If an employer has 100 or fewer employees in the current year but more than 100 employees in either of the two preceding years, the employer cannot adopt a simple cafeteria plan for the current year but will be able to do so in the succeeding year. Leased employees within the meaning of Code Sections 414(n) and (o) are counted as employees.[1] However, the Code is silent as to whether an employer can disregard (or count on a full-time equivalent basis) part-time, temporary, or seasonal employees when determining whether it is an eligible employer. Pending guidance, the conservative approach is to count all employees when making an eligible employer determination.

There is no lower limit on the size of the employer. Additionally, an employer whose only employees are prohibited group members (key employees or HCEs), or with only one owner-employee, could qualify as an eligible employer. However, the prohibition against sole proprietors, partners, and more-than-2 percent shareholders in a Subchapter S Corporation participating in a cafeteria plan applies, so, in general, only owner (shareholder)-employees of C corporations can participate in a simple cafeteria plan. Moreover, it is not clear whether such an employer could meet the required employer contributions test discussed below in Q 129.

124. What happens when an employer with a simple cafeteria plan ceases to qualify to sponsor such a plan?

Employers with simple cafeteria plans will cease to qualify as eligible employers as their workforces expand beyond 200 employees. Thus, employers that maintain simple cafeteria plans must monitor their status as eligible employers. If an employer ceases to be an eligible employer, the regular concentration and nondiscrimination tests will apply. Employers that cease to qualify as eligible employers will need to determine whether to amend or discontinue their cafeteria plan.

125. What aggregation rules apply in defining an employer?

The employer aggregation rules under Code Section 52 and Code Section 414 (controlled and affiliated service groups) generally apply for purposes of determining an eligible employer.[2] Additionally, an employer includes a "predecessor employer," but the term is undefined.[3]

126. Who are "qualified employees" that must be eligible to participate in a simple cafeteria plan?

For purposes of a simple cafeteria plan, "qualified employees" are all non-excludable employees who had at least 1,000 hours of service during the preceding plan year, except a highly compensated employee under Code Section 414(q)[4] or key employee under Code Section 416(i) and who is eligible to participate in the plan.[5]

---

1. IRC Sec. 125(j)(5)(D)(ii).
2. IRC Sec. 125(j)(5)(D)(ii).
3. IRC Sec. 125(j)(5)(D)(i).
4. IRC Sec. 125(j)(3)(D)(iii).
5. IRC Sec. 125(j)(3)(D)(iv).

This definition of qualified employee is relevant only to the two alternative minimum contribution requirements, discussed below in Q 129, and to highly compensated employees (HCEs) and key employees. HCEs and key employees may participate like everyone else so long as they are "employees" and do not receive disproportionate employer nonelective or matching contributions. Comparable contributions must be made for all eligible employees.

Code Section 414(q) defines an HCE as an employee who:

- was a more-than-5 percent owner of the employer at any time during the current or preceding plan year, or

- for the preceding plan year, had compensation in excess of a specified dollar threshold ($115,000 for 2012).

If elected by the employer, an HCE may also be an employee in the "top-paid group" (generally constituting the top 20 percent ranked by compensation) of employees.

Code Section 416 defines a key employee as an employee who, during the plan year, was:

- an officer of the employer with annual compensation in excess of a specified dollar threshold ($160,000 for 2010),

- a more-than-5-percent owner of the employer, or

- a more-than-1-percent owner of the employer with annual compensation in excess of $150,000.

127. Which employees are excludable employees?

Excludable employees (employees who need not be allowed to participate) are those who:

- have not attained age 21 (or a younger age provided in the plan) before the end of the plan year;

- have less than 1000 hours of service in the prior plan year;

- have less than one year of service as of any day during the plan year;

- are covered under a clective bargaining agreement; or

- are nonresident aliens working outside the United States.[1]

---

1. IRC Sec. 125(j)(4)(B).

An employer may have a shorter age and service requirement but only if such shorter service or younger age applies to all employees.[1]

Employees who worked 1,000 hours in a previous plan year but who do not have a year of service in the current plan year can be excluded for the current year.[2] However, since the rule is that they can be excluded if they do not have a year of service on any day in the year, they may have 1,000 hours if they go from full-time to part-time during the current plan year. This is an important point when the employee's salary is less than the health benefits. Employees should be entitled to the entire maximum benefit if elected, even if greater than their compensation in order to safeguard simple status for the cafeteria plan.

128. What is the benefit nondiscrimination requirement?

Each participating employee must be able to elect any benefit under the plan under the same terms and conditions as all other participants.[3] Again, if the special requirements of a specific benefit apply, such as adoption assistance, they must be met as well.

129. What is the employer minimum contribution requirement?

There are two alternative employer contribution requirements. Employer contributions to a simple cafeteria plan must be sufficient to provide benefits to qualified employees of at least either:

- A uniform percentage of at least 2 percent of compensation (defined as it is under Code Section 414(s) for retirement plan purposes, whether or not the employee makes salary reduction contributions to the plan);[4] or

- The lesser of a 200 percent matching contribution (or more, if specified by the plan) or 6 percent of the employee's compensation.[5]

Additional contributions can be made, but the rate of any matching contribution for HCEs or key employees cannot be greater than the rate of the match for the qualified employees (the participating employees other than key and highly compensated employees).[6]

The minimum contribution must be available for application toward the cost of any qualified benefit (any permitted benefit other than a taxable benefit) offered under the plan.[7]

---

1. IRC Sec. 125(j)(4)(B)(iv).
2. IRC Sec. 125(j)(4)(B)(ii).
3. IRC Sec. 125(j)(4)(A)(ii).
4. IRC Sec. 125(j)(3)(A)(i).
5. IRC Sec. 125(j)(3)(A)(ii).
6. IRC Sec. 125(j)(3)(B).
7. IRC Sec. 125(j)(3)(A).

130. Does the Matching Contribution Method require a 100 percent or 200 percent employer match?

The 200 percent matching requirement may be only a 100 percent requirement. An argument may be made for counting an employee's salary reduction contributions when determining whether an employer has contributed "twice the amount of the [employee's] salary reduction contributions." Arguably, the law calls for the employer to contribute the employee's salary reductions (which are employer contributions for tax purposes[1]) plus a 100 percent match, for a total contribution equal to twice the employee's salary reductions. Another reading is that the employer must contribute twice the amount of the employee's salary reductions as matching contributions. The 6 percent of compensation limit applies under either interpretation. The report on health reform by the Joint Committee on Taxation supports the 100 percent view and states that the minimum matching contribution is the lesser of 100 percent of the employee's salary reduction contribution, or 6 percent of the employee's compensation for the plan year.[2]

Compensation for purposes of the minimum contribution requirement is compensation within the meaning of Code Section 414(s).[3]

131. What happens when an employer has all HCEs, all Key Employees and no qualified employees?

An employer whose workforce consists of only one or more HCEs or Key Employees would not have any qualified employees.[4] The Code's simple cafeteria plan provisions require a contribution for each qualified employee. Thus, if the plan provides for that contribution but there is no qualified employee, it is not clear whether such an employer would be exempt from this requirement (in which case the plan could be funded entirely with salary reductions) or would be disqualified from having a simple cafeteria plan.

No Employer Mandate

132. Is there an employer mandate for small employers?

As discussed in Part VIII, the employer mandate ("play or pay") tax penalty on employers failing to provide specified health coverage for employees only applies to employers with fifty or more full-time equivalent employees. Thus, small employers have no tax penalty for not offering health insurance. Instead, certain small employers who would otherwise be eligible for the tax credit for health insurance will not obtain that benefit if they provide no health insurance or if they provide health insurance that does not meet the requirements to obtain the tax credit.

---

1. Prop. Treas. Reg. §1.125-1(r).
2. Technical Explanation of the Revenue Provisions of the "Reconciliation Act of 2010," as amended, in Combination With the "Patient Protection and Affordable Care Act," p. 119 (JCX-18-10) (Mar. 21, 2010) at https://www.jct.gov/publications.html?func=startdown&id=3673. Kevin Knopf, Attorney-Advisor, Office of Tax Policy of the Treasury Department, ECFC Annual Conference (Mar. 4, 2011), has also unofficially expressed this view.
3. IRC Sec. 125(j)(7).
4. See Q 126 for definition of qualified employees.

Automatic Enrollment Exclusion

133. Which employers are not required to provide automatic enrollment into their health plans?

Employers with 200 or fewer full-time employees are exempt from the automatic enrollment requirement. Section 18A of the Fair Labor Standards Act (FLSA),[1] directs an employer with more than 200 full-time employees to which the FLSA applies to automatically enroll new full-time employees in one of the employer's health benefits plans (subject to any waiting period authorized by law), and to continue the enrollment of current employees in a health benefits plan offered through the employer. FLSA Section 18A further requires adequate notice and the opportunity for an employee to opt out of any coverage in which the employee was automatically enrolled.[2]

On December 22, 2010, the Treasury, Labor, and HHS departments issued frequently asked questions (FAQs) on FLSA Section 18A, which noted that the statute provides that employer compliance with the automatic enrollment provisions of Section 18A are to be carried out "[i]n accordance with regulations promulgated by the Secretary [of Labor]." That FAQ also stated that it is the view of the Department of Labor that, until such regulations are issued, employers are not required to comply with Section 18A. Finally, the FAQ indicated that the Department of Labor intends to complete this rulemaking by 2014.[3]

W-2 Reporting Exemption

134. Which employers are exempt from the W-2 reporting requirement?

Employers filing fewer than 250 Forms W-2 for the preceding calendar year are exempt from the W-2 reporting requirement until further notice. Otherwise, employers must comply with the W-2 requirements for the W-2 forms issued for the 2012 calendar year.[4]

Employers that provide "applicable employer-sponsored coverage" under a group health plan are subject to a W-2 reporting requirement. This includes businesses, tax-exempt organizations, and federal, state, and local government entities (except with respect to plans maintained primarily for members of the military and their families).

The health reform law requires the value of the health care coverage to be reported in Box 12 of Form W-2, with Code DD to identify the amount. There is no reporting on the Form W-3 of the total of these amounts for all the employer's employees. In general, the amount reported should include both the portion paid by the employer and the portion paid by the employee.

1. Added by PPACA §1511.
2. IRS Technical Release No. 2012-01.
3. See www.dol.gov/ebsa/faqs/faq-aca5.html.
4. IRS Notice 2012-9, Q&A-3.

PART VI: GRANDFATHERED HEALTH PLANS

135. What is a grandfathered health plan?

A grandfathered plan is:

- one continuously in existence since March 23, 2010,

- with at least one person (need not be the same person) covered at all times, and

- not changed except as permitted, as discussed hereafter.

Grandfathered plans are exempt from many, but not all, health reform rules,[1] described in more detail below, as long as grandfather status is maintained, which can last indefinitely. A self-insured group plan, an insured group plan, and an individual insurance policy may each be grandfathered.

A plan that is grandfathered may permit employees to re-enroll and their family members to enroll after March 23, 2010.[2] While new employees can join the plan, there are restrictions on whether new groups of employees can be transferred to the plan without tainting grandfathered status.[3]

For plan or insurance changes made before March 23, 2010, the changes will be considered to be part of the coverage on March 23, 2010, though they were not in effect on such date, and will not cause the plan to lose grandfathered status, if:

- The changes were effective after March 23, 2010, pursuant to a legally binding contract entered into on or before March 23, 2010,

- The changes were effective pursuant to a filing with the state insurance department that was filed on or before March 23, 2010, or

- The changes were effective after March 23, 2010, pursuant to written amendments to the plan that were adopted on or before March 23, 2010.[4]

Changes that would cause a plan to lose grandfathered status adopted after March 23, 2010, but before June 14, 2010, had to be undone for the first year beginning on or after Sept. 23, 2010, for grandfather status to be maintained.[5]

---

1. PHSA §§2701, 2702, 2703, 2705, 2706, 2707, 2709, 2713, 2715A, 2716, 2717, 2719, and 2719A. See also Treas. Reg. §54.9815-1251T(c)(1); DOL Reg. §2590.715-1251(c)(1); HHS Reg. §147.140(c)(1).
2. Treas. Reg. §54.9815-1251T(a)(4).
3. Treas. Reg. §54.9815-1251T(b).
4. Treas. Reg. §54.9815-1251T(g)(2)(i); DOL Reg. §2590.715-1251(g)(2)(i); HHS Reg. §147.140(g)(2)(i).
5. Treas. Reg. §54.9815-1251T(g)(2)(ii); DOL Reg. §2590.715-1251(g)(2)(ii); HHS Reg. §147.140(g)(2)(ii).

136. How does an employer or other plan sponsor decide whether to maintain grandfathered status?

The sponsor should review the benefits obtained by grandfathered status, i.e., the rules that would otherwise apply that do not apply to grandfathered plans. A plan sponsor should evaluate the relative cost versus the benefit of preserving grandfathered status, including business objectives, such as employee recruitment and retention. In cases in which a collective bargaining agreement or other contract restricts changes that can be made to coverage or contributions, the decision to retain grandfathered status will be relatively easy. Otherwise, the new mandates' increased costs will need to be evaluated. For instance, an employer that already provides rich preventive care benefits should experience less of a cost increase from the preventive care requirements than an employer that provides little or no preventive care coverage. Additionally, an employer that pays the same amount for individual and family coverage for all employees would not be impacted by the new rules preventing discrimination in insured group plans in favor of highly compensated individuals. This analysis will need to be repeated in a year in which changes are contemplated.

137. Has the DOL provided any tools to assist in determining grandfathered status?

The Department of Labor's Employee Benefits Security Administration (EBSA) has published an online self-help tool to enable group health plans, plan sponsors, plan administrators, and health insurance issuers comply with the healthcare reform's group health plan requirements, namely, the "Self-Compliance Tool for Part 7 of ERISA: Affordable Care Act Provisions."[1]

It provides a detailed question and answer checklist addressing the various Affordable Care Act (ACA) provisions applicable to group health plans and health insurance issuers. Various questions allow users to assess their plan's compliance with ACA provisions addressing grandfather plan status, extension of dependent coverage to adult children, prohibitions on lifetime limits and restrictions on annual limits, prohibition on preexisting condition exclusions for individuals under 19, summary of benefits and coverage (SBC) and uniform glossary, preventive services, internal claims and appeals, and external review.

138. What are the details for the DOL self-help healthcare reform tool and grandfathered plan checklist?

Section A. Determining Grandfather Status[2]

Grandfather status is intended to allow people to keep their coverage as it existed on March 23, 2010, while giving plans some flexibility to make "normal" changes while retaining grandfather status. Grandfathered health plan coverage provides individuals' protection from significant reductions in coverage, provides for coverage to include numerous protections

---

1. See http://www.dol.gov/ebsa/pdf/part7-2.pdf.
2. See http://www.dol.gov/ebsa/pdf/part7-2.pdf.

implemented through the Affordable Care Act, and allows employers the flexibility to manage costs.

The analysis for determining grandfather status applies separately to each benefit package or option. Accordingly, grandfather status might be retained for some benefit packages or options and relinquished for others. By contrast, if an employer relinquished grandfather status for self-only, family, or any other tier within a benefits package, it would relinquish grandfather status for the entire package.[1]

There are transitional rules regarding grandfather status as related to recent changes to plan terms.

- Specifically a plan will not relinquish grandfather status for changes effective after March 23, 2010, pursuant to a legally binding contract entered into on or before March 23, 2010; changes effective after March 23, 2010, pursuant to a filing on or before March 23, 2010, with a State insurance department; or changes effective after March 23, 2010, pursuant to written amendments to a plan that were adopted on or before March 23, 2010.

- If after March 23, 2010, a group health plan or issuer made changes to the terms of the plan or coverage and the changes were adopted prior to June 14, 2010, the changes will not cause the plan or coverage to relinquish grandfather status, if the changes were revoked or modified effective as of the first day of the first plan year beginning on or after September 23, 2010, and the terms of the plan or health insurance coverage on that date, as modified, would not cause the plan or coverage to otherwise cease to be a grandfathered health plan.[2]

If the answer is "yes" to questions 1 and 2 below the group health plan may be a grandfathered health plan.

Question 1 – Did the plan exist with at least one individual enrolled on March 23, 2010? A grandfathered group health plan must have been in existence with an enrolled individual on March 23, 2010. Any plan that does not meet this requirement is not in grandfathered status.[3]

Question 2 – Has the plan continuously covered someone (not necessarily the same person) since March 23, 2010? A group health plan will not relinquish its grandfather status merely because one or more (or all) individuals enrolled on March 23, 2010, cease to be covered. However, a grandfathered health plan must continuously cover someone (not necessarily the same person) since March 23, 2010, to maintain its status.[4]

---

1. See 29 CFR 2590.715-1251(a)(1)(i).
2. See 29 CFR 2590.715-1251(g)(2).
3. See 29 CFR 2590.715-1251(a)(1)(i).
4. See 29 CFR 2590.715-1251(a)(1)(i).

Question 3 – Has the plan eliminated all or substantially all benefits to diagnose or treat a particular condition? For the purpose of determining grandfather status, the elimination of benefits for any necessary element to diagnose or treat a condition is considered the elimination of all or substantially all benefits to diagnose or treat a particular condition.[1]

Question 4 – Has the plan increased a percentage cost-sharing requirement (such as an individual's coinsurance)? Any increase measured from March 23, 2010, in a percentage cost-sharing requirement causes a plan to relinquish grandfather status.[2]

Question 5 – Has the plan increased a fixed-amount cost-sharing requirement other than a copayment (such as a deductible or out-of-pocket limit) such that the total percentage increase measured from March 23, 2010 exceeds the maximum percentage increase? The maximum percentage increase is medical inflation, expressed as a percentage, plus 15 percentage points.[3] Medical inflation is the increase since March 2010, in the overall medical care component of the Consumer Price Index for All Urban Consumers (CPI-U) (unadjusted) published by the Department of Labor using the 1982-1984 base of 100.[4]

Question 6 – Has the plan increased a fixed-amount copayment such that the increase measured from March 23, 2010 exceeds the greater of: the maximum percentage increase, or an amount equal to $5 plus medical inflation? The maximum percentage increase is medical inflation, expressed as a percentage, plus 15 percentage points.[5] Medical inflation is the increase since March 2010 in the overall medical care component of the Consumer Price Index for All Urban Consumers (CPI-U) (unadjusted) published by the Department of Labor using the 1982-1984 base of 100.[6]

Question 7 – Has there been a decrease in the contribution rate by the employer (or employee organization) towards the cost of any tier of coverage for any class of similarly situated individuals by more than 5 percentage points below the contribution rate for the coverage period that includes March 23, 2010? If the contribution rate is based on a formula, was the decrease in the contribution rate based on a formula by more than 5 percent below the contribution rate for the coverage period that includes March 23, 2010?[7]

If a group health plan modifies the tiers of coverage it had on March 23, 2010 (for example, from self-only and family to a multi-tiered structure of self-only, self-plus-one, self-plus-two, and self-plus-three-or-more), the employer contribution for any new tier would be tested by comparison to the contribution rate for the corresponding tier on March 23, 2010. If the plan adds one or more new coverage tiers without eliminating or modifying any previous tiers and those new coverage tiers cover classes of individuals that were not

---

1. See 29 CFR 2590.715- 1251(g)(1)(i).
2. See 29 CFR 2590.715-1251(g)(1)(ii).
3. See 29 CFR 2590.715-1251(g)(3)(ii).
4. See 29 CFR 2590.715-1251(g)(3)(i).
5. See 29 CFR 2590.715-1251(g)(3)(ii).
6. See 29 CFR 2590.715-1251(g)(3)(i).
7. See 29 CFR 2590.715-1251(g)(1)(v)(B).

covered previously under the plan, the new tiers would not be analyzed under the standards of paragraph (g)(1).[1]

In cases of a multiemployer plan that has either a fixed-dollar employee contribution or no employee contribution towards the cost of coverage, if the employer's contribution rate changes, provided any changes in the coverage terms would not otherwise cause the plan to cease to be grandfathered and there continues to be no employee contribution or no increase in the fixed-dollar employee contribution towards the cost of coverage, the change of the employer's contribution rate will not, in and of itself, cause a plan that is otherwise a grandfathered health plan to relinquish grandfather status.[2]

Question 8 – Has the plan added or decreased an overall annual limit on benefits? A plan will relinquish its grandfathered status if it:

- Adds an overall annual limit on the dollar value of all benefits when it did not previously impose an overall annual limit;[3]

- Previously imposed an overall lifetime limit on the dollar value of benefits (but no overall annual limit) and adopts an overall annual limit at a dollar value that is lower than the dollar value of the lifetime limit on March 23, 2010;[4] or

- Decreases the dollar value of the overall annual limit that was in place on March 23, 2010.[5]

If the answer to any of questions 3-8 was "yes", the plan is NOT a grandfathered plan.

Question 9 – Did the plan change issuers after March 23, 2010? If the answer to question 9 is "yes", if the group health plan changed issuers after March 23, 2010, and the change in issuer was effective on or after November 15, 2010, the plan will continue to be a grandfathered plan provided no other changes that would relinquish grandfather status are made.[6]

If a group health plan changed issuers after March 23, 2010, and the change was effective prior to November 15, 2010, the plan will have relinquished grandfather status. The operative date is the effective date of the new contract, not the date the new contract was entered into. Special rules apply for collectively bargained plans.[7]

---

1. See DOL FAQs About the Affordable Care Act Implementation Part II, question 3 at http://www.dol.gov/ebsa/faqs/faq-aca2.html.
2. See DOL FAQs About the Affordable Care Act Implementation Part I, question 4 at http://www.dol.gov/ebsa/faqs/faqaca.html.
3. See 29 CFR 2590.715-1251(g)(1)(vi)(A).
4. See 29 CFR 2590.715-1251(g)(1)(vi)(B).
5. See 29 CFR 2590.715-1251(g)(1)(vi)(C)).
6. See 29 CFR 2590.715-1251(a)(1)(ii), as amended.
7. See 29 CFR 2590.715-1251(f) for collectively bargained plans.

Question 10 – Did the plan change from self-insured to fully-insured after March 23, 2010? If the group health plan was self-insured and changed to fully insured after March 23, 2010, and the change was effective on or after November 15, 2010, the plan will continue to be a grandfathered plan provided no other changes are made that would relinquish grandfather status.[1] Proceed to question 11. If a group health plan was self-insured and changed to fully-insured after March 23, 2010, and the change was effective prior to November 15, 2010, the plan will have relinquished grandfather status.

Question 11 – If the group health plan changed issuers (including a plan that was self-insured and changed to fully insured) and has maintained grandfather status did the plan provide documentation to the new issuer of the plan terms under the prior health coverage sufficient to determine whether any other change was made that would relinquish grandfather status? To maintain status as a grandfathered health plan, the plan must provide to the new issuer (and the new issuer must require) documentation of plan terms (including benefits, cost sharing, employer contributions, and annual limits) under the prior health coverage sufficient to determine whether any other change is being made that would relinquish grandfathered status.[2]

Question 12 – Does the plan include a statement that it believes it is a grandfathered health plan in any plan materials provided to participants and beneficiaries that describe the benefits provided under the plan? To maintain status as a grandfathered group health plan, the plan must include a statement, in any plan materials provided to a participant or beneficiary describing the benefits under the plan, that the plan believes it is a grandfathered health plan within the meaning of section 1251 of the Affordable Care Act and must provide contact information for questions and complaints. Model language is available.[3]

Question 13 – Is the plan maintaining records documenting the terms of the plan in connection with the coverage in effect on March 23, 2010, and are these records made available upon request? To maintain status as a grandfathered group health plan the plan must maintain records documenting the terms of the plan in connection with the coverage that was in effect on March 23, 2010, and any other documents necessary to verify, explain, or clarify its status as a grandfathered health plan. These records must be maintained for as long as the plan takes the position that it is grandfathered, and must be available for examination upon request.[4]

---

1. See 29 CFR 2590.715-1251(a)(1)(ii), as amended.
2. See 29 CFR 2590.715-1251(a)(3)(ii), as amended.
3. See 29 CFR 2590.715-1251(a)(2).
4. See 29 CFR 2590.715-1251(a)(3)(i)(A) & (i)(B), as amended.

139. What health reform requirements apply to grandfathered plans?

These seven requirements apply to all health plans, including grandfathered plans.

Health Reform Rules That Apply to All Plans, Including Grandfathered Plans
Pre-existing condition exclusions (PCE) prohibited.[1] Grandfathered individual coverage can continue to apply these exclusions, but group health plans and group health insurance issuers cannot impose PCEs for plan years beginning on or after January 1, 2014. This prohibition took effect for plan years beginning on or after September 23, 2010, (i.e., January 1, 2011, for calendar-year plans) with respect to individuals enrolled in the plan who are younger than nineteen years of age.
Excessive waiting periods of more than ninety days are prohibited for plan years beginning in 2014.[2]
Annual/lifetime limits are prohibited for plan years beginning in 2014.[3] These rules apply to grandfathered plans, but the annual limit prohibition does not apply to grandfathered individual coverage. For benefits that are not "essential health benefits," both lifetime and annual limits are allowed if not prohibited by other federal and state laws.[4] Failure to provide any services for a condition is allowed, but if any benefits are provided for a condition, these prohibitions apply.[5] While grandfathered health plans are not required to offer essential health benefits, they cannot impose either annual or lifetime dollar limits on the essential health benefits they do offer. Individual grandfathered policies may continue annual limits but not lifetime limits.
Rescission of policies is prohibited except for fraud or misrepresentation beginning in 2014.[6]
Dependent coverage for children under age twenty-six must be offered until 2014, except for adults eligible for coverage through their own employer.[7]
SBC Requirement. The requirement to provide at least a four-page summary of benefits and coverage to plan participants applies to grandfathered plans.[8] This is discussed in more detail in Part VII of this publication.
Medical Loss Ratio (MLR) reporting and rebates, designed to lower health insurance costs apply to grandfathered plans.[9]

---

1. PHSA §2704(a), IRC Sec. 9815 & ERISA Sec. 715.
2. PHSA §2708.
3. PHSA §2711.
4. Treas. Reg. §54.9815-2711T(b)(1);   DOL Reg. §2590.715-2711(b)(1); HHS Reg. §147.126(b)(2).
5. Treas. Reg. §54.9815-2711T(b)(2); DOL Reg. §2590.715-2711(b)(2); HHS Reg. §147.126(b)(2).
6. PHSA §2712.
7. PHSA §2714.
8. PHSA §2715.
9. PHSA §2718.

140. What health reform requirements apply to new plans or plans that lose grandfathered status?

These thirteen requirements do not apply to grandfathered plans. They apply only to new plans or plans that lose grandfathered status.

Additional Rules Applicable to New and Nongrandfathered Health Plans
Fair health insurance premiums.[1] These are the rules that limit insurers in the individual or small group market as to allowable factors to alter premiums: • coverage category (e.g., whether the coverage is individual versus family coverage); • rating area (as established by states); • age (may not vary by more than 3 to 1 for adults); and • tobacco use (may not vary more than 1.5 to 1).[2]
Guaranteed-Availability Rules Applicable to Small and Large Group Markets.[3] Healthcare reform makes changes to these requirements. Through December 31, 2013, the guaranteed-availability rules apply to health insurance issuers in the small group market, but not to issuers in the large group market. These rules require a health insurance issuer that actively markets coverage in the small group market to accept every small employer that applies for coverage and to make all products that it actively markets in the small group market available to all small employers. The issuer also must accept for enrollment every eligible individual who applies for coverage when first eligible. Insurers are permitted to impose employer contribution and minimum participation requirements (to the extent consistent with applicable state law), within certain limitations. As of January 1, 2014, the guaranteed-availability rules are significantly expanded. The statutory changes amended and restructured the guaranteed-availability provisions, making these rules applicable to health insurance issuers in the large and small group markets and effecting certain other changes.[4] Each health insurance issuer that offers health insurance coverage in the individual or group market (regardless of whether the coverage is offered in the large or small group market) is required to accept every employer and individual in the state that applies for such coverage. Enrollment may, however, be restricted to open or special enrollment periods.[5]
Guaranteed renewability, which means that an insurer must renew coverage if requested by the plan sponsor.[6] Prior to January 1, 2014, these rules apply to both the small and large group market. They require group insurance issuers in both the small and large group market to renew coverage at the option of the plan sponsor subject to specified exceptions and restrictions (such as nonpayment of premiums, fraud, or violation of certain employer contribution or group participation requirements).

---

1. PHSA §2701.
2. PHSA §2701(a)(1)(A).
3. PHSA §2702.
4. PPACA renumbered PHSA §2711as PHSA §2731; PPACA §1105 included new PHSA §2702(a); and PPACA §1563(c)(8) made changes to PHSA §2731 and renumbered it as PHSA §2702.
5. PHSA §2702(b).
6. PHSA §2703.

Nondiscrimination based on health status. Group health plans and health insurance issuers offering health insurance coverage are prohibited from discriminating against an individual with regard to eligibility or coverage based on a health status factor.[1] Health reform extended these rules, effective January 1, 2014, to health insurance issuers offering individual health insurance coverage.[2]

Nondiscrimination against healthcare providers, beginning in 2014 if they act within the scope of their license or certification.[3]

Comprehensive health insurance coverage. Effective for plan years beginning on or after January 1, 2014, health insurance issuers offering coverage in the individual or small group market must ensure that such coverage includes the "essential health benefits package."[4] A plan must provide essential health benefits,[5] limit cost-sharing,[6] and provide either bronze, silver, gold, or platinum level coverage (benefits that are actuarially equivalent to 60 percent, 70 percent, 80 percent, or 90 percent of the full actuarial benefits provided under the plan), or a catastrophic plan (also known as "young invincibles" coverage).[7] An insurer that offers bronze, silver, gold, or platinum coverage must offer the same level of coverage in a "child-only plan" designed for persons under age twenty-one.[8]

No denial of coverage for individuals participating in approved clinical trials.[9]

No cost-sharing (copayments) for preventive and wellness services.[10]

Transparency in coverage.[11] A health plan seeking Qualified Health Plan (QHP) certification from an exchange must disclose certain information to the exchange, HHS, and the state insurance commissioner, and make the information available to the public as well as cost-sharing disclosures to participants.

Nondiscrimination is prohibited in favor of highly compensated employees by nongrandfathered insured group plans.[12] Those rules are discussed in detail in Part VII of this book.

Quality of care reporting requires group health plans and health insurance issuers annually to report to HHS about plan or coverage benefits and provider "reimbursement structures" that may affect the quality of care.[13]

---

1. Health status factors are health status; medical condition (including both physical and mental illnesses); claims experience; receipt of health care; medical history; genetic information; evidence of insurability (EOI) (including conditions arising out of acts of domestic violence); disability; and any other health status-related factor determined appropriate by the Secretary of HHS. IRC Sec. 9802(a)(1); ERISA Sec. 702(a)(1); PHSA §2705(a). The last category was added by health reform. PHSA §2705(a).
2. PHSA §2705.
3. PHSA §2706.
4. PHSA §2707(a).
5. PPACA §1302(b).
6. PPACA §1302(c).
7. PPACA §1302(e).
8. PHSA §2707(c).
9. PHSA §2709.
10. PHSA §2713.
11. PHSA §2715A.
12. PHSA §2716, IRC Sec. 9815 & ERISA Sec. 715.
13. PHSA §2717.

Claims appeals[1] and external review[2] rules.[3] These rules apply in addition to the ERISA claims procedures. Insurers will handle this duty for insured plans. Plan documents, summary plan descriptions (SPDs), existing claims procedures, any forms and notices used to communicate benefit determinations, and service contracts with TPAs and insurers will need to be updated. Non-ERISA self-insured plans not previously subject to the ERISA claims procedure requirement must adopt the existing DOL claims procedures and comply with these new requirements, such as governmental and church plans that have not elected to be subject to ERISA. In March 2011, a grace period for some requirements was extended until plan years beginning on or after January 1, 2012, (with one exception).[1]

Patient protections[2] for women to select an OB-GYN and parents to select a pediatrician as their child's primary care provider. Additionally, for group health plans providing for emergency services, the plan:

- may not require preauthorization, including for emergency services provided out-of-network;
- must provide coverage regardless of whether the provider is in- or out-of-network;
- may not impose any administrative requirement or coverage limitation that is more restrictive than would be imposed on in-network emergency services; and
- must comply with cost-sharing requirements.[3]

141. What changes to a plan will not result in loss of grandfather status?

Any change that does not result in loss of grandfathered status will not affect grandfathered status. Changes that are not prohibited do not cause a loss of grandfathered status.[7] Changes to premiums, changes to comply with the law, changes voluntarily to implement healthcare reform changes, and changes by third-party administrators are allowed if they are made without exceeding the standards for changes that terminate grandfather status.[8]

142. Can an insured plan change insurance companies?

The initial regulations provided that if an employer entered into a new policy, certificate, or contract of insurance after March 23, 2010, the new policy, certificate, or contract would not be grandfathered health coverage.[9] This provoked a firestorm of protest because plan sponsors could not improve their plans or decrease costs (in permitted ways) by changing insurers without losing grandfather status. Revised regulations changed this result, but only for changes on or

---

1. DOL Reg. §2590.715-2719(b)(2).
2. DOL Reg. §2590.715-2719(a).
3. PHSA §2719.
4. DOL Technical Release 2011-02.
5. PHSA §2719A.
6. Treas. Reg. §54.9815-2719AT(b)(3)(i); DOL Reg. §2590.715-2719A(b)(3)(i); HHS Reg. §147.138(b)(3)(i).
7. Preamble to Grandfathered Health Plan Regulations, 75 Fed. Reg. 34537 (June 17, 2010); FAQs About the Affordable Care Act Implementation Part II, Q/A-1, available at http://www.dol.gov/ebsa/faqs/faq-aca2.html.
8. Preamble to Grandfathered Health Plan Regulations, 75 Fed. Reg. 34537 (June 17, 2010).
9. Interim Final Treas. Reg. §54.9815-1251T(a)(1)(i) (Mar. 2010); DOL Reg. §2590.715-1251(a)(1)(i) (Mar. 2010); HHS Reg. §147.140(a)(1)(i) (Mar. 2010).

after November 15, 2010.[1] A change entered into prior to November 15, 2010, that is effective thereafter is permitted.[2]

For changes of insurer between March 23, 2010, and June 14, 2010 (when the initial grandfather regulations were issued), changes to group health insurance coverage on or after March 23, 2010, but before June 14, 2010 (the date the regulations were made publicly available), the agencies' enforcement safe harbor remains in effect for good faith efforts to comply with a reasonable interpretation of the statute.[3] If no prohibited change in costs or coverage was made, such a plan should retain its grandfather status because the regulations, as amended, allow such a change.

The amendment to the regulations applies only to group health plans, not to insurers in the individual market.[4]

143. What documentation is required for an insured grandfathered plan to change insurance companies?

In order to maintain status as a grandfathered plan, a group health plan that enters into a new

An insurance contract or policy must provide to the new insurer (and the new insurer must require) documentation of plan terms (including benefits, cost-sharing, employer contributions, and annual limits) under the prior health coverage sufficient to determine whether any change is being made that would cause a loss of grandfather status. This documentation may include a copy of the policy and any summary plan description.[5]

144. Can a grandfathered insured group plan change to become self-insured or a self-insured plan change to an insured plan without losing grandfathered status?

The regulations do not address the scenario of an insured grandfathered plan becoming self-insured. However, they allow a self-insured grandfathered plan to move to an insured plan but only after November 15, 2010.[6] However, the reasonable good faith compliance standard should be in effect between March 23, 2010, and June 14, 2010.

145. What other changes can be made to a grandfathered self-insured plan without losing grandfather status?

A self-insured plan can change its third party administrator without losing grandfather status.[7]

A self-insured plan also should be able to change its stop-loss insurance without losing grandfather status because it is not health insurance when maintained by a self-insured plan.[8]

---

1. Treas. Reg. §54.9815-1251T(a)(1)(i); DOL Reg. §2590.715-1251(a)(1)(i); HHS Reg. §147.140(a)(1)(i).
2. Preamble to the Amendment to the Grandfathered Health Plan Regulations, 75 Fed. Reg. 70114, 70116 (November 17, 2010).
3. Preamble to the Amendment to the Grandfathered Health Plan Regulations, 75 Fed. Reg. 70114, 70116 (November 17, 2010).
4. Preamble to the Amendment to the Grandfathered Health Plan Regulations, 75 Fed. Reg. 70114, 70116 (November 17, 2010).
5. Treas. Reg. §54.9815-1251T(a)(3)(ii); DOL Reg. §2590.715-1251(a)(3)(ii); HHS Reg. §147.140(a)(3)(ii).
6. Treas. Reg. §54.9815-1251T(a)(1)(ii); DOL Reg. §2590.715-1251(a)(1)(ii); HHS Reg. §147.140(a)(1)(ii).
7. Preamble to Grandfathered Health Plan Regulations, 75 Fed. Reg. 34537 (June 17, 2010).
8. Nonbinding comments of Amy Turner, Senior Health Law Specialist, Office of Health Plan Standards and Compliance Assistance of the DOL, Department of Labor Affordable Care Act Compliance Assistance Webcast (September 7, 2010).

146. May enhancements or additions to a grandfathered health plan be made?

Yes. Additions to a grandfathered plan generally will not result in loss of grandfathered status. They are not prohibited changes. Thus, adding domestic partner benefits or a new health coverage option (such as an HMO where employer now only offers a PPO), is allowed, as these are two "benefit packages" and each is analyzed on its own to determine whether it is grandfathered.[1] Thus, the existing PPO option would remain grandfathered.

147. What special rules apply to collectively bargained plans in determining grandfathered plan status?

For insured plans, i.e., health insurance coverage maintained under one or more collective bargaining agreements ratified before March 23, 2010, the coverage will be treated as grandfathered until the last collective bargaining agreement terminates, regardless of whether there is a change that would otherwise destroy grandfathered status.[2] Self-funded collectively bargained plans will be treated the same as non-bargained plans and will need to comply with the grandfathering rules, including the new mandates and the limitations on plan changes, if this date is before the relevant collective bargaining agreement expires.[3]

This collectively bargained plan rule does not provide a delayed effective date for changes required by health reform for collectively bargained plans. Although the grandfather rule allows collectively bargained insured plans to maintain grandfathered plan status during the term of the agreement, they must comply with the rules that apply to grandfathered health plans. Therefore, collectively bargained plans (both insured and self-insured) that are grandfathered plans must comply with all the provisions that apply to grandfathered plans with no extension of any effective dates.[4]

Once the collective bargaining agreement expires, the plan may or may not be a grandfathered health plan. Such status will be determined under the otherwise applicable rules, by comparing the plan in existence at the end of the collective bargaining period with the plan in existence on March 23, 2010.[5] If the plan has made changes that, absent the special collectively bargained rule, would take it out of grandfathered status, then the plan is not a grandfathered plan once the collective bargaining agreement expires.

148. Can new enrollees, including new hires and family members, enroll in a grandfathered health plan?

Yes. An individual who was enrolled in a grandfathered health plan on March 23, 2010, may enroll his or her family members in the grandfathered health plan after March 23, 2010.[6]

---

1. Treas. Reg. §54.9815-1251T(a)(1)(i); DOL Reg. §2590.715-1251(a)(1)(i); HHS Reg. §147.140(a)(1)(i).
2. Treas. Reg. §54.9815-1251T(f)(1); DOL Reg. §2590.715-1251(f)(1); HHS Reg. §147.140(f)(1).
3. Treas. Reg. §54.9815-1251T(f)(1); DOL Reg. §2590.715-1251(f)(1); HHS Reg. §147.140(f)(1); Preamble to Grandfathered Health Plan Regulations, 75 Fed. Reg. 34537 (June 17, 2010).
4. Preamble to Grandfathered Health Plan Regulations, 75 Fed. Reg. 34537 (June 17, 2010).
5. Treas. Reg. §54.9815-1251T(f)(1); DOL Reg. §2590.715-1251(f)(1); HHS Reg. §147.140(f)(1).
6. Treas. Reg. §54.9815-1251T(a)(4); DOL Reg. §2590.715-1251(a)(4); HHS Reg. §147.140(a)(4).

Additionally, new and existing employees and family members may enroll in a grandfathered health plan.[1] Employees not covered in a grandfathered plan option may move into a grandfathered option at open enrollment without jeopardizing its grandfathered status.[2]

149. Can employees transfer from one grandfathered plan to another?

Yes, and when this is voluntary, no change in the grandfathered status occurs.[3] This is like a newly hired employee enrolling in a grandfathered plan.

150. Are there limits on employees moving from one plan to another?

Yes. The regulations state that transferring employees from one grandfathered plan or benefit package (transferor plan) to a transferee plan will cause the transferee plan to relinquish grandfather status if amending the transferor plan to replicate the terms of the transferee plan would have caused the transferor plan to relinquish grandfather status and there was no bona fide employment-based reason to transfer the employees.[4] There may be many other circumstances in which a benefit package can be eliminated for a bona fide employment-based reason. The term "bona fide employment-based reason" includes a variety of circumstances, such as the following, which is not intended to be an exhaustive list:

- A benefit package is eliminated because the issuer is exiting the market.

- A benefit package is eliminated because the issuer no longer offers the product to the employer (for example, because the employer no longer satisfies the issuer's minimum participation requirement).

- Low or declining participation by plan participants in the benefit package makes it impractical for the plan sponsor to continue to offer the benefit package.

- A benefit package is eliminated from a multiemployer plan as agreed upon as part of the collective bargaining process.

- A benefit package is eliminated for any reason and multiple benefit packages covering a significant portion of other employees remain available to the employees being transferred.[5]

- After a plant closing, the employer transfers employees to a new location, eliminating the option offered only at the closed plant, and the employees enroll in another option.[6]

---

1. Treas. Reg. §54.9815-1251T(b)(1); DOL Reg. §2590.715-1251(b)(1); HHS Reg. §147.140(b)(1).
2. Treas. Reg. §54.9815-1251T(b)(3), Example 1; DOL Reg. §2590.715-1251(b)(3), Example 1; HHS Reg. §147.140(b)(3), Example 1.
3. Treas. Reg. §54.9815-1251T(b)(3), Example 1; DOL Reg. §2590.715-1251(b)(3), Example 1; HHS Reg. §147.140(b)(3), Example 1.
4. Treas. Reg. §54.9815-1251T(b)(2)(ii); DOL Reg. §2590.715-1251(b)(2)(ii); HHS Reg. §147.140(b)(2)(ii).
5. HHS, DOL, and the Treasury, Frequently Asked Questions (FAQs), Part VI (April 2011) at http://www.dol.gov/ebsa/faqs/faq-aca6.html.
6. Treas. Reg. §54.9815-1251T(b)(3), Example 3; DOL Reg. §2590.715-1251(b)(3), Example 3; HHS Reg. §147.140(b)(3), Example 3.

However, there is no bona fide employment-based reason when there are two or more health plan options and a higher priced option is eliminated to save money, if that amendment would have resulted in a loss of grandfather status. For example, a group health plan may offer two benefit packages, a more generous PPO and a less generous HMO. The employer eliminates the PPO due to its high cost and transfers the employees to the HMO. There is no bona fide employment-based reason for this transfer, and the PPO would have lost its grandfathered status if, instead of being eliminated, its terms had been modified to match the terms of the HMO. Thus, the HMO will lose its grandfathered status. This loss of grandfathered status applies to all enrollees in the HMO, including those in the plan before the employees were transferred from the PPO.[1]

151. What happens to a grandfathered plan after a merger or acquisition?

An anti-abuse rule provides that a plan will lose grandfathered status if it engages in a transaction, such as a merger, acquisition, purchase of assets, etc., for the principal purpose of covering new individuals under a grandfathered health plan.[2]

152. If grandfather status is lost, when is that change effective?

The status is lost on the date a prohibited change becomes effective, rather than the date it is adopted. Thus, if a plan amendment is effective at the beginning of the next plan year, the status is lost for that next plan year.[3]

153. What changes to a health plan will result in a loss of grandfather status?

A change to a health plan effective after March 23, 2010 (unless legally binding prior to that date, as discussed above), can result in loss of grandfathered status. The regulations provide detailed rules for determining if design changes cause a loss of grandfather status. However, only specified changes result in loss of grandfather status.

Any of the six changes discussed in the following section can result in loss of grandfathered plan status:

- Violation of Anti-Abuse Rules (described in Q 151)

- Elimination of benefits

- Any increase in Percentage Cost-Sharing

- Increase in Fixed-Amount Cost-Sharing

- Decrease in Rate of Employer (or Employee Organization) Contributions

---

1. Treas. Reg. §54.9815-1251T(b)(3), Example 2; DOL Reg. §2590.715-1251(b)(3), Example 2; HHS Reg. §147.140(b)(3), Example 2.
2. Treas. Reg. §54.9815-1251T(b)(2)(i); DOL Reg. §2590.715-1251(b)(2)(i); HHS Reg. §147.140(b)(2)(i).
3. HHS, DOL & Treasury, FAQs About the Affordable Care Act Implementation Part VI (April 2011) at http://www.dol.gov/ebsa/faqs/faqaca6. html. (as visited Oct. 14, 2011).

- Certain changes to Annual Limits

In addition, as discussed after the questions about these impermissible changes, either of the following failures will cause loss of grandfather status:

- Failure to provide the Annual Grandfather Notice to Participants

- Failure to retain Records of the Plan in Effect on March 23, 2010.

Other changes may be made without loss of grandfather status.[1] Thus, a grandfathered plan can adopt one or more of the requirements that apply to nongrandfathered plans, as listed above in Q 140, and discussed in more detail in Part VII, without losing grandfathered status.

154. What is an impermissible elimination of benefits that terminates grandfathered status?

The elimination of all or substantially all benefits to diagnose or treat a particular condition will cause a group health plan or insurance to lose its grandfathered status. For this purpose, elimination of any element necessary to diagnose or treat the condition is considered elimination of all or substantially all of the benefits for that condition.[2] For example, if a plan decides to no longer cover care for a particular condition, e.g., diabetes, cystic fibrosis, or HIV/AIDS, grandfathered status will be lost when that change is effective. Termination will also occur if one of two necessary treatments needed for a condition is deleted, such as elimination of drugs or counseling for a mental disorder when both are required.[3]

It is not clear whether certain changes in prescription drug benefits will result in loss of grandfathered status. For example, before March 23, 2010, a plan covered a specific brand-name drug that is effective for a medical condition. If the plan changes its prescription drug provider and that specific drug is no longer covered, grandfather status may be jeopardized. However, if another drug that treats the condition is available, then arguably there has not been an elimination of the benefits to treat that condition. Similarly, if elimination of one treatment for a condition is made, but another treatment is substituted, that may not terminate grandfather status.

155. What is an increase in percentage cost-sharing (coinsurance) that terminates grandfather status?

Coinsurance requires a patient to pay a fixed percentage of a charge, such as 20 percent of a hospital bill. Grandfathered plans cannot increase this percentage. An increase after March 23, 2010, in participant percentage cost sharing terminates grandfather status for a group health plan.[4] Thus, an increase in the amount that the insured pays for hospitalization from 10 percent to 15 percent causes the plan to lose its grandfathered status.[5]

1. Preamble to Grandfathered Health Plan Regulations, 75 Fed. Reg. 34537 (June 17, 2010).
2. Treas. Reg. §54.9815-1251T(g)(1)(i); DOL Reg. §2590.715-1251(g)(1)(i); HHS Reg. §147.140(g)(1)(i).
3. Treas. Reg. §54.9815-1251T(g)(4), Example 2; DOL Reg. §2590.715-1251(g)(4), Example 2; HHS Reg. §147.140(g)(4), Example 2.
4. Treas. Reg. §54.9815-1251T(g)(1)(ii); DOL Reg. §2590.715-1251(g)(1)(ii); HHS Reg. §147.140(g)(1)(ii).
5. Treas. Reg. §54.9815-1251T(g)(4), Example 1; DOL Reg. §2590.715-1251(g)(4), Example 1; HHS Reg. §147.140(g)(4), Example 1.

If a plan has multiple grandfathered options, and the insured's coinsurance percentage is increased in only one option, the other options remain grandfathered.[1]

If the owner of an individual policy may elect an option to pay reduced premiums in exchange for higher cost sharing, such an election can be made without affecting the individual policy's grandfather status.[2]

Example 1: A grandfathered plan includes prescription drug benefits with different cost sharing divided into tiers as follows:

- o   Tier 1 includes generic drugs only;

- o   Tier 2 includes brand-name drugs with no generic available;

- o   Tier 3 includes brand-name drugs with a generic available in Tier 1; and

- o   Tier 4 includes IV chemotherapy drugs.

A drug was previously classified in Tier 2 as a brand-name drug with no generic available. However, a generic alternative for the drug has just been released and is added to the formulary. The plan moves the brand-name drug into Tier 3 and adds the generic to Tier 1. Does this change terminate the plan's grandfathered status?

No. The increase in the cost sharing for a brand-name drug where it is replaced by a generic drug with the same or less cost sharing does not terminate grandfathered status.[3]

Example 2: A grandfathered plan covers treatment at 80 percent without any precertification requirement. In 2013, the plan is amended so that it will pay for treatment at 70 percent if an out-of-network provider is used unless the individual obtains precertification, but otherwise will pay 80 percent. Does this change terminate grandfather status? This issue has not been addressed as yet.

156. What is an increase in fixed-amount cost-sharing (coinsurance) that terminates grandfather status?

Frequently, plans require patients to pay a fixed dollar amount for doctor's office visits and other services. Compared with the required payments in effect on March 23, 2010, grandfathered plans will be able to increase those copays by no more than a percentage equal to percentage medical inflation since 2010 plus 15 percent.[4]

Medical inflation is defined by reference to the overall medical care component (OMCC) of the Consumer Price Index for All Urban Consumers (CPI-U) (unadjusted) published by

---

1. Treas. Reg. §54.9815-1251T(g)(4), Example 9; DOL Reg. §2590.715-1251(g)(4), Example 9; HHS Reg. §147.140(g)(4), Example 9.
2. HHS, DOL & Treasury FAQs About the Affordable Care Act Implementation Part IV, Q/A-2 at http://www.dol.gov/ebsa/faqs/faq-aca4.html.
3. HHS, DOL & Treasury, FAQs About the Affordable Care Act Implementation Part VI, Q/A-2, at http://www.dol.gov/ebsa/faqs/faq-aca6.html.
4. Treas. Reg. §54.9815-1251T(g)(1)(iv); Treas. Reg. §54.9815-1251T(g)(1)(iii); DOL Reg. §2590.715-1251(g)(1)(iii); HHS Reg. §147.140(g)(1)(iii).

the Department of Labor.[1] The change in medical inflation is measured from March 2010 by taking the greatest value of the unadjusted medical index of the CPI-U within twelve months of the date the increase is effective and subtracting the March 2010 medical component of the unadjusted CPI-U. The difference is divided by the March 2010 medical care component of the CPI-U (387.142), which is then added to 15 percent.

While the increase in fixed-amount cost sharing is determined as of the effective date of the increase, the OMCC is computed using any month in the twelve months before the new change is to take effect.[2] Thus, if a change became effective on July 15, 2011, this was evaluated on the OMCC using the month between July 2010 and June 2011 with the "greatest value," not the OMCC for July 2011.[3]

A plan is allowed a 15 percent cumulative increase, measured from March 23, 2010. Thus, smaller increases may be made annually, but the overall limitation over time is 15 percent.[4]

Example: If medical inflation is 4 percent for 2010 and the copay for 2010 is $30, 4 percent plus 15 percent equals 19 percent. The copay cannot increase more than 19 percent or to a maximum of $35 in 2011.

Beginning in 2012, only medical inflation is added, so assuming medical inflation is again 4 percent, then the 2012 percentage allowed is 23 percent (19 percent plus 4 percent) above the 2010 copay for a maximum copay of $37.

157. How do the fixed-amount cost-sharing limitations apply to HRAs paired with HDHPs?

A health reimbursement arrangement (HRA) is an employer-funded medical expense reimbursement plan, reimbursing specified items not paid by insurance. An HRA may allow unused amounts to carry over into future years. An HRA is sometimes paired with an employer-provided high deductible health plan (HDHP) so that HRA amounts can pay medical expenses not covered by the high deductible plan. The employer HRA contributions likely would be viewed as lowering an otherwise applicable deductible, so long as the HRA balance is available for all expenses subject to the deductible. Similarly, if an employer decreased HRA contributions, this could be treated as an increase in the deductible and subject to the 15 percent limit.

158. How much can a fixed-amount cost-sharing (coinsurance) payment be increased without losing grandfather status?

Some plans have a feature with a fixed-amount cost-sharing requirement, such as a deductible or an out-of-pocket limit, which is based on a percentage-of-compensation. This cost-sharing

---

1. Treas. Reg. §54.9815-1251T(g)(3)(i); DOL Reg. §2590.715-1251(g)(3)(i); HHS Reg. §147.140(g)(3)(i).
2. Treas. Reg. §54.9815-1251T(g)(3)(i); DOL Reg. §2590.715-1251(g)(3)(i); HHS Reg. §147.140(g)(3)(i).
3. Treas. Reg. §§54.9815-1251T(g)(3)(i) and (g)(4), Example (3); DOL Reg. §§2590.715-1251(g)(3)(i) and (g)(4), Example (3); HHS Reg. §§147.140(g)(3)(i) and (g)(4), Example (3).
4. Nonbinding comments of Amy Turner, Senior Health Law Specialist, Office of Health Plan Standards and Compliance Assistance of the DOL, Department of Labor Affordable Care Act Compliance Assistance Webcast (September 7, 2010) at http://www.dol.gov/ebsa/newsroom/webcasts.html.

arrangement will not cause the plan or coverage to cease to be a grandfathered health plan so long as the formula for determining an out-of-pocket limit remains the same as on March 23, 2010.[1] Thus, even if an employee's compensation increases and the employee faces a higher out-of-pocket limit as a result, that change will not cause the plan to relinquish grandfather status.

Any increase after March 23, 2010, in fixed-amount co-payments above the greater of:

- $5, increased by medical inflation; or

- 15 percent above medical inflation,

will cause a group health plan or insurer to lose its grandfathered status.[2] This limit applies even to copayments that are for a single category of service.[3]

Example: On March 23, 2010, a grandfathered health plan has a copayment of $30 per office visit for specialists. The plan is later amended to increase the copay requirement to $40. Within the twelve-month period before the $40 copay takes effect, the greatest value of the OMCC is 475. The percentage increase in the copayment from $30 to $40 is 33.33 percent.

$$40 - 30 = 10$$

$$10 / 30 = 0.3333 \text{ or } 33.33 \text{ percent}$$

Medical inflation from March 2010 is 0.2269, calculated as follows:

$$475 - 387.142 = 87.858$$

$$87.858 \div 387.142 = 0.2269 \text{ or } 22.69\%$$

The maximum percentage increase permitted is 37.69 percent, calculated as follows:

$$22.69\% + 15\% = 37.69\%$$

Because 33.33 percent does not exceed 37.69 percent, the change in the copayment does not cause the plan to cease to be a grandfathered health plan.[4]

159. Are there special rules for value-based insurance design (VBID) copayments?

Yes. A copayment may be imposed for an inpatient treatment for preventive services as a part of value-based insurance design, when there is:

- no increase in copayment for the outpatient treatment for the same condition, and

1. HHS, DOL & TREASURY FAQs About the Affordable Care Act Implementation Part V, Q/A-7 at http://www.dol.gov/ebsa/faqs/faq-aca5.html.
2. Treas. Reg. §54.9815-1251T(g)(1)(iv); DOL Reg. §2590.715-1251(g)(1)(iv); HHS Reg. §147.140(g)(1)(iv).
3. HHS, DOL & TREASURY FAQs About the Affordable Care Act Implementation, Part II, Q/A-4, at http://www.dol.gov/ebsa/faqs/faq-aca2.html.
4. Treas. Reg. §54.9815-1251T (g)(4), Example (3); DOL Reg. §2590.715-1251(g)(4), Example (3); HHS Reg. §147.140(g)(4), Example (3).

- a waiver process allowing a waiver of the new hospital inpatient copayment for individuals for whom the outpatient services are medically inappropriate.

Example 1: One healthcare reform FAQ addressed the interaction of value-based insurance design (VBID) and the no cost-sharing preventive care services requirements.[1] In that example, a group health plan did not impose a copayment for colorectal cancer preventive services when performed in an in-network ambulatory surgery center. However, the same preventive service provided at an in-network outpatient hospital setting generally required a $250 copayment, although the copayment was waived for individuals for whom it would be medically inappropriate to have the preventive service provided in the ambulatory setting. The FAQ indicated that this VBID did not cause the plan to fail to comply with the no cost-sharing preventive care requirements.

Example 2: Under another group health plan, since March 23, 2010, similar preventive services are available both at an in-network ambulatory surgery center and at an in-network outpatient hospital setting without a copayment in either setting. If this plan wished to adopt the VBID approach described in Example 1 by imposing a $250 copayment for these preventive services only when performed in the in-network outpatient hospital setting (i.e., not an in-network ambulatory surgery center), and with the same waiver of the copayment for any individuals for whom it would be medically inappropriate to have these preventive services provided in the ambulatory setting, would implementation of that new design now cause the plan to relinquish grandfather status?

No. This increase in the copayment for these preventive services solely in the in-network outpatient hospital setting (subject to the waiver arrangement described above) without any change in the copayment in the in-network ambulatory surgery center setting would not be considered to exceed the thresholds described in the interim final regulations on grandfather status and thus would not cause the plan to relinquish grandfather status.

160. When will a decrease in the rate of plan sponsor contributions terminate grandfather status?

More Than 5 Percentage Point Decrease in Plan Sponsor Contributions. A grandfathered plan will lose its grandfather status if the employer or an employee organization, such as a union, decreases its contribution rate (whether based on a formula or on cost of coverage) for any tier of similarly situated individuals by more than 5 percent below the contribution rate on March 23, 2010.[2] The regulations indicate that a change from, for instance, 90 percent to 85 percent is permitted, because that is a 5 percent reduction, even though the actual number is 4.5 percent $(.90 \times .05 = 0.45)$.

For a self-insured plan, the cost of coverage is determined by using the COBRA rate of coverage.[3] Contributions by an employer or employee organization to a self-insured plan are

---

1. HHS, DOL & TREASURY FAQs About Affordable Care Act Implementation, Part V Q/A 1 at http://www.dol.gov/ebsa/faqs/faq-aca5.html.
2. Treas. Reg. §54.9815-1251T(g)(1)(v); DOL Reg. §2590.715-1251(g)(1)(v); HHS Reg. §147.140(g)(1)(v).
3. Treas. Reg. §54.9815-1251T(g)(3)(iii)(A); DOL Reg. §2590.715-1251(g)(3)(iii)(A); HHS Reg. §147.140(g)(3)(iii)(A).

equal to the total cost of coverage minus the employee contributions toward the total cost of coverage.[1] Employee salary reduction deferrals through a cafeteria or premium conversion plan are treated as employee contributions for this purpose.[2]

Example – Self-Insured Plan COBRA Cost of Coverage: On March 23, 2010, a self-insured grandfathered health plan has a COBRA premium for the 2010 plan year of $5,000 for self-only coverage and $12,000 for family coverage. The required employee contribution for the coverage is $1,000 for self-only coverage and $4,000 for family coverage. Thus, the contribution rate based on cost of coverage for 2010 is 80 percent for self-only coverage, calculated as follows:

$$5,000 - 1,000 = 4,000$$

$$4,000/5,000 = 80\%$$

The contribution rate based on cost of coverage for 2010 is 67 percent for family coverage calculated as follows:

$$12,000 - 4,000 = 8,000$$

$$8,000/12,000 = 67\%$$

For a subsequent plan year, the COBRA premium is $6,000 for self-only coverage and $15,000 for family coverage. The employee contributions for that plan year are $1,200 for self-only coverage and $5,000 for family coverage. The contribution rate based on cost of coverage remains 80 percent for self-only coverage calculated as follows:

$$6,000 - 1,200 = 4,800$$

$$4,800/6,000 = 80\%$$

The contribution rate based on cost of coverage remains 67% for family coverage, calculated as follows:

$$15,000 - 5,000 = 10,000$$

$$(10,000/15,000) = 67\%$$

There is no change in the employer's contribution rate based on the COBRA cost of coverage. Therefore, the plan retains its status as a grandfathered health plan.[3]

---

1. Treas. Reg. §54.9815-1251T(g)(3)(iii)(A); DOL Reg. §2590.715-1251(g)(3)(iii)(A); HHS Reg. §147.140(g)(3)(iii)(A).
2. Treas. Reg. §54.9815-1251T(g)(4), Example (8); DOL Reg. §2590.715-1251(g)(4), Example (8); HHS Reg. §147.140(g)(4), Example (8).
3. Treas. Reg. §54.9815-1251T(g)(4), Example (8); DOL Reg. §2590.715-1251(g)(4), Example (8); HHS Reg. §147.140(g)(4), Example (8).

161. How is this more than 5 percent reduction test applied if there are multiple health packages offered by the plan sponsor?

The test for loss of grandfather status is applied separately to each health package offered by the plan sponsor. It is possible for one package to lose its grandfathering and the others to remain grandfathered.[1]

Example – Multiple Packages (Options): ABC, Inc. maintains a group health plan that is not maintained pursuant to a collective bargaining agreement. It offered three benefit packages on March 23, 2010. Option F is a self-insured option. Options G and H are insured options. Beginning July 1, 2013, the plan increases employee coinsurance under Option H from 10 percent to 15 percent, which is a reduction in the employer contribution of 5.56 percent. The coverage under Option H loses its grandfather status on the effective date of this change, July 1, 2013. Assuming no other changes to options F and G, they remain grandfathered.[2]

162. What if the employer plan offers several tiers of coverage, such as employee, employee and spouse, and employee and family?

The standards for employer contributions apply on a tier-by-tier basis. The results differ depending on whether tiers are modified or a new tier is added. If a plan modifies its tiers of coverage, such as by changing employee and family to employee, employee and spouse, and employee and family, the employer contribution for any new tier would be tested by comparison to the contribution rate for the corresponding tier on March 23, 2010.[3] All of the tiers for a benefit package must pass the 5 percent test to remain grandfathered.

On the other hand, if the plan merely adds a new tier and does not reduce the sponsor contribution percentage to the existing tier by more than 5 percent, then the existing tier remains grandfathered. The new tier not in existence on March 23, 2010, is not grandfathered, regardless of the contribution rate for the new tier.

Example – One Coverage Option; Several Tiers (Combinations) of Insureds: Prior to March 23, 2010, ABC, Inc. contributed 80 percent of the cost of single and family coverage. Due to premium increases, ABC, Inc. reduces its payment for family coverage from 80 percent to 50 percent, a reduction of 30 percent. The employer payment for single coverage remains at 80 percent. This reduction in employer payments for family coverage is more than 5 percent and causes the entire plan to lose grandfather status.[4]

---

1. HHS, DOL & TREASURY, FAQs About the Affordable Care Act Implementation Part II, Q/A 2 at http://www.dol.gov/ebsa/faqs/faq-aca2.html.
2. Treas. Reg. §54.9815-1251T(g)(4), Example (9); DOL Reg. §2590.715-1251(g)(4), Example (9); HHS Reg. §147.140(g)(4), Example (9); HHS, DOL & TREASURY, FAQs About the Affordable Care Act Implementation Part II, Q/A-2 at http://www.dol.gov/ebsa/faqs/faq-aca2.html.
3. HHS, DOL & TREASURY, FAQs About the Affordable Care Act Implementation Part II, Q/A-3 at http://www.dol.gov/ebsa/faqs/faq-aca2.html.
4. Treas. Reg. §54.9815-1251T(g)(4), Example (7); DOL Reg. §2590.715-1251(g)(4), Example (7); HHS Reg. §147.140(g)(4), Example (7).

If ABC, Inc. alters its options to employee coverage, employee-plus-spouse coverage, and family coverage, and the employer payment for any category is less than 75 percent, the grandfather status would be lost.

163. How do the percentage point plan-sponsor contribution rules relate to wellness programs?

The agencies are studying this but caution that while premium discounts or additional benefits to reward healthy behaviors by participants or beneficiaries are acceptable, the use of penalties (such as cost-sharing surcharges) may trigger a violation of the not more than 5 percent reduction test and should be examined carefully.[1]

164. How do plan sponsor fixed dollar amount contributions work for grandfathered plans?

If an employer's contribution toward the cost of coverage for retirees that is covered by the law is not an excepted benefit (because active employees participate in the same plan) and is a fixed dollar amount multiplied by years of service, subject to a flat dollar cap per retiree, how is the 5 percent threshold for decreases in the rate of employer contributions calculated?

The 5 percent threshold for decreases in employer contributions is not violated so long as the formula for calculating the employer's contribution remains the same.[2]

165. How do insurers know if the 5 percent sponsor contribution reduction test has been violated?

If insurers follow certain requirements, a plan is treated as a grandfathered plan until the first date the insurer knows that the employer has decreased its contribution rate by more than five percent or until grandfathering is lost for another reason. The steps are as follows:

- Upon renewal, the insurer must require the plan sponsor to make a representation regarding its contribution rate for the plan year covered by the renewal, as well as its contribution rate on March 23, 2010 (if the issuer does not already have it); and

- The issuer's policies, certificates, or contracts of insurance must disclose in a prominent and effective manner that plan sponsors are required to notify the issuer if the contribution rate changes at any point during the plan year.[3]

1. HHS, DOL & TREASURY, FAQs About the Affordable Care Act Implementation Part II, Q/A-5 at http://www.dol.gov/ebsa/faqs/faq-aca2.html.
2. See HHS, DOL & TREASURY, FAQs About the Affordable Care Act Implementation Part VI, Q/A-6 at http://www.dol.gov/ebsa/faqs/faq-aca6.html.
3. HHS, DOL & TREASURY, FAQs About the Affordable Care Act Implementation Part I, Q/A-2 at http://www.dol.gov/ebsa/faqs/faq-aca.html.

An insurer may request additional advance notice of a decrease in contribution rate.[1] The impact of this rule is to avoid penalties that might be imposed, for example, if the plan thought to be grandfathered in fact is not and does not adhere to the new nondiscrimination rules for insured plans.

166. How does the 5 percent reduction rule work for collectively bargained plans?

Multiemployer plans and contributing employers will be provided the same relief as insurers if they follow steps similar to those provided for insurers, described in Q 165. In addition, a decrease in an employer's rate of contribution does not necessarily mean that the employee's rate has increased. If there has been no increase in the employee contribution rate, an employer's decrease will not, in itself, cause a plan to lose its grandfathered status.[2]

167. What if a grandfathered plan imposes an annual or lifetime limit on benefits, or increases an existing limit?

Plans that do not have an annual dollar limit cannot add a new one unless they are replacing a lifetime dollar limit with an annual dollar limit that is at least as high as the lifetime limit, as this change benefits participants. However, the regulations prohibit three other changes regarding annual or lifetime limits:

- A grandfathered plan that did not impose an overall annual or lifetime limit on the value of all benefits on March 23, 2010, will lose its grandfathered status if it imposes an annual limit.[3]

- A plan that had an overall lifetime limit on the value of all benefits but no overall annual limit will lose its grandfathered status if it imposes an overall annual limit on the value of all benefits that is lower than the lifetime limit in place on March 23, 2010.[4]

- For plans with an overall annual limit on the value of all benefits on March 23, 2010, grandfathering is lost if that annual limit is lowered, regardless of whether the plan had a lifetime limit).[5]

The regulations address an "overall limit on the value of all benefits." It is unclear whether a limit on nonessential benefits would violate this requirement.

---

1. HHS, DOL & TREASURY, FAQs About the Affordable Care Act Implementation Part I, Q/A-2 at http://www.dol.gov/ebsa/faqs/faq-aca.html.
2. HHS, DOL & TREASURY, FAQs About the Affordable Care Act Implementation Part I, Q/A-4, available at http://www.dol.gov/ebsa/faqs/faq-aca.html, stating: "If multiemployer plans and contributing employers follow steps similar to those outlined in Q/A-2 [for insurers], above, the same relief will apply to the multiemployer plan unless or until the multiemployer plan knows that the contribution rate has changed."
3. Treas. Reg. §54.9815-1251T(g)(1)(vi)(A); DOL Reg. §2590.715-1251(g)(1)(vi)(A); HHS Reg. §147.140(g)(1)(vi)(A).
4. Treas. Reg. §54.9815-1251T(g)(1)(vi)(B); DOL Reg. §2590.715-1251(g)(1)(vi)(B); HHS Reg. §147.140(g)(1)(vi)(B).
5. Treas. Reg. §54.9815-1251T(g)(1)(vi)(C); DOL Reg. §2590.715-1251(g)(1)(vi)(C); HHS Reg. §147.140(g)(1)(vi)(C).

168. What is the notice required for grandfathered plans?

The statute (PPACA §1251) has no provision requiring a notice by the plan or the employer or other entity sponsoring the health plan. The regulations (unless they are changed when issued in final form) do impose a notice requirement that is not well known, which in effect could negate the law for most employers and eliminate grandfathered plans for all but that handful of employers who have sophisticated, specialized healthcare reform legal and benefits advisors and were aware of and in fact issued the grandfathered plan notice each year.

The loss of this important statutory provision far outweighs the Department of Labor "goal that the notice encourages plan sponsors and issuers to identify other communications in which disclosure of grandfather status would be appropriate and consistent with the goal of providing participants and beneficiaries information necessary to understand and make informed choices regarding health coverage."

The regulations issued in 2010 in proposed form[1] require notices to plan participants beginning in the fall of 2010. Failing to distribute the required grandfathered notice will cause a plan to lose its grandfathered status. A plan that intends to maintain grandfathered status must provide, in any plan materials describing benefits for participants or beneficiaries:

1. A statement that the plan or coverage is believed to be a grandfathered plan and

2. Contact information for questions or complaints.

A plan or individual grandfathered policy must provide, in any plan materials describing benefits for participants or beneficiaries, (a) a statement that the plan or coverage is believed to be a grandfathered plan, and (b) contact information for questions or complaints. To maintain grandfather status,[2] group health plans should assume that this requirement applies to enrollment materials, summary plan descriptions, summary of material modifications to an SPD, and perhaps when the SBC (Summary of Benefits & Coverage) is distributed. A grandfathered plan need not provide a disclosure statement regarding its grandfather status every time it sends out a communication, such as an explanation of benefits to participants.[3]

It is not clear when this notice requirement applies. There are a number of possibilities: the first plan year on or after March 23, 2010, or perhaps for the first plan year beginning after June 17, 2010, when the regulations were published in the federal register, or preferably after the regulations are finalized. The latter seems most fair because the law[4] requires no notice of grandfathering and likely most US employers have no knowledge of this notice requirement. Additionally, a plan sponsor may not make the decision on grandfathering until well after March 23, 2010, and perhaps not until subsequent years.

---

1. Treas. Reg. §54.9815-1251T(c)(1); DOL Reg. §2590.715-1251(c)(1); HHS Reg. §147.140(c)(1).
2. Treas. Reg. §54.9815-1251T(a)(2)(i); DOL Reg. §2590.715-1251(a)(2)(i); HHS Reg. §147.140(a)(2)(i).
3. HHS, DOL & TREASURY, FAQs About the Affordable Care Act Implementation Part IV, Q/A-1, available at http://www.dol.gov/ebsa/faqs/faq-aca4.htm.
4. PPACA §1251.

However, the statute has no notice requirement.

PPACA Sec. 1251, Preservation of Right to Maintain Existing Coverage, provides as follows:

(a) No Changes to Existing Coverage—

    (1)   In general. Nothing in this Act (or an amendment made by this Act) shall be construed to require that an individual terminate coverage under a group health plan or health insurance coverage in which such individual was enrolled on the date of enactment of this Act.

    (2)   CONTINUATION OF COVERAGE. With respect to a group health plan or health insurance coverage in which an individual was enrolled on the date of enactment of this Act, this subtitle and subtitle A (and the amendments made by such subtitles) shall not apply to such plan or coverage, regardless of whether the individual renews such coverage after such date of enactment.

(b) Allowance for Family Members to Join Current Coverage. With respect to a group health plan or health insurance coverage in which an individual was enrolled on the date of enactment of this Act and which is renewed after such date, family members of such individual shall be permitted to enroll in such plan or coverage if such enrollment is permitted under the terms of the plan in effect as of such date of enactment.

(c) Allowance for New Employees to Join Current Plan. A group health plan that provides coverage on the date of enactment of this Act may provide for the enrolling of new employees (and their families) in such plan, and this subtitle and subtitle A (and the amendments made by such subtitles) shall not apply with respect to such plan and such new employees (and their families).

(d) Effect on Collective Bargaining Agreements. In the case of health insurance coverage maintained pursuant to one or more collective bargaining agreements between employee representatives and one or more employers that was ratified before the date of enactment of this Act, the provisions of this subtitle and subtitle A (and the amendments made by such subtitles) shall not apply until the date on which the last of the collective bargaining agreements relating to the coverage terminates. Any coverage amendment made pursuant to a collective bargaining agreement relating to the coverage which amends the coverage solely to conform to any requirement added by this subtitle or subtitle A (or amendments) shall not be treated as a termination of such collective bargaining agreement.

(e) Definition. In this title, the term 'grandfathered health plan' means any group health plan or health insurance coverage to which this section applies.

169. What are the recordkeeping requirements for grandfathered plans?

The plan and coverage terms in effect on March 23, 2010, must be documented. [1] Such documentation, plus any additional documentation needed to verify, explain, or clarify grandfathered health plan status must be retained for so long as the plan or coverage takes the position that it is a grandfathered plan. [2] Such documentation may include intervening and current plan documents, health insurance policies, certificate or contracts of insurance, SPDs, and other cost and cost-sharing documentation. [3]

In addition, the plan or coverage must make those records available for examination upon request. [4] The regulations indicate that a participant, beneficiary, individual policy subscriber, or state or federal agency official may inspect the grandfathered plan documentation. [5]

---

1. Treas. Reg. §54.9815-1251T(a)(3)(i); DOL Reg. §2590.715-1251(a)(3)(i); HHS Reg. §147.140(a)(3)(i).
2. Treas. Reg. §54.9815-1251T(a)(3)(i); DOL Reg. §2590.715-1251(a)(3)(i); HHS Reg. §147.140(a)(3)(i).
3. Preamble to Grandfathered Health Plan Regulations, 75 Fed. Reg. 34537 (June 17, 2010).
4. Treas. Reg. §54.9815-1251T(a)(3)(ii); DOL Reg. §2590.715-1251(a)(3)(ii); HHS Reg. §147.140(a)(3)(ii).
5. Preamble to Grandfathered Health Plan Regulations, 75 Fed. Reg. 34537 (June 17, 2010).

PART VII: PHSA COVERAGE MANDATES AND ENFORCEMENT

Coverage Mandates and Enforcement

170. What are the coverage mandates imposed by health reform and incorporated into the Public Health Services Act (PHSA)?

As discussed earlier in connection with grandfathered plans, health reform's revision of the Public Health Services Act imposes numerous coverage mandates for policies and plans covering essential health benefits. These do not include "excepted benefits."[1] In addition to their inclusion in the PHSA, these provisions are incorporated by reference into Section 715 of the Employee Retirement Income Security Act of 1974 (ERISA) and Section 9815 of the Internal Revenue Code (Code). The mandates for essential health benefits for grandfathered plans are as follows:

Health Reform Rules That Apply to All Plans, Including Grandfathered Plans
Pre-existing condition exclusions (PCE) prohibited.[2] Grandfathered individual coverage can continue to apply these exclusions, but group health plans and group health insurance issuers cannot impose PCEs for plan years beginning on or after January 1, 2014. This prohibition took effect for plan years beginning on or after September 23, 2010, (i.e., January 1, 2011, for calendar-year plans) with respect to individuals enrolled in the plan who are younger than nineteen years of age.
Excessive waiting periods of more than ninety days are prohibited for plan years beginning in 2014.[3]
Annual/lifetime limits are prohibited for plan years beginning in 2014.[4] These rules apply to grandfathered plans, but the annual limit prohibition does not apply to grandfathered individual coverage. For benefits that are not "essential health benefits," both lifetime and annual limits are allowed if not prohibited by other federal and state laws.[5] Failure to provide any services for a condition is allowed, but if any benefits are provided for a condition, these prohibitions apply.[6] While grandfathered health plans are not required to offer essential health benefits, they cannot impose either annual or lifetime dollar limits on the essential health benefits they do offer. Individual grandfathered policies may continue annual limits but not lifetime limits.
Rescission of policies is prohibited except for fraud or misrepresentation beginning in 2014.[7]

---

1. Preamble to Grandfathered Health Plan Regulations, 75 Fed. Reg. 34537 (June 17, 2010) and HHS, DOL & TREASURY, FAQs About the Affordable Care Act Implementation Part II, Q/A-6, at http://www.dol.gov/ebsa/faqs/faq-aca2.html.
2. PHSA §2704(a), IRC Sec. 9815 and ERISA Sec. 715.
3. PHSA §2708.
4. PHSA §2711.
5. Treas. Reg. §54.9815-2711T(b)(2); DOL Reg. §2590.715-2711(b)(2); HHS Reg. §147.126(b)(2).
6. Treas. Reg. §54.9815-2711T(b)(1); DOL Reg. §2590.715-2711(b)(1); HHS Reg. §147.126(b)(2).
7. PHSA §2712.

Dependent coverage for children under age twenty-six must be offered until 2014, except for adults eligible for coverage through their own employer.[1]

SBC Requirement. The requirement to provide at least a four-page summary of benefits and coverage to plan participants applies to grandfathered plans.[2]. This is discussed in more detail in Part VII of this publication.

Medical Loss Ratio (MLR) reporting and rebates, designed to lower health insurance costs apply to grandfathered plans.[3]

171. What health reform coverage mandates apply to new plans or plans that lose grandfathered status?

The following thirteen requirements do not apply to grandfathered plans but apply to new and nongrandfathered plans.

Additional Rules Applicable to New and Nongrandfathered Health Plans

Fair health insurance premiums.[4] These are the rules that limit insurers in the individual or small group market as to allowable factors to alter premiums:

- coverage category (e.g., whether the coverage is individual versus family coverage);
- rating area (as established by states);
- age (may not vary by more than 3 to 1 for adults); and
- tobacco use (may not vary more than 1.5 to 1).[5]

Guaranteed-Availability Rules Applicable to Small and Large Group Markets. Healthcare reform makes changes to these requirements.

Through December 31, 2013, the guaranteed-availability rules apply to health insurance issuers in the small group market, but not to issuers in the large group market. These rules require a health insurance issuer that actively markets coverage in the small group market to accept every small employer that applies for coverage and to make all products that it actively markets in the small group market available to all small employers. The issuer also must accept for enrollment every eligible individual who applies for coverage when first eligible. Insurers are permitted to impose employer contribution and minimum participation requirements (to the extent consistent with applicable state law), within certain limitations.

---

1. PHSA §2714.
2. PHSA §2715.
3. PHSA §2718.
4. PHSA §2701.
5. PHSA §2701(a)(1)(A).
6. PHSA §2702.

As of January 1, 2014, the guaranteed-availability rules are significantly expanded. The statutory changes amended and restructured the guaranteed-availability provisions, making these rules applicable to health insurance issuers in the large and small group markets and effecting certain other changes.[1] Each health insurance issuer that offers health insurance coverage in the individual or group market (regardless of whether the coverage is offered in the large or small group market) is required to accept every employer and individual in the state that applies for such coverage. Enrollment may, however, be restricted to open or special enrollment periods.[2]

Guaranteed renewability, which means that an insurer must renew coverage if requested by the plan sponsor.[3] Prior to January 1, 2014, these rules apply to both the small and large group market. They require group insurance issuers in both the small and large group market to renew coverage at the option of the plan sponsor subject to specified exceptions and restrictions (such as nonpayment of premiums, fraud, or violation of certain employer contribution or group participation requirements).

Nondiscrimination based on health status. Group health plans and health insurance issuers offering health insurance coverage are prohibited from discriminating against an individual with regard to eligibility or coverage based on a health status factor.[4] Health reform extended these rules, effective January 1, 2014, to health insurance issuers offering individual health insurance coverage.[5]

Nondiscrimination against healthcare providers, beginning in 2014 if they act within the scope of their license or certification.[6]

Comprehensive health insurance coverage. Effective for plan years beginning on or after January 1, 2014, health insurance issuers offering coverage in the individual or small group market must ensure that such coverage includes the "essential health benefits package."[7] A plan must provide essential health benefits,[8] limit cost-sharing,[9] and provide either bronze, silver, gold, or platinum level coverage (benefits that are actuarially equivalent to 60 percent, 70 percent, 80 percent, or 90 percent of the full actuarial benefits provided under the plan), or a catastrophic plan (also known as "young invincibles" coverage).[10] An insurer that offers bronze, silver, gold, or platinum coverage must offer the same level of coverage in a "child-only plan" designed for persons under age twenty-one.[11]

---

1. PPACA renumbered PHSA §2711 as PHSA §2731; PPACA §1105 included new PHSA §2702(a); and PPACA §1563(c)(8) made changes to PHSA §2731 and renumbered it as PHSA §2702.
2. PHSA §2702(b).
3. PHSA §2703.
4. Health status factors are health status; medical condition (including both physical and mental illnesses); claims experience; receipt of health care; medical history; genetic information; evidence of insurability (EOI) (including conditions arising out of acts of domestic violence); disability; and any other health status–related factor determined appropriate by the Secretary of HHS. IRC Sec. 9802(a)(1); ERISA Sec. 702(a)(1); PHSA §2705(a). The last category was added by health reform. PHSA §2705(a).
5. PHSA §2705.
6. PHSA §2706.
7. PHSA §2707(a).
8. PPACA §1302(b).
9. PPACA §1302(c).
10. PPACA §1302(e).
11. PHSA §2707(c).

No denial of coverage for individuals participating in approved clinical trials.[1]

No cost-sharing (copayments) for preventive and wellness services.[2]

Transparency in coverage.[3] A health plan seeking Qualified Health Plan (QHP) certification from an exchange must disclose certain information to the exchange, HHS, and the state insurance commissioner, and make the information available to the public as well as cost-sharing disclosures to participants.

Nondiscrimination is prohibited in favor of highly compensated employees by nongrandfathered insured group plans.[4] Those rules are discussed in detail in Part VII of this book.

Quality of care reporting requires group health plans and health insurance issuers annually to report to HHS about plan or coverage benefits and provider "reimbursement structures" that may affect the quality of care.[5]

Claims appeals[6] and external review[7] rules.[8] These rules apply in addition to the ERISA claims procedures. Insurers will handle this duty for insured plans. Plan documents, summary plan descriptions (SPDs), existing claims procedures, any forms and notices used to communicate benefit determinations, and service contracts with TPAs and insurers will need to be updated. Non-ERISA self-insured plans not previously subject to the ERISA claims procedure requirement must adopt the existing DOL claims procedures and comply with these new requirements, such as governmental and church plans that have not elected to be subject to ERISA. In March 2011, a grace period for some requirements was extended until plan years beginning on or after January 1, 2012, (with one exception).[9]

Patient protections[10] for women to select an OB-GYN and parents to select a pediatrician as their child's primary care provider. Additionally, for group health plans providing for emergency services, the plan:

- may not require preauthorization, including for emergency services provided out-of-network;
- must provide coverage regardless of whether the provider is in- or out-of-network;
- may not impose any administrative requirement or coverage limitation that is more restrictive than would be imposed on in-network emergency services; and
- must comply with cost-sharing requirements.[11]

---

1. PHSA §2709.
2. PHSA §2713.
3. PHSA §2715A.
4. PHSA §2716, IRC Sec. 9815 and ERISA Sec. 715.
5. PHSA §2717.
6. DOL Reg. §2590.715-2719(b)(2).
7. DOL Reg. §2590.715-2719(a).
8. PHSA §2719.
9. DO L Technical Release 2011-02.
10. PHSA §2719A.
11. Treas. Reg. §54.9815-2719AT(b)(3)(i); DOL Reg. §2590.715-2719A(b)(3)(i); HHS Reg. §147.138(b)(3)(i).

172. How are these coverage mandates enforced?

The health reform requirements discussed in Q 171, i.e., the coverage mandates incorporated into the PHSA, are enforceable by:

- the IRS or the Department of Labor (DOL),

- participants, beneficiaries and plan fiduciaries, and

- the states and HHS, for state and local government plans.

Although the mandates applicable to group health plans and insurers are virtually identical, the consequences of noncompliance differ depending on type of entity and plan because of the different enforcement mechanisms under the Internal Revenue Code (Code), ERISA, the Fair Labor Standards Act (FLSA), and the PHSA.

The PHSA mandates are directly applicable to (and therefore enforceable against) state and local governmental employer group health plans. Insurers in the group and individual markets are subject to the PHSA.[1] Due to incorporation of the mandates into ERISA, they are also applicable to private-sector employer group health plans. Private-sector group health plans are also subject to the mandates incorporated into the Code. While the group health plans of church employers are generally not subject to ERISA (unless they opt in to ERISA coverage), they are subject to the mandates as incorporated into the Code.

Litigation due to violation of these mandates to enforce them could be brought against employers, plan sponsors, and fiduciaries under the PHSA, ERISA, and the FLSA. In addition, there could be other litigation, for example, when an employer moves employees to part-time status (fewer than thirty hours per week) to eliminate or soften the impact of the employer mandate tax penalty. Any such workforce realignment inherently carries with it risks of litigation under ERISA Section 510, which prohibits interference with a participant's benefits or rights under ERISA, as well as potential claims under other antidiscrimination statutes, such as the Age Discrimination in Employment Act and Title VII of the Civil Rights Act.

Internal Revenue Code. The IRS can assess excise taxes upon group health plans that do not comply with the coverage mandates. For group health plans, the penalty tax upon a non-complying plan sponsor is $100 per day of noncompliance per affected individual,[2] and the violations must be self-reported on IRS Form 8928. The tax may be higher where violations occurred or continued during a period under IRS examination or where the violations are more than *de minimis*. The tax does not apply where the failure was based on reasonable cause and not on willful neglect,[3] and the failure is corrected within thirty days after the person knew or should have known that the failure existed.[4] If the plan (other than a church plan)[5] is audited by the

---

1. PHSA §2723.
2. IRC Sec. 4980D, which does not apply to insurers.
3. IRC Sec. 4980D(c)(1).
4. IRC Sec. 4980D(c)(2). See IRC Sec. 4980D(c)(2)(B)(ii), which gives church plans 270 days after the date of mailing by the Secretary of a notice of default with respect to the plan's failure.
5. IRC Sec. 4980D(b)(3)(c).

IRS, the minimum excise tax for a compliance failure discovered after a notice of examination generally is $2,500.[1] The minimum excise tax is increased to $15,000 if violations are "more than de minimis."[2] If not corrected and if the failure was due to reasonable cause and not willful neglect (an unintentional failure), the tax imposed may not exceed the lesser of 10 percent of the amount paid to provide medical care during the taxable year or $500,000. In the case of a multiemployer plan, the tax is levied upon the plan.

The PHSA also imposes an additional new penalty of up to $1,000 per day per affected individual for willful violations of the Summary of Benefits and Coverage (SBC) rules for group health plans.[3] For an insured plan, the insurer and plan administrator are potentially subject to this penalty.[4]

There is an exception for small employers with between two and fifty employees. This exception seems limited to failures by an insurer to comply with the mandates and not because an insured plan violates the rules, for example, the health insurance nondiscrimination rules, discussed at Q 306 to Q 310.

ERISA. Using ERISA's enforcement mechanisms, health reform imposes substantial, complex, and plan-wide coverage mandates on employers. ERISA did this for pension benefits, and health reform has now extended this to the complex world of health benefits. It is quite likely that the plaintiffs' bar, or perhaps even DOL, will test the limits of grandfathered status, as well as of the employers' and plan fiduciaries' good faith efforts to comply with the many coverage mandates.

Health reform allows health plans that were in effect on March 23, 2010, to continue as "grandfathered" plans without having to comply with many of the law's coverage mandates. Under the DOL's regulations, grandfathered plans must include a statement, in any plan materials provided to participants, noting the plan's grandfathered status, describing the plan's benefits, and providing contact information for questions and complaints.[5] When there is more than one grandfathered option or "package," the notice must be given for each grandfathered option.

It is unclear whether technical notice failures, such as being thirty days late, will forfeit grandfathered status, and good faith or substantial compliance on notice and changes in benefits may prevent loss of such status.[6] Because the loss of grandfathered status triggers compliance with certain of the law's coverage mandates on preventative care and, beginning in 2014, imposes limits on cost sharing and deductibles, it is likely that plaintiffs will often look to challenge grandfathering on a class basis. Plaintiffs also will be expected to contend that the "appropriate

1. IRC Sec. 4980D(b)(3)(B).
2. IRC Sec. 4980D(c)(3)(A).
3. PHSA §2715(f).
4. PHSA §2715(f); Treas. Regs. §54.9815-2715(e); DOL Regs. §2590.715-2715(e); 45 CFR §147.200(e).
5. 75 Fed. Reg. 34538 (June 17, 2010).
6. Participant notices are required to "maintain status as a grandfathered health plan." 75 Fed. Reg. 34538, 34541. A representative of the Treasury Department stated in nonbinding remarks that failing to provide the required notices will not automatically revoke a plan's grandfathered status, and that the facts and circumstances surrounding a notice failure will be determinative as to continued grandfathering. See http://www.employersgroup.com/Content.aspx?id=1675.

equitable relief" section of ERISA allows them to seek recovery of benefits that otherwise would have been provided from the date that such status elapsed.

The DOL may enforce the coverage mandates against group health plans by bringing a civil action to enjoin a noncompliant act or practice or for appropriate equitable relief under Part 7 of ERISA.[1] In addition, participants, beneficiaries, and fiduciaries can sue under ERISA, either individually or through class actions, to enforce the PHSA mandates against private-sector group health plans and their insurers.[2] Such lawsuits might include claims for payment of benefits alleged to be due under the plan, and the affected party could seek damages for unpaid benefits, interest, and attorney's fees.

The coverage mandates result in litigation exposure because of their complexity and the uncertainty that surrounds implementation. In addition, many of these mandates will upset existing practices (e.g., the potential lifting of annual limits on durable medical equipment or therapy services), and will impose substantial costs on employers. For example, plaintiffs may be expected to test whether limits on doctor visits, mental health sessions, and the like (which are often imposed by plans) are permitted, or instead constitute impermissible forms of annual limits. Finally, if a court later determines that the benefit at issue was required, the employer or plan fiduciary may face plan-wide exposure, with plaintiffs seeking to use ERISA's remedial provisions to acquire these benefits, including payment of money for any lost benefits.

Beginning in 2014, no essential health benefits (EHB) may have annual or lifetime limits, so plaintiffs may challenge annual or lifetime limits on certain items and services as violating the prohibition on such limits for EHBs. Health plans should be able to show compliance with the "good faith" implementation standard set forth in the regulations[3] until more specific EHB criteria are issued.

ERISA's fee-shifting provision,[4] giving courts the power to award legal fees to plaintiffs who show "some success on the merits"[5] may also increase the likelihood of class litigation. Previous ERISA litigation has resulted in large "common fund" fee awards for class actions,[6] as well as large lodestar fee awards,[7] making ERISA class litigation attractive to plaintiffs.

PHSA. Non-federal (state and local) governmental plans and health insurance issuers are subject to penalties for violations of the PHSA mandates by HHS (but only if the state takes no enforcement action).[8] The PHSA civil money penalties of up to $100 per day may be assessed against the issuer, the sponsoring employer of a non-federal governmental plan, and the plan itself if it is sponsored by more than one employer.[9] Like the tax penalty, there are exceptions if the

---

1. ERISA Sec. 502(a).
2. ERISA Sec. 502(a).
3. Dep't of Labor's FAQs About the Affordable Care Act Implementation Part IV, available at http://www.dol.gov/ebsa/faqs/faq-aca4.html.
4. ERISA Sec. 502(g), 29 U.S.C. §1132(g).
5. See *Hardt v. Reliance Std. Life Ins. Co.*, 130 S. Ct. 2149, 2157-58 (2010).
6. E.g., *IBM Personal Pension Plan v. Cooper*, 2005 WL 1981501 (S.D. Ill. Aug. 16, 2005) (settling cash balance conversion case for $314.3 million, with attorney's fees of 29% of first $250 million, and 25% of remainder).
7. *Continental Group v. McClendon*, 872 F. Supp. 142 (D.N.J. 1994) (ERISA 510 claim settled for $415 million, with $33.3 million fee award based on "enhanced" lodestar method).
8. PHSA §§2723(a) and (b)(1).
9. PHSA §2723(b)(2).

failure was not discovered with the exercise of reasonable diligence.[1] Failures due to reasonable cause that are self-corrected within thirty days of the date the entity knew or should have known of the failure have no penalty.[2] Like the tax penalty, this penalty is capped at 10 percent of the aggregate amount paid or incurred by the employer during the preceding taxable year for the group health plan or $500,000, whichever is less.[3]

FLSA. The Department of Labor and individuals denied their rights may sue to enforce the FLSA. Health reform amended the FLSA to protect employees reporting or otherwise opposing violations of the healthcare reform law. That amendment prohibits an employer from discharging or otherwise discriminating against an employee who:

- has received a premium tax credit or subsidy for a qualified health plan;

- provided information or is about to provide information to the employer, the federal government, or the state attorney general about any violation of significant portions of the PPACA;

- testified or is about to testify in a proceeding concerning such a violation;

- has otherwise participated or is about to assist or participate in such a proceeding; or

- has objected to, or refused to participate in, any activity, policy, practice, or task that the employee reasonably believes to be such a violation.[4]

This amendment adopts the complaint procedures of the already existing whistleblower protection provision of the federal Consumer Product Safety Improvement Act. Under that provision, an employee who believes that he or she has been retaliated against may file a complaint with the U.S. Department of Labor.

The employee may also file suit in federal court within 90 days after receiving a written determination or within 210 days of the filing of the complaint, if the DOL has not issued a final decision.

Annual Limits on Essential Health Benefits Limited, Then Eliminated

173. What changes has health reform imposed on annual limits in health plans?

Health reform prohibits health plans from putting a lifetime dollar limit on essential health benefits for individual insurance and insurance issued in the small group market.[5]

---

1. PHSA §2723(b)(2)(C)(iii)(I).
2. PHSA §2723(b)(2)(C)(iii)(II).
3. PHSA §2723(b)(2)(D).
4. FLSA §18C.
5. Treas. Reg. §54.9815-2711T(b)(1); DOL Reg. §2590.715-2711(b)(1); HHS Reg. §147.126(b)(2).

Essential health benefits do not include "excepted benefits," which are not subject to health reform provisions. (See Part I, Q 12 to Q 22, for more information on "excepted benefits.") Self-funded, large group market, and grandfathered health plans are not required to offer essential health benefits.

The law also restricts and phases out the annual dollar limits a health plan, other than a grandfathered plan, can place on essential health benefits.[1] Annual limits are prohibited completely in 2014 except for grandfathered plans, as long as they do not reduce the dollar limit and otherwise retain their grandfather status. Beginning in 2014, all insurance coverage available on the exchanges will provide essential health benefits.

Before the healthcare law, many health plans set an annual limit — a dollar limit on their yearly spending for covered benefits. Many plans also set a lifetime limit — a dollar limit on what they would spend for covered benefits during the entire time a participant was enrolled in that plan.

Under the law, lifetime limits on most benefits are prohibited in any health plan or insurance policy issued or renewed on or after September 23, 2010.

The law restricts and phases out the annual dollar limits that all employment-related plans, and individual health insurance plans issued after March 23, 2010, can put on most covered health benefits. Specifically, the law says that none of these plans can set an annual dollar limit lower than:

- $750,000: for a plan year or policy year starting on or after September 23, 2010, but before September 23, 2011.

- $1.25 million: for a plan year or policy year starting on or after September 23, 2011, but before September 23, 2012.

- $2 million: for a plan year or policy year starting on or after September 23, 2012, but before January 1, 2014.

No annual dollar limits are allowed on most covered benefits beginning January 1, 2014. The ban on lifetime dollar limits for most covered benefits applies to *every* health plan, whether individual or group coverage.

174. What are essential health benefits?[2]

Insurance policies must cover these benefits in order to be certified and offered in exchanges, and all Medicaid state plans must cover these services by 2014. A definition of essential health benefits is found in Part I, Q 2.

---

1. PHSA §2711.
2. See http://cciio.cms.gov/programs/marketreforms/annuallimit/index.html.

175. What exceptions to the annual limit rules are there?

The annual limit rules do not apply to "excepted benefits." The rules are not specific as to whether there can be non-dollar limits, such as limits on certain types of visits to providers. As noted, self-funded, large group market, and grandfathered health plans are not required to offer essential health benefits, but they are not subject to the prohibition on annual limits on the essential health benefits they do offer.[1] The rule does not apply to health flexible spending arrangements, medical savings accounts, or health savings accounts. If a health reimbursement arrangement (HRA) is integrated with other coverage as part of a group health plan, and the other coverage standing alone would comply with this rule, then the HRA will not be subject to the rule.[2]

The rule generally does not apply to retiree-only stand-alone HRAs. The tri-agency task force (HHS, DOL, and Treasury) has requested comments regarding the application of the rule to non-retiree-only stand-alone HRAs.

The regulations clarify that the rule does not preclude a plan from excluding all benefits with respect to a particular condition. If the plan provides any benefits for a condition, however, the rule applies.

176. Are any waivers to the annual limit rule available?

Yes. Some plans (typically "mini-med" plans offering restricted benefits) were eligible for a waiver from the rules concerning annual dollar limits, if complying with the limit would mean a significant decrease in benefits coverage or a significant increase in premiums. On June 17, 2011, the Centers for Medicare & Medicaid Services (CMS) introduced a process for plans that have already received waivers and want to renew those waivers for plan or policy years beginning before January 1, 2014. Revised guidance extends the duration of waivers that have been granted through 2013, if applicants submitted annual information about their plan and comply with requirements to ensure that their enrollees understand the limits of their coverage.

As a condition of receiving a waiver, a plan must provide a notice explaining to participants that the plan does not meet the annual limit requirements.[3]

Lifetime Limits on Essential Health Benefits Eliminated

177. When are the rules against lifetime limits effective?

Unlike the rules for annual limits, there is no waiver procedure for the rules against lifetime limits. Effective for plan years beginning on or after September 23, 2010, group health plans and insurers, other than grandfathered plans, may not impose any lifetime limit on the dollar

---

1. Frequently Asked Questions on Essential Health Benefits Bulletin, Q/A-10, at http://cciio.cms.gov/resources/files/Files2/02172012/ehb-faq-508.pdf.
2. Preamble to Interim Final Rules Relating to Preexisting Condition Exclusions, Lifetime and Annual Limits, Rescissions, and Patient Protections Under PPACA, 75 Fed. Reg. 37188, 37190 (June 28, 2010).
3. OCIIO Sub-Regulatory Guidance (OCIIO 2010-1A): Supplemental Guidance, at http://cciio.cms.gov/resources/files/annual_limits_waiver_guidance.pdf.

amount of essential health benefits for any individual.[1] As noted, self-funded, large group market, and grandfathered health plans are not required to offer essential health benefits but are subject to the prohibition on lifetime limits on the essential health benefits they offer.[2] As noted above in Q 173, plans are not prohibited, however, from placing lifetime dollar limits on specific covered benefits that are not essential health benefits to the extent such limits are otherwise permitted under applicable federal or state law.[3] The rules against lifetime limits apply to both in-network and out-of-network benefits.[4] All coverages offered on the exchanges will offer essential health benefits.

The applicable essential health benefits benchmark for the state in which the insurance policy is issued would determine the essential health benefits for all participants, regardless of the employee's state of residence or domicile.[5] The preventive services described in Section 2713 of the PHS Act are part of essential health benefits.[6] Beginning January 1, 2014, all Medicaid benchmark and benchmark-equivalent plans must include at least the ten statutory categories of EHBs.[7]

Dependent Coverage Extended to Children until Age Twenty-six

178. What are the rules that require extending coverage to children of the insured until the child reaches age twenty-six?

The until age 26 adult child coverage requirement is the following:

A group health plan and a health insurance issuer offering group or individual health insurance coverage that provides dependent coverage of children shall continue to make such coverage available for an adult child until the child turns 26 years of age. Nothing in this section shall require a health plan or a health insurance issuer described in the preceding sentence to make coverage available for a child of a child receiving dependent coverage.[8]

Thus, coverage is available until the day before the child's twenty-sixth birthday. Therefore, unless extended by the plan until the end of the year, coverage terminates at age twenty-six.

Like all of health reform, the age twenty-six rules do not apply to "excepted benefits," but only to major medical coverage.

---

1. PHSA §2711(a)(1)(A); Treas. Reg. §54.9815-2711T(a)(1); DOL Reg. §2590.715-2711(a)(1); HHS Reg. §147.126(a)(1).
2. Frequently Asked Questions on Essential Health Benefits Bulletin, Q/A-10, at http://cciio.cms.gov/resources/files/Files2/02172012/ehb-faq-508. pdf.
3. PHSA §2711(b); Treas. Reg. §54.9815-2711T(b); DOL Reg. §2590.715-2711(b); HHS Reg. §147.126(b).
4. Nonbinding comments of James Mayhew, Office of Consumer Information and Insurance Oversight, Centers for Medicare & Medicaid Services of HHS, Department of Labor Affordable Care Act Compliance Assistance Webcast Series: Part I(September 7, 2010).
5. Frequently Asked Questions on Essential Health Benefits Bulletin, Q/A-11, at http://cciio.cms.gov/resources/files/Files2/02172012/ehb-faq-508. pdf.
6. Frequently Asked Questions on Essential Health Benefits Bulletin, Q/A-12, at http://cciio.cms.gov/resources/files/Files2/02172012/ehb-faq-508. pdf.
7. Frequently Asked Questions on Essential Health Benefits Bulletin, Q/A-20, at http://cciio.cms.gov/resources/files/Files2/02172012/ehb-faq-508. pdf.
8. PHSA §2714.

179. When was the until age twenty-six coverage requirement effective?

The until age twenty-six rule is effective for plan years beginning on or after September 23, 2010.[1] For policies in the individual market, the mandate is applicable for the initial period of coverage beginning on or after September 23, 2010, regardless of what the policy year is.[2] Grandfathered plans only need to cover children not eligible for coverage from their own employer's health plan (other than coverage as a dependent child) until the plan year beginning in 2014.[3]

For income tax purposes, the change is effective March 30, 2010.[4]

180. What about adult children who were previously ineligible for coverage who became eligible for the first plan year beginning on or after September 23, 2010?

The regulations required a notice to these newly eligible adult children and an enrollment period for plans meeting specified conditions.[5]

181. What is the definition of a child for this purpose?

There is no statutory or regulatory definition of the term "child" for this purpose as there is for income tax purposes. The plan and summary plan description (SPD) should provide a clear definition of "child" that accurately reflects the plan sponsor's intent as to the categories of individuals for whom coverage is intended to be extended until age twenty-six.

In defining which children under age twenty-six are eligible for coverage, the interim final regulations prohibit a plan from requiring a child to satisfy any conditions other than "a relationship between a child and the participant."[6] No further guidance was offered as to the meaning of "child."

Relatives such as nephews and nieces are not required to be covered to age twenty-six, even if the plan grants them eligibility.[7] Thus, it is permissible for a plan that covers them to impose a lower age limit with respect to coverage for them.

However, some plans permit or prohibit coverage of stepchildren, grandchildren, foster children, or other categories of children. If a plan provides coverage to children in these categories, it is not clear whether the plan can impose satisfaction of additional conditions before providing coverage. For example, if a plan provides coverage for stepchildren, is it required to cover all

---

1. PPACA §1004(a).
2. HHS, DOL & TREASURY, FAQs About the Affordable Care Act Implementation Part II, Q/A-9, at http://www.dol.gov/ebsa/faqs/faq-aca2.html.
3. PPACA, Pub. L. No. 111-148, §1251(a).
4. IRS Notice 2010-38.
5. DOL Reg. §2590.715-2714(f); Treas. Reg. §54.9815-2714T(f); HHS Reg. §147.120(f); Interim Final Rules Relating to Dependent Coverage of Children to Age 26 Under PPACA, 26 CFR Parts 54 and 602; 29 CFR Part 2590; 45 CFR Parts 144, 146, and 147; 75 Fed. Reg. 27121 (May 13, 2010).
6. Interim Final Rules Relating to Dependent Coverage of Children to Age 26 Under PPACA, 26 CFR Parts 54 and 602; 29 CFR Part 2590; 45 CFR Parts 144, 146, and 147; 75 Fed. Reg. 27121, 27134 (May 13, 2010).
7. HHS, DOL & TREASURY, FAQs About the Affordable Care Act Implementation Part I, Q14, available at http://www.dol.gov/ebsa/faqs/faq-aca.html.

stepchildren, or can it limit coverage to those stepchildren who reside with or are financially dependent on a plan participant?

182. Must all health plans now offer the until age twenty-six coverage?

No. Plans are not required to offer any dependent care coverage. However, if a group health plan or insurer provides coverage of children, the plan must make such coverage available for a child until age twenty-six. In addition, a "uniformity rule" requires that coverage for children under age twenty-six cannot vary based on age.[1] So a copay can be charged (so long as it is not for preventive services) for all persons age nineteen and over.

183. If adult child coverage is provided, must it eliminate prohibitions against preexisting conditions for adult children before 2014?

While this is not specifically addressed, it seems that the answer is "no." Health reform prohibits preexisting condition exclusions for children under age nineteen, effective for the first plan year beginning on or after September 23, 2010.[2]

184. Does this rule require the elimination of preexisting condition exclusions for all Code Section 152(f)(1) children up to age twenty-six?

The IRS has informally indicated that HHS, DOL, and Treasury agree that the prohibition on benefit variance does not mandate an elimination of preexisting condition exclusions up to age twenty-six.[3]

185. May a plan exclude, for the up to age twenty-six rule, children based on tax-dependent status, residency, age, income, employment, marital, or tax-filing status?

If a plan covers dependents, then the answer is no, at least not for children who are Code Section 152(f) children, i.e., dependents.[4] These factors cannot be used whether the child is a minor or an adult. The statute itself makes clear that marriage is not a disqualification.[5] However, coverage need not be offered to the child's spouse.[6]

Generally, a plan cannot deny eligibility to a Code Section 152(f) child because that child is eligible for other coverage.[7] Thus, if a plan offers dependent coverage to Code Section 152(f) children of employees, it must extend coverage even to Code Section 152(f) children who are eligible for coverage through another parent's employer or a spouse's employer. As discussed at Q 179, for a limited time, grandfathered plans need not offer dependent coverage to a child

1. DOL Reg. §2590.715-2714(a); Treas. Reg. §54.9815-2714T; HHS Reg. §147.120(a).
2. PHSA §2704.
3. Nonbinding comments of Russ Weinheimer, IRS Attorney, Department of Labor Affordable Care Act Compliance Assistance Webcast (September 7, 2010).
4. DOL Reg. §2590.715-2714(b); Treas. Reg. §54.9815-2714T(b); HHS Reg. §147.120(b).
5. PHSA §2714(b) because the phrase "who is not married" was removed.
6. Interim Final Rules Relating to Dependent Coverage of Children to Age 26 Under PPACA, 26 CFR Parts 54 and 602; 29 CFR Part 2590.45 CFR Parts 144, 146, and 147, 75 Fed. Reg. 27121 (May 13, 2010).
7. DOL Reg. §2590.715-2714(b); Treas. Reg. §54.9815-2714T(b); HHS Reg. §147.120(b).

under age twenty-six who is eligible to enroll in another employer-sponsored group health plan, other than that of the other parent's employer.[1]

186. Given the uncertain definition of a child, what should an employer or other health plan sponsor do?

Given the potential for litigation and liability for medical care for someone who should have been covered but was not, the plan sponsor should not impose conditions beyond the relationship with the participant on any child within the Code section 152(f)(1) dependent definition. This means, for example, that a plan should treat all stepchildren and foster children equally. i.e., cover all or none until they turn twenty-six.

187. May a plan allow a choice of coverage as an employee or dependent coverage as a child, but not both?

This provision would seem permissible, since the child could choose whether to enroll for dependent coverage (through an employed parent) or for the child's own employee coverage. Again, absent a clear answer, the prudent course would be not to use this plan provision.

188. What about the children of a person's same-sex partner?

Stepchildren are the children of an individual's spouse, and in states that recognize same-sex marriage, the child of an employee's same-sex spouse would likely be treated as a stepchild. It is unclear whether the stepchild status under state law would carry over for federal law purposes given the Defense of Marriage Act (DOMA) and its prohibition on treating same-sex couples as spouses for purposes of federal law. Arguably, DOMA's effect should be confined to determining who is a spouse for federal law purposes and not who is a stepchild; however, the issue is uncertain.

189. What if a plan covers grandchildren? Does the until age twenty-six requirement apply to them?

No. The coverage mandate does not require coverage to be offered to a grandchild of an employee.[2] Some plans previously extended eligibility to an employee's grandchild if the grandchild was the employee's tax dependent. A plan may place eligibility conditions on grandchildren (e.g., requiring that they be qualifying children or qualifying relatives of the employee), since they are not within the definition of Code Section 152(f) children.[3]

190. Who is a child for income tax purposes and what is the tax treatment of the until age twenty-six coverage?

Health reform revised IRC Section 105(b) now makes excludable from an employee's income employer and health plan reimbursements for medical care attributable to the employee's child

---

1. PPACA, Pub. L. No. 111-148, §1001(5).
2. DOL Reg. §2590.715-2714(c); Treas. Reg. §54.9815-2714T(c); HHS Reg. §147.120(c).
3. HHS, DOL & TREASURY, FAQs About the Affordable Care Act Implementation Part I, Q14, at http://www.dol.gov/ebsa/faqs/faq-aca. html.

to the extent such child is not yet age twenty-seven during the taxable year. The 2010 law also included numerous conforming changes to the IRC regarding voluntary employees beneficiary associations (VEBAs), IRC Section 401(h) transfer accounts, and the deduction for medical insurance for self-employed persons under IRC Section 162(l). As discussed in Q 194, health reform inadvertently failed to amend IRC Section 106, but the IRS is treating that provision as if it were amended.

IRS Notice 2010-38 addresses these tax changes in connection with the adult child coverage provisions of the PHSA. Employer-provided coverage for an employee's Code Section 152(f) children under age twenty-seven is now nontaxable[1] for the "taxable year" (see discussion in Q 192 for meaning of "taxable year") in addition to coverage for an employee's Code Section 105(b) dependents. For income tax purposes, a "child" is "a son, daughter, stepson, or stepdaughter of the taxpayer, or ... an eligible foster child of the taxpayer."[2] This definition is used when determining the taxability of employer-provided coverage for children under age twenty-seven.[3] So children who have their twenty-sixth birthday mid-year still enjoy favorable income tax treatment, as does the plan, until the end of the plan year or the policy year for individual policies.

191. Do the Internal Revenue Code's dependency tests apply in determining qualifying adult child status?

No. Notice 2010-38 makes clear that the age, limit, residency, and support tests applicable to IRC Section 152 dependents do not apply in determining whether an individual qualifies as an adult child for purposes of tax-free employer-paid coverage. Thus, to qualify, an adult child need only be younger than twenty-seven for the taxable year at issue and be a legal child, stepchild, or eligible foster child of the employee in order to qualify.

192. What is a "taxable year" for employees?

The law amended IRC Section 105(b) to make excludable from an employee's income any employer-paid coverage attributable to the employee's child to the extent such child is not yet age twenty-seven during the "taxable year" at issue. Notice 2010-38 makes clear that "taxable year" means the employee's taxable year and that employers may assume that an employee's taxable year is the calendar year.[4]

193. How does a plan sponsor know the age of adult children?

Employers may rely on employees' representations regarding their children's date of birth.[5] The guidance is silent as to whether such representations must be in writing, but requiring a written statement would be prudent for employers.

1. IRS Notice 2010-38.
2. IRC Sec. 152(f)(1).
3. IRS Notice 2010-38.
4. IRS Notice 2010-38.
5. IRS Notice 2010-38.

194. Will the employer's payments to a health plan for adult children also be given favorable tax treatment?

Yes, although health reform inadvertently failed to amend IRC Section 106. Nevertheless, the IRS will issue regulations for IRC Section 106 that make excludable the employer-paid coverage itself.[1] "On and after March 30, 2010, both coverage under an employer-provided accident or health plan and amounts paid or reimbursed under such a plan for medical care expenses of ... an employee's [qualifying adult] child ... are excluded from the employee's gross income."[2]

195. Can mid-year election changes be made to cafeteria plans due to the new adult child until age twenty-six rules?

Yes, such changes can be made on and after March 30, 2010. Although existing rules[3] do not permit mid-year changes to cafeteria plan elections when a coverage change results from an individual either qualifying or no longer qualifying as an adult child (because such election changes may only apply with respect to an employee, spouse, and dependents based on a modified IRC Section 152 definition), the IRS will provide relief. Notice 2010-38 expressly states that "IRS and Treasury intend to amend the regulations under §1.125-4, effective retroactively to March 30, 2010, to include change in status events affecting nondependent children under age 27, including becoming newly eligible for coverage or eligible for coverage beyond the date on which the child otherwise would have lost coverage."

196. What was the deadline for amending a cafeteria plan for the until age twenty-six law change?

If an employer wanted to permit adult children's coverage to be offered in its cafeteria plan in 2010, the plan could have been operated to do so as long as it was amended by December 31, 2010, and retroactively effective to the date when this provision was implemented, but no earlier than March 30, 2010.

Notice 2010-38 provides a transition rule for cafeteria plan amendments. Generally, cafeteria plan amendments must be made prior to a change becoming effective.[4] Nevertheless, Notice 2010-38 states as follows:

> Notwithstanding this general rule, as of March 30, 2010, employers may permit employees to immediately make pre-tax salary reduction contributions for accident or health benefits under a cafeteria plan (including a health FSA) for children under age 27, even if the cafeteria plan has not yet been amended to cover these individuals. However, a retroactive amendment to a cafeteria plan to cover children under age 27 must be made no later than December 31, 2010, and must be effective retroactively to the first date in 2010 when employees are

---

1. Notice 2010-38 addresses this issue and notes that "[t]here is no indication that Congress intended to provide a broader exclusion in Code section 105(b) than in Code section 106," and that, therefore, "IRS and Treasury intend to amend the regulations under Code section 106, retroactively to March 30, 2010, to provide that coverage for an employee's child under age 27 is excluded from gross income."
2. Notice 2010-38.
3. Treas. Reg. §1.125-4(c).
4. Prop. Treas. Reg. §1.125-1(c).

permitted to make pre-tax salary reduction contributions to cover children under age 27 (but in no event before March 30, 2010).

197. What other changes were made for HRAs, FICA, FUTA, VEBAs, and Section 401(h) accounts?

Notice 2010-38 states the following:

- Its principles apply to health reimbursement arrangements (HRAs).

- Adult Child coverage is excepted from wages for FICA/FUTA purposes.

- Its principles apply to VEBAs,[1] IRC Section 401(h) transfer accounts, and deductions for self-employed individuals under IRC Section 162(l).

Regarding VEBAs, for purposes of providing for the payment of sick and accident benefits to members of a VEBA and their dependents, the term "dependent" includes any qualifying adult child (i.e., a child who has not attained age twenty-seven by the close of the calendar year).

As amended by the health reform law, IRC Section 401(h) "provides that the term dependent includes any individual who is a retired employee's [qualifying adult] child" (i.e., a child who has not attained age twenty-seven by the close of the calendar year).

IRC Section 162(l), as amended, covers expenses associated with medical insurance attributable to a qualifying adult child (i.e., a child who has not attained age twenty-seven by the close of the calendar year).

198. Do the until age twenty-six adult child rules apply to HSAs?

No. Health savings accounts (HSAs) are not group health plans. However, the law does apply to an underlying high deductible health plan (HDHP) offered in conjunction with the HSA. The HSA rules were not amended by healthcare reform to allow medical expenses of nondependent children under age twenty-seven to be reimbursed tax-free from a parent's HSA.[2]

Example: A parent has coverage under her employer's HDHP and enrolls her twenty-four-year-old daughter, in the coverage. The coverage provided by the HDHP is not taxable to the employee, because it is a group health plan. However, distributions from the parent's HSA are not taxed only if they reimburse or pay medical expenses of the HSA account holder, spouse, or dependents. If the daughter incurs medical expenses that are not paid by the HDHP, any distributions that the parent takes from the HSA to cover those expenses will be taxable because the daughter does not qualify as her dependent for HSA purposes. She is not a qualifying child, nor a qualifying relative unless she is disabled

---

1. Voluntary Employees Beneficiary Associations, which are governed by IRC Sec. 501(c)(9).
2. IRC Sec. 223(d)(2)(A).

or the parent provides more than 50 percent of the daughter's support.[1] However, the daughter could create an HSA and the parent could fund it.

Civil Rights Discrimination by Health Programs Prohibited

199. What existing anti-discrimination laws were affected by health reform?

Health reform[2] prohibits discrimination by any health program or activity. A plan may not exclude persons from participation in, or deny benefits under, any health program or activity for a reason that is discriminatory under the Civil Rights Act (race, color, or national origin), the Education Amendments Act (sex), the Age Discrimination in Employment Act (age), or the Rehabilitation Act (disability).

200. What guidance has been issued on these rules?

Although health programs and activities are subject to these nondiscrimination requirements, the terms are undefined in the statute. On August 6, 2012, HHS issued seven questions and answers (Q&As) addressing nondiscrimination rules under healthcare reform that apply to health programs and activities receiving federal financial assistance.[3]

Examples of these, HHS clarified that people who claim that they are not getting health care because of how they look can file a complaint. There will be no Section 1557 regulation on the definition of what is masculine or feminine,[4] and sex-change surgery need not be covered.[5]

The Office for Civil Rights (OCR) has enforcement authority for health programs and activities that receive federal financial assistance from HHS.[6]

Preventive Health Services Required

201. What does health reform do to encourage preventive care?

To encourage people to be treated as early as possible, health reform added Section 2713 of the Public Health Service Act (PHSA). It provides that a group health and a health insurance issuer (as to both group and individual coverage) must provide benefits for, and may not impose cost-sharing (with certain out-of-network exceptions) with respect to, preventive care and screening.

This rule is effective for plan years (policy years in the individual market) beginning on or after September 23, 2010, and it affects all health plans that are not grandfathered health plans or that provide "excepted benefits."

---

1. IRC Sec. 223(d)(2)(A) (for HSA purposes, dependent is as defined in IRC Sec. 152 without regard to subsections (b)(1), (b)(2), and (d)(1)(B).
2. PPACA §1557.
3. http://www.hhs.gov/ocr/civilrights/resources/laws/section1557_questions_answers.html.
4. http://www.hhs.gov/ocr/civilrights/resources/laws/section1557_questions_answers.html, Q/A-3.
5. http://www.hhs.gov/ocr/civilrights/resources/laws/section1557_questions_answers.html, Q/A-4.
6. http://www.hhs.gov/ocr/civilrights/resources/laws/section1557_questions_answers.html, Q/A-1.

Women's preventive service rules are generally effective August 1, 2012, although, as discussed in Q 204, there is an exemption for contraception and sterilization for religious organizations and a one-year delay for social organizations sponsored by religious organizations.

Health plans that violate Section 2713 could be subject to the assessment of penalties of $100 per day per affected employee as long as the violation continues.[1]

202. What guidance has been issued by the agencies regarding the preventive care coverage requirements?

The Departments of Health and Human Services (HHS), Treasury and Labor (collectively the agencies) issued interim final regulations regarding the new preventive care coverage requirements.[2] As discussed in Q 208, they were later amended as to contraceptive services.

203. What preventive services are covered?

Generally, group health plans that are not "grandfathered health plans" must cover and waive all cost-sharing requirements for the following "recommended preventive services":

- Evidence-based items or services with an "A" or "B" rating from the U.S. Preventive Services Task Force (USPSTF) ;[3]

- Immunizations for routine use in children, adolescents, and adults with a recommendation in effect from the Advisory Committee on Immunization Practices of the Centers for Disease Control and Prevention;[4]

- Evidence-informed preventive care screenings for infants, children, and adolescents provided in guidelines supported by the Health Resources and Services Administration (HRSA);[5] and

- Evidence-informed preventive care and screening for women provided in guidelines supported by HRSA and not otherwise addressed by the USPSTF.[6]

The complete list of recommendations and guidelines that must be covered by plans is at http://www.healthcare.gov/law/resources/regulations/prevention/recommendations.html (the List) and will be continually updated to reflect both new recommendations and guidelines and revised or removed guidelines.

---

1. IRC Sec. 4980D, and the penalty must be self-reported on Form 8928.
2. Interim Final Rules for Group Health Plans and Health Insurance Issuers Relating to Coverage of Preventive Health Services Under PPACA, 26 CFR Part 54; 29 CFR Part 2590; 45 CFR Part 147, 75 Fed. Reg. 41726 (July 19, 2010).
3. PHSA §2713(a)(1); Treas. Reg. §54.9815-2713T(a)(1)(i); DOL Reg. §2590.715-2713(a)(1)(i); HHS Reg. §147.130(a)(1)(i).
4. PHSA §2713(a)(2); Treas. Reg. §54.9815-2713T(a)(1)(ii); DOL Reg. §2590.715-2713(a)(1)(ii); HHS Reg. §147.130(a)(1)(ii).
5. PHSA §2713(a)(3); Treas. Reg. §54.9815-2713T(a)(1)(iii); DOL Reg. §2590.715-2713(a)(1)(iii); HHS Reg. §147.130(a)(1)(iii).
6. PHSA §2713(a)(4); Treas. Reg. §54.9815-2713T(a)(1)(iv); DOL Reg. §2590.715-2713(a)(1)(iv); HHS Reg. §147.130(a)(1)(iv). The regulations note that HHS is developing these.

Plans are not required to provide coverage (or waive cost-sharing) for any item or service that ceases to be a recommended preventive service, for example, if the USPSTF downgrades a recommended preventive service from a rating of "B" to a rating of "C" or "D." Likewise, plans may provide coverage for items and services in addition to those included in the recommendations and guidelines (and such services may be subject to cost sharing).

204. Are there any limits on the frequency, method, treatment, or setting for preventive services to prevent patients from abusing this rule?

Yes. Reasonable medical management techniques can be used when the applicable recommendations and guidelines do not specify the frequency, method, treatment, or setting for a particular preventive service. Plans and insurers may use reasonable medical management techniques to determine any coverage limitations.[1]

205. What are the requirements as to the prohibition on patient payment, i.e., cost-sharing requirements?

Generally, cost sharing for network providers with respect to "recommended preventive services" is prohibited. "Cost sharing" for these rules includes deductibles, copayments, and coinsurance. Cost sharing is permitted for any item or service that ceases to be a recommended preventive service or for services or treatments in addition to those included in the specified recommendations.

Cost-sharing is permitted for office visits when preventive services are billed or tracked as individual encounter data separately or are not the primary purpose of an office visit. Conversely, cost-sharing cannot be imposed when preventive services are not billed or not tracked as individual encounter data separately and are the primary purpose of an office visit.

Example: A child visits an in-network pediatrician for a preventive care screening. As a result of the screening, the pediatrician recommends that the child undergo surgery for a heart disorder. Because the preventive care screening is a recommended preventive service, the plan cannot impose a cost-sharing requirement. However, the plan may impose a cost-sharing requirement for the child's heart surgery, which resulted from the preventive care screening.

Example: A child covered by a group health plan visits an in-network pediatrician to receive an annual physical exam that is a recommended preventive service. During the office visit, the child receives additional services that are not recommended preventive services. The provider bills the plan for the office visit. Because the primary purpose for the office visit was to provide recommended preventive services, and the plan was not billed separately for the additional services, the plan may not impose a cost-sharing requirement with respect to the office visit.

---

1. Treas. Reg. §54.9815-2713T(a)(4); DOL Reg. §2590.715-2713(a)(4); HHS Reg. §147.130(a)(4).

Example: A patient is covered by a group health plan and visits an in-network healthcare provider. While visiting the provider, the patient is screened for cholesterol abnormalities with a rating of A or B (which are recommended preventive services). The provider bills the plan separately for the office visit and for the laboratory work of the cholesterol screening test. The plan may not impose any cost-sharing requirements with respect to the separately billed laboratory work of the cholesterol screening test. However, the plan may impose cost-sharing requirements for the office visit since it was billed separately from the recommended preventive service.

Example: A patient visits his network provider for abdominal pain. During the visit, he has a blood pressure screening that is a recommended preventive service. The provider bills the plan for the office visit, and there is no separate bill for the blood pressure screening. The plan may impose cost sharing on the office visit because the primary purpose of the office visit was not the delivery of a recommended preventive service.

206. How do these rules deal with in-network and out-of-network providers?

The regulations clarify that a network-based plan is not required to provide coverage for recommended preventive services delivered by an out-of-network provider and may impose cost-sharing requirements for any such out-of-network services that are offered.[1]

207. What rules apply for women's preventive services?

New rules went into effect for women's preventive health benefits on August 1, 2012, and for health plans, other than grandfathered plans, for the first plan year beginning on or after August 1, 2012, except for contraception and sterilization services for women employed by certain religious organizations or social organizations operated by religious organizations, which are exempt or have a delayed effective date, respectively.

In addition to previously discussed mandated preventive services the enhanced services mandate requires no cost sharing for women for:

- Well-woman visits

- Screening for gestational diabetes

- HPV and DNA testing for women thirty years and older

- Sexually transmitted infection counseling

- HIV screening and counseling

- FDA-approved contraceptive methods and contraceptive counseling. (Some religious groups may qualify for a complete or temporary exemption from covering contraceptive counseling and methods as discussed in Q 208.)

---

1. Treas. Reg. §54.9815-2713T(a)(3); DOL Reg. §2590.715-2713(a)(3); HHS Reg. §147.130(a)(3).

- Breastfeeding support, supplies, and counseling

- Domestic violence screening and counseling

As changes occur, an updated list can be found at http://www.hrsa.gov/womensguidelines.

208. How does health reform deal with contraception and sterilization services for employees of religious organizations and social organizations sponsored by religious groups?

Section 2713(a)(4) of the PHS Act requires that non-grandfathered group health plans and health insurance issuers offering non-grandfathered group or individual health insurance coverage provide benefits for certain women's preventive health services without cost sharing, as provided by Health Resources and Services Administration (HRSA) guidelines. The August 1, 2011, HRSA Guidelines include all FDA approved contraceptive methods, sterilization procedures, and patient education and counseling for women with reproductive capacity, as prescribed by a health care provider (collectively, contraceptive services). The HRSA guidelines do not cover men.

The final contraception regulations promote two goals. First, they provide women with access to contraceptive coverage without cost sharing, thereby advancing the compelling government interests in safeguarding public health and ensuring that women have equal access to health care. Second, they protect certain not-for-profit religious organizations with religious objections to providing contraceptive coverage from having to contract, arrange, pay, or refer for such coverage.

In July 2013, the agencies (DOL, HHS, and IRS) issued revised final regulations, changing how the previous 2012 regulations applied the contraceptive coverage mandate to not-for-profit religious organizations. Under the 2013 final regulations, a religious employer includes (1) churches, their integrated auxiliaries, and conventions or associations of churches[1] or (2) the exclusively religious activities of any religious order[2] and is exempt from the mandate.[3] With the exception of the amendments to the religious employer exemption, which apply to group health plans and health insurance issuers for plan years beginning on or after August 1, 2013, these 2013 final regulations apply to group health plans and health insurance issuers for plan years beginning on or after January 1, 2014.

The prior exemption requirements that the organization had to have as its purpose the inculcation of religious values and had to primarily employ and serve persons who share its religious tenets were removed. Under the 2013 final regulation, an eligible organization is an organization that (1) opposes providing coverage for some or all of the contraceptive services required to be covered under section 2713 of the PHSA on account of religious objections; (2) is

---

1. IRC Sec. 6033(a)(3)(A)(i).
2. IRC Sec. 6033(a)(3)(A)(iii).
3. The revised religious employer exemption applies to group health plans and health insurers for plan years beginning on or after August 1, 2013. HHS Reg. §147.131(a): Coverage of Certain Preventive Services Under the Affordable Care Act, 26 CFR Part 54; 29 CFR Part 2590; 45 CFR Parts 147, 148, and 156; 78 Fed. Reg. 39869 (July 2, 2013).

organized and operates as a not-for-profit entity; (3) holds itself out as a religious organization; and (4) certifies that it satisfies the first three criteria. An eligible organization also includes student health insurance coverage arranged by eligible organizations that are institutions of higher learning.

Therefore, group health plans of not-for-profit houses of worship that provide educational, charitable, or social services to their communities qualify for the exemption. An employer that is a not-for-profit entity is not limited to any particular form of entity under state law, and it is not necessary to determine the federal tax-exempt status of a not-for-profit entity in determining whether the religious employer exemption applies.

The accommodation for eligible organizations with nongrandfathered insured plans requires the insurer to assume sole responsibility for providing separate payment for contraceptive services directly to participants and beneficiaries, without cost-sharing, premium, fee, or other charge to plan participants, beneficiaries, or to the religious organization or its plan. The payments are not individual health insurance policies.

For eligible organizations with self-insured plans, the TPA becomes an ERISA plan administrator and claims administrator solely for the purpose of providing payments for contraceptive services for participants and beneficiaries at no cost to plan participants or beneficiaries or to the eligible organization. The TPA must provide or arrange separate payments for contraceptive services for participants and beneficiaries in the plan without cost-sharing, premium, fee, or other charge to plan participants, beneficiaries, the eligible religious organization, or its plan. The TPA can provide the payments on its own, or it can arrange for an insurer or other entity to provide the payments. Like the payments for contraceptive services under the accommodation for insured plans, the payments are not health insurance policies.[1]

Any organization seeking accommodation as an eligible organization certifies to its insurer or TPA that it meets the definition of an eligible organization. In turn, insurers or TPAs provide an annual notice of the availability of the coverage to participants and beneficiaries.[2]

Employers participating in a multiple employer plan are required to independently qualify as religious employers or eligible organizations to take advantage of the exemption or accommodations.[3]

Not-for-profit employers that do not fit within the previously outlined exemption and do not currently cover contraceptive services are not required to provide contraception coverage until plan years beginning on or after Jan. 1, 2014.[4]

---

1. Treas. Reg. §54.9815-2713(b); DOL Reg. §2590.715-2713(b); Coverage of Certain Preventive Services Under the Affordable Care Act, 26 CFR Part 54; 29 CFR Part 2590; 45 CFR Parts 147, 148, and 156; 78 Fed. Reg. 39869, 39879 (July 2, 2013).
2. HHS Reg. §147.131(d); Treas. Reg. §54.9815-2713(d); DOL Reg. §2590.715-2713(d).
3. Coverage of Certain Preventive Services Under the Affordable Care Act, 26 CFR Part 54; 29 CFR Part 2590; 45 CFR Parts 147, 148, and 156; 78 Fed. Reg. 39869, 39886 (July 2, 2013).
4. CCIIO Bulletin: Guidance on the Temporary Enforcement Safe Harbor for Certain Employers, Group Health Plans and Group Health Insurance Issuers with Respect to the Requirement to Cover Contraceptive Services Without Cost Sharing Under PHSA §2713, ERISA §715(a)(1), and Code §9815(a)(1) (June 28, 2013) at http://www.cms.gov/CCIIO/Resources/Regulations-and-Guidance/Downloads/preventive-services-guidance-6-28-2013.pdf.

- The safe harbor is also available to not-for-profit organizations with religious objections to some but not all contraceptive coverage;

- Group health plans will not be ineligible for the safe harbor merely because an attempt made before February 10, 2012, to exclude or limit contraceptive coverage proved unsuccessful; and

- The safe harbor may be invoked without prejudice by not-for-profit organizations that are uncertain whether they qualify for the religious employer exemption (i.e., doing so will not preclude an otherwise-eligible employer from later invoking the exemption).[1]

The HHS bulletin requires specific notice and certification requirements that these organizations must meet in order to qualify. Specific language must be used to satisfy these requirements. The notice must be distributed "in connection with enrollment (or re-enrollment)" for coverage that is effective beginning each plan year before January 1, 2014. Thus, for a calendar-year plan with an open enrollment period beginning November 1, the notice must be provided to participants on or after November 1, 2013. The notice is required to be provided by the plan, although the plan may delegate this responsibility to its insurer or TPA. With respect to insured coverage, unless it accepts in writing the responsibility to provide the notice, an insurer does not lose protection under the temporary enforcement safe harbor solely because the notice is not distributed by the plan or because the insurer relies in good faith on a representation by the plan that turns out to be incorrect.

209. Are there any other options for religious organizations that object to these rules?

Employers that do not intend to comply with Section 2713 could terminate their group health plan and encourage their employees to obtain individual policies. As of January 1, 2014, such individual policies must be offered on state health insurance exchanges on a guaranteed issue, guaranteed renewability basis. However, employers with at least fifty full-time equivalent employees or with at least thirty-one full-time employees that do not offer health coverage are subject to penalties.[2]

Rescissions Limited

210. How does health reform limit insurers' ability to terminate coverage?

Before enactment of health reform in 2010, the Public Health Service Act (PHSA) included some protections regarding cancellation of coverage. Additional protections were also provided

---

1. Id.
2. Employers with at least 50 full-time equivalent employees must offer insurance meeting specified requirements or pay a $2,000 penalty per full-time worker (in excess of 30 full-time workers) if any of its full-time employees receive a federal premium subsidy through a Health Care Exchange. IRC Sec. 4980H(c)(2)(D). A different penalty applies for employers of at least 50 full-time equivalent employees that offer insurance that does not meet federal requirements. IRC Sec. 4980H(b)(1).

in the HIPAA nondiscrimination rules. This new rescission regulation builds on the existing protections, and sets a federal floor on rescissions.

The restriction limiting rescissions is effective for plan years (for individual policies in the individual market, policy years) beginning on or after September 23, 2010.

States may limit rescissions beyond the limits of the federal health reform law.[1] The federal law prohibiting rescissions does not apply to "excepted benefits."

211. What is a rescission?

A "rescission" is a retroactive cancellation or discontinuance of coverage of an "enrollee," i.e., a person who is covered by the policy. Whether an individual or group policy, the statute indicates that a rescission can only apply to the individual who committed the fraud or intentional misrepresentation of a material fact.[2] However, the regulations contemplate that a group policy can be rescinded as well.[3] A cancellation or discontinuation of coverage is not a rescission if it:

- has only a prospective effect; or

- is effective retroactively to the extent it is attributable to a failure to timely pay required premiums or contributions toward the cost of coverage.[4]

A rescission is an adverse benefit determination that is subject to the healthcare reform internal claims and appeals and external review requirements discussed at Q 216 to Q 226.

212. When is an insurer allowed to rescind or terminate an individual or group policy retroactively?

An insurer may retroactively terminate a policy for fraud or an intentional misrepresentation of a material fact with notice.[5] Misrepresentations that are inadvertent are not intentional.[6]

The regulations require a group health plan or an issuer offering group coverage to provide at least thirty days' advance written notice to each participant who would be affected before coverage may be rescinded—regardless of whether the coverage is insured or self-insured, or whether the rescission applies to an entire group or only to an individual within the group (same rules apply with respect to a rescission of individual coverage).[7] The purpose of the waiting period is to provide individuals and plan sponsors with an opportunity to explore their rights to contest the rescission, or look for alternative coverage, as appropriate."[8]

---

1. Preamble, 75 Fed. Reg. 37188, 37192 (June 28, 2010).
2. PHSA §2712.
3. Preamble, 75 Fed. Reg. 37188, 37192 (June 28, 2010).
4. Treas. Reg. §54.9815-2712T(a)(2); DOL Reg. §2590.715-2712(a)(2); HHS Reg. §147.128(a)(2).
5. PHSA §2712.
6. Treas. Reg. §54.9815-2712T(a)(3), Example 1; DOL Reg. §2590.715-2712(a)(3), Example 1; HHS Reg. §147.128(a)(3), Example 1.
7. Treas. Reg. §54.9815-2712T(a)(1); DOL Reg. §2590.715-2712(a)(1); HHS Reg. §147.128(a)(1).
8. Preamble, 75 Fed. Reg. 37188, 37193 (June 28, 2010).

213. If an employer with an insured group plan covering employees working thirty hours or more a week forgets to advise the insurer that a covered employee's hours are reduced below thirty, can this individual's policy be rescinded?

No because there is no fraud or intentional material misrepresentation. However, the insurer could cancel the employee's coverage prospectively, subject to requirements of state and federal laws.[1]

214. What should the sponsor of an insured group plan do if the plan wants to be able to rescind coverage retroactively?

If a plan wants to be able to cancel coverage retroactively, the plan document and summary plan description (SPD) should define what constitutes fraud and what will be considered an intentional misrepresentation of material fact, consistent with the statute that will trigger the plan's right to rescind coverage. A frequent reason for retroactive cancellation of coverage is the enrollment of an ineligible dependent or adult child. In order to retain the right to rescind coverage of ineligible children and dependents, the SPD should clearly describe who is eligible for coverage and the requirements for documenting eligibility. The SPD should state that intentionally enrolling or continuing coverage for an ineligible individual constitutes fraud and an intentional misrepresentation of a material fact that will trigger rescission. In addition, the SPD should describe the results of rescission, including but not limited to liability for improper benefits paid.

215. Has the government declared any coverage terminations not to be rescissions?

Yes. An FAQ clarified several eligibility matters. For example, some employers' human resource departments may reconcile lists of eligible individuals with their plan or issuer via data feed only once per month. If a plan covers only active employees (subject to the COBRA continuation coverage provisions) and an employee pays no premiums for coverage after termination of employment, the agencies do not consider the retroactive elimination of coverage back to the date of termination of employment, due to delay in administrative record-keeping, to be a rescission.

Similarly, if a plan does not cover ex-spouses (subject to the COBRA continuation coverage provisions), the plan is not notified of a divorce, and the full COBRA premium is not paid by the employee or ex-spouse for coverage, the agencies do not consider a plan's termination of coverage retroactive to the divorce to be a rescission of coverage.[2]

New Claims and Appeals Procedures

216. What are health reform's required claims and appeals procedures?

Nongrandfathered group health plans (excluding those for "excepted benefits") are required to have internal claims and external appeals procedures in place for plan years beginning on

---

1. Treas. Reg. §54.9815-2712T(a)(3), Example 2; DOL Reg. §2590.715-2712(a)(3), Example 2; HHS Reg. §147.128(a)(3), Example 2.
2. See FAQs About the Affordable Care Act Implementation Part II, Q/A-7, at http://www.dol.gov/ebsa/faqs/faq-aca2.html.

and after September 23, 2010.[1] PPACA in the Public Health Service Act (PHSA) Section 2719 set forth standards for non-grandfathered group health plans, insured and self-insured, and for internal claims and appeals and external reviews. The Employee Benefits Security Administration (EBSA), IRS, and Department of Health and Human Services (HHS) published the interim final regulations implementing PHSA Section 2719 on July 23, 2010.[2] The regulations were updated and revised in June 2011.[3]

217. Were any of the requirements postponed?

Yes. The DOL's Employee Benefits Security Administration (EBSA) in Technical Release 2010-02 initially provided group health plans and self-funded nonfederal governmental health plans relief until July 1, 2011, from enforcement actions by IRS (including the otherwise applicable excise tax for noncompliance) and by EBSA for plans that work in good faith to implement the new regulatory internal claims and appeals rules. EBSA extended this grace period until January 1, 2012, in Technical Release 2011-01. The original grace period and new extension are, however, only for three minor new standards, less than 1 percent of the entire PPACA Claims Regulations, and have no effect on the PPACA statutory effective date of September 23, 2010, for the bulk of the PPACA Claims Regulations. Specifically, Technical Release 2011-01 extends the enforcement grace period until plan years beginning on or after January 1, 2012, with respect to standard #2 (regarding the timeframe for making urgent care claims decisions), standard #5 (regarding providing notices in a culturally and linguistically appropriate manner), and standard #7 (regarding substantial compliance).

Plans of a private-sector or church employer and those health plans subject to the Internal Revenue Code did not have to report any excise tax liability on Form 8928 for the rules extended by the grace period.[4]

Many state insurance departments offer claims assistance.[5]

218. Is there a minimum claim threshold under these new claim and appeal rules?

No. There is no *de minimis* exception for small claims eligible for external review, including some HRAs and dental and vision plans that do not qualify as excepted benefits. The appeals regulations specifically provide that the "state process may not impose a restriction on the minimum dollar amount of a claim for it to be eligible for external review."[6] Thus, there can be no minimum claims threshold. Although the appeals regulations and guidance are silent on this point for federal standards for external review, plans subject to the federal standards similarly are likely not permitted to impose minimum thresholds for claims.

---

1. Appeals Regulations, 75 Fed. Reg. 43329, 43337–38 (July 23, 2010).
2. Interim Final Rule on Internal Claims and Appeals and External Review Processes, 75 Fed. Reg. 43329 (July 23, 2010).
3. Amendment to Interim Final Rule on Internal Claims and Appeals and External Review Processes, 76 Fed. Reg. 37208 (June 24, 2011).
4. See DOL Technical Release 2011-01.
5. See Technical Release 2011-01, Appendix, at http://www.dol.gov/ebsa/newsroom/tr11-01.html.
6. Treas. Reg. §54.9815–2719T(c)(2)(v); DOL Reg. §2590.715–2719(c)(2)(v); HHS Reg. §147.136(c)(2)(v).

219. How are health reimbursement account claims handled?

For many HRAs, the claim decision simply is whether the expense meets the definition of "medical expense" under Code Section 213(d). As a result, HRA claims are simpler and less urgent than many other health plan claims. As a practical matter, there are fewer appeals for HRAs than other types of plans.

220. How do these claims and appeal rules relate to the ERISA claims and appeal rules?

The ERISA claims procedure continues to apply.[1] Non-ERISA self-insured plans, such as church plans, while not subject to ERISA (assuming they have not affirmatively made themselves subject to ERISA), are subject to these new health reform rules. The health reform regulations expand on the 2000 DOL claims regulations, add several new requirements, and extend application of the requirements to non-ERISA group plans and to issuers of individual health insurance.

The health law claims and appeal regulations apply to group health plans and group and individual health insurance issuers for plan or policy years beginning after September 23, 2010. For nongrandfathered ERISA plans, these new requirements are in addition to existing claims procedures in the ERISA internal claim procedure rules at 29 CFR 2560.503-1. Where applicable, if an internal appeal is denied, patients may choose to have the claim reviewed by an independent reviewer. The regulations do not require the plan to provide continued coverage during the claim and any internal appeal, other than the coverage for an ongoing course of treatment. Plans are generally prohibited from reducing or terminating an ongoing course of treatment without notice and an opportunity to review. Individuals in urgent care situations and those receiving an ongoing course of treatment may be allowed to proceed with an expedited external review at the same time as the internal appeals process. However, the regulations do not make it clear whether this continued coverage requirement applies to appeals of eligibility claims and rescissions.

221. Can state versus federal standards apply?

Yes. Group health plans must determine whether they are subject to state standards or federal standards. For health insurance coverage (i.e., fully insured group health plans), if a state's external review process is binding on an insurer and includes the consumer protections in the NAIC Uniform Model Act in place as of July 23, 2010, the insurer must comply with the applicable state standards. This requirement is imposed on the insurer and not the plan. If a state's process does not meet such requirements, then the federal process will apply. The federal external review process generally will apply to ERISA-covered, self-insured plans. However, the preamble to the final regulations also notes that this would not preclude a state from applying its external review process to self-insured group health plans not covered by ERISA or subject to other state insurance law (i.e., nonfederal governmental plans, church plans and multiple employer welfare arrangements).

---

1. DOL Reg. §2560.503-1.

222. Which external review process (state or federal) applies to plans?

Type of Plan	What Process Applies?	Who Is Liable?
Insured Plan	State process (if state process applies and is binding)	Insurer (not plan)
	Federal process (if no state process applies and is binding)	Insurer or plan**
Self-Insured ERISA Plan	Federal process (unless plan voluntarily complies with an applicable state process, if available)	Plan
Self-Insured Non-ERISA Plan (e.g., nonfederal governmental plans and church plans)	State process (if state process applies and is binding)	Plan
	Federal process (if no state process applies and is binding)	Plan

** Although the federal external review requirement applies by its terms to plans or insurers, as a practical reality, insured plan sponsors will use the process used by their insurers to comply with this requirement.

223. What are the requirements of the new claims and appeals rules?

These regulations amended ERISA claims procedures applicable to group health plans, and made the new standards applicable to both group health plans and health insurance issuers. Specifically, the regulations provide the following new rules for internal claims and appeals processes:

- The appeals process provision under the law imposes obligations owed to health plan "enrollees."[1] The appeals regulations, however, generally use the term "claimant." A claimant is an individual (participant or beneficiary) who makes a claim under the rules for internal claims and appeals and external review procedures, which may include a claimant's authorized representative.[2] This is the same definition as under the DOL claims procedure regulations.[3]

- As part of full and fair review, a claimant must be permitted to review his or her claim file.[4] This is in addition to the right under the DOL claims procedures to have access to and copies of "documents, records, and other information relevant" to the claim.[5] Existing DOL regulations permit claimants to present written comments,

---

1. PHSA §2719(a).
2. DOL Reg. §2590.715-2719(a)(2)(iii).
3. DOL Reg. §2560.503-1(a).
4. PHSA §2719(a)(1)(C).
5. DOL Reg. §2560.503-1(h)(2)(iii).

records, and information relating to a benefits claim.[1] Claimants also must be permitted to present evidence and testimony;[2] however, the law and regulations do not define testimony. The term "testimony" likely includes personal and written testimony from a witness, for example, by affidavit.[3] It generally is made by oath or affirmation under penalty of perjury.[4] Informally, the DOL has indicated that the appeals regulations were not intended to add a new rule requiring plans to hold hearings and allow claimants to make oral statements.[5]

- An adverse benefit determination eligible for internal claims and appeals was expanded to include a rescission of coverage, whether or not the rescission has an adverse effect on any particular benefit at the time.[6]

- A final internal adverse benefit determination is either an adverse benefit determination that has been upheld by a plan or insurer at completion of the plan's internal appeals procedures or an adverse benefit determination for which the internal appeals procedures have been exhausted.[7] Typically, most plans a claim and one internal appeal.

- A plan or issuer must notify a claimant of a benefit determination, whether or not adverse, for a claim involving urgent care as soon as possible, taking into account the medical exigencies, but not later than seventy-two hours after the receipt of the claim by the plan or issuer. The original standard of twenty-four hours was amended to seventy-two hours.[8]

- The appeals regulations require plans or insurers to provide claimants, free of charge, and without any requirement of a claimant's request, with "any new or additional evidence considered, relied upon, or generated by" the plan or insurer (or at the direction of the plan or insurer) in connection with a claim.[9] This evidence must be provided as soon as possible and soon enough so the claimant can respond.[10] These rules must be followed at each stage of the process.

- Decisions regarding hiring, compensation, termination, promotion, or other similar matters by decision-makers, such as claims adjudicators and medical experts, must

---

1. DOL Reg. §2560.503-1(h)(2)(ii).
2. PHSA §2719(a)(1)(C).
3. Black's Law Dictionary (9th ed. 2009) ("testimony").
4. Black's Law Dictionary Free Online 2nd Ed. at http://thelawdictionary.org/testimony.
5. Nonbinding comments, Amy Turner, EBSA, ABA Joint Committee on Employee Benefits teleconference, "Health Plans: Compliance with PPACA's Health Claims and Appeals Process" (Nov. 17, 2010).
6. DOL Reg. §2590.715-2719(b)(2)(ii)(A).
7. DOL Reg. §2590.715-2719(a)(2)(v).
8. Preamble to amended Appeals Regulations, 76 Fed. Reg. 37208, 37212 (June 24, 2011).
9. DOL Reg. §2590.715-2719(b)(2)(ii)(C)(1).
10. DOL Reg. §2560.503-1(i).

avoid any conflict of interest and not be based upon the likelihood that the individual will support the denial of benefits.[1]

- Notices must be provided in a culturally and linguistically appropriate manner,[2] including notices in a non-English language if 25 percent of all participants are literate in the same non-English language. For plans with 100 or more participants, the notices must be provided in a non-English language if the lesser of 500 participants or 10 percent of all participants are literate in the same non-English language.[3]

- Notices to claimants must comply with certain content requirements:

  o Any notice of an adverse benefit determination or a final internal adverse benefit determination must include information sufficient to identify the claim involved, including the date of the service, the healthcare provider, the claim amount (if applicable), the diagnosis code and its corresponding meaning, and the treatment code and its corresponding meaning;

  o The plan or issuer must ensure that the reasons for an adverse benefit determination or final internal adverse benefit determination include the denial code and its corresponding meaning, as well as a description of the plan's or issuer's standard, if any, that was used in denying the claim; and in the case of a final internal adverse benefit determination, this description must also include a discussion of the decision;

  o The plan or issuer must provide a description of the available internal appeals and external review processes, including information regarding how to initiate an appeal; and

  o The plan or issuer must disclose the availability of, and contact information for, an applicable office of health insurance consumer assistance or ombudsman established under PHSA Section 2793.

224. What if a plan fails to follow these claims and external review rules?

Prior to filing a lawsuit, a claimant must exhaust the appeals process. If a plan or issuer fails to adhere strictly to all requirements of the interim final regulations, the claimant is deemed to have exhausted the plan's or issuer's internal claims and appeals process, regardless of whether the plan or issuer asserts that it has substantially complied. The claimant may initiate any available external review process and remedies available under ERISA and state law.

---

1. DOL Reg. §§2560.503-1(b) and (h).
2. PHSA §2719(a)(1)(B); Reg. §54.9815-2719T(e); 2012 Culturally and Linguistically Appropriate Services (CLAS) County Data, at http://www.cciio.cms.gov/resources/factsheets/clas-data.html.
3. HHS Reg. §147.136(e)(3).

The claimant may request a written explanation of a violation of the procedures from the plan or insurer, and the plan or insurer must provide such explanation within ten days, including a specific description of its bases for asserting that the violation should not cause the internal claims and appeals process to be deemed exhausted.[1]

If an external reviewer or court rejects a claimant's request for immediate review on the basis that the plan met the standards for the exception described above, the claimant has the right to resubmit and pursue the internal appeal of the claim. In such a case, within a reasonable time after the external reviewer or court rejects the claim for immediate review (not to exceed ten days), the plan must provide the claimant with notice of the opportunity to resubmit and pursue the internal appeal of the claim. Time periods for re-filing the claim begin to run when the claimant receives the notice.[2]

225. Have model notices been issued?

Yes. Three model notices have been issued by the Labor Department[3] and are reproduced in Appendix B.

226. What are the requirements for SPDs to incorporate the new claims and appeals rules?

The enhanced internal claims and appeals requirements and external review procedures will require that existing SPDs and other plan communications that describe the plan's claims procedures be updated. In March 2011, the agencies modified and extended the enforcement grace period for certain internal claims and appeals requirements.[4] SPDs and plan communications should provide participants and beneficiaries with information relating to internal claims and appeals requirements and external review procedures, as updated in June 2011.[5]

Wellness Program Rules

227. What are wellness programs?

Some wellness programs are stand-alone programs and others are offered as part of or in conjunction with a group health plan. Wellness programs encourage good health and healthy lifestyles. Additionally, some may provide physical examinations, cholesterol screening, flu shots, nutrition counseling and education, and similar benefits. To the extent that a wellness program provides such medical benefits, it will likely be treated as a group health plan subject to the PHSA mandates in ERISA and the Internal Revenue Code for private employers or in the PHSA for state and local government employers.

The 2014 prohibition against discriminating based on a health status-related factor means, among other things, that plans and insurers may not charge individuals different premiums

---

1. DOL Reg. §2590.715-2719(b)(2)(ii)(F)(2).
2. DOL Reg. §2590.715-2719(b)(2)(ii)(F)(2).
3. Technical Release No. 2011-02 at http://www.dol.gov/ebsa/newsroom/tr11-02.html.
4. DOL Technical Release 2011-01 (Mar. 18, 2011).
5. Amendment to Interim Final Rule on Internal Claims and Appeals and External Review Processes, 76 Fed. Reg. 37208 (June 24, 2011).

or impose different costs based on the presence or absence of a health status-related factor. However, nondiscrimination provisions were not meant to prevent a group health plan or insurer from establishing premium discounts or reduced copayments or deductibles in return for "adherence to programs of health promotion and disease prevention."[1] Thus, certain programs of health promotion or disease prevention (referred to as "wellness programs") are an exception to the general prohibition on discrimination based on a health status-related factor.

228. How are stand-alone wellness programs treated?

Stand-alone wellness programs are not subject to the PHSA mandates if they are not group health plans. A wellness plan is not a group health plan if it does not provide or pay for health or medical benefits. Examples of types of stand-alone wellness programs that are not group health plans include programs that pay for health or weight-loss club dues, award prizes to persons who walk a certain number of miles, or provide health information. Even when a wellness plan offers incentives, this does not make it a group health plan if the incentives are unrelated to the group health plan, such as a plan offering extra vacation days or bonuses to those who do not smoke or have a good cholesterol level, for example.

On the other hand, stand-alone wellness programs that provide or pay for medical benefits (such as a physical exam program) are group health plans[2] and are subject to the PHSA mandates unless they qualify for an exception.

229. How are wellness programs that relate to group health plans regulated?

A wellness program that relates to, or is a part of, a larger group health plan is subject to the PHSA mandates, if the group health plan to which it is connected is subject to the mandates and is not an excepted benefit, such as a stand-alone vision or dental plan.

A wellness program is related to a group health plan if it is actually one of the benefits under the larger group health plan or if any of the incentives or rewards that it offers affect the benefits or contributions under the larger group plan. For example, an employer-sponsored wellness program that offers, as an incentive for undergoing certain testing, a discount on the amount that an employee must pay for major medical coverage is subject to the PHSA mandates.

The permissible reward under a health-contingent wellness program—from 20 percent to 30 percent of the cost of individual coverage under the group health plan, and up to 50 percent for programs designed to prevent or reduce tobacco use. The codified rules are effective for plan years beginning on or after January 1, 2014.[3] The regulations apply the same standards to both grandfathered and nongrandfathered plans, except grandfathered plans in the individual market.[4]

---

1. IRC Sec. 9802(b)(2); ERISA Sec. 702(b)(2); PHSA §2705(b)(2).
2. See, e.g., DOL Information Letter to Joseph S. Dunn (Nov. 17, 1993).
3. Incentives for Nondiscriminatory Wellness Programs in Group Health Plans, 26 CFR Part 54, 29 CFR Part 2590, 45 CFR Parts 146 and 147, 78 Fed. Reg. 33158 (June 3, 2013).
4. HHS Reg. §147.110(b).

Additional rules apply to certain wellness programs under HIPAA's health status nondiscrimination rules. Employers offering wellness programs must also comply with the Americans with Disabilities Act (ADA). Wellness programs or discounts may violate the ADA if the discounts or other rewards are not available to individuals with disabilities. A wellness program could also violate the ADA provisions limiting an employer's ability to make disability related inquiries and to require medical examinations during employment.

Bringing Down the Cost of Coverage

Medical Loss Ratio (MLR) Rules; PHSA, ERISA and Tax Ramifications

230. What are the health reform provisions relating to reducing the cost of health insurance?

Health reform added PHSA Section 2718 entitled "Bringing Down Cost Of Health Care Coverage." The purpose of the law is to limit the amount insurers can spend on administrative costs. If an insurer exceeds the limit, it is required to rebate the excess. The medical loss ratio (MLR) is the cost of claims plus amounts expended on health care quality improvement as a percentage of total premiums, excluding taxes, fees, and adjustments for risk adjustments and risk corridors, as well as reinsurance.[1]

Health care reform's Medical Loss Ratio rules became effective January 1, 2011, and the first rebates were required to be issued on August 1, 2012. These rules apply to individual insurance policies and insured group plans but not self-insured health plans. Insurers must provide rebates (refunds)[2] if their percentage of premiums spent on medical claims (and quality improvement) for policies issued in a state is less than 80 percent in the small group and individual markets or 85 percent in the large group market.[3]

Until 2014, the rebate is to be calculated using the figures for the reporting year. Beginning on January 1, 2014, the calculation to determine rebate amounts will be based on the average ratio over the previous three years.[4] Notices of rebates must be sent to both plan sponsors and participants in the plan to which the rebate relates.

Rebates must be paid by August 1 of the year following the year for which the medical loss ratio (MLR) data are calculated.[5] Insurers must also report how the rebate was calculated. Insurers who fail to comply with the law are subject to civil fines to be assessed by HHS up to $100 per day per individual affected by the violation.

---

1. PHSA §2718(a) and (b)(1)(A).
2. PHSA §2718(b)(1)(A).
3. PHSA §§2718(b)(1)(A)(i) and (ii). This ratio is determined on a state-by-state basis and it is measured in the state in which the policy is issued. States can require higher minimum MLR percentages, but HHS can also adjust state MLR requirements downward where necessary to prevent destabilization of the individual market. State MLR targets tend to be lower than the health reform law targets.
4. PHSA §2791(e)(4).
5. 45 CFR §158.240(d).

231. When were the final MLR regulations issued?

In December 2011, HHS issued final MLR regulations,[1] and the DOL has issued related guidance on healthcare reform's MLR rules, making changes for employer-sponsored group health plans, including who receives the rebates and how such amounts may be applied.[2] Insurers must provide the rebates for individuals covered by group health plans subject to ERISA or the PHSA to the policyholder, which is generally the employer for a group plan. The effective date of this final regulation was January 3, 2012.

232. How may the insurance company rebates be paid to persons ("enrollees") purchasing individual policies in the individual market?

For current individual policy owners, insurers may issue rebates in the form of either a premium credit, a reduction in the premium, or a lump-sum payment.[3] For former individual policy owners, only a lump-sum payment is permitted.[4] If an insurer finds that its MLR is lower than the standard required during an MLR reporting year, it may also institute a premium holiday to avoid paying rebates, but only if permitted under state law.[5] An insurer seeking to suspend or reduce premiums must obtain permission from the governing state agency and do so in a non-discriminatory manner. An "enrollee" for rebate purposes is the policyholder or government entity that paid the premium for healthcare coverage received by an individual during the respective MLR reporting year.[6]

In addition to a premium credit or a lump-sum payment, if the premium is paid using a credit or debit card, an insurer is permitted to return the entire rebate to the account used to pay the premium[7] and no additional fees are charged.[8]

233. How are insurers to pay rebates in connection with employer health insurance plans?

If an employer selects the insurer and administers the health insurance plan, it is an employee welfare benefit plan and subject to ERISA. Section 3(l) of ERISA describes an employee welfare plan as "any plan, fund, or program which was heretofore or is hereafter established or maintained by an employer or by an employee organization, or by both, to the extent that such plan, fund, or program was established or is maintained for the purpose of providing for its participants or

---

1. On November 22, 2010, the Department of Health and Human Services (HHS) issued its interim final regulations implementing the MLR requirements of section 2718 of the Public Health Services Act (PHSA) entitled "Bringing Down the Cost of Health Care Coverage." The term "medical loss ratio" does not appear in Section 2718.
2. Medical Loss Ratio Requirements under PPACA, 45 CFR Part 158, 76 Fed. Reg. 76574 (Dec. 7, 2011); Medical Loss Ratio Rebate Requirements for Non-Federal Governmental Plans, 45 CFR Part 158, 76 Fed Reg. 76596 (Dec. 7, 2011); DOL Technical Release 2011-04 (Dec. 2, 2011); HHS Fact Sheet: Medical Loss Ratio: Getting Your Money's Worth on Health Insurance (Dec. 2, 2011).
3. 45 CFR §158.241(a).
4. 45 CFR §158.241(b).
5. CCIIO Technical Guidance (CCIIO 2012-002): Questions and Answers Regarding the Medical Loss Ratio Regulation, Q/A-30, at http://cciio.cms.gov/resources/files/mlr-qna-04202012.pdf.
6. 45 CFR §158.240(b).
7. 45 CFR §158.241.
8. CCIIO Technical Guidance (CCIIO 2012-002): Questions and Answers Regarding the Medical Loss Ratio Regulation, Q/A-37, at http://cciio.cms.gov/resources/files/mlr-qna-04202012.pdf.

their beneficiaries, through the purchase of insurance or otherwise, ... medical, surgical, or hospital care or benefits..." [1]

Insurers must provide rebates for group health plans subject to ERISA (private employers) or the PHSA (state and local governments) to the policyholder, which is generally the employer sponsoring the plan. [2] For these plans, the rebates can have both ERISA and income tax ramifications, both of which are discussed in more detail below, in Q 247 and Q 248.

234. What if the plan has been terminated when the rebate is due?

If a group health plan, regardless of whether it is subject to ERISA, has been terminated at the time of rebate payment and the insurer cannot, despite reasonable efforts, locate the policyholder (the employer), the insurer must distribute the entire rebate, including the employer's share, to the participants who were enrolled in the terminated plan during the MLR reporting year on which the rebate was calculated by dividing the rebate equally among the individuals entitled to a rebate. [3] If an insurer is able to locate the policyholder with respect to a terminated ERISA plan, the policyholder would need to comply with ERISA's fiduciary provisions when handling any rebate. Despite the fact that the plan has been terminated, the plan document should be consulted and its terms followed. If the plan document does not provide direction, the employer must pay the employees' portion to them unless it is not cost effective. [4]

235. What if the MLR limits on insurers cause financial problems for insurers?

HHS may "adjust" (but not waive) the MLR target [5] in individual states where enforcement of the 80 percent target would "destabilize" the individual market. [6] HHS must provide detailed, public information as to its conclusions and the public may comment. HHS may elect to hold a hearing and must respond promptly to state requests.

236. Do the MLR rules limit commissions paid to brokers and agents?

Brokers and agents commissions reportedly may account for 5 percent or more of premiums as of this writing. The statute requires that sales commissions be counted as administrative costs, although HHS could consider such compensation in assessing market destabilization. [7]

237. How is the MLR computed?

The numerator of the MLR formula includes reimbursement of claims for clinical services and expenditures for quality improvement activities. Clinical services reimbursement includes

---

1. ERISA Sec. 3(1), 29 U.S.C. §1002(1).
2. 45 CFR §158.242(b). ERISA generally applies to private employer plans, while the PHSA applies to non-federal governmental employer plans.
3. 45 CFR §158.242(b)(4).
4. DOL Technical Release No. 2011-04, Guidance on Rebates for Group Health Plans Paid Pursuant to the Medical Loss Ratio Requirements of the Public Health Service Act (Dec. 2, 2011), at http://www.dol.gov/ebsa/newsroom/tr11-04.html.
5. CCIIO Technical Guidance (CCIIO 2011-002): Questions and Answers Regarding the Medical Loss Ratio Interim Final Rule, Q/A-17, at http://cciio.cms.gov/resources/files/2011_05_13_mlr_q_and_a_guidance.pdf.
6. OCIIO Technical Guidance (OCIIO 2010-2A): Process for a State to Submit a Request for Adjustment to the Medical Loss Ratio Standard of PHS Act Section 2718, at http://cciio.cms.gov/resources/files/12-17-2010ociio_2010-2a_guidance.pdf.
7. 75 Fed. Reg. 74863, 74877 (Dec. 1, 2010).

direct payments for services and supplies as well as changes in contract reserves (where an issuer holds reserves for later years when claims are expected to rise as experience deteriorates) and reserves for contingent benefits and lawsuits. Payments under capitation contracts with providers may be counted fully as claims, but insurers must count as administrative costs rather than claims costs payments made to third party vendors (such as behavioral health or pharmacy benefit managers) that are attributable to administrative services.

The definition of quality improvement activities found in Section 2717 of the health reform law is used for the MLR rules. Quality improvement activities include activities that:

- improve health care outcomes,

- reduce medical errors,

- improve patient safety,

- encourage wellness and prevention, and

- reduce rehospitalizations.

- MLR quality improvement costs also include:

- related IT expenses,

- the cost of healthcare hotlines,

- the cost of collecting and reporting quality data for accreditation purposes, and

- expenditures for facilitating the "meaningful use" of certified electronic health record technologies.

Prospective utilization review may be considered quality improvement to the extent it is intended to ensure appropriate treatment, but concurrent and retrospective utilization review activities are administrative costs.

The regulations provide that the MLR is calculated as follows:

$$\frac{\text{medical care claims} + \text{quality improvement expenses}}{\text{premiums} - (\text{federal and state taxes} + \text{licensing and regulatory fees})^1}$$

Fraud Prevention. PPACA does not allow insurers to count fraud prevention costs in the numerator as quality improvement expenses. However, the rule allows insurers to offset their fraud detection and recovery expenses against successful fraud recoveries.

---

1. 103 45 CFR §158.140, 104 45 CFR §158.150.105, 45 CFR §§158.161 and 158.162, 106 45 CFR §158.240(c); see also http://www.gao.gov/new.items/d1290r.pdf, page 4.

Quality Improvement Expenses Must Be Verifiable and Objective. The HHS rule states that only activities "capable of being objectively measured and of producing verifiable results and achievements" can be counted as quality improvement. The preface to the HHS rule states: "While an issuer does not have to present initial evidence proving the effectiveness of a quality improvement activity, the issuer will have to show measurable results stemming from the executed quality improvement activity."

238. What if an insurer has several entities licensed in a state?

MLRs are calculated separately for each licensed entity within a state by market segment (individual, small, or large group). Experience can be aggregated to the state in which the contract is located for employers with employees in multiple states. Affiliated insurers can also aggregate their experience where they combine to offer an employer in- and out-of-network coverage. No national reporting is allowed. Association health plans selling individual coverage must report their experience in the state in which individual certificates of coverage are issued.[1]

239. What are the rules for MLR rebates for state and local government (non-federal) group health plans?

Group health plans maintained by non-federal governmental employers, including state and local governments, are not subject to ERISA. HHS issued separate interim final regulations for these plans.[2] The plan policyholder is required to use the portion of rebates attributable to the amount of premium paid by plan subscribers for the benefit of subscribers. At the option of the policyholder, this portion of the rebate must be used either to reduce employee premium contributions or to provide cash refunds to employees covered by the group health policy on which the rebate is based. In either case, however, the rebate is to be used to reduce premiums for (or pay refunds to) employees enrolled during the year in which the rebate is actually paid (rather than the MLR reporting year, i.e., the prior year, on which the rebate was calculated).

240. What are the rules for group insured health plans sponsored by employers and subject to ERISA?

Most employer-provided health plans are subject to ERISA. The exceptions for state and local governments and church plans are discussed in Q 220.

Where the health plan is funded by a trust, the rebate is paid to that trust. If the plan is not funded by a trust, DOL Technical Release 2011-04, excuses insured group health plans from the obligations to hold participant contributions in trust and to file Form 5500 *if* the MLR rebates are used within three months of receipt to make employee refunds (the preferred option, as discussed in Q 234) or to pay the employees' share of premiums, in each case to the extent premiums were paid by employees.[3]

---

1. 45 CFR §158.120(a).
2. Vol. 76 Federal Register No. 235, pp. 76596-76599 (December 7, 2011) at http://www.gpo.gov/fdsys/pkg/FR-2011-12-07/pdf/2011-31291.pdf.
3. DOL Technical Release No. 2011-04, Guidance on Rebates for Group Health Plans Paid Pursuant to the Medical Loss Ratio Requirements of the Public Health Service Act (Dec. 2, 2011), at http://www.dol.gov/ebsa/newsroom/tr11-04.html.

241. How does an employer comply with the three-month rule?

To be safe under the three-month rule, rebates belonging to participants must be used to benefit plan participants within three months. An employer that decides to distribute the rebate to plan participants must issue checks, by regular payroll or special checks, within three months of the employer's receipt of the rebate. If the employer decides to use the portion of the rebate belonging to employees to reduce required participant contributions, it must adjust payroll deductions for affected participants within three months of the rebate's receipt. Thus, a plan that receives a rebate on August 1 cannot wait until the next plan year begins to reduce employee contributions if the beginning of the next year is more than three months after receipt of the rebate.

242. How does an employer decide whether an MLR belongs to the employer or the employees when the health plan is not funded through a trust?

DOL Technical Release 2011-04[1] discusses MLR payments relating to ERISA health insurance plans and explains the fiduciary and plan asset rules that apply. As noted in Q 240, plans without a trust need to dispose of the rebates belonging to participants within three months of receipt. Plan sponsors should review plan documents to determine if they address how the plan assets portion of a rebate is determined and to verify whether such provisions are consistent with the final regulation.

The DOL states that MLR rebates may be ERISA plan assets in whole or part, depending on various factors, including the terms of the insurance contract and plan documents. Quite often, there will be no specific provisions in either the insurance contract or the employer's health insurance plan. In that case, the 2011 Technical Release offers guidance on how to deal with the MLR refunds.

Assuming the plan documents, the insurance contract, and other extrinsic evidence do not resolve the allocation issue, the DOL says the portion of a rebate that is attributable to employee contributions belongs to the participants. Any portion of a rebate that constitutes ERISA plan assets must be used for the exclusive benefit of plan participants and beneficiaries.

For an ERISA plan, the employer may never retain more than the amount of premiums and plan expenses paid by the employer. Otherwise, this would be a breach of fiduciary duty and a prohibited transaction under ERISA. The DOL guidance directs employers to look to who paid the premiums for the health plan for the year to which the MLR rebate relates to determine whether the rebate is owned by the plan if a trust, the employer, or the employees.

- If the employer paid entire premium, the employer may retain the entire rebate.

- If a trust or the employees paid the entire premium, the entire rebate belongs to the trust or employees.

---

1. DOL Technical Release No. 2011-04, Guidance on Rebates for Group Health Plans Paid Pursuant to the Medical Loss Ratio Requirements of the Public Health Service Act (Dec. 2, 2011), at http://www.dol.gov/ebsa/newsroom/tr11-04.html.

- If the employer and employees each paid a specified percentage of the premium, they each are entitled to the rebate based on those percentages.

- If the employer was required to pay a fixed amount and participants were responsible for paying any additional costs, then the portion of the rebate under such a policy that does not exceed the participants' total amount of prior contributions during the relevant period would be attributable to participant contributions.

- If participants paid a fixed amount and the employer was responsible for paying any additional costs, then the portion of the rebate under such a policy that did not exceed the employer's total amount of prior contributions during the relevant period would not be attributable to participant contributions.

243. How does an employer decide how amounts belonging to employees are used?

The preferred option for participant rebate funds is to return them to the participants. If that is not cost effective, then the employee's share of the rebate can be used to reduce participant contributions due within the three months after the rebate is received, or to enhance benefits. DOL Technical Release 2011-04 states that if a fiduciary finds that the cost of distributing shares of a rebate to former participants (terminated employees who participated in the program during the year for which the rebates are paid), approximates the amount of those proceeds, the fiduciary may properly decide to allocate the proceeds to current participants based upon a reasonable, fair and objective allocation method If there are former participants who cannot be located after use of a locator service, then the plan should be followed. If the plan is silent, it would seem reasonable to add those funds to the amounts being distributed to current and former participants.

Making Payment to Employees Is Fail-Safe. As a practical matter, employers may return 100 percent of the MLR rebate to participants, even when the employers legally could retain all or a portion of the rebate as the employer's share under the rules discussed in Q 242. This approach assures compliance with ERISA's fiduciary requirements and allows the employer to communicate positive news to employees. When there are terminated employees who were participants during the year to which the rebate is attributable, they too are entitled to their share of the rebate unless they cannot be located with reasonable effort (a locator service should be used) or the refund is not cost-effective, as discussed above in Q 234.

244. What are the special considerations when an employer has a plan with several insurance options?

Where an employer has several health insurance plans, such as an HMO, PPO, and high deductible options, those employers must distribute the rebates only to participants that were covered by the specific policy for which the rebate is issued. The DOL states that using rebates to benefit non-participants is a breach of ERISA fiduciary duties.[1]

---

1. *See, e.g.*, Advisory Opinions 2001-02A (Feb. 15, 2001); 99-08A (May 20, 1999); 94-31A (Sept. 9, 1994); and 92-02A (Jan. 17, 1992).

245. What are the special issues if insurance is paid in part by employee pre-tax cafeteria plan payments?

With respect to an MLR rebate to a cafeteria plan under Code Section 125, refunding part or all of the rebate to participants should not be a violation of the "use it or lose it" rule of the regulations because that rule applies to healthcare and dependent care flexible spending accounts, not to premium conversion amounts that are plan assets. The rebate should not be used to reduce the employees' contribution for the next three months. That would be an impermissible election change unless this is done by virtue of the fact that the employee's share of the premiums are reduced, and the plan allows for changing payroll deductions based on changes in the insurance premiums.

246. How do the rebate rules differ for non-ERISA plans?

Plans of state and local governments and churches are exempt from ERISA unless their plan documents make them subject to ERISA. If not subject to ERISA, they are not bound by the three-month rule and can apply the rebates to reduce the costs for the upcoming plan year.

247. What is the income tax treatment for rebates paid to owners of individual health insurance policies issued in the individual market?

For individual market coverage (non-group individual policies), the rebate is not taxed if the individual did not deduct the premiums for that year to which the rebate relates.[1] If the individual did deduct the premium, the rebate is taxable,[2] including a premium deducted by a sole proprietor or partner.[3]

248. What are the income tax rules for rebates paid to employees in employer-sponsored group health insurance plans?

For those participating in insured group plans, the concepts are the same: the rebates are not taxable if paid with after-tax (no deduction taken) dollars, whether paid directly to the employee by the insurer or by the insurer to the employer and in turn by the employer to the employee.[4] However, if the employee deducted the premium on the employee's personal income tax return, the rebate is taxable income.[5] If a person participates in the plan in the year in which the rebate is paid, but not the prior year, and receives a share of the rebate, the rebate is not taxed.[6]

Where the insurance policy is a group policy, and the employee paid the employee's share of the premium with pre-tax dollars (amounts not taxed to an employee, such as a salary reduction

---

1. IRS Medical Loss Ratio (MLR) FAQs Q/A-2 at http://www.irs.gov/newsroom/article/0,,id=256167,00.html.
2. IRS Medical Loss Ratio (MLR) FAQs Q/A-3 at http://www.irs.gov/newsroom/article/0,,id=256167,00.html.
3. IRS Medical Loss Ratio (MLR) FAQs Q/A-4 at http://www.irs.gov/newsroom/article/0,,id=256167,00.html.
4. IRS Medical Loss Ratio (MLR) FAQs Q/A-5&6 at http://www.irs.gov/newsroom/article/0,,id=256167,00.html.
5. IRS Medical Loss Ratio (MLR) FAQs Q/A-7 at http://www.irs.gov/newsroom/article/0,,id=256167,00.html.
6. IRS Medical Loss Ratio (MLR) FAQs Q/A-8&9 at http://www.irs.gov/newsroom/article/0,,id=256167,00.html.

payment through a cafeteria plan that is not reported as taxable income to the employee) in the plan year to which the rebate relates, the following rules apply:

- If the employer applies the employee's share of the rebate to reduce the employee's share of the premium, this is taxed to the employee.[1]

- The rebate is also taxable in the year paid if it is paid to the employee and is "wages" subject to payroll and employment taxes.[2]

Where the insurance policy is a group policy, the rebate is paid to participants regardless of whether they participated in the plan in the year generating the rebate, and the employee pays the employee's share of the premium in the current plan year with pre-tax dollars:

- If the employee's share of the rebate is allocated to reduce the cost of insurance for the year in which the rebate was received, the rebate is taxable and is wages in the year paid subject to employment taxes.[3]

- If the rebate is paid to the employee, who participated in the plan in the year for which the rebated is paid, the rebate is taxable and is wages in the year paid subject to employment taxes.[4]

If the rebate is paid to the employee, who did not participate in the plan in the year for which the rebated is paid, the rebate is taxable and is wages in the year paid subject to employment taxes.[5]

Summary of Benefits and Coverage (SBC) Requirement for Insurers and Employers

249. Are insurance companies and health plans required to prepare and distribute to participants/insureds a Summary of Benefits and Coverage (SBC)?

Yes, for those providing essential health benefits, and they also must provide a Uniform Glossary, a list of important defined terms. This health reform requirement[6] applies to essential health benefits and not "excepted benefits." Where a plan is insured, the insurer is required to prepare the SBC, and the employer or other plan sponsor is required to distribute it annually in a timely manner. A self-funded plan must prepare its own SBC. Where an employer has several health benefit package options, this requirement will require coordination.

---

1. IRS Medical Loss Ratio (MLR) FAQs Q/A-10 at http://www.irs.gov/newsroom/article/0,,id=256167,00.html.
2. IRS Medical Loss Ratio (MLR) FAQs Q/A-11 at http://www.irs.gov/newsroom/article/0,,id=256167,00.html.
3. IRS Medical Loss Ratio (MLR) FAQs Q/A-12 at http://www.irs.gov/newsroom/article/0,,id=256167,00.html.
4. IRS Medical Loss Ratio (MLR) FAQs Q/A-13 at http://www.irs.gov/newsroom/article/0,,id=256167,00.html.
5. IRS Medical Loss Ratio (MLR) FAQs Q/A-14 at http://www.irs.gov/newsroom/article/0,,id=256167,00.html.
6. PHSA §2715(a), ERISA Sec. 715, and IRC Sec. 9815.

250. What guidance has been provided for the SBC requirement?

The DOL, HHS, and IRS issued on Apr. 23, 2013 (1) FAQs, Part XIV,[1] addressing changes to the summary of benefits and coverage (SBC) effective for coverage beginning on or after January 1, 2014, and before January 1, 2015, (2) an updated SBC template,[2] and (3) sample completed SBC.[3]

251. What is new in the updated SBC template (beginning on or after January 1, 2014, and before January 1, 2015?

The updated sample SBC template (and sample completed SBC) require information about whether the plan or coverage provides "minimum essential coverage" and satisfies the "minimum value" standard. The SBC template for the first year of applicability did not require this information. A copy of a completed updated sample SBC template is located in Appendix A.

To the extent that it would be administratively burdensome for a plan or insurer to modify its SBCs to add this new information, the agencies indicate that no enforcement action will be taken for using the previous template, provided that the necessary minimum essential coverage and minimum value information is set forth in a cover letter or other disclosure furnished with the SBC. Model language is provided for this purpose.

The SBC disclosures of minimum essential coverage and minimum value is important for employees. Enrollment in minimum essential coverage is required to avoid individual mandate penalties. Additionally, information about minimum value is needed for determining potential eligibility for subsidized Exchange coverage. An employee is not eligible for subsidies for health insurance purchased on an Exchange if he or she is offered employer minimum essential coverage that provides minimum value and is affordable.

It is notable that the SBC does not require any information about affordability. The draft Individual Exchange Application by HHS includes an "Employer Coverage Form" to request information from an employer on how much an employee would have to pay under the employer's lowest cost self-only health plan providing minimum value.

252. Are there any changes to the Glossary, Instructions, or Coverage Examples as a result of the April 23, 2013, guidance?

The agencies have indicated that no changes have been made to the uniform glossary (a separate document that is a companion to the SBC) or to the instructions for completing the SBC. Also, no additional coverage examples are required with this guidance. The same two coverage examples previously provided—relating to having a baby and managing diabetes—must be included. See Q 263.

---

1. FAQs at http://www.dol.gov/ebsa/faqs/faq-aca14.html.
2. SBC Template at http://www.dol.gov/ebsa/pdf/correctedsbctemplate2.pdf.
3. Sample Completed SBC at http://www.dol.gov/ebsa/pdf/CorrectedSampleCompletedSBC2.pdf.

253. What impact do the SBC changes have on annual limits?

While no changes have been made to the SBC template or the sample completed SBC regarding annual limits, there is recognition that, for plan years beginning on or after January 1, 2014, the prohibition on imposing annual limits on the dollar value of essential health benefits will take effect. Thus, the agencies have indicated that no enforcement action will be taken against a plan or insurer that modifies its SBC for the second year of applicability by removing the entire row containing the question "Is there an overall annual limit on what the plan pays?"

254. What other issues does the April 23, 2013, guidance address?

The agencies have extended existing enforcement relief relating to various facets of SBC compliance (e.g., the circumstances in which the SBC may be provided electronically, penalties for failure to provide the SBC or uniform glossary) through the end of the second year of applicability, i.e., coverage beginning on or after January 1, 2014, and before January 1, 2015.

255. What if there is more than one benefit package for essential health benefits?

A plan sponsor may offer more than one essential health benefits benefit package, such as a choice among an HMO, a PPO, and a self-insured option, or a high deductible option paired with an HSA. In such a case, for a newly eligible participant, SBCs for each benefit package must be distributed. For those already enrolled, the SBC for the option previously selected must be distributed.[1] In addition, the SBC for any benefit package must be provided within seven days of a participant or insured's request.[2]

256. Does the SBC/Uniform Glossary requirement apply to grandfathered plans?

Yes.[3]

257. What plans are exempt from the SBC and Uniform Glossary requirements? What about HSAs, HRAs, MERPs, health FSAs, EAPs, and wellness programs?

Any plan or policy that is not an essential health benefit need not comply with these rules.[4] Thus, policies and plans that provide "excepted benefits" need not comply. Generally, health savings accounts, health reimbursement accounts (medical expense reimbursement accounts), and health flexible spending accounts are "excepted benefits." Where the employer provides a high deductible health plan (HDHP) that funds HSAs, the role of the HSA is mentioned when discussing the HDHP.[5] When stand-alone HRAs and health FSAs are not excepted benefits,

---

1. Treas. Reg. §54.9815-2715(a)(1)(ii); DOL Reg. §2590.715-2715(a)(1)(ii); HHS Reg. §147.200(a)(1)(ii).
2. Treas. Reg. §54.9815-2715(a)(1)(ii)(F); DOL Reg. §2590.715-2715(a)(1)(ii)(F); HHS Reg. §147.200(a)(1)(ii)(F).
3. PPACA, §§1251(a) and 10101(d) (2010).
4. Preamble to Final Rule: Summary of Benefits and Coverage and the Uniform Glossary, 77 Fed. Reg. 8668, 8670 (Feb. 14, 2012).
5. Preamble to Final Rule: Summary of Benefits and Coverage and the Uniform Glossary, 77 Fed. Reg. 8668, 8670–8671 (Feb. 14, 2012).

they must comply with the SBC/Uniform Glossary rules.[1] Plans in which HRAs are integrated with other coverage may use one SBC.[2] In this case, the HRA plan administrator is responsible for the SBC's description of the HRA's coverage.[3]

The SBC rules do not discuss employee assistance programs (EAPs). Whether the SBC requirements apply depends on whether the EAP is a group health plan. EAPs offer a range of benefits, such as counseling for alcohol and substance abuse, marital, family, and personal problems, stress, anxiety, grief, finances, retirement as well as childcare and elder care. These benefits are not included in the model SBC. Thus, EAPs are governed by the rule that where a plan's terms cannot reasonably be described in a manner consistent with the template and instructions, the plan or insurer must describe the terms using its best efforts to do so in accordance with the instructions and prescribed format.[4] Where an EAP is offered to employees, whether or not they are covered in the plan providing essential health benefits, it should seem that the SBC would not mention the EAP.

A wellness program may or may not be part of a group health plan. The FAQs refer to a wellness program that is an "add on" to major medical coverage that could affect the individual's cost-sharing and other information on the SBC. In such circumstances, the agencies explain that the coverage examples (discussed in Q 263) should note the assumptions used in creating them.[5] The sample SBC provides an example of how to describe a diabetes wellness program.[6]

258. What is the reason for the SBC requirement?

The SBC and a Uniform Glossary[7] of commonly used terms are to be distributed to all persons with essential health benefits in an individual policy or group plan. It applies to grandfathered policies and plans. The purpose is to provide a uniform summary of important provisions to assist individuals in understanding their coverage and provide the ability to compare it to other available options on an "apples to apples" basis.

259. Who must distribute the SBC and Glossary, and what happens if they fail to do so?

For insured plans, the insurer must distribute them to the plan administrator, which is often the employer. The plan administrator must distribute them to the participants. For a self-insured plan, the plan administrator, unless the plan says otherwise, is responsible to prepare and

1. Preamble to Final Rule: Summary of Benefits and Coverage and the Uniform Glossary, 77 Fed. Reg. 8668, 8671 (Feb. 14, 2012).
2. HHS, DOL & TREASURY, FAQs About the Affordable Care Act Implementation Part VIII, Q/A-6, at http://www.dol.gov/ebsa/faqs/faq-aca8.html.
3. HHS, DOL & TREASURY, FAQs About the Affordable Care Act Implementation Part IX, Q/A-10, at http://www.dol.gov/ebsa/faqs/faq-aca9.html
4. Preamble: Summary of Benefits and Coverage and the Uniform Glossary, 77 Fed. Reg. 8668, 8674–8675 (Feb. 14, 2012).
5. HHS, DOL & TREASURY, FAQs About the Affordable Care Act Implementation Part VIII, Q/A-6, at http://www.dol.gov/ebsa/faqs/faq-aca8.html.
6. See http://www.dol.gov/ebsa/pdf/correctedsbctemplate2.pdf and http://www.dol.gov/ebsa/pdf/CorrectedSampleCompletedSBC.pdf.
7. Final Rule: Summary of Benefits and Coverage and Uniform Glossary, 77 Fed. Reg. 8668 (Feb. 14, 2012); Summary of Benefits and Coverage and Uniform Glossary – Templates, Instructions, and Related Materials; and Guidance for Compliance, 77 Fed. Reg. 8706 (Feb. 14, 2012).

distribute the SBC and glossary.[1] Thus, employers with insured plans should seek contractual protection by requiring the insurer to deliver the SBC with sufficient lead time that the plan's plan administrator can timely deliver the SBC and Glossary to participants. Alternatively, the employer contractually can require the insurer to distribute the SBC to participants, which eliminates the employer and plan administrator for any penalty liability.[2]

Those responsible for preparation and delivery of the SBC and glossary are subject to substantial penalties for failure timely to do so. As discussed earlier in Q 172 as to the enforcement of the health reform coverage mandates, the law imposes a penalty of up to $1,000 per day per affected individual (per participant) for willful violations of the SBC rules for group health plans. For an insured plan, the insurer and plan administrator are each potentially subject to this penalty because the insurer must distribute the SBC to the plan administrator, and the plan administrator must distribute it to the participants. Additionally, the penalty tax upon a non-complying plan sponsor is $100 per day of noncompliance per affected individual,[3] and the violations must be self-reported on IRS Form 8928. The tax may be higher where violations occurred or continued during a period under IRS examination or where the violations are more than minimal. The tax does not apply where the failure was based on reasonable cause and not on willful neglect,[4] and the failure is corrected within thirty days after the person knew or should have known that the failure existed.[5]

260. When is the SBC required to be distributed?

Insurers must distribute SBCs to holders of individual market coverage and to insured group health plans beginning September 23, 2012. *For group health plans, the requirement applies beginning with the first open enrollment period beginning on or after September 23, 2012,* for participants and beneficiaries enrolling or re-enrolling through open enrollment. For individuals enrolling other than through open enrollment (such as newly eligible individuals or special enrollees), the requirement applies beginning on the first day of the first plan year that begins on or after September 23, 2012.[6] Thus, when an open enrollment period begins prior to September 23, 2012, the SBC and Uniform Glossary would only need to be distributed on and after September 23, 2012, to newly eligible persons. All others would receive the SBC and Uniform Glossary in 2013 at the open enrollment.[7]

Enrollment and Re-Enrollment. All health plans and insurers will provide an SBC to enrollees at important points in the enrollment process, including application and renewal. The SBC requirements apply to disclosures made to those enrolling or re-enrolling in group health plan coverage through an open enrollment period beginning on or after September 23, 2012.

---

1. Treas. Reg. §54.9815-2715(a)(1)(iii)(A); DOL Reg. §2590.715-2715(a)(1)(iii)(A); HHS Reg. §147.200(a)(1)(iii)(A).
2. Treas. Reg. §54.9815-2715(a)(1)(iii)(A); DOL Reg. §2590.715-2715(a)(1)(iii)(A); HHS Reg. §147.200(a)(1)(iii)(A).
3. IRC Sec. 4980D, which does not apply to insurers.
4. IRC Sec. 4980D(c)(1).
5. IRC Sec. 4980D(c)(2). See IRC Sec. 4980D(c)(2)(B)(ii), which gives church plans 270 days after the date of mailing by the Secretary of a notice of default with respect to the plan's failure.
6. Treas. Reg. §54.9815-2715(f); DOL Reg. §2590.715-2715(f); HHS Reg. §147.200(f).
7. The distribution date was postponed twice. The law required HHS to provide guidance by March 23, 2011, although HHS did not do so until August 18, 2011, when it issued proposed regulations. The August 18, 2011, SBC proposed regulations required that the SBCs be distributed to health plan participants beginning March 23, 2012. Many comments to the proposed regulations were made, and the deadline was again postponed until final regulations were later issued.

For enrollments occurring outside of open enrollment, the requirements apply beginning on the first day of the first plan year that begins on or after September 23, 2012.

SBC and Glossary on Demand. Whether shopping for health insurance or already enrolled in coverage, consumers will be able to request the SBC at any time, and health plans will have to provide it within seven business days. Consumers will also be able to request and receive the Uniform Glossary within seven business days.[1]

Material Modification: Mid-Year Change. To the extent a plan or policy implements a mid-year change that is a material modification that affects the content of the SBC, and that occurs other than in connection with a renewal or reissuance of coverage, a notice of modification must be provided sixty days in advance of the effective date of the change.[2]

A group health plan or insurer must provide notice of a plan change if it makes a material modification in any of the terms of the plan that is not reflected in the most recently provided SBC. A material modification[3] is any modification to the coverage offered under a plan that alone or in conjunction with other modifications is an important change in benefits or other terms of coverage to an average plan participant, including diminished or enriched benefits, coverage of previously excluded benefits, changes to cost sharing (copays or deductibles), premiums, or referrals requirements. However, only material modifications that would affect SBC content require plans and insurers to provide this notice. The notice may be provided in paper or electronic form, in accordance with the requirements discussed previously for providing the SBC.[4]

This requirement can be satisfied either by a separate notice describing the material modification or an updated SBC containing it. For ERISA-covered group health plans, this will satisfy the requirement to provide a Summary of Material Modification under ERISA. [Preamble to Final Rule: Summary of Benefits and Coverage and the Uniform Glossary, 77 Fed. Reg. 8668, 8677 (Feb. 14, 2012)]

COBRA Continuation Notice. As discussed in Q 265, the SBC must contain a verbatim statement about state and COBRA continuation options.

261. To whom must an SBC be provided?

The SBC requirement applies to all health insurance plans, individual and group, and all employer sponsored plans, both insured and self-insured, grandfathered and non-grandfathered. Persons in any such plan or arrangement must receive an SBC.

262. May the SBC be distributed electronically?

Yes. The SBC can be distributed electronically to participants in an ERISA welfare benefit plan if the Department of Labor's requirements are met.[5] See Q 254.

---

1. Treas. Reg. §54.9815-2715(a)(1)(ii)(F); DOL Reg. §2590.715-2715(a)(1)(ii)(F); HHS Reg. §147.200(a)(1)(ii)(F).
2. Treas. Reg. §54.9815-2715(b); DOL Reg. §2590.715-2715(b); HHS Reg. §147.200(b).
3. ERISA Sec. 102.
4. Treas. Reg. §54.9815-2715(b); DOL Reg. §2590.715-2715(b); HHS Reg. §147.200(b).
5. DOL Reg. §2590.715-2715(a)(4)(ii)(A); Treas. Reg. §54.9815-2715(a)(4)(ii)(A). The requirements of the DOL are in DOL Reg. §2520.104b-1(c).

263. What is the required format for the SBC?

A specified format is required, and detailed instructions for the format are provided.[1] Form language and formatting must be precisely reproduced, unless instructions allow or instruct otherwise. Unless otherwise provided, the plan or insurance company must use 12-point font, and replicate all symbols, formatting, bolding, and shading on the specimen formats, which are provided later in this question. While the law requires four pages, the agencies (HHS, DOL, and Treasury) have interpreted this to be eight pages because the pages have a front and back side. Surprisingly, the size of the paper that one can use is not specified.

To the extent a plan's terms that are required to be described in the SBC template cannot reasonably be described in a manner consistent with the template and instructions, the plan or insurance company must accurately describe the relevant plan terms while using its best efforts to do so in a manner that is still as consistent with the instructions and template format as reasonably possible. Such situations may occur, for example:

- if a plan provides a different structure for provider network tiers or drug tiers than is represented in the SBC template,

- if a plan provides different benefits based on facility type (such as hospital inpatient versus non-hospital inpatient),

- in a case where a plan is denoting the effects of a related health flexible spending arrangement or a health reimbursement arrangement, or

- if a plan provides different cost sharing based on participation in a wellness program.

Plans and insurance companies must customize all identifiable company information throughout the document, including Web sites and telephone numbers.

The items shown on pages 1 and 2 must always appear on pages 1 and 2, and the rows of the chart must always appear in the same order. However, the chart rows shown on page 2 may extend to page 3 if space requires, and the chart rows on page 3 may extend to the beginning of page 4 if space requires. The Excluded Services and Other Covered Services section may appear on page 3 or page 4, but must always immediately follow the chart starting on page 2. The Excluded Services and Other Covered Services section must be followed by the Your Rights to Continue Coverage section, the Your Grievance and Appeals Rights section, and the Coverage Examples section, in that order.

A footer must appear at the bottom left of every page with the appropriate telephone number and Web site information.

---

1. http://www.cms.gov/CCIIO/Programs-and-Initiatives/Consumer-Support-and-Information/Summary-of-Benefits-and-Coverage-and-Uniform-Glossary.html.

The language used must be plain language and present the information in a culturally and linguistically appropriate manner, utilizing terminology understandable by the average individual.

Plans and insurance companies with questions about completing the SBC may contact the Department of Health and Human Services at SBC@cms.hhs.gov or the Department of Labor at 866-444-EBSA(3272).

Two coverage examples are required. CMS provides the information necessary to perform the two coverage example calculations for having a baby (normal delivery) and managing type 2 diabetes (routine maintenance of a well-controlled condition).[1]

The SBC for a group health plan need not be a standalone document. Plans or insurance companies may provide the SBC as a separate document or in combination with other summary materials, such as a summary plan description (SPD), so long as the SBC information is "intact and prominently displayed at the beginning of the materials," such as after the Table of Contents in a SPD. However, SBCs issued for a plan in the individual market must be provided as a standalone document.[2]

A model SBC[3] and Uniform Glossary[4] of health coverage and medical terms has also been provided by CMS. These are provided in English, Chinese, Navajo, Spanish, and Tagalog.[5] An updated model SBC and Uniform Glossary are provided in Appendix A.

264. Can a state impose its own requirements on the SBC or Uniform Glossary?

No. Any state law that requires less information is preempted.[6] However, a state can impose additional disclosure requirements unless the plan is subject to ERISA, which preempts any contrary state law.[7] Private employer plans will be welfare benefit plans governed by ERISA. Government plans, church plans, and insurance policies purchased by individuals without significant employer involvement are not subject to ERISA.

265. Is the SBC used in connection with COBRA continuation coverage?

Yes. The exact language in the SBC template must be used without change.[8] The SBC template includes a section called "Your Rights to Continue Coverage." The instructions to this section of the template provide different required language for group and for individual

---

1. http://cciio.cms.gov/resources/other/index.html#sbcug.
2. See http://cciio.cms.gov/resources/other/index.html#sbcug.
3. http://cciio.cms.gov/resources/files/sbc-sample.pdf.
4. http://cciio.cms.gov/resources/files/Files2/02102012/uniform-glossary-finhttp://cciio.cms.gov/resources/files/sbc-sample.pdfal.pdf.
5. http://cciio.cms.gov/resources/other/index.html#sbcug.
6. PHSA §2715(e).
7. Preamble to Final Rule: Summary of Benefits and Coverage and the Uniform Glossary, 77 Fed. Reg. 8668, 8678 (Feb. 14, 2012); ERISA Sec. 514(b)(2)(B).
8. See What This Plan Covers and What it Costs: Instruction Guide for Group Coverage, February 2012, athttp://www.dol.gov/ebsa/pdf/SB-CInstructionsGroup.pdf.

coverage. For group coverage, the language provides a general statement about state and federal continuation coverage rights that "must appear without alteration," as follows:

> If you lose coverage under the plan, then, depending upon the circumstances, Federal and State laws may provide protections that allow you to keep health coverage. Any such rights may be limited in duration and will require you to pay a premium, which may be significantly higher than the premium you pay while covered under the plan. Other limitations on your rights to continuation coverage may also apply. For more information on your rights to continue coverage, contact the plan at [contact number]. You may also contact your state insurance department, the U.S. Department of Labor, Employee Benefits Security Administration at 1-866-444-3272 or www.dol.gov/ebsa, or the U.S. Department of Health and Human Services at 1-877-267-2323 x61565 or www.cciio.cms.gov.[1]

This section must be placed, as indicated in the template and instructions, after the section entitled "Other Covered Services" and before the section entitled "Your Grievance and Appeals Rights."

Exchange Notice Required

266. What is the Exchange notice requirement for employers?

FAQ guidance[2] provides that Exchange notices will not be required until after regulations on this requirement are issued and become applicable, which is by Oct. 1, 2013, and each year thereafter. Employers of all sizes, whether or not they have health plans, that are subject to the Fair Labor Standards Act must provide all new hires and current employees with a written notice about the health benefit Exchange and some of the consequences if an employee decides to purchase a qualified health plan through the Exchange in lieu of employer-sponsored coverage.[3] (Regulations implementing the Notice of Exchange requirement will be issued by the Secretary of Labor; the FLSA is enforced by the DOL).

267. When must employers give employees this Exchange Notice?

This disclosure requirement was to go into effect for employers beginning on March 1, 2013. In January 2013, the DOL announced a delay in the statutorily prescribed March 1, 2013 effective date.[4] The effective date is now Oct. 1, 2013, and each year thereafter. See Q 266.

The Exchange Notice will inform the employees about the existence of the health benefit exchange and give a description of the services provided by the exchange. Additionally, it will explain how the employee may be eligible for a premium tax credit or a cost-sharing reduction if the employer's plan does not meet certain requirements. The Exchange Notice must inform employees that if they purchase a qualified health plan through the exchange, then they may lose any employer contribution toward the cost of employer-provided coverage, and that all or

---

1. What This Plan Covers and What it Costs: Instruction Guide for Group Coverage, February 2012, at http://www.dol.gov/ebsa/pdf/SBCInstructionsGroup.pdf.
2. See FAQs About the Affordable Care Act Implementation Part V, Q/A-2, at http://www.dol.gov/ebsa/faqs/faqaca5.html.
3. FLSA §18B.
4. FAQs About the Affordable Care Act Implementation Part XI, Q/A-1 at http://www.dol.gov/ebsa/faqs/faq-aca11.html.

a portion of the employer contribution to employer-provided coverage may be excludable for federal income tax purposes. Finally, the Exchange Notice will include contact information for customer service resources within the exchange and an explanation of appeal rights.

268. Which employers are subject to the Exchange Notice requirement?

The Exchange Notice requirement applies to employers that are subject to the FLSA. Although the FLSA's minimum wage and maximum hour provisions are generally limited to entities that are engaged in interstate commerce and have a gross annual volume of sales that is not less than $500,000[1] it is not clear that the Exchange Notice has this same limitation. As a result, its scope appears to be determined by the FLSA's definition of "employer," which generally includes "any person acting directly or indirectly in the interest of an employer in relation to an employee."[2]

269. What is the penalty for failing to give the Exchange Notice?

The law provides no specific penalty for noncompliance.

HIPAA Electronic Transactions and Operating Rules

270. How has health reform expanded HIPAA's electronic transaction requirements?

HIPAA's provisions include standards for electronic transactions to reduce healthcare costs by encouraging the use of electronic data interchange (EDI), standardize the electronic processing of health care claims, and improve overall communication in the health care industry. Health reform[3] includes an expansion of HIPAA's electronic transaction requirements and requires HHS to adopt uniform standards and operating rules governing transactions with health plans. HHS issued regulations[4] adopting operating rules for two HIPAA electronic transactions: (1) eligibility for a health plan and (2) healthcare claim status.

271. When is compliance required with these expanded requirements?

Compliance is required by January 1, 2013, for (1) eligibility for a health plan and (2) healthcare claim status.[5] Additional regulations will be issued for other electronic requirements with their own due dates from 2014 through 2016.[6]

272. What should group health plan sponsors do to comply with these expanded requirements?

Most health plans do not process their own electronic transactions but instead engage a third party (called a "business associate") to process them. In this case, plan sponsors should ensure the relevant documents (such as a business associate agreement, a trading partner agreement,

---

1. 29 U.S.C. §§206 and 207.
2. 29 U.S.C. §203(d).
3. PPACA §1104.
4. 76 Fed. Reg. 40458 (July 8, 2011).
5. 76 Fed. Reg. 40458 (July 8, 2011).
6. SSA §1173(g)(4)(B).

and policies and procedures) are consistent with these rules. Plan sponsors' business associate agreements should require that the business associates as well as their agents and contractors comply with the rules.

273. What requirements are there for electronic funds transfer and health claims attachment transactions?

HHS must establish standards for electronic funds transfer and health claims attachment transactions. HHS has issued regulations called "health care electronic funds transfers (EFT) and remittance advice."[1] These new standards deal with EFT payments made through the Automated Clearing House (ACH) Network, and the remittance advice that explains the payment, the explanation of benefits (EOB).

274. What are the rules relating to HPIDs and OEIDs?

As required by health reform,[2] HHS issued regulations[3] establishing standards for a national unique health plan identifier (HPID) and implementation of the HPID. The regulations also establish another entity identifier (OEID) for non-health plan entities that may need to be identified in standard transactions.[4] The standards are based on recommendations from the National Committee on Vital and Health Statistics (NCVHS).

Large health plans must use the HPID in standard transactions beginning October 1, 2014, and small health plans must the HPID in standard transactions no later than October 1, 2015.[5]

275. What are the HPID rules for a controlling health plan (CHP) and a subhealth plan (SHP)?

A CHP is a health plan that controls its own business activities, actions, or policies, or is controlled by an entity that is not a health plan. Additionally, a CHP is an entity that directs the business activities, actions, or policies of one or more SHPs. All CHPs must obtain an HPID. An SHP is defined as a health plan whose business activities, actions, or policies are directed by a CHP. Health plans include group health plans, health insurance issuers, and HMOs.[6]

A controlling health plan (CHP), which includes a self-insured CHP, would be required to obtain an HPID. A subhealth plan (SHP) would not be required to obtain an HPID but could obtain an HPID at the direction of its CHP or on its own initiative. A CHP also would be able to obtain HPIDs for its SHPs.[7]

---

1. Administrative Simplification: Adoption of Standards for Health Care Electronic Funds Transfers (EFTs) and Remittance Advice, 77 Fed. Reg. 1556, 1564 (Jan. 10, 2012).
2. PPACA §1104(c)(1).
3. Administrative Simplification: Adoption of a Standard for a Unique Health Plan Identifier; Addition to the National Provider Identifier Requirements; and a Change to the Compliance Date for ICD-10-CM and ICD-10-PCS Medical Data Code Sets, 77 Fed. Reg. 22950 (Apr. 17, 2012).
4. Prop. HHS Reg. §162.514.
5. Prop. HHS Reg. §162.504(b).
6. Prop. HHS Reg. §162.103.
7. Prop. HHS Reg. §162.512.

If a CHP uses a single data processing center for all of its SHPs, the CHP may use one HPID for itself and its SHPs. Alternatively, if an SHP has its own processing center, the CHP could obtain a separate HPID for such SHPs or ask them to do so.

276. How are HPIDs and OEIDs used?

A covered entity is required to use an HPID when it identifies a health plan in a standard transaction. If a covered entity uses one or more business associates to conduct standard transactions, the covered entity would require them to use an HPID to identify the health plan in the standard transactions.[1]

Other uses for the HPID that are permitted, including in internal files, are to facilitate processing of healthcare transactions; on an enrollee's health insurance card; as a cross-reference in healthcare fraud and abuse files and other program integrity files; in patient medical records to identify patients' healthcare benefit packages; and for reporting purposes.[2]

The OEID is a voluntary identifier for entities that are not health plans but need to be identified in standard transactions. HHS asked for comments as to whether use of an OEID should be required.[3]

277. What are the penalties for failure to comply with the requirements and operating rules?

Through the Social Security Act (SSA) HHS will conduct audits to ensure that health plans (including third parties, such as business associates) comply with requirements and operating rules.[4] HHS can assess a penalty against a health plan for failing to meet the certification and documentation requirements.[5] HHS will assess a penalty of $1 per covered life up to a ceiling until the certification is complete.[6] The penalty doubles for any health plan that knowingly provides inaccurate or incomplete information in a statement of certification or documentation of compliance.[7] The annual penalty against a health plan may not exceed $20 per covered life and $40 per covered life if the plan knowingly has provided inaccurate or incomplete information.[8]

Automatic Enrollment

278. When are employers required to enroll employees automatically in their health benefits plan?

Starting in 2014 or when the DOL issues regulations, if later,[9] specified employers are required to enroll new full-time employees automatically in one of the "health benefits plans"[10]

---

1. Prop. HHS Reg. §162.510.
2. 77 Fed. Reg. 22950, 22958 (Apr. 17, 2012).
3. 77 Fed. Reg. 22950, 22962-63 (Apr. 17, 2012).
4. SSA §1173(i).
5. SSA §1173(j)(1)(A).
6. SSA §1173(j)(1)(B).
7. SSA §1173(j)(1)(C).
8. SSA §1173(j)(1)(E).
9. See FAQs About the Affordable Care Act Implementation Part V, Q/A-2, at http://www.dol.gov/ebsa/faqs/faq-aca5.html.
10. The term "health benefits plan" is not defined under the FLSA, although the term is used periodically in other provisions of healthcare reform, for example, in the new requirement to report health insurance coverage.

offered through the employer and must continue the enrollment of current employees in such plans.[1] This provision applies to employers that have more than 200 full-time employees and that offer employees enrollment in one or more health benefit plans.[2] Automatic enrollment may be subject to the plan's waiting period. The automatic enrollment program must include adequate notice and the opportunity for an employee to opt out of coverage.[3] Employers may ask employees to provide proof of alternative coverage, but the legislation does not require employees to provide this documentation.

The Fair Labor Standards Act (FLSA) does not define "full-time employee." For purposes of the FLSA, the employer makes that determination. It is likely that DOL regulations[4] will adopt the employer mandate definition of a full-time employee, which is a person who, for any month, is employed on average for at least thirty hours of service per week.[5]

The general FLSA preemption rule supersedes those state laws that are less beneficial to workers than the FLSA, but requires compliance with state laws that are more beneficial to workers than the FLSA.[6] Employers that have 200 or fewer employees and require employees to pay a portion of the health insurance premium must have employees authorize the payroll deduction in writing and cannot automatically enroll their employees in their group health plan without this authorization. Employers that have 200 or fewer employees and pay 100 percent of the health insurance premium may follow their policy or practice for automatic enrollment, including requiring the necessary information to be provided by employees for coverage.

New Health Insurance Nondiscrimination Provisions

279. What are the new health insurance income tax nondiscrimination rules?

Prior to the health reform law, the Internal Revenue Code only imposed nondiscrimination rules on self-insured health plans. No benefits-related nondiscrimination rules applied to an insured health plan. Thus, an insured group health plan could cover management and other highly paid employees under terms that were more favorable than those applicable to other employees, or not even cover the other employees.

Self-insured plans and employers' medical expense reimbursement plans are subject to the nondiscrimination provisions of Code Section 105(h), in effect since 1980. Congress originally believed that insurance underwriting considerations limited abuses favoring the highly paid in insured plans. However, underwriting practices in fact allowed plans to favor the highly compensated.

Health reform imposes similar rules to those that apply to self-insured plans or insured group health plans, other than grandfathered plans. The law does this in a very circular way.

---

1. FLSA §18A.
2. FLSA §18A.
3. FLSA §18A.
4. FAQs About the Affordable Care Act Implementation Part V, Q/A-2, at http://www.dol.gov/ebsa/faqs/faq-aca5.html.
5. IRC Sec. 4980H(c)(4)(A).
6. 29 U.S.C. §218.

Health reform law[1] added new ERISA Section 715 and Code Section 9815, respectively. Both ERISA Section 715 and Code Section 9815 incorporate by reference Public Health Service Act (PHSA) Section 2716, which incorporates by reference the concepts of Code Section 105(h). The law leaves the details of the insured plan nondiscrimination rules to the regulations. It merely requires "rules similar to" those in Code Section 105(h), regarding nondiscrimination eligibility, nondiscriminatory benefits, and controlled groups.[2] These rules prohibit discrimination in favor of highly compensated individuals (HCIs), who are generally the highest paid 25 percent of the employer's workforce.

280. When are the income tax nondiscrimination rules for nongrandfathered group health insurance plans applicable?

The law provides that these nondiscrimination rules are effective for nongrandfathered plans for plan years beginning on or after September 23, 2010. However, the IRS postponed the effective date until regulations are issued and the IRS announces a new effective date.[3] This had not yet occurred.

281. What is the consequence of violating the new health insurance nondiscrimination rules?

As a result of incorporating the HIPAA penalty, the excise tax that applies in the event of a violation of the HIPAA requirements also applies in the event of a violation of these new nondiscrimination requirements.[4] The health insurance nondiscrimination rules for nongrandfathered plans have different and potentially much harsher sanctions than for self-insured plans that fall under Code Section 105(h). For discriminatory self-insured plans, the highly compensated employees have taxable income based on the benefits paid by the employer. However, with respect to the new health insurance nondiscrimination requirements, the sanction is a $100 per day excise tax[5] on the "affected employees" and is paid by the employer or the plan in the case of a multiemployer plan. While the IRS has not yet issued any regulations on the penalty, its request for comments indicates that the term "affected employees" means all those who are not highly compensated. Thus, if an employer has an insured health plan that is not grandfathered and violates these new nondiscrimination rules for the plan year beginning on or after September 23, 2010, and if that employer has twenty non-highly compensated employees, the penalty will be $2,000 per day (20 employees X $100/day) as a result of having a discriminatory non-grandfathered health insurance plan.

---

1. PPACA §§1001 and 1562(e), (f).

2. PHSA §2716(a), which imposes such requirements in IRC Sec. 9815, and ERISA Sec. 715. PHSA §2716(a) requires nongrandfathered insured group health plans to satisfy the requirements of Code section 105(h)(2) (relating to prohibition on discrimination in favor of highly compensated individuals). For this purpose, "rules similar to the rules contained in" Code section 105(h)(3) (relating to nondiscriminatory eligibility), (4) (relating to nondiscriminatory benefits) and (8) (apply the rules to controlled groups). Code section 105(h)(5) (relating to which employees are "highly compensated") is not included, which means that the regulations are not bound to the highest paid 25 percent text in defining the group in favor of which a nongrandfathered insured plan cannot discriminate.

3. IRS Notice 2011-1.

4. Joint Committee Staff Technical Explanation of the Revenue Provisions of the Reconciliation Act of 2010, as amended, in combination with the Patient Protection and Affordable Care Act. (JCX-18-10) 3/21/10, p. 50.

5. IRC Sec. 4980D.

282. What is the small employer exception to the application of the excise tax, and does it apply to avoid the nondiscrimination tax penalty?

Code Section 4980(D)(d)(1) contains an exception to the excise tax for small employers, but the language is somewhat ambiguous. It states:

> In the case of a group health plan of a small employer which provides health insurance coverage solely through a contract with a health insurance issuer, no tax shall be imposed by this section on the employer on any failure (other than a failure attributable to §9811) *which is solely because of the health insurance coverage offered by such issuer.* (Emphasis added.)

It is not clear whether this exception applies to the new nondiscrimination rules or simply to a health insurance policy that does not meet federal requirements. The italicized language may mean that the exception will apply only if the insurance policy is discriminatory as opposed to the employer's plan being discriminatory. In other words, the small business exception may not apply if the plan, rather than the insurance policy, is nondiscriminatory. For the purpose of this exception, a small employer is defined as one with two to fifty employees.[1]

283. What are the issues involved in applying the nondiscrimination excise tax?

Code Section 4980D(a) imposes an excise tax on the failure of a group health plan to meet the requirements of Chapter 100 relating to group health plans. The amount of tax is $100 for each day in the noncompliance period with respect to each individual to whom such failure relates.[2] As noted in Q 280, Notice 2011-1 deferred the effective date of the insured plan nondiscrimination rules and indicates that the penalty will apply to nonhighly compensated individuals ("NHCIs"). Notice 2011-1 states:

> [I]f an insured group health plan fails to comply with Code Sec. 105(h), it is subject to a civil action to compel it to provide nondiscriminatory benefits and the plan or plan sponsor is subject to an excise tax or civil money penalty of $100 per day *per individual discriminated against.* [Emphasis added.][3]

The noncompliance period is the period beginning on the date on which the failure occurs,[4] and ends on the date the failure is corrected.[5] A failure is treated as corrected if it is retroactively undone to the extent possible,[6] and the person to whom the failure relates is placed in a financial position that is as good as the position such person would have been in had the failure not occurred.[7]

---

1. IRC Sec. 4980D(d)(1).
2. IRC Sec. 4980D(b)(1).
3. See also Notice 2010-63.
4. IRC Sec. 4980D(b)(2)(A).
5. IRC Sec. 4980D(b)(2)(B).
6. IRC Sec. 4980D(f)(3)(A).
7. IRC Sec. 4980D(f)(3)(B).

284. What are the limits or exceptions to the application of the nondiscrimination excise tax on nongrandfathered insured plans?

There are a number of limitations on the amount of the tax. First, no tax is imposed on any failure during any period for which it is established to the satisfaction of the IRS that the person liable for the tax did not know, and, exercising reasonable diligence, would not have known that such failure existed.[1] For church plans,[2] no tax is imposed if the failure is corrected before the end of the correction period.[3] For most plans, no tax is imposed if the failure was due to reasonable cause and not to willful neglect,[4] and such failure is corrected during the thirty-day period beginning on the first date the person otherwise liable for such loss knew, or exercising reasonable diligence would have known, that such failure existed.[5]

Notwithstanding these limits on the Code Section 4980D excise tax, in the case of one or more failures for an individual before the date a notice of examination of income tax liability is sent to the employer, and when such failure occurred or continued during the period under examination, there is a minimum tax with respect to such individual of not less than the lesser of $2,500, or the amount of tax that would have been imposed without regard to the limitations on tax.[6] To the extent that the violations are more than *de minimis* (an undefined term), $15,000 is substituted for $2,500.[7]

With respect to unintentional failures (i.e., those due to reasonable cause and not to willful neglect), the tax imposed on single employers for failures during the employer's tax year cannot exceed the lesser of:

- 10 percent of the aggregate amount paid or incurred by the employer (or predecessor employer) during the preceding tax year for group health plans, or

- $500,000.[8]

With respect to specified multiple employer health plans,[9] the excise tax cannot exceed the lesser of

---

1. IRC Sec. 4980D(c)(1).
2. Defined in IRC Sec. 414(e).
3. IRC Secs. 414(e)(4)(c) and 4980D(c)(2)(B)(ii).
4. IRC Sec. 4980D(c)(2)(A).
5. IRC Sec. 4980D(c)(2)(B)(i).
6. IRC Sec. 4980D(b)((3)(A).
7. IRC Sec. 4980D(b)(3)(B).
8. IRC Sec. 4980D(c)(3)(A)(i).
9. A specified multiple employer health plan is a group health plan that is either a multiemployer plan or a multiple employer welfare arrangement (MEWA), as defined in Section 3(40) of ERISA , as in effect on March 23, 2010. IRC Sec. 4980D(f)((2). IRC Sec. 4980D(c)(3)(ii) provides that if not all persons who are treated as a single employer for purposes of IRC Sec. 4980D have the same tax year, the tax years taken into account are determined under principles similar to the principles of IRC Sec. 1561. However, IRC Sec. 414(t), which provides for application of controlled group rules to various sections of the Code, references IRC Sec. 4980B, but not IRC Sec. 4980D. IRC Sec. 4980(D)(2)(A), for purposes of determining if an entity is a small employer, references Sections 414(b)(c), (m), and (o).

- 10 percent of the amount paid or incurred by such trust during the tax year to provide medical care directly or through insurance, reimbursement, or otherwise, or

- $500,000.[1]

However, if an employer is assessed a tax by reason of failure with respect to a specified multiple employer health plan, the limit is determined in the same manner as for a single employer plan, rather than for a specified multiple employer health plan.[2] For a failure due to reasonable cause and not to willful neglect, the IRS may waive all or a portion of the tax "to the extent that the payment of such tax would be excessive relative to the failure involved."[3]

The excise tax does not apply to a group health plan of a small employer[4] that provides health insurance coverage[5] solely through a contract with a health insurance issuer[6] with respect to any failure[7] that is solely because of the health insurance coverage offered by such issuer. The issues about the scope of this exception are discussed previously.

285. Who is liable to pay the excise tax?

Liability for the tax is generally imposed on the employer.[8] However, with respect to a multiemployer plan[9] or a failure under Code Section 9803 relating to guaranteed renewability with respect to a multiple employer welfare arrangement,[10] the tax is imposed on the plan.

286. How is the liability for the excise tax reported?

Employers subject to the excise tax must file Form 8928.[11] For single employer plans, the employer must file the return on or before the due date for filing the employer's income tax return, without any extensions unless a separate extension request is filed properly for Form 8928.[12] It also must reflect the portion of the noncompliance period for each failure that occurs during the employer's tax year.[13] If the person liable for the excise tax is a specified multiple employer health plan, the return must be filed on or before the last day of the seventh month

---

1. IRC Sec. 4980D(c)(3)(B)(i). For purposes of this section, all plans of which the same trust forms a part are treated as one plan.
2. IRC Sec. 4980D(C)(3)(B)(ii).
3. IRC Sec. 4980D(C)(4).
4. IRC Sec. 4980D(d)(2)(A) defines a small employer as an employer who, with respect to a calendar year and a plan year, employed an average of at least two but not more than fifty employees on business days during the preceding calendar year and who employed at least two employees on the first day of the plan year. For these purposes, as for tax-qualified plans, all persons treated as a single employer under Sections 414(b), (c), (m), and (o) are treated as one employer. With respect to an employer that was not in existence during the preceding calendar year, the determination of whether such employer is a small employer is based on the average number of employees that it is reasonably expected such employer will employ on business days in the current year. IRC Sec. 4980D(d)(2)(B). All references to "employer" include a reference to any predecessor of such employer. IRC Sec. 4980D(d)(2)(C).
5. IRC Sec. 4980D(d)(3) provides that health insurance coverage has the meaning set forth in IRC Sec. 9832.
6. IRC Sec. 4980D(d)(3) provides that health insurance issuer has the meaning set forth in IRC Sec. 9832.
7. The exemption for certain insured small employer plans does not apply to a failure described in IRC Sec. 9811, i.e. standards relating to benefits for mothers and newborns.
8. IRC Sec. 4980D(e)(1).
9. IRC Sec. 4980D(e)(2).
10. IRC Sec. 4980D(e)(3).
11. Reg. §§54.6011-2 and 54.4980D-1, A-1(a).
12. Reg. §54.6151-1. An automatic six-month extension for filing Form 8928 is available for applications filed on or after June 24, 2011, by submitting a Form 7004 on or before the prescribed day for filing the return and remitting the amount of the estimated tax liability. Reg. §54.6081-1(b).
13. Reg. 54.6071-1(b)(1). An extension for filing the employer's income tax return does not extend the time for filing Form 8928. Reg. 54.4980D-1, A-1(b).

following the end of the plan's plan year.[1] The return is filed at the place specified in Form 8928 and the instructions, and the tax shown on the return is paid to the IRS office with which the return is filed, at the time and place for filing each return.

287. What is the penalty if an insured plan incorrectly believes that it is grandfathered, but it is not?

How should Code Section 4980D be applied if a nongrandfathered health plan fails one of the technical requirements because the employer believes it to be grandfathered? For example, if a nongrandfathered plan provides coverage for obstetrical or gynecological care or both and requires the designation of an in-network primary care provider, the plan may not require authorization or referral by the plan or any person for a female participant who seeks gynecological or obstetrical care provided by an in-network specialist i.e., an obstetrician or a gynecologist. Additionally, the plan must advise each participant that the plan cannot require authorization or referral for gynecological care.

What if the employer believes that the plan is grandfathered but it is not grandfathered because it was unaware of the notice or recordkeeping requirements of the regulations or because it inadvertently failed to satisfy them? As a result, when Alice, a plan participant, requests a gynecological exam with Dr. Brady, an in-network OB-GYN, the plan requires prior authorization from Alice's designated primary care provider, Dr. Colby, for the exam. Dr. Colby provides the authorization, and Alice sees Dr. Brady. This prior authorization for a woman to see an OB-GYN is not permitted for a nongrandfathered plan.

In the example in the preceding paragraph, when did the failure occur? A failure cannot occur until the status as a grandfathered health plan is lost, but the regulations do not specify when this occurs. No precise time is provided for the required notice, but presumably, it should have been provided during the open enrollment period, but it was not. Therefore, (1) every female participant and dependent (at least those above a certain age) was affected by the failure to receive the notice and (2) at least all individuals in that category who saw a gynecologist or obstetrician in that period and had requested an authorization from the primary care physician were affected by that failure.

However, the IRS could argue that the latter failure related to all female plan participants and dependents because they may not have sought to obtain authorization from their primary care physician for the OB-GYN treatment. It is not clear if, with respect to one individual, there can be multiple failures relating to one Code requirement.

Assuming there was a failure, when would it be corrected, if at all? The first requirement is that the failure be retroactively undone to the extent possible. The second requirement is that the person to whom the failure relates be placed in the same financial position in which he or she would have been had the failure not occurred. However, unless the primary care physician charged the participant for obtaining that authorization/referral, there was no financial detriment to the participant unless the referral process caused a delay in seeing the OB/GYN, and the

---

1. Reg. §§54.6071-1(b)(2) and 54.4980D-1, A-1(c).

OB/GYN increased its fees in the interim. If so, the detriment is the difference between those fees. Absent this, the failure arguably is self-correcting but it is unknown whether the IRS will recognize this concept.

288. What if the failure to meet the nondiscrimination rules is due to reasonable cause and not willful neglect?

As to whether the failure was due to reasonable cause and not to willful neglect, the issue in all likelihood will not be whether the plan sponsor had some reasonable basis for a position that it took, but rather a matter of inadvertence (in the example above about a plan that the employer thought was grandfathered but was not), whether a participant failed to receive an SPD or open enrollment material, or whether some documents relating to verification, or clarification of grandfathered health plan status were not maintained. In the context of an inadvertent error, it may not be clear that, by exercising reasonable diligence, the employer would have known if the failure occurred. If a participant fails to receive a summary plan description or a document is improperly discarded, it is unclear if reasonable diligence would have located the errors. The issue of what constitutes "reasonable diligence" is based on all relevant facts and circumstances.

If the failure to provide notice or retain records was due to erroneous advice from a plan's advisor, many cases address what constitutes reasonable cause and not willful neglect.

A failure to give a notice or to maintain records is not as serious as a HIPAA violation, such as discrimination due to health status, which was the type of action that initially resulted in the imposition of this excise tax that was enacted with HIPAA. At a minimum, the amount of excise tax for the violation of the group health plan rules applicable only to non-grandfathered group health plans that do not violate HIPAA should depend on whether the plan administrator believed in good faith, albeit erroneously, that the plan had grandfathered status.

Waiting Period Limits and Eligibility Requirements

289. What is a waiting period?

A waiting period is the time that must pass before coverage for a person who is otherwise eligible for coverage under the terms of the plan is effective if the person applies for it. Being eligible for coverage means having met the plan's eligibility conditions other than any waiting period, such as being in a job category that is covered by the plan's terms).[1]

290. What is the maximum waiting period for essential health benefits in 2014?

Eligibility conditions based solely on the lapse of time are permissible for ninety days and no more. Other eligibility conditions are permitted unless the condition is designed to avoid

---

1. DOL Tech. Rel. 2012-01 (Feb. 9, 2012); IRS Notice 2012-17 (Feb. 10, 2012); HHS Bulletin: Frequently Asked Questions from Employers Regarding Automatic Enrollment, Employer Shared Responsibility, and Waiting Periods (Feb. 9, 2012) at http://cciio.cms.gov/resources/files/Files2/02102012/employer_faq_bulletin_2_9_12_final.pdf.

compliance with the ninety-day waiting period limitation. If an employee may elect coverage and be covered on a date that does not exceed a ninety-day waiting period, the ninety-day limit is met.

Group health plans and insurers offering group or individual coverage, including grandfathered plans or individual policies, are prohibited from applying a waiting period that exceeds ninety days for plan years beginning on or after January 1, 2014.[1] The prohibition on excessive waiting periods does not apply to "excepted benefits."[2] The prohibition applies regardless of the size of the employer/plan sponsor.

Compliance guidance was issued by the IRS, DOL, and HHS. This guidance is effective at least through 2014.

291. When does a waiting period begin?

The ninety-day waiting period begins when an employee is otherwise eligible for coverage under the terms of the group health plan.[3] If a plan provides that full-time employees are eligible for coverage without satisfying any other condition, and an employee was hired as a full-time employee, the waiting period for that employee would begin on the date of hire. Any eligibility condition based solely on the lapse of a time period is permitted for no more than ninety days.[4]

292. Is the ninety-day limit extended if employees take additional time to elect coverage?

A plan or insurer does not violate the ninety-day limit if employees take additional time to elect coverage.[5] Thus, if employees are eligible on the first day of the month following completion of enrollment forms, the fact that an employee hired on the first day of the month does not complete the forms that day does not violate the excessive waiting period rule.[6] Thus, if employees are eligible on the first day of the month following completion of enrollment forms, the fact that an employee hired on the first day of the month does not complete the forms that day does not violate the excessive waiting period rule.[7]

It is not permissible to allow eligibility on the first weekday, the first day of the month, or the beginning of the first pay period after a ninety-day waiting period ends even though the statute provides that a waiting period may not exceed ninety days. No guidance exists as to whether the ninety-day waiting period must be continuous.

1. PHSA §2708.
2. PHSA §2708.
3. Treas. Reg. §54.9801-3(a)(3)(iii); DOL Reg. §2590.701-3(a)(3)(iii); HHS Reg. §146.111(a)(3)(iii).
4. DOL Tech. Rel. 2012-01, Q/A-7 (Feb. 9, 2012), available at http://www.dol.gov/ebsa/newsroom/tr12-01.html.
5. IRS Notice 2012-59 (Aug. 31, 2012); DOL Tech. Rel. 2012-02 (Aug. 31, 2012); HHS Guidance on 90-Day Waiting Period Limitation PHSA §2708 (Aug. 31, 2012) at http://cciio.cms.gov/resources/files/Files2/2708-guidance-8-31-2012.pdf.
6. IRS Notice 2012-59, Q/A-1 (Aug. 31, 2012); DOL Tech. Rel. 2012-02, Q/A-1 (Aug. 31, 2012); HHS Guidance on 90-Day Waiting Period Limitation PHSA §2708, Q/A-1 (Aug. 31, 2012), at http://cciio.cms.gov/resources/files/Files2/2708-guidance-8-31-2012.pdf.
7. IRS Notice 2012-59, Q/A-1 (Aug. 31, 2012); DOL Tech. Rel. 2012-02, Q/A-1 (Aug. 31, 2012); HHS Guidance on 90-Day Waiting Period Limitation PHSA §2708, Q/A-1 (Aug. 31, 2012), at http://cciio.cms.gov/resources/files/Files2/2708-guidance-8-31-2012.pdf.

293. What other eligibility requirements can an employer have?

The law permits other eligibility conditions unless the condition is designed to avoid compliance with the ninety-day waiting period rule. For example, eligibility conditions such as full-time status or a bona fide specified job category are permitted. While employers and other plan sponsors who are subject to the employer mandate,[1] as discussed previously, may choose to base eligibility on full-time status (thirty hours or more), they are not required to do so.

In determining an eligibility requirement such as full-time status, a plan may use a reasonable measurement period of up to twelve months to determine whether a new employee with variable hours meets the condition. This period will not be considered to be designed to avoid compliance if coverage is available no later than thirteen months from the employee's start date (plus, if applicable, the time between the start date and the first day of the next month). If a plan requires a cumulative number of hours to become eligible, that requirement will not be considered to be designed to avoid compliance if the required hours do not exceed 1,200.

294. What other prohibitions apply to the eligibility requirements?

It is not permissible to allow eligibility on the first weekday, the first day of the month, or the beginning of the first pay period after a ninety-day waiting period ends even though the statute provides that a waiting period may not exceed ninety days. No guidance exists as to whether the ninety-day waiting period must be continuous.

295. How are permissible eligibility requirements applied to part-time and variable hour employees?

If a plan conditions eligibility on an employee regularly working a specified number of hours per period or working full-time, and the employer cannot determine that a new employee is reasonably expected regularly to work that number of hours or work full-time, the plan may take a reasonable amount of time to determine whether the employee meets the plan's eligibility condition. This may include a measurement period that is consistent with the timeframe used for purposes of the employer shared responsibility (employer mandate or "play or pay" penalty) provision.[2]

A period is reasonable if coverage is effective no later than thirteen months from the employee's start date, plus, if applicable, the time remaining until the first day of the next calendar month. Where cumulative hours of service are required for eligibility, up to 1,200 hours may be required; more than 1,200 hours would be considered designed to avoid compliance with the ninety-day waiting period limitation.

Illustration 1: Going from Part-Time to Full-Time Employment. Employer's plan limits eligibility for coverage to full-time employees. Coverage becomes effective on the first day of the calendar month following the date the employee becomes eligible. Employee begins working

---

1. IRC Sec. 4980H.
2. IRS Notice 2012-59 (Aug. 31, 2012); DOL Tech. Rel. 2012-02 (Aug. 31, 2012); HHS Guidance on 90-Day Waiting Period Limitation PHSA §2708 (Aug. 31, 2012) at http://cciio.cms.gov/resources/files/Files2/2708-guidance-8-31-2012.pdf.

full-time on May 15. Prior to this date, employee worked part-time for employer. Employee enrolls in the plan, and coverage is effective June 1. The period while employee was working part-time is not part of the waiting period because employee was not in a class of employees eligible for coverage while working part-time. Full-time employment is a condition that is not designed to avoid compliance with the ninety-day waiting period rule.[1]

Illustration 2: Part-Time Employee Satisfies Cumulative Hours of Service Requirement. Employee begins working twenty-five hours per week for Employer on January 1 as a part-time employee for purposes of employer's plan. Employer sponsors a plan that provides coverage to part-time employees after they have completed a cumulative 1,200 hours of service. Employee satisfies the plan's cumulative hours of service condition on December 15. The cumulative hours of service condition for part-time employees is not designed to avoid compliance with the ninety-day waiting period rule. Accordingly, coverage for employee under the plan must begin no later than the ninety-first day after employee works 1,200 hours. If the plan's cumulative hours of service requirement were more than 1,200 hours, that requirement would be deemed designed to avoid compliance with the ninety-day waiting period limitation.[2]

Illustration 3: Variable Hour Employee to Full-Time Status. Under employer's group health plan, employees who work full-time (defined as regularly working thirty hours per week or more) are eligible for coverage. Employee begins work for employer on May 15 of Year 1. Employee's hours are expected to vary between twenty and forty-five hours per week depending on work and employee's availability. Thus, it cannot be determined at employee's start date that employee is reasonably expected to work full-time. Under the terms of the plan, variable hour employees are eligible to enroll in the plan if they are determined to be full-time after a measurement period of twelve months. Coverage is made effective no later than the first day of the first calendar month after the applicable enrollment forms are received.

Employee's twelve-month measurement period ends May 14 of Year 2. Employee is determined to be full-time and is notified of his plan eligibility. If employee then elects coverage, his first day of coverage will be July 1 of Year 2. Here, the measurement period is permissible and not considered to be designed to avoid compliance with the ninety-day waiting period limitation because the plan may use a reasonable period of time to determine whether a variable hour employee is full time if the period of time is consistent with the timeframe permitted for such determinations under the employer shared responsibility rules. In such circumstances, the time period for determining whether an employee is full time will not be considered to avoid the ninety-day waiting period limitation if coverage can become effective no later than thirteen months from employee's start date, plus the time remaining until the first day of the next calendar month.[3]

---

1. IRS Notice 2012-59, Q/A-2 (Aug. 31, 2012; DOL Tech. Rel. 2012-02, Q/A-2 (Aug. 31, 2012); HHS Guidance on 90-Day Waiting Period Limitation PHSA §2708, Q/A-2 (Aug. 31, 2012) at http://cciio.cms.gov/resources/files/Files2/2708-guidance-8-31-2012.pdf.
2. IRS Notice 2012-59, Q/A-4 (Aug. 31, 2012); DOL Tech. Rel. 2012-02, Q/A-4 (Aug. 31, 2012); HHS Guidance on 90-Day Waiting Period Limitation PHSA §2708, Q/A-4 (Aug. 31, 2012) at http://cciio.cms.gov/resources/files/Files2/2708-guidance-8-31-2012.pdf.
3. IRS Notice 2012-59, Q/A-3 (Aug. 31, 2012); DOL Tech. Rel. 2012-02, Q/A-3 (Aug. 31, 2012); HHS Guidance on 90-Day Waiting Period Limitation PHSA §2708, Q/A-3 (Aug. 31, 2012) at http://cciio.cms.gov/resources/files/Files2/2708-guidance-8-31-2012.pdf (as visited Oct. 23, 2012).

Guaranteed Coverage
No Preexisting Conditions or Health Status Discrimination for Essential Health Benefits

296. How does health reform affect the ability of a health insurance policy or plan covering essential health conditions not to deny coverage or reimbursement for preexisting conditions (PCEs)?

Health reform eliminated the ability of a health insurance policy or plan covering essential health conditions to deny coverage or reimbursement for preexisting conditions for plan years beginning on or after September 23, 2010, for persons under age nineteen.[1] Group health plans and group health insurance companies, as well as individual policies cannot impose PCEs for plan years beginning on or after January 1, 2014.[2] A PCE may still be imposed for excepted benefits.

297. What is a preexisting condition (PCE)?

A PCE is "a limitation or exclusion of benefits (including a denial of coverage) based on the fact that the condition was present before the effective date of coverage (or if coverage is denied, the date of the denial)."[3] Thus, the prohibition covers (1) denial of enrollment and (2) denial of specific benefits based on a preexisting condition. A preexisting condition can be a serious medical condition, such as cancer, diabetes, or high blood pressure, or something relatively minor, such as tendonitis.

A PCE includes any limitation or exclusion based on information relating to an individual's health status, "such as a condition identified as a result of a pre-enrollment questionnaire or physical examination given to the individual, or review of medical records relating to the pre-enrollment period."[4]

298. Are certificates of creditable coverage still required?

Under HIPAA rules relating to preexisting conditions coverage, group health plans and health plan issuers are required to issue certificates of creditable coverage. Beginning on or after January 1, 2014, PPACA's prohibition on preexisting condition exclusions applies and a certificate of creditable coverage need no longer be issued. However, the current regulations will continue to apply until December 31, 2014, so that individuals needing to offset a preexisting condition exclusion under a plan that operates with a plan year beginning later than January 1, 2014, would still have access to the certificate for proof of coverage.[5]

---

1. PPACA §10103(e)(2) (2010).
2. PHSA §2704(a); IRC Sec. 9815, and ERISA Sec. 715.
3. Treas. Reg. §54.9801-2; DOL Reg. §2590.701-2; HHS Reg. §144.103.
4. Treas. Reg. §54.9801-2; DOL Reg. §2590.701-2; HHS Reg. §144.103.
5. Prop. Reg. §54.9801-5.

Cost-Sharing Limits

299. What are the cost-sharing limits on out-of-pocket expenses and annual deductibles?

For plan years beginning in 2014, except as discussed subsequently, the cost sharing for self-only and coverage other than self-only coverage cannot exceed the maximum out-of-pocket expense limits for self-only and family coverage for HSA-compatible high deductible health plans (HDHPs) for taxable years beginning in 2014,[1] namely $6,350 for individuals and $12,700 for families. The HDHP deductible amount is adjusted for increases in the cost of living. This sets the maximum out-of-pocket expense limit, i.e., the plan's annual deductible (which is separately limited, as discussed in Q 300) and other annual out-of-pocket expenses (such as copayments) the insured is required to pay. The agencies interpret the annual limit as applying only to employers and insurers in the individual and small group markets for nongrandfathered plans.[2] In the case of a plan using a network of providers, cost sharing paid by, or on behalf of, an individual for benefits provided outside of such network does not count toward the annual limitation on cost sharing or the annual limitation on deductibles.[3]

However, employer plans that have "separately administered" benefits, such as a primary package of health benefits and a different insurer or administrator for other benefits such as prescription drugs, need not comply until 2015.[4] Employer plans with separately administered benefits that qualify for the delay must apply some out-of-pocket limits in 2014. These plans must ensure that their primary package of health benefits has an out-of-pocket limit of no more than $6,350 for individuals and $12,700 for families. A separately administered benefit, such as prescription drugs, that already has an existing limit on out-of-pocket costs must also comply with the limits of $6,350 for individuals and $12,700 for families in 2014.[5]

For a plan year beginning in a calendar year after 2014, the cost-sharing limit for self-only coverage is the amount for self-only coverage for plan years beginning in 2014, increased by an index amount equal to the product of that amount and the "premium adjustment percentage" for the calendar year. For coverage other than self-only coverage, the cost-sharing limit for a plan year beginning in a calendar year after 2014 is twice the amount for self-only coverage.[6] The premium adjustment percentage for a calendar year is determined by HHS and is the percentage by which the average per capita premium for health insurance coverage in the United States for the preceding calendar year exceeds the average per capita premium for 2013.[7]

---

1. PPACA §1302(c)(1)(A) (2010); IRC Sec. 223(c)(2)(A)(ii).
2. HHS Reg. §156.130(b); Standards Related to Essential Health Benefits, Actuarial Value, and Accreditation, 45 CFR Parts 147, 155, and 156, 78 Fed. Reg. 12834, 12837 (Feb. 25, 2013).
3. HHS Reg. §156.130(c).
4. FAQs About the Affordable Care Act Implementation Part XII, Q/A-2 at http://www.dol.gov/ebsa/faqs/faq- aca12.html.
5. Id.
6. PPACA §1302(c)(1)(B) (2010); PPACA §1302(c)(4) (2010).
7. PPACA §1302(c)(4) (2010).

300. What are the 2014 limits for annual deductibles?

The deductible cannot exceed $2,000 for a plan covering one individual and $4,000 for any other plan.[1] The annual limitation on deductibles is to be applied in such a manner so as to not affect the actuarial value of any health plan, including a plan in the bronze level, as explained previously.[2] Furthermore, the allowance of an annual deductible does not allow a plan to have a deductible for preventive health services.

While one might conclude from the statute that the annual deductible limit is solely for plans in the small group market,[3] it most likely applies to any "group health plan."[4] These amounts may be increased by the maximum amount of reimbursement that is reasonably available to a participant under a flexible spending arrangement to the extent funded by the employer and not the employee.[5]

Clinical Trials and Coverage

301. What patient protections does the law create for persons participating in clinical trials?

Specifically, a group health plan may not:

- deny any qualified individual the right to participate in a clinical trial as described below,

- deny, limit, or impose additional conditions on the coverage of "routine patient costs" for items and services furnished in connection with participation in the clinical trial;[6] or

- discriminate against any qualified individual who participates in a clinical trial.[7]

A plan can require a "qualified individual" to use an in-network provider participating in a clinical trial if the provider will accept the individual as a participant. A person participating in an approved clinical trial conducted outside the state of the individual's residence is also protected if the plan otherwise provides out-of-network coverage for routine patient costs.[8]

---

1. PPACA §1302(c)(2)(A) (2010).
2. PPACA §1302(c)(2)(C) (2010).
3. PPACA §1302(c)(2)(A).
4. PHSA §2707(b). The DOL Web site states that PHSA §2707(b) requires "all group health plans to comply with limitations on allowable cost sharing." See Application of the New Health Reform Provisions of Part A of Title XXVII of the PHS Act to Grandfathered Plans, at http://www.dol.gov/ebsa/pdf/grandfatherregtable.pdf.
5. PPACA §1302(c)(2)(A) (2010) refers to a health flexible spending arrangement described in IRC Sec. 106(c)(2) and the maximum amount of reimbursement which is reasonably available to a participant for such coverage is less than 500 percent of the value of such coverage. In the case of an insured plan, the maximum amount reasonably available is determined by underlying coverage.
6. PHSA §2709(a)(1)(B).
7. PHSA §2709(a)(1)(C).
8. PHSA §§2709(a)(3),(4) and 2709(c).

"Routine patient costs" include items and services provided for a person not enrolled in a clinical trial. However, such items and services do not include:

- the investigational item, device or service itself;

- items and services not included in the direct clinical management of the patient, but rather in connection with data collection and analysis; or

- a service clearly not consistent with widely accepted and established standards of care for the particular diagnosis.[1]

A "qualified individual" is a group health plan participant or beneficiary who is eligible to participate in an approved clinical trial for the treatment of cancer or other life-threatening disease or condition and:

- The referring healthcare professional is a participating provider and has concluded that the participant's or beneficiary's participation in the clinical trial would be appropriate, or

- The participant or beneficiary provides medical and scientific information establishing that the individual's participation in the clinical trial would be appropriate.[2]

An "approved clinical trial" is a Phase I, Phase II, Phase III, or Phase IV clinical trial that:

- is conducted in connection with the prevention, detection, or treatment of cancer or other life-threatening disease or condition[3] and is federally funded through a variety of entities or departments of the federal government, including the National Institutes of Health, the CDC, the Centers for Medicare & Medicaid Services, a cooperative group or center of any of the previous entities or the Department of Defense or the Department of Veterans Affairs, a qualified nongovernmental research entity identified in guidelines issued by the National Institutes of Health for center support grants and, if certain conditions are met, the Department of Veterans Affairs, the Department of Defense, and the Department of Energy;[4]

- is conducted in connection with an investigational new drug application reviewed by the Food and Drug Administration;[5] or

- is exempt from investigational new drug application requirements.[6]

---

1. PHSA §2709(a)(2).
2. PHSA §2709(b).
3. A "life-threatening condition" is a disease or condition likely to result in death unless the disease or condition is interrupted. PHSA §2709(e).
4. PHSA §2709(d)(1)(A).
5. PHSA §2709(d)(1)(B).
6. PHSA §2709(d)(1)(C).

Fair Insurance Premiums
Health Insurance Rating Rules

302. What are the health insurance rating rules imposed by health reform?

Effective in 2014, health reform imposes new federal rules on how health insurers may "rate" or price their products. Grandfathered plans and plans in the large group and self-insured markets are not subject to these rules. However, if large group market insurance plans are offered on an exchange, they will be subject to these rating rules.[1]

Under the new rules, insurers will be allowed to vary premiums for coverage in the individual and small group markets using only four factors:

- Self-only versus family coverage,

- Geographic "rating area," established by each state,[2]

- Age, and

- Tobacco use.

In the cases of age and tobacco use, the new rules also limit the extent of the permitted premium variations.[3]

For tobacco use, the maximum allowed variation will be 1.5 to 1, meaning that a plan will not be allowed to charge a tobacco user more than one and a half times (or 50 percent above) the rate charged to a non-tobacco user. With respect to age rating, the maximum allowed variation for adults will be 3 to 1, meaning that a plan will not be allowed to charge a sixty-four-year-old more than three times the premium charged a twenty-one-year-old for the same coverage.

Under the law, premiums also may vary based only on self-only or family enrollment and rating area, as specified by the state.[4] Factors such as gender and health status are not allowed.[5]

Additionally, health reform[6] prohibits employer-sponsored health plans and commercial health insurers from imposing a preexisting-condition exclusion on the coverage of any enrollee or applicant under any circumstances.[7] This blanket prohibition took effect for children (under age nineteen) on September 23, 2010, and will take effect for adults on January 1, 2014.[8] Under prior law, insurers and employer self-insured health plans are required to provide coverage

---

1. PHSA §2701(a)(5).
2. PHSA §2701(a)(2)(A).
3. PPACA §1201(4).
4. PHSA §2701.
5. PHSA §2701(a)(1)(B).
6. PPACA §1201(2)(A).
7. PHSA §2701.
8. PPACA §1255.

to enrollees in employer-sponsored plans on a guaranteed-issue basis and are prohibited from varying premiums based on individual health status.[1] Sections 1201(2) and (4) of PPACA (the health reform law) extend those requirements to the individual market as well, effective January 1, 2014.[2]

Health Insurance Coverage Transparency Reporting and Cost-Sharing Disclosure

303. What are the "transparency in coverage" reporting and cost-sharing disclosures?

Health reform requires each state to have a health insurance exchange for the purchase of qualified health plans (QHPs).[3] A health plan seeking QHP certification must disclose certain information to the exchange, HHS, and the state insurance commissioner, and make the information available to the public ("transparency in coverage" reporting and cost-sharing disclosures).[4] Both exchange QHPs and health plans and insurers outside an exchange must comply.[5] The requirements for QHPs and plans and insurers outside of the exchange are identical to the requirements for QHPs on an exchange, except that with respect to transparency in coverage reporting, non-exchange plans and insurers are not required to provide the information to the exchange.

Grandfathered policies and group plans are not required to comply[6] except for QHPs sold on an exchange.[7]

304. What information must be provided for transparency in coverage reporting?

Health plans and insurers subject to the transparency in coverage reporting requirement must make accurate and timely disclosure of the following information to HHS, the state insurance commissioner, and the public:

- claims payment policies and practices;

- periodic financial disclosures;

- data on enrollment and disenrollment;

- data on the number of claims denied;

- data on rating practices;

---

1. 42 U.S.C. §§300gg, 300gg-1, and 300gg-11.
2. PHSA §§2701 and 2702.
3. PPACA §1311(b)(1).
4. PPACA §1311(e)(3)(A).
5. PHSA §2715A.
6. PPACA §§1251(a) and 10103(d)(1); Treas. Reg. §54.9815-1251T(c)(1).
7. PPACA §§1251(a) and 10103(d)(1); Treas. Reg. §54.9815-1251T(c)(1).

- information on cost-sharing and payments regarding any out-of-network coverage;

- information on enrollee and participant rights under Title I of PPACA; and

- other information as determined by HHS.[1]

Additionally, exchange-based QHPs must disclose this information to the exchange.

The information must be disclosed using "plain language" that the intended audience, including individuals with limited English proficiency, can readily understand and use because that language is concise, well-organized, and follows other best practices of plain language writing.[2]

305. What cost-sharing disclosures to individuals must be made?

Health plans and insurers subject to this requirement must provide certain cost-sharing (including deductibles, copayments, and coinsurance) information in a timely manner on request by an individual.[3] At a minimum, the information must be made available to the individual through an Internet Web site. However, for those individuals who do not have access to the Internet, the information must be provided in some other means.[4]

No Discrimination against Providers

306. How does health reform prohibit discrimination against healthcare providers, such as physicians?

A group health plan and a health insurance issuer offering group or individual health insurance coverage cannot discriminate as to participation under the plan or coverage against any healthcare provider acting within the scope of that provider's license or certification under applicable state law. However, this rule does not require that a group health plan or health insurance issuer contract with any healthcare provider willing to abide by the terms and conditions for participation established by the plan or issuer.[5]

In addition, this law does not prevent HHS, a group health plan, or a health insurance issuer, from establishing varying reimbursement rates based on quality or performance measures.[6]

This law is the first federal provider non-discrimination law applicable to non-government and to self-insured ERISA plans. "Group health plans" and "health insurance issuers offering group or individual health insurance coverage" include self-insured employee health benefit plans, group health insurance, individual health insurance, and likely the federal employees health benefits program. This nondiscrimination requirement applies to products sold through the new health insurance exchanges starting in 2014.

---

1. PPACA §1311(e)(3)(A).
2. PPACA §1311(e)(3)(B).
3. PPACA §1311(e)(3)(C).
4. PPACA §1311(e)(3)(C).
5. PHSA §2706(a).
6. PHSA §2706(a).

307. What are some examples of prohibited discrimination against providers?

Possible prohibited activities could include the following:

- Health insurer requires that optometrists seeking to be participating providers in health plan provider network must also contract to be participating providers in free-standing vision plan, but does not impose same requirement on ophthalmologists or other physicians.

- Health insurer maintains "closed" or "limited" network of podiatrists but has "open panel" approach to participation by qualified orthopedic physicians and primary care physicians.

  o Could be vulnerable to charge of discrimination.

  o Could perhaps be defended on ground that law does not impose "any willing provider requirement" and plan has different needs for orthopedic surgeons than for podiatrists or achieves legitimate business objectives by varying contracting approach taking into account services provided by orthopedists compared to podiatrists, and is not discriminating based on license.

- Health insurer includes optometrists or nurse midwives in network only in rural areas but not in urban areas.

- Health insurer has different fee schedule for same CPT code service based on whether service is performed by psychologist or M.D.

- Insurer has limited network for provision of certain eye exams for which it uses an RFP bid process to choose a vendor, but has a separate provider network for a different set of eye care services some of which are not performed in that state by optometrists, such as eye surgery. If optometrists are able to participate in bid activity for the former, but are not able to qualify for the second, is this federal law violated?

- What if insurer imposes new credentialing criteria that are hard for non-MDs to meet, and it grandfathers people in its existing network, which includes a few non-MDs?

308. What is the effective date of the provider nondiscrimination requirements?

This provision is effective January 1, 2014, or, for group plans, plan years beginning on or after January 1, 2014.[1]

---

1. PPACA §1255.

309. How will the nondiscrimination requirement be enforced?

HHS enforces the PHSA for government plans, and the states enforce the law for its private health insurance requirements.[1] Sanction for insurers that violate the law would depend on state law. HHS enforces the PHSA for self-insured group health plans and, if the state does not enforce it, for health insurers.[2]

For HHS enforcement, HHS may impose a civil monetary penalty on insurance issuers that fail to comply with the PHSA requirements. The maximum penalty imposed under the PHSA is $100 per day per individual with respect to which such a failure occurs.[3] Similar to the Internal Revenue Code, certain minimum penalty amounts may apply to a plan or employer if the violation is not corrected within a specified period, or if a violation is considered to be more than *de minimis*. In determining the amount of the penalty, HHS must take into account the entity's previous record of compliance with the PHSA provisions.

In addition, a penalty may not be imposed for a violation if it is established to the Secretary's satisfaction that none of the entities knew (or if exercising reasonable diligence would have known) that the violation existed. If the violation was due to reasonable cause and not willful neglect, a penalty would not be imposed if the violation were corrected within thirty days of discovery.[4] Entities found to violate the PHSA requirements may challenge the penalty in a hearing subject to a decision by an administrative law judge.[5] Following this administrative hearing, entities may file an action for judicial review.[6]

310. To what products or programs do these provider nondiscrimination rules not apply?

These provider nondiscrimination rules do not apply to Medicare, Medicare Advantage, Medicare Supplement or Medicaid. Medicare Advantage plans already are prohibited from discriminating, in terms of participation, reimbursement, or indemnification, against any healthcare professional who is acting within the scope of his or her license or certification under state law, solely on the basis of the license or certification. Additionally, the requirement does not apply to "excepted benefits," such as stand-alone dental and vision coverage, workers compensation, long-term-care insurance, insurance for a specific disease or illness, or hospital indemnity insurance, for example.

---

1. 42 U.S.C. §300gg-22(a)(1).
2. 42 U.S.C. §300gg-22(a)(2).
3. 42 U.S.C. §300gg-22(b)(2)(C)(i).
4. 42 U.S.C. §300gg-22(b)(2)(C)(iii).
5. 42 U.S.C. §300gg-22(b)(2)(D).
6. 42 U.S.C. §300gg-22(b)(2)(E).

PART VIII: REQUIRED DISCLOSURES AND INFORMATION REPORTING

W-2 Reporting Beginning 2013

311. What is the W-2 reporting requirement and when is it effective?

Employers, including those with grandfathered plans,[1] must report the "aggregate cost" of "applicable employer sponsored coverage" on an employee's Form W-2.[2] This cost generally consists of employer-sponsored coverage under a group health plan (insured or self-funded) that is excludable from the employee's gross income.[3] IRS Notice 2012-9 supersedes earlier notices[4] that delayed and created exceptions to the PPACA W-2 reporting requirement, which originally was to apply for 2011 W-2s that normally would be issued by employers in January 2012. The W-2 reporting requirement, which was delayed by the IRS, first applies to 2012 W-2s that generally will be issued in January 2013 unless an exception (discussed in Q 315) applies.

312. What is the income tax impact of this requirement to employers and employees?

None. This requirement is merely designed to provide information to the federal government. It does not change any rules regarding the employer's deductions or the taxation to the employee. Failure to properly report will not cause coverage that is excludible from gross income under Code Section 106 or any other Code provision to become taxable or to be reported in any other box on Form W-2.[5]

313. Which employers must comply with the expanded W-2 reporting?

This requirement includes employers that are federal, state and local government entities, churches and other religious organizations, and employers that are not subject to the COBRA continuation coverage requirements under Code Section 4980B.[6]

314. Is the amount reported on the W-2 the amount for health coverage paid by the employer?

No. The reportable cost generally includes the amounts paid by both the employer and employee, regardless of whether paid through pre-tax or after-tax contributions. The aggregate reportable cost is reported on Form W-2 in Box 12, using Code DD.[7]

---

1. PPACA §1251(a) lists the requirements for which an employer is exempt and does not include the W-2 requirement.
2. PPACA §9002.
3. IRC Sec. 6051(a)(14).
4. IRS Notices 2010-69 and 2011-28.
5. Notice 2012-9, Q&A 2.
6. Notice 2012-9, Q&A 3.
7. Notice 2012-9, Q&A 5.

315. Which employers are exempt from the W-2 reporting requirement?

The W-2 reporting requirement does not apply to the following:

- Employers with fewer than 250 W-2s issued for the prior calendar year until further notice.[1]

- An employer that would have filed only 100 Forms W-2 for the previous year had it not used an agent under Code Section 3504[2] will not be subject to the reporting requirement for the year, nor will an agent under Code Section 3504 with respect to that employer's Forms W-2 for the year. In contrast, if the same employer would have filed 300 Forms W-2 for the previous year had it not used an agent under Code Section 3504, that employer would be subject to the reporting requirement for the year. If an agent under Code Section 3504 is used again, the information will need to be provided to the agent and reported on the Form W-2.[3]

- An employer is not required to report any amount in Box 12 using Code DD for an employee who, pursuant to §31.6051-1(d)(1)(i), has requested to receive a Form W-2 before the end of the calendar year during which the employee terminated employment.[4]

- Coverage under a flexible spending arrangement if contributions occur only through employee salary reductions.[5]

- "Excepted benefits," which include dental and vision plans offered under a separate policy, certificate, or contract of insurance, or if the participants have the right to elect the dental or vision benefits and, if they do, pay an additional premium or contribution.[6]

- Excess reimbursements that are includible in the income of highly compensated individuals under Code Section 105(h) or payments or reimbursements of health insurance premiums for a 2 percent shareholder-employee of an S corporation.[7]

---

1. Notice 2012-9, Q&A 3. Tribally chartered corporations wholly owned by a federally recognized Indian tribal government are also exempt .Id.
2. This agent is not a payroll service that prepares paychecks for the employer's signature. Rather, an agent under IRC Sec. 3504 performs acts such as the withholding, reporting and paying of federal employment taxes with regard to wages paid by the agent for the employer, as well as the agent's own employees. A Section 3504 agent agrees to assume liability along with the employer for the employer's Social Security, Medicare and federal income tax withholding responsibilities. An agent is appointed using IRS Form 2678 and files aggregate returns using the agent's EIN. The Section 3504 designation does not apply to FUTA tax, with a limited exception provided for certain household workers. See IRS Notice 2003-70.
3. Notice 2012-9, Q&A 3.
4. Notice 2012-9, Q&A 6.
5. Notice 2012-9, Q&A 19.
6. Notice 2012-9, Part II and Q&A 20.
7. Notice 2012-9, Q&A 23.

- The cost of hospital or other fixed indemnity coverage, or coverage only for a specified disease or illness, is not reportable if the coverage is offered as an independent, noncoordinated benefit and is includible in the employee's income or paid for on an after-tax basis. However, the cost of such coverage is reportable when paid for on a pre-tax basis under a cafeteria plan or with employer contributions that are excludable from income.

316. What about related employers that each employ and pay the same person?

Related employers that do not use a common paymaster can either provide the full reportable cost to an employee on a single Form W-2 or allocate the cost and reporting among the employers.[1] The notice does not define the term "related employers." Presumably, it means related employers as defined for W-2 purposes.[2] This definition includes the following types of corporations if they satisfy any one of the following four tests at any time during a calendar quarter:

(i)   The corporations are members of a "controlled group of corporations", as defined in Code Section 1563, or would be members if Code Section 1563(a)(4) and (b) did not apply and if the phrase "more than 50 percent" were substituted for the phrase "at least 80 percent" wherever it appears in Code Section 1563(a).

(ii)   In the case of a corporation that does not issue stock, either 50 percent or more of the members of one corporation's board of directors (or other governing body) are members of the other corporation's board of directors (or other governing body), or the holders of 50 percent or more of the voting power to select such members are concurrently the holders of more than 50 percent of that power with respect to the other corporation.

(iii)   Fifty percent or more of one corporation's officers are concurrently officers of the other corporation.

(iv)   Thirty percent or more of one corporation's employees are concurrently employees of the other corporation.[3]

317. How is the amount of reportable cost determined?

Employers that use a composite rate to determine premiums for active employees and another method to determine COBRA premiums may use either rate to determine the reportable cost, but they must use that method consistently when reporting the cost for each applicable group.[4]

---

1. Notice 2012-9, Q&A 7 provides that if two or more related corporations concurrently employ the same individual and compensate such individual through a common paymaster which is one of such corporations, each such corporation shall be considered to have paid as remuneration to such individual only the amounts actually disbursed by it to such individual and shall not be considered to have paid as remuneration to such individual amounts actually disbursed to such individual by another of such corporations.
2. Reg. §31.3121(s)-1.
3. Reg. §31.3121(s)-1.
4. Notice 2012-9, Q&A34.

An employer may also include in the reportable cost of coverage certain amounts that need not be reported, such as the cost of coverage for a Health Reimbursement Account.

The reportable cost of coverage may be based on the information available to the employer on December 31, and need not be adjusted for later elections or notifications, such as a divorce or other change in family status that retroactively affects coverage during the prior year.[1]

318. How do employers with self-insured health plans calculate the aggregate cost of applicable employer-sponsored coverage?

There are COBRA rules governing how a self-insured plan determines its applicable premium, generally requiring that such plans calculate the applicable premium through the actuarial method or the past cost method.[2] Presumably these are the methods used, as the IRS notices provide no special guidance.[3]

319. How is the cost for EAPs, wellness programs, and on-site medical clinics reported?

The cost of EAPs (employee assistance programs), wellness programs, and on-site medical clinics is includible in the reported cost of coverage to the extent that the program is a group health plan. However, such coverage is not reportable if the employer does not charge a premium for that coverage for purposes of COBRA (or other federally required continuation coverage) or if the employer is not subject to COBRA.[4]

320. What is the penalty for failure to follow the W-2 reporting requirements?

There is no special penalty for failure properly to report healthcare costs. Presumably, the normal W-2 penalties will apply.[5]

321. What about health costs paid for retirees not entitled to a W-2?

Employers are not required to issue a W-2 to report health plan costs to persons not otherwise required to receive a W-2.[6]

322. Has the IRS provided a chart summarizing the W-2 health cost reporting requirements?

Yes. It is as follows:[7]

---

1. Notice 2012-9, Q&A 35.
2. ERISA Sec. 604(2); IRC Sec. 4980B(f)(4)(B); PHSA §2204(2).
3. IRS Notices 2011-28 and 2012-9.
4. Notice 2012-9, Q&A 32.
5. IRC Secs. 6721, 6722, and 6674.
6. Notice 2012-9, Q&A 9.
7. See http://www.irs.gov/newsroom/article/0,,id=257101,00.html.

Form W-2 Reporting of Employer-Sponsored Health Coverage			
	Form W-2, Box 12, Code DD		
Coverage Type	Report	Do Not Report	Optional
Major medical	X		
Dental or vision plan not integrated into another medical or health plan			X
Dental or vision plan which gives the choice of declining or electing and paying an additional premium			X
Health Flexible Spending Arrangement (FSA) funded solely by salary-reduction amounts		X	
Health FSA value for the plan year in excess of employee's cafeteria plan salary reductions for all qualified benefits[1]	X		
Health Reimbursement Arrangement (HRA) contributions			X
Health Savings Arrangement (HSA) contributions (employer or employee)		X	
Archer Medical Savings Account (Archer MSA) contributions (employer or employee)		X	
Hospital indemnity or specified illness (insured or self-funded), paid on after-tax basis		X	
Hospital indemnity or specified illness (insured or self-funded), paid through salary reduction (pre-tax) or by employer	X		
Employee Assistance Plan (EAP) providing applicable employer-sponsored healthcare coverage	Required if employer charges a COBRA premium		Optional if employer does not charge a COBRA premium

---

1. X's cafeteria plan offers permitted taxable benefits (including cash), qualified nontaxable benefits (including a health FSA), and an employer flex credit of $1,000. John makes a $2,000 salary reduction election for several qualified benefits under the plan, including a health FSA for $1,500. The cost of his qualified benefits under the plan for the year is $3,000. The amount of John's salary reduction election for the plan year ($2,000) equals or exceeds the amount of the health FSA for the plan year ($1,500), so none of the health FSA amount is taken into account when determining the aggregate reportable cost. See IRS Notice 2012-9 Q&A 19 (Example 2).

On-site medical clinics providing applicable employer-sponsored healthcare coverage	Required if employer charges a COBRA premium		Optional if employer does not charge a COBRA premium
Wellness programs providing applicable employer-sponsored healthcare coverage	Required if employer charges a COBRA premium		Optional if employer does not charge a COBRA premium
Multi-employer plans			X
Domestic partner coverage included in gross income	X		
Governmental plans providing coverage primarily for members of the military and their families		X	
Federally recognized Indian tribal government plans and plans of tribally charted corporations wholly owned by a federally recognized Indian tribal government		X	
Self-funded plans not subject to Federal COBRA			X
Accident or disability income		X	
Long-term care		X	
Liability insurance		X	
Supplemental liability insurance		X	
Workers' compensation		X	
Automobile medical payment insurance		X	
Credit-only insurance		X	
Excess reimbursement to highly compensated individual, included in gross income		X	
Payment/reimbursement of health insurance premiums for 2% shareholder-employee, included in gross income		X	
Other Situations	**Report**	**Do Not Report**	**Optional**
Employers required to file fewer than 250 Forms W-2 for the preceding calendar year (determined without application of any entity aggregation rules for related employers)			X

| Forms W-2 furnished to employees who terminate before the end of a calendar year and request, in writing, a Form W-2 before the end of that year | | | X |
| Forms W-2 provided by third-party sick-pay provider to employees of other employers | | | X |

Exchange Notice Required Beginning October 1, 2013

323. What is the Exchange Notice that employers must give and when is the requirement effective?

The health insurance exchanges will be operational on January 1, 2014. PPACA requires employers to provide a notice prior to the beginning date of the exchange. Originally required March 1, 2013, this notice must be provided by all employers, regardless of size, subject to the Fair Labor Standards Act (virtually all employers) to employees by Oct. 1, 2013.[1] Notices must be provided by employers, including those without a group health plan, to both active part-time and full-time employees (not spouses or dependents), regardless of whether eligible for the employer's health plan, if any.[2]

New employees hired on and after October 1, 2013, must receive the notice within fourteen days of hire. This fourteen-day notification period for new hires is in effect from October 1, 2013, through 2014 (the timing to be revisited at that point).

The employer's health plan year is not relevant in regard to the required delivery of this exchange notice. Notice may be sent first class mail or electronically.

There are 2 model notices. For employers with a health plan, see http://www.dol.gov/ebsa/pdf/FLSAwithplans.pdf. For employers with no health plan, see http://www.dol.gov/ebsa/pdf/FLSAwithoutplans.pdf. These model notices are reproduced in Appendix B.

324. Who is an employer for this purpose?

The notice requirement applies to employers that are subject to the Fair Labor Standards Act (FLSA). The term "employer" is defined in the FLSA as "any person acting directly or indirectly in the interest of an employer in relation to an employee." This broad definition will likely encompass most employers.

325. What is the purpose and content of the Exchange Notice?

The notice is intended to inform the employees about the existence of the health benefit exchange and give a description of the services provided by the exchange. The notice also will explain how the employee may be eligible for a premium tax credit or a cost-sharing reduction if the employer's plan does not meet certain requirements. The

---

1. DOL Technical Release No. 2013-02; FAQs about Affordable Care Act Implementation Part XI, Q&A 1, available at http://www.dol.gov/ebsa/faqs/faq-aca11.html.
2. FLSA § 18B.

notice must inform employees that if they purchase a qualified health plan through the exchange:

- They may lose any employer contribution toward the cost of employer-provided coverage, and

- All or a portion of the employer contribution to employer-provided coverage may be excludable for federal income tax purposes.

Lastly, the notice will include contact information for customer service resources within the exchange and an explanation of appeal rights. The regulations clarified that the notice must meet certain accessibility and readability requirements, as well as be in writing.

The DOL is expected to release a model notice, along with additional guidance, prior to the March 1, 2013, effective date.

326. Which employees must receive the notice?

All employees, not just those eligible for health coverage must receive the notice. The FLSA broadly defines an employee as "an individual employed by an employer."[1]

327. What are the penalties for failure to give the Exchange Notice to employees?

There is no known penalty at this time.

Reporting of Health Insurance Coverage (Insurers and Employers that Self-Insure) for 2015 and Thereafter

328. In addition to the W-2 reporting, what other reporting must employers make to the IRS and covered individuals?

Healthcare reform requires any person who provides "minimum essential coverage"[2] to an individual during a calendar year to report certain health insurance coverage information to the IRS.[3] Reporting is required for grandfathered plans.[4] No reporting is required for "excepted benefits."[5] The employer must also provide a written statement to the covered individual, as discussed in Q 342.

---

1. FLSA §3(e)(1), 29 USC §203(e)(1).
2. IRC Sec. 5000A.
3. IRC Sec. 6055.
4. IRC Sec.5000A(f)(1)(D).
5. IRC Sec.5000A(f)(3).

329. When does this reporting requirement go into effect?

The requirement for Reporting of Health Insurance Coverage originally was to be effective in 2014. However, IRS Notice 2013-45, issued in July 2013, provided a one-year delay to three reporting requirements under the healthcare reform law.

The first reporting requirement that was postponed was the annual obligation under Section 6055 of the Internal Revenue Code (Code) for insurers, self-insuring employers and other parties that provide "minimum essential coverage" to provide certain information to the IRS.

The other two requirements that were postponed were

- The annual obligation under Code Section 6056 for applicable large employers to report to the IRS and to the employer's full-time employees as to whether and what healthcare coverage is offered to such employees.

- The requirement under Code Section 4980H for applicable large employers to offer healthcare coverage to full-time employees or pay penalties, commonly known as the "play-or-pay" penalties (POP).

(See Q 344 through Q 347 for discussions of the Code Section 6056 for applicable large employers.)

330. What type of information must be reported to the IRS?

The type of information includes the name and address of the primary insured and other individuals covered under an applicable policy, the dates of coverage, and whether and by what method Minimum Essential Coverage is provided. This information is used to determine various employer and individual penalties, when applicable.

331. Did the July 2013 IRS Notice postpone all elements of the PPACA reporting requirements?

No. The Notice postpones compliance with only these three requirements until 2015. Everything else scheduled to become effective in 2014 will go into effect in 2014. See PPACA Timeline, Part III, Q 98.

332. What new effective dates did the July 2013 IRS Notice provide?

The Notice advises that the IRS will in the summer of 2013 propose regulations for the two information-reporting provisions now effective in 2015. The IRS encourages employers, insurers and other reporting entities to voluntarily comply with the proposed rules for information reporting for 2014, but no penalties for failure to comply with these reporting provisions now exist for 2014.

333. Why were the reporting requirements postponed?

The information reporting required by Code Sections 6055 and 6056 must occur in order for the IRS to enforce and administer the employer mandate requirements under Code Section

4980H. The employer mandate penalties are triggered if one or more of an applicable large employer's full-time employees are entitled to premium tax credits for the purchase of insurance on a state exchange marketplace under Code § 36B and (1) the employer fails to offer 95 percent of full-time employees and their dependents the opportunity to enroll in minimum essential coverage or (2) the employer offers full-time employees and dependents the opportunity to enroll in minimum essential coverage but the coverage is not affordable or does not provide minimum value. The second penalty can never exceed the first penalty.

An employer typically will not know whether a full-time employee has received such a tax credit, and the employer will not have all the information needed to determine whether it owes an employer mandate penalty. Therefore, applicable large employers do not have to calculate employer mandate penalties or file returns submitting payment for such penalties in 2014.

Instead, the IRS, after receiving the information returns filed by applicable large employers under Code Section 6056 and the information about employees claiming the premium tax credit for any given calendar year, will determine whether any of the employer's full-time employees received the premium tax credit and, if so, whether any employer mandate penalty is due. The IRS will thus contact any applicable large employer if the employer owes a penalty, and the employer will have an opportunity to respond to the information provided by IRS before any penalty is assessed. (See Q 344 through Q 347 for information on the Code 6056 requirements affecting certain large employers.)

334. What were other reasons for the postponement of the reporting requirements?

An employer typically will not know whether a full-time employee has received such a tax credit, and the employer will not have all the information needed to determine whether it owes an employer mandate penalty. Therefore, applicable large employers do not have to calculate employer mandate penalties or file returns submitting payment for such penalties. Instead, the IRS, after receiving the information returns filed by applicable large employers under Code Section 6056 and the information about employees claiming the premium tax credit for any given calendar year, will determine whether any of the employer's full-time employees received the premium tax credit and, if so, whether any employer mandate penalty is due. The IRS will thus contact any applicable large employer if the employer owes a penalty, and the employer will have an opportunity to respond to the information provided by IRS before any penalty is assessed.

335. Is an employees' ability to receive premium tax credits in 2014 effected by the reporting requirement delay?

No. The Notice states that the transition relief does not affect an individual's eligibility for a premium tax credit if he or she purchases health insurance through one of the health insurance exchange marketplaces established under the Act. Participants in the exchanges will continue to qualify for premium tax credits if their household income is within the specified range and they are not eligible for other minimum essential coverage. Such other minimum essential coverage includes eligible employer-sponsored group health plans that are affordable and provide minimum value.

336. Were any 2014 requirements of the PPACA affected by the extension of the effective date of these reporting requirements?

No. The Notice makes clear that the 2014 transition relief is limited solely to these three items and has no effect on the effective date or application of other provisions under the Act, many of which go into effect in 2014. For example, the transition relief has no effect on the provisions taking effect in 2014 as to premium tax credits for those purchasing subsidized health insurance on an exchange marketplace or the individual mandate requirements under Code § 5000A for individuals to maintain healthcare coverage for themselves or pay penalties.

337. What are some of the 2014 requirements that were not affected by the postponement of these three reporting requirements?

Provisions taking effect for Plan Years beginning on or after Jan. 1, 2014 include the following:

- Group health plans, whether or not "grandfathered" under the Act, may not impose dollar limits on "essential health benefits."

- Non-grandfathered health insurance plans in the small group market must offer essential health benefits.

- Group health plans and health insurance issuers offering group health insurance coverage may not establish rules for initial or continued eligibility of an individual to enroll in the plan or discriminate as to coverage based on the individual's or dependent's health status-related factors, such as medical condition (both physical and mental illnesses); claims experience; receipt of healthcare; medical history; genetic information; evidence of insurability (including conditions arising out of acts of domestic violence); and disability. Nevertheless, premium or contribution provisions for similarly-situated individuals in connection with a wellness program that satisfies certain requirements are permitted

- Group health plans and health insurance issuers offering group health insurance coverage, including grandfathered plans and policies, may not impose any preexisting condition exclusion.

- Group health plans, including grandfathered plans, cannot apply waiting periods for coverage that are greater than 90 days.

- Non-grandfathered group health plans may not impose annual cost-sharing that exceeds the maximum out-of-pocket expense limits for health savings account-compatible high-deductible health plans.

(See Part III, Q 98, for a complete PPACA implementation timeline.)

338. What is "minimum essential coverage" that must be reported?

Most employer-provided group health coverage is "minimum essential coverage." The definition includes any "eligible employer-sponsored plan." This includes a group health plan or group health insurance coverage offered by an employer to an employee that is a governmental plan or any other plan or coverage offered in a state's small or large group market.[1]

339. Who is subject to this reporting requirement?

Employers sponsoring insured and self-insured plans must file reports.[2] It is possible that insurers will be required to make this reporting on behalf of employers with insured group health plans. Additionally, these requirements must be coordinated with the additional reporting required for large employers, discussed in Q 344 to Q 347, to prevent redundant reporting.

340. When is this reporting requirement effective?

The Code Section 6055 reporting requirement is first required for coverage provided on or after January 1, 2014. The first information returns will be filed in 2015.

341. What information must be reported to the IRS?

The return is on a form provided by the IRS and must contain the following information:

- the name, address, and taxpayer identification number (TIN) of the primary insured (this term is undefined but most likely refers to employees and not family members), and the name and TIN of each other individual obtaining coverage under the policy;

- the dates during which the individual was covered during the calendar year;

- if the coverage is health insurance coverage, whether the coverage is a qualified health plan (QHP) offered through a health benefit exchange;

- if the coverage is health insurance coverage and that coverage is a QHP, the amount of any advance cost-sharing reduction payment or of any premium tax credit with respect to such coverage; and

- any other information required by the IRS.[3]

In addition, if health insurance coverage is through an employer-provided group health plan, the return must contain the following information:

- the name, address, and employer identification number (EIN) of the employer maintaining the plan;

---

1. IRC Sec. 5000A(f)(2).
2. Joint Committee on Taxation, "Technical Explanation of the Revenue Provisions of the 'Reconciliation Act of 2010,' as Amended, in Combination with the 'Patient Protection and Affordable Care Act,'" at p. 35 (2010).
3. IRC Sec. 6055(b)(1).

- the portion of the premium (if any) required to be paid by the employer; and

- any other information the IRS may require to administer the new tax credit for health insurance for eligible small employers.[1]

342. What statement must be furnished to covered individuals?

The person who is required to report the health insurance coverage to the IRS (as described above in Q 339) must also furnish a written statement to each individual whose name must be included in the information return. This statement must include:

- the name, address, and contact information of the reporting person; and

- the information required to be shown on the return with respect to that individual (discussed in Q 341).[2]

This statement must be furnished to the covered individual on or before January 31 of the year following the calendar year for which the information was required to be reported to the IRS.[3]

343. What is the sanction for noncompliance with this reporting requirement?

An employer that fails to comply with these reporting requirements is subject to penalties for failure to file an information return and failure to furnish payee statements.[4]

Health Insurance Coverage Reporting by Large Employers and Offering Employers for 2015 and Thereafter

344. In addition to the requirements described above in Q 323 to Q 343 for employers to report to the IRS and employees, what other similar reporting requirements exist?

Internal Revenue Code Section 6056 contains requirements similar to those described in Q 341 that are imposed by Code Section 6055. The Code Section 6056 requirements apply to "applicable large employers" and "offering employers." The IRS may allow for any return or written statement required under this provision (i.e., large employers and "offering employers") to be provided as part of a return or written statement required under Code Section 6055, discussed above in Q 341.[5]

Applicable Large Employers. "Applicable large employers" are the employers with fifty or more full-time equivalent employees (on average, during the preceding year) that may be liable for the employer mandate penalty tax under Code Section 4980H if they provide no health

---

1. IRC Sec. 6055(b)(2).
2. IRC Sec. 6055(c)(1).
3. IRC Sec. 6055(c)(2).
4. IRC Sec. 6724(d) defines "information return" for the penalty provisions in IRC Secs. 6721, 6722, and 6723.
5. IRC Sec. 6056(d)(2).

coverage or do not provide affordable health coverage to their full-time employees (and their dependents).[1]

Offering Employers. The reporting requirement also applies to "offering employers," which are employers that offer "minimum essential coverage" to employees under an eligible employer-sponsored plan and the employee contribution of any employee exceeds 8 percent of the wages paid to that employee by the employer.[2]

345. What information is reported by the applicable large employers and offering employers?

The employer files an information return with the IRS with the following information:

- the employer's name, date, and employer identification number (EIN);

- a certification of whether the employer offers its full-time employees and their dependents the opportunity to enroll in "minimum essential coverage" under an "eligible employer-sponsored plan;"[3]

- the number of full-time employees the employer has for each month during the calendar year;

- the name, address, and taxpayer identification number (TIN) of each full-time employee employed by the employer during the calendar year and the months (if any) during which the employee and any dependents were covered under a health benefit plan sponsored by the employer during the calendar year; and

- any other information required by the IRS.[4]

Employers that offer the opportunity to enroll in "minimum essential coverage" must also report:

- the months during the calendar year for which coverage under the plan was available;

- the monthly premium for the lowest cost option in each of the enrollment categories under the plan;

- the employer's share of the total allowed costs of benefits provided under the plan;

---

1. IRC Sec. 4980H.
2. IRC Sec. 6056(f)(1).
3. Defined in IRC Sec. 5000A(f)(2).
4. IRC Sec. 6056(b).

- in the case of an employer that is an applicable large employer, the length of any waiting period for such coverage;

- for an offering employer, the option for which the employer pays the largest portion of the cost of the plan and the portion of the cost paid by the employer in each of the enrollment categories under such option; and

- any other information required by the IRS.[1]

346. Which statements must be furnished to employees by "applicable large employers" and "offering employers?"

Employers required to submit a report of health insurance coverage to the IRS under Code Section 6056 must also furnish a written statement to each of their full-time employees whose name was required to be included in the report to IRS. This statement includes:

- the name, address, and contact information of the reporting employer; and

- the information required to be shown on the return with respect to the individual.[2]

The written statement must be furnished to full-time employees on or before January 31 of the year following the calendar year for which the information was required to be reported to the IRS.[3]

347. What are the consequences for failure to comply with the Code Section 6056 reporting requirements?

An employer that fails to comply with these reporting requirements is subject to penalties for failure to file an information return and failure to furnish payee statements.[4]

Annual Report by DOL about Self-Insured Plans (Using Form 5500 Information)

348. What information must the DOL report to Congress regarding self-insured health plans?

Healthcare reform requires the DOL to prepare and submit to Congress an aggregate annual report that includes general information collected from Form 5500 filings by self-insured group health plans, including plan type, number of participants, benefits offered, funding arrangements, and benefit arrangements.[5]

---

1. IRC Sec. 6056(b).
2. IRC Sec. 6056(c)(1).
3. IRC Sec. 6056(c)(2).
4. IRC Sec. 6724(d) defines "information return" for the penalty provisions in IRC Secs. 6721, 6722, and 6723.
5. PPACA §1253.

Insured Health Plan Transparency in Coverage and Cost-Sharing Reporting

349. What are the transparency in coverage and cost-sharing reporting requirements?

The transparency in coverage reporting and the cost-sharing disclosure rules apply to individual policies and group health plans, both qualified health plans (QHPs), and those outside of the exchanges.[1] The requirements are the same except that non-exchange health plans need not report to the exchange. These health plan reports are made to HHS, the state insurance commissioner, and the public.[2] The rules do not apply to grandfathered plans,[3] although if a QHP sold on an exchange were grandfathered, it would need to make a report to the exchange.[4] In addition, a health plan seeking QHP certification on an exchange must provide certain cost-sharing disclosures to participants.[5]

350. What information must be reported under these rules?

Health plans and insurers subject to the transparency in coverage reporting requirement must disclose all of the following information:

- claims payment policies and practices;

- periodic financial disclosures;

- data on enrollment and disenrollment;

- data on the number of claims denied;

- data on rating practices;

- information on cost-sharing and payments regarding any out-of-network coverage;

- information on enrollee and participant rights under Title I of PPACA; and

- other information as determined appropriate by the Secretary of HHS.[6]

351. Must any of this information be disclosed to individuals?

Yes. Health plans and insurers subject to this requirement must provide certain cost-sharing information (including deductibles, copayments, and coinsurance) in a timely manner on request

---

1. PHSA §2715A (plans and insurers outside of the Exchange) and PPACA §1311(e)(3)(A)(requirement for exchange-certified health plans).
2. PHSA §2715A.
3. PPACA §§1251(a), 10103(d)(1).
4. PPACA §1311(e)(3)(A).
5. PPACA 1311(e)(3)(C).
6. PPACA §1311(e)(3)(A).

by an individual.[1] The information generally may be provided on a Web site, but for individuals who do not have access to the Internet, the information must be provided another way.[2]

SPD Content Requirements for ERISA Group Health Plans

352. Does health reform make any changes in the SPD requirements for group health plans?

The law does not make changes directly, but it does direct the DOL to update and harmonize its rules governing disclosures to group health plan participants (e.g., plan terms and conditions or periodic financial disclosure) with standards established by HHS.[3] Thus, some additional SPD disclosure requirements are expected.

Quality of Care Reporting by Group Health Plans and Insurers

353. What reporting is required by group health plans and insurers that is designed to improve the quality of care?

Group health plans and health insurance companies must submit an annual report to HHS addressing plan or coverage benefits and provider reimbursement structures that may affect the quality of care in certain specified ways. The reporting requirements are to be developed in consultation with health care quality experts and representatives of care providers, care recipients, insurers, and employers. This requirement will be enforced by "appropriate penalties" developed by HHS.[4] Grandfathered plans are not subject to these rules.[5]

HHS was required to "develop" the reporting requirements and issue regulations no later than March 23, 2012.[6] HHS missed the deadline.[7]

354. What information must be reported and when?

The quality of care report will address whether plan or coverage benefits as well as provider reimbursement structures satisfy several criteria related to the cost and quality of health care. These will include whether the plan or coverage:

- improves health outcomes for treatment or services under the plan or coverage through such activities as quality reporting, effective case management, care

---

1. PPACA §1311(e)(3)(C).
2. PPACA §1311(e)(3)(C).
3. PPACA §1311(e)(3)(D).
4. PHSA §2717(a).
5. PPACA §§1251(a) and 10103(d)(1).
6. PHSA §2717.
7. The Government Accountability Office (GAO) released a report on January 13, 2012 stating that HHS has failed to properly supervise the development of quality measures that are required by PPACA. The report, "Health Care Quality Measurement: HHS Should Address Contractor Performance and Plan for Needed Measures" (GAO-12-136), also criticized the National Quality Forum (NQF), a nonprofit group that has a 4-year, $100 million contract with HHS to develop quality measures, for missing deadlines and exceeding contract cost estimates. The 75-page GAO report expresses concern that if HHS does not exert more control over NQF's performance, it "may be unable to ensure that [HHS] receives the quality measures needed to meet PPACA requirements," including deadlines for the implementation of new programs and initiatives to control healthcare costs.

coordination, chronic disease management, and medication and care compliance initiatives (including the medical homes model);

- implements activities to prevent hospital re-admissions using a comprehensive discharge program and post-discharge reinforcement;

- improves patient safety and reduces medical errors through best clinical practices, evidence-based medicine, and health information technology; and

- implements wellness and health promotion activities.[1]

Cadillac Plan Excise Tax Determination

355. What is the "Cadillac Tax" and what reporting is required?

The "Cadillac Tax" is effective in 2018 and its intent is to discourage expensive health plans that require enrollees to pay little for their own care. It is discussed in more detail in Part IX of this book.

An employer will have to determine whether the following costs for each employee for each year exceed $10,200 (individual) and $27,500 (family):

- Health care coverage;

- Employer health FSA contributions and any reimbursements in excess of the employer contributions;

- Employer and employee pretax HSA contributions; and

- HRA contributions.

If the cost is above the threshold, the employer is required to determine the excess amount and report it to the Secretary of the Treasury and each third-party administrator or insurer, including the excess amounts attributable to each third-party administrator or insurer.

List of Required Disclosures and Notices to Health Plan Participants

356. What are the various notices required to be made to health plan participants?

In addition to the mandates discussed earlier in Part VII of this book that need to be described in the health plan SPD, the following notices must be given:

Grandfather Status (effective for plan years beginning on and after September 23, 2010). Grandfathered plans must include a statement in any plan material provided to participants and beneficiaries each year describing benefits under the plan that the plan believes it is grandfathered

---

1. PHSA §2717(a)(1).

and contact information for questions and complaints. See Q 168. The DOL provided model language as follows:

> This [group health plan or health insurance issuer] believes this [plan or coverage] is a "grandfathered health plan" under the Patient Protection and Affordable Care Act (the Affordable Care Act). As permitted by the Affordable Care Act, a grandfathered health plan can preserve certain basic health coverage that was already in effect when that law was enacted. Being a grandfathered health plan means that your [plan or policy] may not include certain consumer protections of the Affordable Care Act that apply to other plans, for example, the requirement for the provision of preventive health services without any cost sharing. However, grandfathered health plans must comply with certain other consumer protections in the Affordable Care Act, for example, the elimination of lifetime limits on benefits.

> Questions regarding which protections apply and which protections do not apply to a grandfathered health plan and what might cause a plan to change from grandfathered health plan status can be directed to the plan administrator at [insert contact information]. [For ERISA plans, insert: You may also contact the Employee Benefits Security Administration, U.S. Department of Labor at 1-866-444-3272 or www.dol.gov/ebsa/healthreform. This website has a table summarizing which protections do and do not apply to grandfathered health plans.] [For individual market policies and nonfederal governmental plans, insert: You may also contact the U.S. Department of Health and Human Services at www.healthreform.gov.]

Rescission Prohibition (effective for plan years beginning on and after September 23, 2010). All plans must provide at least thirty days' advance written notice to each participant who would be affected by a rescission, whether the rescission applies to the entire group or to an individual.

Primary Care Designation Notice (plan years beginning on or after September 23, 2010). All non-grandfathered plans must provide notice of the following: If a plan requires the designation of a primary care provider, the plan must allow each participant or beneficiary to elect a primary care provider who will accept him/her, including a pediatrician for a child. A plan also must allow direct access to an in-network OB/GYN for female participants or beneficiaries. The following is a model notice:

> For plans and issuers that require or allow for the designation of primary care providers by participants or beneficiaries, insert:

> [Name of group health plan or health insurance issuer] generally [requires/allows] the designation of a primary care provider. You have the right to designate any primary care provider who participates in our network and who is available to accept you or your family members. [If the plan or health insurance coverage designates a primary care provider automatically, insert: Until you make this designation, [name of group health plan or health insurance issuer] designates one for you.] For information on how to select a primary care provider, and for a list of the participating primary care providers, contact the [plan administrator or issuer] at [insert contact information].

For plans and issuers that require or allow for the designation of a primary care provider for a child, add:

For children, you may designate a pediatrician as the primary care provider.

For plans and issuers that provide coverage for obstetric or gynecological care and require the designation by a participant or beneficiary of a primary care provider, add:

You do not need prior authorization from [name of group health plan or issuer] or from any other person (including a primary care provider) in order to obtain access to obstetrical or gynecological care from a health care professional in our network who specializes in obstetrics or gynecology. The health care professional, however, may be required to comply with certain procedures, including obtaining prior authorization for certain services, following a pre-approved treatment plan, or procedures for making referrals. For a list of participating health care professionals who specialize in obstetrics or gynecology, contact the [plan administrator or issuer] at [insert contact information].

PPACA Prohibition on Lifetime Dollar Limits; Re-enrollment Right (plan years beginning on or after September 23, 2010). If an individual was no longer eligible for coverage under the plan because of reaching the lifetime dollar limit, the plan must allow the individual into the plan on the first plan year on and after September 23, 2010. The plan must provide notice of the right to reenroll to this individual. The following model notice can be used:

The lifetime limit on the dollar value of benefits under [Insert name of group health plan or health insurance issuer] no longer applies. Individuals whose coverage ended by reason of reaching a lifetime limit under the plan are eligible to enroll in the plan. Individuals have 30 days from the date of this notice to request enrollment. For more information contact the [insert plan administrator or issuer] at [insert contact information].

Annual Limits (effective for plan years beginning on or after September 23, 2010). For plan years beginning before January 1, 2014, a plan may impose restricted annual dollar limits on essential benefits. However, a plan may obtain a waiver of the dollar limits if it can show that these restrictions would increase cost or limit access to benefits. If a plan receives a waiver, it must provide a notice to all participants that, in a 14-point font:

- states that the plan or policy does not meet the minimum annual limits for essential benefits and received a waiver of this requirement;

- specifies the dollar amount of the annual limit;

- describes the plan benefits to which the limits apply; and

- states that the waiver is only granted until the last day of the plan year before January 1, 2014.

For waivers received for plan years on or after February 1, 2011, the notice must be provided as part of any informational or educational materials and included in the SPD. HHS provided a model notice. Waiver recipients must receive permission to use language that is different from the model notice.

Adult Child Coverage Opportunity (effective for plan years beginning on or after September 23, 2010). The following model notice can be used:

Individuals whose coverage ended, or who were denied coverage (or were not eligible for coverage), because the availability of dependent coverage of children ended before attainment of age 26 are eligible to enroll in [Insert name of group health plan or health insurance coverage]. Individuals may request enrollment for such children for 30 days from the date of notice. Enrollment will be effective retroactively to [insert date that is the first day of the first plan year beginning on or after September 23, 2010.] For more information contact the [insert plan administrator or issuer] at [insert contact information].

Claims and Appeals Process. Health reform adds additional requirements for claims and appeals procedures for non-grandfathered plans. These requirements were effective for plan years beginning on and after September 23, 2010, but the DOL provided an enforcement grace period for certain provisions for plan years beginning on and after the date noted below. This notice must:

- be written in a culturally and linguistically appropriate manner (effective January 1, 2012).

- provide the following additional content:

  ○ Information sufficient to identify the claim involved, including the date of service, the healthcare provider, the claim amount, and a statement that the diagnosis code and its corresponding meaning and the treatment code and its corresponding meaning are available on request.

  ○ An explanation of the reason for the adverse benefit determination or final adverse benefit determination, including the denial code and its meaning and a description of the plan's standard that was used in denying the claim or making the final adverse determination (effective July 1, 2011).

  ○ Describe the internal appeals and external review process (effective July 1, 2011).

  ○ Describe the availability of and contact information for an applicable office of health insurance consumer assistance or ombudsman as established under PPACA (effective July 1, 2011).

If a plan does not meet all of the requirements in the regulations, the claimant is deemed to have exhausted the internal claims and appeals process and may initiate any available external review or remedies under ERISA or state law. The strict adherence standard will not apply if the errors were:

- de minimis;

- nonprejudicial or nonharmful;

- for good cause or because of matters beyond the plan's control;

- in the context of an ongoing, good-faith exchange of information; and

- not a pattern or practice of non-compliance.

If a plan asserts the exception, it must provide an explanation in response to a written request from the claimant (effective January 1, 2012).

Summary of Benefits and Coverage (SBC) (effective for open enrollments beginning for plan years beginning on and after September 23, 2012 and new enrollments). The SBC must be provided to employees. The SBC must not exceed eight pages (four sheets front and back), be in 12-point font, be presented in "culturally and linguistically" appropriate language, and include the following:

- A Uniform Glossary, i.e., definitions of standard insurance terms and medical terms.

- A description of coverage and any cost sharing (including any deductibles, coinsurance, and copayments, but not premiums).

- Any exceptions, reductions, and limitations on coverage.

- Renewability and continuation coverage provisions.

- Coverage examples (currently only childbirth and diabetes, but up to four more may be added in the future).

- A statement of whether the plan provides minimum essential coverage and has an actuarial value of at least 60 percent (effective for plan years beginning on and after January 1, 2014).

- A contact number to call and an Internet address or Web site for a copy of the policy or the SPD for self-funded plans).

- If a plan has multiple networks, contact information for obtaining a list of network providers.

- If a plan uses a prescription drug formulary, contact information for obtaining information on prescription drug coverage.

- An Internet address or Web site for obtaining the Uniform Glossary, a contact number to obtain a paper copy of the Uniform Glossary, and a disclosure that paper copies are available.

A sample SBC and Uniform Glossary are provided in the Appendix A of this book. If any material modification of any of the terms of the plan coverage is made and it is not reflected in the most recent SBC, notice of the modification must be provided no later than sixty days before the modification becomes effective.

W-2 Reporting 2012 Calendar Year Health Care Coverage (reportable by January 31, 2013). See Q 311 to Q 327.

Explanation of Exchange, the Exchange Notice. Effective March 1, 2013 and for all new hires thereafter.

Reporting of Health Insurance Coverage Effective for Plan Years beginning on and after January 1, 2014. An employer must file a return with the IRS showing:

- The name, address, and TIN of the participant and the name and TIN of each beneficiary

- The date of coverage

- The employer's name, address, and EIN

- The portion of the premium paid by the employer.

An employer must provide to a participant the following before January 31 of the year following the reporting year:

- The name and address of the employer and a phone number of the contact for the information provided to the participant

- The information that is required to be on the return to the IRS.

Automatic Enrollment (presumably plan years beginning on and after January 1, 2014). An employer with more than 200 employees must automatically enroll each new full-time employee and continue such enrollment, unless the employee opts out or changes the coverage. The employer must provide notice of the automatic enrollment and the procedures for opting out. Employers do not have to comply with this provision until the DOL issues regulations, which will not be before 2014.

Disclosure of Plan Data and Financials. The Secretary of Labor will update the participant and plan disclosure requirements to be consistent with the standards established by the Secretary of HHS for exchange plans, relating to the following:

- Claims payment policies and practices

- Periodic financial disclosures

- Data on enrollment

- Data on disenrollment

- Data on the number of claims that are denied

- Data on rating practices

- Information on cost-sharing and payments with respect to any out-of-network coverage

- Information on enrollee and participant rights

- Any other information the Secretary of HHS determines appropriate.

PART IX: TAX INCREASES AND REVENUE RAISERS

Additional Requirements for Nonprofit Hospitals

357. When are health reform's additional requirements for Code Section 501(c)(3) hospitals effective?

All of the new requirements, with the exception of the Community Health Needs Assessment (CHNA) requirements (see Q 360), will apply to taxable years after March 23, 2010.[1] The CHNA requirements become effective for taxable years after March 23, 2012.[2]

358. Why were these additional requirements enacted?

Charitable hospital organizations seeking to qualify for federal tax-exempt status must now satisfy not only Code Section 501(c)(3) criteria but also health reform's additional requirements.

Among other things, these requirements impose transparency on hospital organizations and require a level of accountability for providing adequate charity care. Those charitable hospital organizations seeking the benefits of tax-exempt status must prove they are fulfilling their charitable missions.

359. What are the requirements for the establishment of a financial assistance policy?

Health reform imposed additional requirements on charitable hospitals to qualify for Code Section 501(c)(3) tax-exempt status. Specifically, tax-exempt hospital organizations must establish a written financial assistance policy, to include:

(a)   The criteria for eligibility for financial assistance,

(b)   The method for applying for financial assistance,

(c)   The basis for calculating amounts charged to patients,

(d)   The action to be taken in the event of nonpayment, and

(e)   A description of the procedures to publicize the policy.[3]

In addition, the hospitals must establish a written policy concerning emergency medical care, requiring the organization to provide care for emergency medical conditions regardless of the patient's ability to pay.[4]

Moreover, the organizations must limit the amounts charged for emergency or non-emergency medical care to patients eligible for financial assistance to not more than the amount generally billed and prohibit the use of gross charges.[5]

---

1. PPACA §§9007(f), 10903; IRC Sec. 501(r).
2. PPACA §9007(f)(2); IRC Sec. 501(r).
3. PPACA §9007(a)(1)(4)(A); IRC Sec. 501(r).
4. PPACA §9007(a)(1)(4)(B); IRC Sec. 501(r).
5. PPACA §§9007(a)(1)(5), 10903(a); IRC Sec. 501(r).

Finally, nonprofit hospitals must refrain from engaging in extraordinary billing and collection actions until after reasonable efforts have been made to determine whether a patient is eligible for financial assistance.[1]

360. What are the community health needs assessment requirements?

For taxable years after March 23, 2012, tax-exempt hospitals must conduct a "community health needs assessment" (CHNA) every three years and then adopt and implement a strategic plan to meet the community's health needs identified through the assessment. The CHNA must take into account input from public health experts and individuals in the community who represent the broad interests of the community in the area served by the organization. The CHNA must be made available to the public.[2]

In addition, these hospitals must include on their IRS Form 990 a description of how the organization is addressing the needs identified in the CHNA and a description of any such needs that are not being addressed, together with the reasons why such needs are not being addressed.[3]

Not only must a hospital organization satisfy the above additional requirements, but the organization's community benefit activities will be subject to review by the Department of the Treasury at least once every three years.[4] Any organization that fails to meet the CHNA requirements for any taxable year will be subject to an excise tax of $50,000.[5] The amount of the excise tax must be reported on the organization's annual tax return.[6]

Penalty for Lack of Economic Substance

361. What is the economic substance doctrine?

The term "economic substance doctrine" means the common-law doctrine established by court decisions under which income tax benefits are not allowed if the transaction does not have economic substance or lacks a business purpose.[7] As part of health reform, Congress codified the economic substance doctrine in the Internal Revenue Code[8] and imposed penalties for its violation.[9] The law adopts a two-prong test used by most, though not all, of the federal circuit courts. A transaction has economic substance only if:

    (i)   the transaction changes in a meaningful way (apart from federal income tax effects) the taxpayer's economic position, and

---

1. PPACA §9007(a)(1)(6); IRC Sec. 501(r).
2. PPACA §9007(a)(1)(3); IRC Sec. 501(r).
3. PPACA §9007(d); IRC Sec. 501(r).
4. PPACA §9007(c); IRC Sec. 501(r).
5. IRC Sec. 4959.
6. IRC Sec. 6033(b)(10).
7. IRC Sec. 7701(o)(5)(A).
8. IRC Sec. 7701(o).
9. IRC Secs. 6662, 6662A, 6664, and 6676.

(ii)   the taxpayer has a substantial purpose (apart from federal income tax effects) for entering into the transaction.[1]

Additionally, the law adopts a strict liability penalty if the taxpayer violates the doctrine (40 percent if not disclosed; 20 percent if disclosed). This will impose a significant downside risk for those who continue to indulge in tax-shelter transactions because there will be no reasonable cause defense available. However, aggressive positions might be tested in refund actions without risk of the penalty imposed under Code Section 6676 on excessive refund claims.[2]

The IRS has announced that there will be no "angel list" (specific transactions to which the penalty does not apply).[3] By avoiding "bright lines," few rational taxpayers should want to test the "tax lottery" in this area.

362. When are the economic substance penalties effective?

The law applies with respect to transactions entered into on or after March 31, 2010.[4]

Tanning Bed Tax

363. What is the new tanning bed tax?

Effective July 1, 2010, a 10 percent tax on indoor tanning salons' tanning sessions is imposed.[5] Recipients of any indoor tanning service are responsible for paying an excise tax equal to 10 percent of the amount paid for the indoor tanning services, whether or not the amounts to be paid by insurance.[6] The tax is imposed at the time of payment for any indoor tanning service[7] and is collected by the service provider.[8] The tax is 10 percent of the amount of the services and is not grossed up.[9]

364. Which tanning services are covered and which are exempt from the indoor tanning services tax?

An "indoor tanning service" is a service that uses any electronic product designed to incorporate one or more ultraviolet lamps, and intended for the irradiation of an individual by ultraviolet radiation, with wavelengths in air between 200 and 400 nanometers, to induce skin tanning.[10]

---

1. IRC Sec. 7701(o)(1).
2. Susswein, "Is There a Disclosure Exception to The Economic Substance Penalty?" 133 Tax Notes 871 (Nov. 14, 2011), which discusses the ability to obtain administrative or judicial review of economic substance issues without risk of penalty via refund claims.
3. IRS Notice 2010-62.
4. IRS Notice 2010-62.
5. PPACA §10907.
6. IRC Sec. 5000B(a); Reg. §49.5000B-1T(d)(1).
7. Reg. §49.5000B-1T(b)(1).
8. "Excise Tax on Indoor Tanning Services Frequently Asked Questions," (June 30, 2010) at www.irs.gov.
9. IRC Sec. 5000B(a).
10.IRC Sec. 5000B(b)(1); Reg. §49.5000B-1T(c)(1).

The term "indoor tanning service" excludes any phototherapy service performed by a licensed medical professional, on the medical professional's premises.[1] Phototherapy services performed by a licensed medical professional on the medical professional's premises are exempt from the indoor tanning services excise tax. Phototherapy service means a service that exposes an individual to specific wavelengths of light for treatment of:

- dermatological conditions (e.g., acne, psoriasis, or eczema);[2]

- sleep disorders;[3]

- seasonal affective disorder (SAD) or other psychiatric disorder;[4]

- neonatal jaundice;[5]

- wound healing;[6] or

- other medical condition determined by a licensed medical professional to be treatable by exposing the individual to specific wavelengths of light.[7]

Indoor tanning services also do not include spray tans or topical creams[8] and tanning lotions.[9]

Limits on Reimbursement of Nonprescription Over-the-Counter Drugs

365. How have the rules changed on the ability to reimburse for over-the-counter (OTC) drugs?

Health reform limits the payment for over-the-counter drugs to insulin or those that are prescribed by a physician beginning January 1, 2011.[10] Thus, the cost of OTC medicines cannot be reimbursed with excludable income through a health flexible spending account (FSA), health reimbursement account (HRA), health savings account (HSA), or Archer medical savings account (MSA) unless the medicine is insulin or the non-prescription medicine is, in fact, prescribed by a doctor.

IRS Notice 2011-5 states that health FSA and HRA debit cards may continue to be used after January 15, 2011, to purchase prescribed over-the-counter medicines or drugs at drug

---

1. IRC Sec. 5000B(b)(1); Reg. §49.5000B-1T(c)(1).
2. Reg. §49.5000B-1T(c)(3)(i).
3. Reg. §49.5000B-1T(c)(3)(ii).
4. Reg. §49.5000B-1T(c)(3)(iii).
5. Reg. §49.5000B-1T(c)(3)(iv).
6. Reg. §49.5000B-1T(c)(3)(v).
7. Reg. §49.5000B-1T(c)(3)(vi).
8. "Excise Tax on Indoor Tanning Services Frequently Asked Questions," (June 30, 2010) at www.irs.gov.
9. Reg. §49.5000B-1T(c)(2).
10. See IRC Secs. 106(f), 220(d)(2)(A), and 223(d)(2)(A), as amended by PPACA §9003.

stores and pharmacies, at non-healthcare merchants that have pharmacies, and at mail order and Web-based vendors that sell prescription drugs, if:

(1)   prior to purchase:

      o   the prescription for the OTC medicine or drug is presented (in any format) to the pharmacist;

      o   the OTC medicine or drug is dispensed by the pharmacist in accordance with applicable law and regulations; and

      o   a prescription number is assigned;

(2)   the pharmacy or other vendor retains, in a manner that meets IRS's recordkeeping requirements:

      o   the prescription number;

      o   the name of the purchaser or person for whom the prescription applies; and

      o   the date and amount of the purchase;

(3)   all of these records are available to the taxpayer's employer or its agent upon request;

(4)   the debit card system will not accept a charge for an OTC medicine or drug unless a prescription number has been assigned; and

(5)   the additional requirements regarding the use of health FSA or HRA debit cards[1] are met.

Use of Debit Cards. After January 15, 2011, health FSA and HRA debit cards may also continue to be used to purchase OTC medicines or drugs from vendors other than those described previously that have healthcare-related "Merchant IRCs,"[2] including physicians, pharmacies, dentists, vision-care offices, hospitals, and other medical care providers. If all other requirements in the previous list are satisfied, then these debit card transactions will be considered fully substantiated at the time and point-of-sale.

Health FSA and HRA debit cards may also be used to purchase OTC medicines and drugs at "90 percent pharmacies" with at least 90 percent of the store's gross receipts during the prior tax year consisting of qualified medical care expenses.[3]

---

1. Prop. Reg. §1.125-6, Rev. Rul. 2003-43, Notices 2006-69, 2007-2, and 2008-104.
2. Described in Rev. Rul. 2003-43.
3. IRC Sec. 213(d).

Doubled HSA and MSA Penalty for Spending for Non-Health Care and Nonprescription Over-the-Counter Items

366. How has health reform changed the penalty for a health savings account (HSA) or an Archer medical savings account (MSA) regarding payment for non-medical items?

The health reform law revised the rules with respect to HSAs[1] and MSAs[2] to provide that for amounts paid after December 31, 2010, a distribution for a medicine or drug is a tax-free qualified medical expense only if the medicine or drug is a prescribed drug or insulin. Thus, to be reimbursed, over-the-counter (OTC) drugs must have a prescription or be insulin. Thus, a distribution from an HSA or an Archer MSA for a medicine or drug is a tax-free qualified medical expense only if the medicine or drug:

- requires a prescription,

- is an OTC medicine or drug and the individual obtains a prescription, or

- is insulin.

If amounts are distributed from an HSA or Archer MSA for any medicine or drug that does not satisfy this requirement, the amounts will be distributions for nonqualified medical expenses, which are includable in gross income and generally are subject to a 20 percent additional tax.

The IRS has stated that items that are not medicines or drugs – including equipment such as crutches, supplies such as bandages, and diagnostic devices such as blood sugar test kits – are not reimbursable[3] unless they qualify for medical care expenses. Such items may qualify if they otherwise meet the definition of medical care, which includes expenses for the diagnosis, cure, mitigation, treatment, or prevention of disease, or for the purpose of affecting any structure or function of the body. Expenses for items that are merely beneficial to the general health of an individual, such as expenditures for a vacation, are not expenses for medical care.[4]

367. When were the new HSA and Archer MSA rules effective?

These new rules are effective for items purchased on or after January 1, 2011.[5] This change does not affect HSA or Archer MSA distributions for medicines or drugs made before January 1, 2011, nor does it affect distributions made after December 31, 2010, for medicines or drugs purchased on or before that date.

1. IRC Sec. 223(d)(2)(A).
2. IRC Sec. 220(d)(2)(A).
3. IRS Notice 2010-59.
4. IRC Sec. 213(d)(1); Treas. Reg. §1.213-1(e)(1)(ii).
5. PPACA §9003(d)(2).

368. What is a prescription for purposes of these rules?

For the prescription requirement, a "prescription" for a medicine or drug, including one sold over the counter, is a written or electronic order that satisfies the legal requirements for a prescription in the state in which the expense is incurred, including that it be issued by someone who is legally authorized to issue a prescription in that state.[1] In later guidance, the IRS indicated that a prescription could be presented to the pharmacist "in any format."[2] This modification means that if state law allows oral prescriptions by telephone, then the telephone qualifies as a prescription.

Annual Fee on Manufacturers and Importers of Branded Drugs

369. What is the annual fee on manufacturers and importers of branded drugs?

Health reform[3] imposes an annual flat fee starting at $2.5 billion in 2011, increasing to $4.1 billion by 2018, and $2.8 billion in 2019 and thereafter on the branded pharmaceutical manufacturing sector, including foreign corporations and importers. This nondeductible fee is allocated across the industry according to market share and does not apply to companies with sales of branded pharmaceuticals of $5 million or less or certain orphan drugs.

For sales of branded prescription drugs between $5 million and $125 million, only 10 percent of such sales are taken into account when determining the applicable fee. For sales between $125 million and $225 million, 40 percent of such sales are taken into account; and for sales between $225 and $400 million, 75 percent of such sales are considered. To the extent that a covered entity's sales of branded prescription drugs to a specified government program exceed $400 million, 100 percent of such excess sales are taken into account to compute the entity's market share.[4]

This nondeductible excise tax is paid to the Medicare Part B trust fund.[5] The IRS issued guidance on this tax.[6]

370. When is this new tax effective?

The first calculation period is the calendar year beginning January 1, 2011. The fee for 2011 must be paid to the IRS no later than September 30, 2012.

---

1. IRS Notice 2010-59.
2. IRS Notice 2011-5.
3. PPACA §9008.
4. PPACA §9008(b).
5. PPACA §9008(c).
6. Notices 2010-71 and 2011-9 and Rev. Proc. 2011-24.

Repeal of Employer-Paid Retiree Prescription Drug Rebate Income Tax Exclusion

371. What was the employer-paid retiree prescription drug rebate income tax exclusion?

Before taxable years beginning in 2013, employers providing retiree drug coverage to their former employees could both exclude from income the federal subsidy they received and also deduct all of the costs of the retiree drug coverage, including the costs paid by the subsidy. This rule was enacted in 2003 when the Medicare Part D drug coverage program was enacted. This double benefit was intended to encourage employers to continue coverage for retirees and lessen the number of people switching to Medicare Part D coverage. Many retirees preferred the employer-provided coverage to the Medicare coverage because it is usually more generous than Medicare Part D and does not have "doughnut holes" in coverage. Doughnut holes are the gaps in prescription drug coverage under Medicare after subscribers reach a certain level of expenses and before coverage kicks in again.

For taxable years beginning in 2013 and thereafter, the rule that the exclusion from taxable income for Medicare Part D federal subsidy payments to employers is not taken into account in determining the deduction is allowable for an employer's retiree prescription drug expenses is eliminated.[1] Thus, the amount otherwise allowable as a deduction for an employer's retiree prescription drug expenses will be reduced by the amount of the excludible subsidy payments received from the federal government by that employer. Some employers that are losing this double benefit say they will discontinue the retiree drug coverage benefit.

The elimination of the exclusion will result in treating the subsidy the same as most items that may be excluded from income. Thus, for example, while medical insurance reimbursements are not included in a taxpayer's income, they also are not deductible as medical expenses under Code Section 213.

Example: A company receives a $28 federal subsidy for $100 of eligible drug expenses. The $28 is excludable from income under Code Section 139A, and the amount otherwise allowable as a deduction will be reduced by the $28. If the company otherwise meets the Code Section 162 requirements for its eligible retiree drug expenses, it is entitled to a $72 ordinary business expense deduction.[2]

Tax on Sale of Medical Devices

372. What is the new tax on the sale of taxable medical devices?

The healthcare reform law amends Chapter 32 of the Internal Revenue Code establishing a new excise tax on manufacturers or importers of taxable medical devices.[3] The tax is equal to

---

1. IRC Sec.139A as amended by PPACA §9012(a).
2. Joint Comm. Staff, Tech Explanation of the Revenue Provisions of the Reconciliation Act of 2010, as Amended, in Combination With the Patient Protection and Affordable Care Act (JCX-18-10), p. 95 (3/21/2010).
3. IRC Sec. 4191(a).

2.3% of the sale price of medical devices sold after December 31, 2012. Certain medical devices, such as contact lenses and hearing aids purchased by the general public at retail stores, are exempt.

373. What is a taxable medical device?

A "taxable medical device" means any device[1] intended for humans.[2] Several specific devices are exempted from the tax, including eyeglasses, contact lenses, hearing aids, and any other medical device determined by the Secretary to be of a type that is generally purchased by the general public at retail for individual use.[3]

In addition, the following sales by a manufacturer are exempt:

- For use by the purchaser for further manufacture, or for resale by the purchaser to a second purchaser for use by such second purchaser in further manufacture.

- For export, or for resale by the purchaser to a second purchaser for export.

- For use by the purchaser as supplies for vessels or aircraft.

- To a state or local government for the exclusive use of the state or local government.

- To a nonprofit educational organization for its exclusive use.

- To a qualified blood collector organization for such organization's exclusive use in the collection, storage, or transportation of blood.[4]

Expanded Medicare Tax on Wages

374. What is the expanded Medicare tax on wages that goes into effect January 1, 2013?

An additional 0.9 percent Medicare tax (called the hospital insurance tax) on wages in excess of the $250,000/$125,000/$200,000 thresholds for married taxpayers filing jointly, married taxpayers filing separately, and all other taxpayers, respectively, is imposed on individuals in 2013. There is a corresponding 0.9 percent increase in the self-employment tax for self-employed individuals, except that the $250,000/$125,000/$200,000 thresholds are reduced (but not below zero) by the taxpayer's wages.[5] This additional 0.9 percent tax on wages and self-employment income above the applicable thresholds is not deductible for income tax purposes.[6] In this respect, it is like the "employee" portion of the FICA tax, which

---

1. Federal Food, Drug and Cosmetic Act (FFDCA) §201(h).
2. IRC Sec. 4191(b).
3. IRC Sec. 4191(c).
4. IRC Sec. 4221.
5. IRC Sec. 1401(b)(2).
6. IRC Sec. 164(f).

generally comes out of after-tax wages, as opposed to the "employer" portion of the FICA tax that is deductible by the employer (and not included in the employee's wages).

The net effect of this new 0.9 percent Medicare tax is to put the higher-income wage earner in roughly the same position as the higher-income passive investor who must pay a 3.8 percent Medicare tax on investment income above the same dollar thresholds. They both will effectively now pay an additional 3.8 percent tax above the "high-income" thresholds.

However, a taxpayer subject to this extra 0.9 percent tax is effectively allowed to "deduct" the 1.45 percent "employer" portion of the FICA tax when applying the increased 3.8 percent rate, even above the income thresholds, whereas the investor subject to the 3.8 percent tax on net investment income cannot deduct it. All wages and self-employment income are subject to the existing 2.9 percent Medicare tax (the 1.45 percent "employer" portion, which is "deductible," and the 1.45 percent employee portion, which is not), not just the portion of such income above the thresholds.

The new Medicare tax rate structure, including both the new 3.8 percent Medicare tax on investment income, discussed beginning with Q 375, and the 0.9 percent increased FICA/SECA (Self Employment Contributions Act) rate should not have a big impact on most other closely held business tax planning issues. However, it increases the advantage of wages versus dividends from a C corporation. Ironically, a passive investor in a partnership subject to the self-employment tax actually pays tax at a slightly lower marginal rate (43.95 percent) than that same investor in a partnership whose activities are not subject to the self-employment tax (44.59 percent), because of the deductibility of the 1.45 percent amount.[1]

Additionally, an S corporation shareholder receiving a dividend distribution from S corporation trade or business income (as opposed to self-employment income) pays even less (40.79 percent) as this dividend is not subject to either the expanded Medicare tax on wages or the new Medicare tax on investment income, discussed in Q 375. The rates above are based on the maximum 2012 income tax rate of 35 percent. If that increases, the marginal rates above will increase as well.

New 3.8 Percent Medicare Tax on Investment Income

375. What is the new 3.8 percent Medicare tax on investment income, effective in 2013?

For taxable years starting on or after January 1, 2013, the health reform law imposes a new 3.8 percent Medicare tax on "net investment income" (this excludes trade or business income, except from passive activities and trading in financial instruments or commodities) for higher income individuals, estates, and trusts through Code Section 1411. For individuals, such "net investment income" is subject to this new tax to the extent that "modified adjusted gross income" exceeds $250,000 in the case of joint returns, $125,000 in the case of married filing separate returns, and $200,000 in all other cases.[2] Modified adjusted gross income is adjusted

---

1. IRC Sec. 1411(c)(6), Illustration #4.
2. IRC Sec. 1411(a)(1), (b).

gross income increased by the net foreign earned income exclusion.[1] Although the new tax is called a "Medicare" tax in the health reform statute, legislative history, and Internal Revenue Code, the IRS refers to this new tax as the "net investment income tax." Nonresident aliens are not subject to the new tax.

Example: A married couple filing jointly has $300,000 of AGI, $100,000 of which is net investment income. They will pay $1,900 in the new tax – i.e., 3.8 percent of the lesser of the amount of net investment income ($100,000) or $50,000 which is the excess of the $300,000 AGI over the $250,000 threshold amount.

Example: Same as Example # 1 above, except only $25,000 of the AGI is net investment income. They will pay $950 in the new tax – i.e., 3.8 percent of the lesser of the amount of net investment income ($25,000) or $50,000 which is the excess of the $300,000 AGI over the $250,000 threshold amount.

376. Does this new Medicare tax on investment income apply to estates and trusts also?

Yes. For estates or trusts, this new tax applies to the lesser of (1) undistributed net investment income or (2) the excess of (i) AGI (as defined in Code Section 67(e)) over (ii) the dollar amount at which the highest trust/estate tax rate begins.[2] The highest tax bracket in Code Section 1(e) for estates and trusts during calendar year 2012 is taxable income over $11,650.[3] Additionally, as explained below, "net investment income" for purposes of this new tax is defined to include passive activity income.[4] No tax is imposed on tax-exempt trusts, however, where principal and income goes to charity.[5]

Example: For 2013, a trust has $250,000 in AGI and $100,000 in undistributed net investment income. Assume that the top federal rate for trusts starts at $11,650 in 2013. The trust pays $3,800 in this tax, namely, 3.8 percent of the lesser of its undistributed net investment income ($100,000) or $238,350 which is the excess of its $250,000 AGI over $11,650.

Example: Same as above, except that the trust's AGI equals $100,000. It would pay $3,357 in this tax, namely, 3.8 percent of the lesser of its undistributed net investment income ($100,000) or $88,350 which is the excess of its $100,000 AGI over $11,650.

377. How does this new Medicare tax on investment income apply to S corporation electing small business trusts?

It is not clear how this new Medicare tax should apply to net investment income passed through from an S corporation to a shareholder that is an electing small business trust shareholder. First, such a trust may distribute some or all of this net investment income, even though it is

---

1. IRC Sec. 1411(d). Unlike the definition of "modified adjusted gross income" for purposes of the individual premium tax credit, this definition makes no adjustment for tax-exempt interest.
2. IRC Sec. 1411(c)(6). The tax brackets are in IRC Sec. 1(e) for estates and complex trusts.
3. IRC Secs. 1411(a)(2)(i); 1(e). *See* Rev. Proc. 2011-52 (providing tax brackets for calendar year 2012).
4. *See* IRC Sec. 469(a)(2)(A); Treas. Reg. §1.469-8.
5. IRC Sec. 1141(e)(2).

taxed inside the trust at the "highest rate set forth in Section 1(e)."[1] Second, for purposes of determining "the distributable net income of the entire trust," such pass through items are "excluded."[2]

378. What is "net investment income?"

Net investment income does not include trade or business income except income except from Code Section 469 passive activities and trading in financial instruments or commodities.[3] "Net investment income" means the following items, less deductions "properly allocable"[4] to them:

- Interest, Dividends, Annuities, Royalties and Rents.[5] However, these types of income are not subject to this new tax if they are "derived in the ordinary course of a trade or business," as long as that trade or business does not constitute a passive activity with respect to the taxpayer and does not constitute "trading in financial instruments or commodities."[6] Thus, interest on customer receivables and interest derived in an active lending business should not be subject to this new tax. Moreover, royalties earned in the active conduct of a software business should be exempt. However, net investment income attributable to working capital will be subject to the tax.[7]

- Passive Activity Income.[8] Until 2013, passive activity income was a favorable tax classification because it, unlike non-passive trade or business income, could be offset by passive losses.[9] Thus, taxpayers often preferred this income classification. This new tax may cause taxpayers to attempt to avoid passive activity classification. Net investment income includes trade or business income that is a passive activity under Code Section 469.[10]

  For example, an individual might be engaged in 10 separate activities, and actively participate in several of them for less than 500 hours per year. If each of these activities is treated as a separate activity, then those activities in which the taxpayer spends more than 100, but less than 500, hours per year (and which generate an overall net loss), along with those in which the taxpayer spends less

---

1. IRC Sec. 641(c)(2)(A), (C).
2. IRC Sec. 641(c)(3).
3. IRC Sec. 1411(c)(2).
4. Taxpayers are entitled to subtract "deductions allowed by this subtitle which are properly allocable to such gross income." For many taxpayers some or all "properly allocable" investment expenses are not "allowed by this subtitle" because they are only deductible to the extent that they exceed 2 percent of adjusted gross income.
5. IRC Sec. 1411(c)(1)(A)(i).
6. IRC Sec. 1411(c)(1)(A)(i), (2).
7. See IRC Secs. 1411(c)(3); 469(e)(1)(b).
8. IRC Sec. 1411(c)(1)(A)(ii), (B); (2)(A).
9. IRC Sec. 469(d)(1)(B).
10. IRC Sec. 1411(c)(2)(A).

than 100 hours per year, should be classified as passive activities generating passive activity income.[1] However, treating all of the activities in which the taxpayer participates as one single activity for passive activity purposes could avoid this new tax on all of the income from the activities in which he or she participates (though probably not for his or her outside passive activities), because the taxpayer's aggregate material participation in all of these activities totals more than 500 hours.[2]

Such planning considerations are important because the Internal Revenue Service now requires all taxpayers who form new groups of activities or add new activities to existing groups to disclose how they are aggregating or segregating their activities under the passive activity loss rules.[3] These disclosure requirements apply for taxable years beginning after January 15, 2010.[4]

Incorporation of the passive activity rules into this new Medicare Tax structure also creates a number of open issues. For example, the passive activity regulations provide that gross income from each significant participation activity "equal to a ratable portion of the taxpayer's net passive income from such activity for the taxable year shall be treated as not from a passive activity if the taxpayer experiences net taxable income from such significant participation activities."[5] Does this mean that such income is not subject to this new Medicare Tax on "net investment income"? There are no clear answers yet.

• The Business of Financial Instruments and Commodities. The "trade or business of trading in financial instruments or commodities (as defined in Code Section 475(e)(2)) is "net investment income," regardless of whether a taxpayer materially participates.[6] This seemingly would include hedge fund income. Although commodities are defined by reference to a specific Code section, the term "financial instruments" will be defined by regulation. Treasury Regulation Section 1.1275-6 (b)(3) defines "financial instrument" as "a spot, forward, or future contract, an option, a notional principal contract, a debt instrument, or a similar instrument, or combination or series of financial instruments," but specifically excludes stock. Similarly, Code Section 475(c)(2)(E) and Treasury Regulation Section 1.988-1(a) (2)(iii) describe financial instruments in terms of what are commonly considered

---

1. Treas. Reg. §1.469-5T(a)(1), (3), (c).
2. Treas. Reg. §1.469-5T(a)(1).
3. Rev. Proc. 2010-13.
4. Rev. Proc. 2010-13. Taxpayers who do not add new activities or alter their existing activity groups are grandfathered in, and do not need to disclose their existing grouping decisions.
5. Treas. Reg. §1.469-2T(f)(2).
6. IRC Sec. 1411(c)(1)(A)(ii), (2)(B).

to be financial derivatives. On the other hand, Code Section 731(c)(2)(C) defines financial instrument more broadly as including stocks and other equity investments, evidences of indebtedness, options, forward or futures contracts, notional principal contracts, and derivatives.

Another issue is what constitutes "trading" in financial instruments or commodities? Does the extensive case law relating to the treatment of "dealers" and "traders" come into play, perhaps with individual investors not subject to this new tax?[1]

- Net Gain from Non-Business Property. "Net gain (to the extent taken into account in computing taxable income) attributable to the disposition of property other than property held in a trade or business," is subject to this tax, unless that trade or business is a passive activity with respect to the taxpayer or involves trading in financial instruments or commodities.[2] In general, this is a broad category. This income includes gain from the disposition of nonbusiness assets, such as houses, boats, and airplanes. However, excluded gain from the sale of a personal residence of $250,000 or $500,000[3] is not subject to this Medicare tax on investment income because it is not "taken into account in computing taxable income."[4] Gain from the disposition of stock in a C corporation should be taxable under this provision unless excluded under Code Section 1202.

  Significantly, "property held in a trade or business" is excluded unless the trade or business does not fall within the disfavored passive activity or trading category.[5] There is also an exception for the disposition of interests in partnerships and S corporations (i.e., pass-through entities), which provides that gain on such dispositions will be taken into account "only to the extent of the net gain which would be so taken into account by the transferor if all property of the partnership or S corporation were sold for fair market value immediately before the disposition of such interest."[6] The Technical Explanation concludes that "[t]hus only net gain or loss attributable to property held by the entity which is not properly attributable to an active trade or business is taken into account."[7]

---

1. *See, e.g., Holsinger v. Comm'r,* T.C. Memo 2008-191 (married couple not traders due to insubstantial trading activity and lack of profit motive); *George R. Kemon,* 16 T.C. 1026 (1951) (partnership found to be a trader); *United States v. Diamond,* 788 F.2d 1025 (4th Cir. 1986) (recognizing the difference between "dealers" who sell to customers and "traders" who do not).
2. IRC Sec. 1411(c)(1)(A)(iii).
3. IRC Sec. 121.
4. *See* IRC Sec. 121; Joint Committee On Taxation, Technical Explanation Of The Revenue Provisions Of The Reconciliation Act Of 2010, As Amended In Combination With The Patient Protection And Affordable Care Act, p. 135 n. 285 (Mar. 21, 2010) at http://www.jct.gov/publications. html?func=startdown&id=3673).
5. IRC Sec. 1411(c)(1)(A)(iii).
6. IRC Sec. 1411(c)(4).
7. Technical Explanation, at 135.

379. How does the Medicare tax on investment income apply to pass-through entities?

The tax is not intended to apply at all to non-passive, non-trading businesses conducted by S corporations, partnerships, or sole proprietorships.[1] Thus, for pass-through entities that do not have passive investors and do not engage in any financial instrument or commodity trading business, "net investment income" will include only non-business income from interest, dividends, annuities, royalties, rents, and capital gains, minus the allocable deductions. Therefore, business income earned or distributed by such pass-through entities will not be subject to the new Medicare tax.

An S corporation shareholder's allocable share of trade or business income is not net earnings from self-employment and will not be subject to the extra 0.9 percent Medicare tax on wages nor to the 3.8 percent on net investment income.[2] One technique that clearly does not work is for a professional to form a partnership or LLC "with himself or herself." or otherwise try to "fractionalize" personal services into a large "passive" component and a small "residual" component, and then claim that the income flowing through the "passive" or limited liability ownership is not subject to SECA.[3]

380. What items are not subject to the Medicare tax on net investment income?

Active Trade or Business Income. Active trade or business income is not subject to the 3.8 percent Medicare net investment income tax. The net investment income tax makes extremely important the distinction between activities that are a trade or business on the one hand and not so characterized on the other hand. Activities entered into for profit are not necessarily trade or business activities.[4]

IRA and Qualified Plan Distributions. "Net investment income" does not include any distribution from a plan or arrangement described in Code sections 401(a) (pension,

---

1. Technical Explanation, at 135.
2. Rev. Rul. 59-221; see also IRC Sec. 1402(a)(2) (excluding "dividends on shares of stock issued by a corporation" from "net earnings from self-employment); Letter Ruling 871606 (Jan. 21, 1987) (income derived by a shareholder-employee from an "S" corporation did not constitute net earnings from self-employment for self-employment tax purposes and taxpayer was not eligible to adopt a qualified pension plan based on the income derived from "S" corporation since such income did not constitute earned income).
3. *Robucci v. Comm'r.*, 101 T.C. Memo. (CCH) 1060 (Jan. 24, 2011), a psychiatrist on the advice of his CPA set up a structure whereby he formed an LLC between himself and his wholly-owned professional corporation. The Tax Court held that the professional corporation had no business purpose and should be ignored (meaning that the LLC had only one member (the taxpayer) and therefore that all income passed through was subject to SECA) and further upheld the IRS's imposition of negligence penalties. In *Renkemeyer, Campbell & Weaver LLP v. Comm'r.*, 136 T.C. 137 (2011), three attorneys were partners in an LLP. Initially, 10 percent of the LLP was owned by an "S" corporation owned by an ESOP of which the three attorneys were beneficiaries; later, the "S" corporation was eliminated and, in an apparent attempt to come under the Proposed Section 1402 Regulations, the partners split their interests into de minimis general managing partner interests and the remainder into "investing partner" interests. The bulk of the LLP's income was allocated to the "investing" interests and the partners did not pay SECA tax on the amounts so allocated. The Tax Court agreed with the IRS's contention that all income was subject to SECA and that the partners' active involvement in and performance of legal services for the LLP was inconsistent with what Congress had intended in enacting relief under Code section 1402(a) (13) for limited partners as passive investors.
4. See, e.g. *Estate of Roger Stangeland v. Comm'r.*, T.C. Memo. 2010-185, 100 T.C. Memo. (CCH) 156 (Aug. 16, 2010) (consulting enterprise operated by petitioners to manage petitioner's other business interests was not itself a trade or business; instead, its purpose and the nature of its operations was to increase the investment value of petitioners' other businesses); cf. *Wilbur Langford v. Comm'r.*, T.C. Memo. 1988-300, 55 T.C. Memo. (CCH) 1267 (July 19, 1988) (college professor's royalties from co-authorship of one textbook were "royalties" not subject to SECA tax because petitioner's activities did not rise to the level of a "trade or business"; citing Rev. Rul. 55-385 and Rev. Rul. 68-498.

profit-sharing, 401(k) and stock bonus plans), 403(a) or 403(b) (employee annuity plans), 408 (IRAs), 408A (Roth IRAs), or 457(b) (state and local government and tax-exempt organization deferred compensation plans).[1] Distributions from such plans also do not constitute "wages" for purposes of FICA taxes and withholding,[2] However, distributions from these plans (except for Roth IRAs) enter into a taxpayer's adjusted gross income (AGI) and, therefore, increase AGI above the applicable threshold amount for purposes of determining tax on net investment income from taxable mutual funds and other non-sheltered sources.

Other Exempt Income. The explanation of the Joint Committee on Taxation states that gross income for purposes of computing net investment income does not include items excluded from gross income for income tax purposes, such as interest on tax-exempt bonds or gain excluded under Code Section 121 from the sale of a principal residence.[3] Similarly, proceeds from a life insurance policy (subject to the "transfer-for-value" rules of Code Section 101), and the "inside buildup" in a life insurance policy, should be exempt from the new tax.

Cafeteria Plan Changes
$2,500 Cap on Employee FSA Contributions
381. What are the cafeteria plan changes enacted in health reform?

For tax years beginning in 2011, the new SIMPLE cafeteria plan, discussed earlier in Part V (Small Business Provisions) is an option for smaller employers.

In taxable years beginning after 2012, health reform limits annual employee contributions to a health flexible spending account (FSA) offered under a cafeteria plan to $2,500 (adjusted for inflation).[4]

In addition, effective beginning in 2014, Code Section 125(f)(3) permits a qualified employer to offer employees the opportunity to enroll in a qualified health insurance plan of a health exchange through the employer's cafeteria plan, even though reimbursement of expenses paid to a health exchange-participating qualified health plan otherwise is not a permissible benefit under a cafeteria plan.

382. To what does the new $2,500 FSA limit apply?

The $2,500 cap is for employee contributions to health flexible spending accounts (FSAs) for plan years beginning in 2013 and thereafter.[5] Health FSAs are used to reimburse medical and dental expenses not paid by insurance, whether due to copays, deductibles,

---

1. IRC Sec. 1411(c)(5).
2. IRC Sec. 3121(a)(5).
3. Joint Committee On Taxation, Technical Explanation Of The Revenue Provisions Of The Reconciliation Act Of 2010, As Amended In Combination With The Patient Protection And Affordable Care Act, p. 135 n. 285 (Mar. 21, 2010) at http://www.jct.gov/publications.html?func=s tartdown&id=3673).
4. IRC Sec. 125(i).
5. IRC Sec. 125(i).

or otherwise. The $2,500 health FSA limit does not apply to a cafeteria plan health insurance premium conversion (Premium Only Plans or "POP") option and other various options in a cafeteria plan, such as dependent care FSAs and adoption assistance FSAs. The limit also does not apply to employer contributions ("flex credits") to cafeteria plan health FSAs.

383. What clarifications has the IRS made regarding issues relating to the $2,500 health FSA employee deferral limit?

IRS Notice 2012-40 provides:

- The $2,500 limit applies only to salary reduction contributions under a health FSA, and does not apply to certain employer non-elective contributions (flex credits) or to any types of contributions or amounts available for reimbursement under other types of FSAs, health savings accounts, or reimbursement arrangements, including salary reduction contributions used to pay an employee's share of health coverage (insured or self-insured) dependent care, or adoption assistance.

- The cap applies to health FSA plan years that begin on or after January 1, 2013. Thus, the new cap will not apply to non-calendar year plans until the plan year beginning in 2013. However, a plan sponsor cannot change from a calendar year to a non-calendar plan year to postpone the new cap without a *bona fide* business reason for the change.

- For plans that have adopted the optional cafeteria plan two-and-a-half month grace period,[1] amounts carried over during the grace period do not count toward the cap.

- The employer can correct employee deferral contributions that exceed the limit if due to a reasonable mistake and not willful misconduct as long as the cafeteria plan is not under IRS audit. To correct the error, the employer pays the excess amount to the employee, which is reported as wages for income tax withholding and employment taxes on the employee's Form W-2 for the employee's taxable year that ends with or after the cafeteria plan year in which the correction is made.

- The relief provided for erroneous excess contributions is not available for an employer if a federal tax return of the employer is under examination with respect to benefits provided under a cafeteria plan.

- If both spouses have an FSA, whether at the same or different employers, each can fund his/her health FSA to the full amount of the $2,500 limit.

---

1. See Notice 2005-42, 2005-1 C.B. 1204, and Prop. Treas. Reg. §1.125-1(e).

- An individual employed by separate employers that are not members of the same controlled group or affiliated service group may establish and fund an FSA at each employer up to the $2,500 limit.

- If a cafeteria plan has a short plan year (fewer than twelve months) that begins after 2012, the $2,500 limit is prorated based on the number of months in that short plan year.

384. What is the deadline to amend a cafeteria plan to limit employee deferrals into health FSAs?

Employers have until the end of 2014 to amend their plan documents to incorporate the $2,500 limit, but this change must be effective for the plan year beginning in 2013.[1]

385. What is the penalty if a cafeteria plan is not timely amended or does not comply with the $2,500 employee deferral limit?

A cafeteria plan that fails to comply with Code Section 125(i) for plan years beginning in 2013 is not a valid Code Section 125 cafeteria plan and the value of the taxable benefits that an employee could have elected to receive under the plan during the plan year is includible in employee's gross income, regardless of the benefit elected by the employee.[2]

Health Insurers Executive Compensation

386. How does health reform increase taxes on executive compensation for health insurance companies?

The law limits the amount that certain health insurers may deduct for a tax year starting after 2012 for compensation to any employee in excess of $500,000. Congress enacted this limitation as part of the Patient Protection and Affordable Care Act of 2010, which, among many other things, essentially requires every individual to be covered by health insurance. Congress included the $500,000 cap to ensure that companies providing mandatory coverage do not utilize premiums received for this coverage to overcompensate executives.

Although the law only applies to certain healthcare insurers, it otherwise has a broader impact than the general deduction limit under Code Section 162(m). Section 162(m) limits the amount a publicly held corporation may deduct for compensation paid to a narrow group of executives to $1 million per year per executive, makes an exception for performance-based compensation and commissions, and excludes the compensation paid to former covered executives once they are no longer covered.

However, the new health insurance company provision applies regardless of whether the health insurer's stock is publicly traded, limits the deduction to $500,000 per individual, and

---

1. IRS Notice 2012-40. Cafeteria plan amendments generally must be effective only prospectively. See Prop. Treas. Reg. §1.125-1(c).
2. IRS Notice 2012-40. See also Prop. Treas. Reg. §1.125-1(b).

makes no exception for performance-based compensation or commissions. In addition, the limit applies to compensation, including deferred compensation, paid to all current and former employees and most independent contractors, not just to compensation paid to a narrow group of current top executives.

387. What is a covered health insurance provider?

The $500,000 cap only applies to an employer for a "disqualified taxable year,"[1] which is a taxable year during which the employer is a "covered health insurance provider."[2] A covered health insurance provider is a "health insurance issuer" that writes "minimum essential coverage" and receives premiums for this coverage that account for at least 25 percent of its gross premiums from providing health insurance coverage.[3] A "health insurance issuer" is an insurance company, service, or organization (including a health maintenance organization (HMO)) that is licensed to engage in the business of insurance in a U.S. state and is subject to state law regulating insurance.[4] "Minimum essential coverage" is coverage satisfying the individual mandate, applicable for years after 2013, that every individual have health insurance coverage.[5] For example, employer-sponsored health insurance satisfies the mandate for covered employees and is therefore minimum essential coverage.[6]

Aggregation Rules for Related Employers. A broad range of related persons are aggregated in applying the definition of "covered health insurance provider" by controlled group and affiliated service group rules.[7] Assume an insurance company writes health insurance through two subsidiaries, one of which issues primarily minimum essential coverage and the other of which only issues health insurance that is not minimum essential coverage. The two subsidiaries (and all other members of the corporate group) are treated as one employer for this purpose. Thus, if premiums for minimum essential coverage are at least 25 percent of the gross health insurance premiums received by the group, the $500,000 cap applies to both of the health insurance subsidiaries, including the subsidiary that writes no minimum essential coverage.

388. What is applicable individual remuneration for purposes of the $500,000 annual limit?

The $500,000 cap generally applies to an employer's deductions for "applicable individual remuneration" for services performed by an "applicable individual" during a disqualified taxable year beginning after 2012.[8] The term "applicable individual" includes all employees, officers, and directors of a covered health insurance provider, and it also includes any other

---

1. IRC Sec. 162(m)(6)(A).
2. IRC Sec. 162(m)(6)(B).
3. IRC Sec. 162(m)(6)(C)(i)(II). This definition applies for years beginning after 2012. Another definition applies for years beginning during the period 2010 through 2012. IRC Sec. 162(m)(6)(C)(i)(I). "Solely for purposes of determining whether a taxpayer is a 'covered health insurance provider,'...premiums received under an indemnity reinsurance contract are not treated as premiums from providing health insurance coverage." Notice 2011-2, III.D.
4. IRC Sec. 9832(b)(2). A "group health plan" is not a health insurance issuer. For the term HMO, see Code Section 9832(b)(3).
5. IRC Sec. 5000A(f).
6. IRC Sec. 5000A(f)(1)(B).
7. IRC Sec. 162(m)(6)(C)(ii). Specifically, two or more persons are treated as a single employer for this purpose if they are so treated under Code sections 414(b), 414(c), 414(m), or 414(o).
8. IRC Sec. 162(m)(6)(A)(i).

person "who provides services for or on behalf of such covered health insurance provider."[1] An individual performing services as an independent contractor can therefore be an applicable individual.[2]

"Applicable individual remuneration" includes "the aggregate amount" that would, but for the $500,000 cap, be allowed as a deduction for remuneration for services performed by an applicable individual for a disqualified taxable year, whether or not the services were performed during the taxable year.[3] Remuneration paid on a commission basis and other performance-based compensation may be applicable individual remuneration.

Applicable individual remuneration does not include "deferred deduction remuneration," which is remuneration for services performed during one disqualified taxable year that is deductible for a later disqualified taxable year.[4] Deferred deduction remuneration is taken into account for the year of the deduction (usually the year during which the compensation is paid), not the year during which the services are performed. Deferred deduction remuneration may include remuneration, otherwise deductible for a disqualified taxable year beginning after 2012 that is paid for services performed during any disqualified year beginning after 2009.

389. How is the $500,000 cap applied? Does it make any difference if compensation is earned and paid later as deferred compensation?

The cap applies separately to "deferred deduction remuneration" and applicable individual remuneration. For applicable individual remuneration (compensation that is deductible for the year during which the services are performed), remuneration in excess of $500,000 for any individual is not deductible for the current year or at any other time.[5]

The rule for deferred deduction remuneration applies to any such remuneration that is attributable to services performed by an applicable individual during a disqualified taxable year beginning after 2009, but deductible for a disqualified year after 2012. For such compensation otherwise deductible for a particular year, the maximum deduction is the excess of $500,000 over the sum of (1) the applicable individual remuneration for the year during which the services were performed, and (2) any portion of the deferred deduction remuneration for such services that was taken into account under this rule for a preceding post-2009 taxable year.[6]

In other words, deferred deduction remuneration is taken into account for the year for which it is otherwise deductible, but the deduction is only allowed to the extent of the unused cap for the individual from the year during which the services were performed.

---

1. IRC Sec. 162(m)(6)(F).
2. An independent contractor is not, however, an applicable individual if he or she provides substantial services to multiple unrelated customers, as described in Reg. §1.409A-1(f)(2). Notice 2011-2, 2011-2 IRB 260, III.C.
3. IRC Sec. 162(m)(6)(D).
4. IRC Secs. 162(m)(6)(D), 162(m)(6)(E).
5. IRC Sec. 162(m)(6)(A)(i).
6. IRC Sec. 162(m)(6)(A)(ii).

Example: Assume an employee's compensation for disqualified taxable year 1 is cash compensation of $400,000 plus nonqualified deferred compensation of $300,000, which the employer may only deduct when paid; the deferred compensation is paid to the employee in two installments: $150,000 during disqualified taxable year 2 and $150,000 during disqualified taxable year 3.

Taxable years 1, 2, and 3 all begin after 2012. The cash compensation is fully deductible for year 1 because it does not exceed $500,000. The deferred compensation would normally be deductible for years 2 and 3 in the amounts paid during each of those years. The maximum deduction for the deferred compensation paid during year 2 is $100,000: the excess of $500,000 over the amount deductible for the year during which the services were performed ($400,000).

The employer is allowed no deduction for the deferred compensation paid during year 3 because the cap is $500,000, less the amount deductible for the year the services were performed ($400,000) and less amounts deductible before year 3 for compensation deferred from year 1 ($100,000 deducted for year 2).

390. What rules apply to a covered health insurance provider for compensation earned in 2010 through 2012?

The application of Code Section 162(m)(6) to deferred compensation earned prior to 2013 but paid out after 2012 is different because the law defines a "covered health insurance provider" in broader terms for 2010, 2011, and 2012 than for 2013 and later. Starting in 2013, a health insurance provider is "covered" only if 25 percent or more of its gross premiums received from providing health insurance coverage is from "minimum essential coverage," which, as defined in Code Section 5000A(f), generally means group or individual medical coverage needed to satisfy the individual coverage. The pre-2013 definition of covered health insurance provider (receiving any premium) applies to more employers than the post-2012 definition (receiving at least 25 percent of premiums from offering minimum essential coverage).

For a taxable year beginning during the years 2010 through 2012, an employer is a covered health insurance provider, and the year is therefore disqualified, if the employer is a health insurer and receives premiums from providing health insurance coverage.[1] For such a year, in other words, the portion of the gross premiums received from providing minimum essential coverage is not relevant. The cap never applies to compensation that is deductible for a year beginning before 2013. An employer's status as a covered health insurance provider for a year during the period 2010 through 2012 is only relevant for the purpose of tainting remuneration for services performed during those years but is not deductible by the employer (e.g., is not paid) until a year after 2012.

If an employer is a health insurance issuer for all years after 2009, it is a covered health insurance provider for the years 2010 through 2012. If at least 25 percent of its gross premiums from health insurance coverage for years after 2012 is for minimum essential coverage, it is also

---

1. IRC Sec. 162(m)(6)(C)(i)(I).

a covered health insurance provider for post-2012 years. The cap can apply to remuneration for services performed during the years 2010 through 2012, but paid during a post-2012 year.[1] In contrast, if premiums for minimum essential coverage are less than 25 percent of the employer's gross premiums for each post-2012 year, it is not a health insurance issuer for any such year, and the cap cannot apply to any remuneration that it pays, regardless of when the services are performed.[2]

The cap applies to deferred deduction remuneration only if the employer is a covered health insurance provider for both the year during which the services are performed and the year for which the remuneration would normally be deductible (e.g., the year of payment), but the employer's status for other years is not relevant. An entity that was not a covered health insurance provider after 2012 does not have its deductions limited if compensation deferred from 2010, 2011, or 2012 was paid out after 2012.[3]

> **Example:** An employer is a health insurance issuer for all years after 2009, and premiums for minimum essential coverage are less than 25 percent of the employer's gross premiums for the years 2013 through 2015. These premiums account for at least 25 percent of gross premiums for 2016 and later years.[4] The employer is a covered health insurance provider for 2010 through 2012 and for years after 2015, but not for the years 2013 through 2015. The cap applies to deferred deduction remuneration for services performed during a 2010–2012 year if the remuneration becomes deductible for a year after 2015, but not if the deduction is allowed for a year during the period 2013 through 2015.

De Minimis Rule. The IRS has administratively provided a *de minimis* rule not found in the statute.[5] An employer is deemed not to be a covered health insurance provider for a taxable year beginning during the period 2010 through 2012 if the premiums it receives for providing health insurance coverage are less than 2 percent of its gross revenues for the year.[6] For a taxable year beginning after 2012, an employer is not considered a covered health insurance provider if health insurance premiums received for providing minimum essential coverage are less than 2 percent of its gross revenues for the year.

Increase Threshold for Personal Deduction for Medical Expenses

391. How does health reform limit individual income tax deductions for health care?

In 2013 and thereafter, individual itemized deductions for unreimbursed medical care expenses, including premiums for health, long-term-care, and dental insurance are only deductible to the extent they exceed 10 percent of adjusted gross income. In 2012 and before, the threshold

---

1. Notice 2011-2,, III.A, Ex. 1.
2. Notice 2011-2, III.A, Ex. 2.
3. Notice 2011-02.
4. Notice 2011-2, III.A, Ex. 3.
5. IRC Sec. 162(m)(6)(H) (Treasury "may prescribe such guidance, rules, or regulations as are necessary to carry out the purposes of this paragraph").
6. Notice 2011-2, III.B.

was 7.5 percent.[1] However, through 2016, taxpayers age 65 and older will continue to be able to use the old 7.5 percent threshold.[2]

These taxpayers could claim an itemized deduction to the extent that their unreimbursed medical expenses exceeded 7.5 percent of adjusted gross income. Use of this deduction requires taxpayers to itemize deductions and forgo the standard deduction, and the 7.5 percent threshold made the deduction of minimal value for most taxpayers. The Joint Committee on Taxation estimated the value of this limited itemized deduction for medical expenses to be only $8.7 billion in 2007, as compared to the combined value of $250.9 billion for the exclusion for employer-provided health insurance and the self-employed health insurance deduction.[3]

Further, many taxpayers will receive a tax subsidy for buying insurance on a health insurance exchange beginning in 2014.[4]

The Individual Mandate

392. What is the individual mandate?

As discussed in detail in Part I of this book, the individual mandate requires individuals, unless excluded, to have minimum essential health coverage through their employer or individually or pay a tax penalty.

If an "applicable individual" does not have "minimum essential coverage" for that individual or dependents who also are an "applicable individual," a tax "penalty"[5] equal to the greater of:

(i)   the "applicable dollar amount" for the individual and all such dependents (up to a maximum of three applicable dollar amounts) or

(ii)   a specified percentage of the applicable individual's "household income," but in no event more than "the national average premium for qualified health plans which have a bronze level (see Q 67) of coverage with coverage for the applicable family size involved, that are offered through exchanges."[6]

The minimum penalty ranges from $95 in calendar year 2014 up to $695 in calendar year 2016, and is inflation-adjusted thereafter.[7] Moreover, the applicable percentage of income increases from 1 percent in calendar year 2014, to 2 percent in calendar year 2015, and to 2.5 percent for calendar year 2016 and thereafter.[8]

---

1. PPACA §9013(d) amended IRC Sec. 213(a).

2. IRC Sec. 213(f).

3. Joint Committee on Taxation, Tax Expenditures for Health Care, JCX-66-08, pp. 22-24, (July 30, 2008) at http://www.jct.gov/publications.html?func=startdown&id=1193.

4. IRC Sec. 36B.

5. IRC Sec. 5000A(f).

6. IRC Sec. 5000A(b)(1), (c)(1), (2). Use of the national average for bronze coverage means that calculation might not bear much relationship to the actual cost of coverage available in a specific location. However, the premium amounts likely will not be lower than the penalty.

7. IRC Sec. 5000A(c)(3)(A), (B), (D).

8. IRC Sec. 5000A(c)(2)(B). The net effect of these percentage increases for taxpayers who do not procure minimum essential coverage and whose income is sufficient to be above the minimum penalty is an increase in their marginal tax rate by 1% in calendar year 2014 rising to a 2.5 percent marginal tax rate increase for subsequent years.

For low-income employees, the minimum penalty is small in comparison to the actual cost of coverage, thereby increasing the likelihood that an individual without minimum essential coverage will not purchase health insurance, although the tax credit subsidies will make the insurance less expensive.

Applicable Individual. The individual mandate tax penalty applies only to "applicable individuals," and the definition of that term excludes designated categories of individuals, including:

- members of certain religious faiths already exempt from self-employment tax,

- members of healthcare-sharing ministries which, among other things, share medical expenses among members and have been in continuous existence since December 31, 1999,

- illegal aliens, and

- incarcerated individuals after they have been convicted.[1]

Affordability. Another major exemption is the one for applicable individuals whose "required contribution (determined on an annual basis) for coverage for the month exceeds 8 percent of such individual's household income for the taxable year."[2] For this exemption, the "required contribution" for an individual eligible to participate in an employer-sponsored plan is equal to "the portion of the annual premium which would be paid by the individual (without regard to whether paid through salary reduction or otherwise) for self-only coverage."[3]

Taxpayers whose household income for a taxable year is less than the gross income necessary to trigger an income tax return filing requirement[4] are also not applicable individuals and are not subject to the employee mandate. These gross income levels are unlikely to exempt many applicable individuals who are not already exempt under the 8 percent affordability exemption discussed above. However, many such individuals are also likely to be eligible for Medicaid and thus exempt from the penalty as long as they apply to procure such coverage.

393. What is the purpose of the individual mandate?

One purpose is to provide incentives to individuals to have health coverage to reduce the burdens imposed by free medical care. If they do not have minimum essential coverage, unless exempt, they must pay a tax penalty. Additionally, a primary goal of health reform was to fix the problems in the market for individual health insurance policies.

---

1. IRC Sec. 5000A(d)(2), (3), (4).
2. IRC Sec. 5000A(e)(1)(A). It is not clear why the "affordability test "for employers is 9.5 percent whereas this individual "affordability test" is 8 percent.
3. IRC Sec. 5000A(e)(1)(B)(i). This affordability test based on the premium for "self-only coverage" will be integrated into the penalty calculation under which an individual may also be responsible for providing coverage for a spouse and/or dependents. *See* Preamble to Proposed Regulations for Code section 36B.
4. IRC Sec. 5000A(e)(2).

Most critically, the law imposes open enrollment[1] and guaranteed renewal[2] requirements on all health insurance plans offered in the individual and small group markets so that these plans must accept all applicants for health insurance. The law will further limit insurance issuers' ability to charge applicants different prices based on their expected health risks. The law will only allow health insurance issuers to vary their prices based on four factors:

- the size of the applicant's family (for applicants seeking family coverage),

- the geographic region in which the applicant resides,

- the applicant's age, and

- whether the applicant uses tobacco.[3]

Even with respect to these factors, insurance issuers will be limited to charging their oldest applicants no more than three times the prices charged to their youngest applicants and to charging tobacco users no more than one and a half times the prices charged to non-smokers.[4] In effect, the law prevents insurance plans from discriminating against applicants with preexisting health conditions.

These provisions of the law that will significantly limit insurers' ability to engage in risk classification could undermine the individual market. However, health reform does several things to bolster this market, including penalties and incentives, such as:

- the individual mandate tax penalty,

- state-based health insurance exchanges,

- generous tax subsidies for those lower income individuals purchasing insurance, and

- the expansion of state Medicaid programs (in effect made optional by the U.S. Supreme Court).

If these provisions are effective, insurance policies offered on the exchanges could potentially be of better quality and lower cost than employer-provided offerings. Perhaps more likely, if the provisions are only partially effective, employer-provided insurance might retain its advantages over insurance policies offered on the exchanges, but with the advantages of employer-provided insurance being significantly reduced as compared to the advantages employer-provided insurance previously enjoyed over the insurance policies available on the individual market due to income tax advantages as well as bargaining power.

---

1. PPACA §1201.
2. PPACA §1201.
3. PPACA §1201.
4. PPACA §1201.

The Employer Mandate

394. How does the employer mandate improve health care?

The details of the employer mandate, which potentially affects employers (including related employers) with fifty or more full-time equivalent employees, are discussed in Part I and in detail in Part XI. It is designed to induce employers to offer affordable coverage for essential health benefits.

Maintaining the previous system of employer-sponsored coverage for lower-income employees was critically important for realizing health reform's financial targets because additional lower-income employees qualifying for the exchange subsidies drive up federal costs. Thus, the employer mandate, coupled with the health insurance nondiscrimination rules and the grandfathered plan rules were designed to induce employers to provide care to employees and their families.

395. What are the incentives created by health reform for employers, including but not limited to the employer mandate?

An employer avoids the Code Section 4980H(a) "all employee" $2,000 penalty by offering health insurance to all full-time employees regardless of how much the employees would be charged for that insurance. The Code Section 4980H(b) penalty will be triggered when an employer does offer health insurance, but when that insurance is "unaffordable" or fails the minimum value test, namely, that the employer's share of the total allowed costs of benefits provided under the plan is less than 60 percent of such costs.[1]

An employer with few low- and moderate-income employees could face the full Code Section 4980H(b) penalty of $3,000 annually per employee that qualifies for the exchange subsidies. An employer with many low- and moderate-income employees is more likely to have the Code Section 4980H(b) assessable payments limited to the Code Section 4980H(a) penalty amount of $2,000 times the total number of full-time employees over thirty.

The Code Section 4980H(a) penalty will not prevent employers from providing health insurance to their higher-income employees while sending their lower-income employees to the exchanges. The employers can avoid the Code Section 4980H(a) penalty by offering their lower income employees "unaffordable" health insurance. Only the Code Section 4980H(b) penalties will apply to an employer who offers "unaffordable" health insurance to its lower-income employees. Although employers often may not know a family's household income, nevertheless, the law somewhat encourages an employer to offer the tax benefits of employer coverage for high earners and provide unaffordable coverage to lower income employees to allow them to benefit from the exchange subsidies. A critical question is whether the health insurance nondiscrimination rules will result in the additional $100 per day per affected (nonhighly compensated) employee.

---

1. IRC Sec. 36B(c)(2)(C)(ii).

An offer of "affordable" employer-sponsored health insurance will result in an employee's entire family being ineligible for the premium tax credits, not just the employee.[1] Moreover, whether an employer's offer of family coverage is considered "affordable" is determined based on the cost the employee would need to contribute for self-only coverage.[2] In other words, if an employer offers an insurance policy with an option for family coverage, and if the amount an employee would need to contribute to pay for the portion of the policy covering only the employee (and not also the other members of the employee's family) is less than 9.5 percent of the employee's household income, then the employee's entire family is ineligible for the premium tax credits.

Comparing just the exchange subsidies (tax credits for lower income individuals) to the tax exclusions (employer tax deduction and individual exclusion from income and payroll taxes) based on the Tax Policy Center's estimates for 2016, the breakeven point for an individual is when household income is somewhere between 350 percent and 375 percent of the federal poverty line. The breakeven point for a family of four is when household income reaches 400 percent of the federal poverty line.[3]

For household incomes below these breakeven points, the exchange subsidies will generally offer more value than the tax exclusions. Conversely, for household incomes above these breakeven points, the tax exclusions will generally offer more value than the exchange subsidies. These breakeven analyses assume that the health-insurance policies offered on the exchanges will be of equivalent cost and quality to employer-sponsored health insurance policies. If all of the exchange coverage options are inferior to employer-sponsored options, then the breakeven thresholds would need to be adjusted.

These breakeven analyses assume that employers offer their employees subsidized health insurance as a form of employee compensation. When comparing the premiums they must pay for exchange coverage against the premiums they must pay for employer-sponsored coverage, many employees will prefer employer-sponsored coverage to the extent that employers continue to subsidize this coverage. Yet, in effect, these employer subsidies come out of the employees' income.

Health Insurance Premium Tax

396. What is the health insurance premium "tax" that begins in 2014?

Beginning in 2014, Americans will indirectly start paying a new fee on health insurance that will be assessed against health insurers but likely will be paid through increased premium rates. Health reform[4] requires individuals, families, and others to help pay a total of $73 billion over five years. The tax is not deductible.[5] This means that health insurers must pay the tax and then pay federal, state, and local taxes on the taxed amount, which increases the amount by which they must increase premiums to break even.

---

1. IRC Sec. 36B(c)(2)(C)(i)(II); Prop. Treas. Reg. §36B, 76 Fed. Reg. 50931, 50935 (Aug. 17, 2011).
2. IRC Sec. 36B(c)(2)(C)(i)(II); Prop. Treas. Reg. §36B, 76 Fed. Reg. 50931, 50935 (Aug. 17, 2011).
3. Stephanie Rennane & C. Eugene Steurle, Health Reform: A Two-Subsidy System, Urban Institute and Brookings Institution: Tax Policy Center S10-001, (2010), at http://www.taxpolicycenter.org/library/displayatab.cfm?Docid=2699.
4. PPACA §9010.
5. PPACA §9010(f), providing that the tax is nondeductible under IRC Sec. 275(A)(6).

The health insurance (HI) premium tax is an annual fee on insurers beginning in 2014. The fee (equivalent to a sales tax) applies to U.S. health insurance providers and is intended to collect roughly $90 billion in revenue through 2020. A predetermined amount of revenue will be collected each year:

- $8 billion in 2014,

- $11.3 billion in 2015 and 2016,

- $13.9 billion in 2017, and

- $14.3 billion or more annually in years 2018 and beyond.

After 2018, the HI tax in any particular year will equal the fee levied during the previous year, increased by the rate of premium growth for the preceding calendar year. The aggregate fee is apportioned among the providers based on a ratio designed to reflect relative market share of U.S. health insurance business.

A study by former Congressional Budget Office Director Douglas Holtz-Eakin released in March 2011 found that the HI tax can be expected to raise premiums for employer-sponsored insurance by as much as 3 percent, a price increase that is nearly $475 per family per year and $5,000 per family over the first decade.[1] Additionally, the Joint Committee on Taxation estimated that repealing the tax would reduce premiums of insurance plans offered by covered entities by 2.0 percent to 2.5 percent.[2]

The new tax is not assessed on self-funded ERISA health plans, nonprofit insurers that meet specific criteria, and certain voluntary employee beneficiaries associations (VEBAs).

Tax on "Cadillac" Policies

397. Why did Congress decide to tax generous health plans?

Beginning in 2018, health reform imposes a tax on high-cost health plans. In addition to being a revenue raiser, the reason for this provision is to reduce the demand for high-cost ("Cadillac") coverage where the individual has little out-of-pocket cost so as to encourage employers, providers, and consumers to control health costs.

398. What type of plans are taxed?

For purposes of the excise tax on employer-sponsored health insurance, coverage is health coverage under any group health plan offered by an employer to an employee (plus any former employee, surviving spouse, and any other primary insured individual[3]) without regard to whether

---

1. Douglas Holtz-Eakin, "Higher Costs and the Affordable Care Act: The Case of the Premium Tax", American Action Forum (March 9, 2011) at http://americanactionforum.org/sites/default/files/Case%20of%20the%20Premium%20Tax.pdf.
2. Thomas A. Barthold, letter to Senator Jon Kyl, Joint Committee on Taxation, Washington, DC, 3 June 3, 2011 at http://www.ahipcoverage.com/wp-content/uploads/2011/11/Premium-Tax-JCT-Letter-to-Kyl-060311-2.pdf.
3. IRC Sec. 4980I(d)(3).

the employer provides the coverage (and thus the coverage is excludable from the employee's income) or the employee pays for the coverage with after-tax dollars.[1]

Employer-sponsored health insurance coverage includes coverage under any group health plan established and maintained primarily for the civilian employees of the federal government or any of its agencies or instrumentalities and, generally, of any state government or political subdivision or any state agencies or instrumentalities.[2]

Employer-sponsored health insurance coverage includes both fully insured and self-insured health coverage excludable from the employee's gross income, including, in the self-insured context, on-site medical clinics that offer more than a minimal amount of medical care to employees and executive physical programs. In the case of a self-employed individual, employer-sponsored health insurance coverage is coverage for any portion of which a deduction is allowable to the self-employed individual under Code Section 162(l).

399. How does the Cadillac tax on expensive health plans work?

Beginning in 2018, a 40 percent nondeductible excise tax is imposed on "coverage providers" that provide high-cost health care coverage to the employer's employees. Coverage providers include:

- health insurer for fully insured plans,

- the employer with respect to self-insured plans, HSA or Archer MSA contributions, and

- in all other cases, the "person that administers the plan."

The tax applies to "applicable employer-sponsored coverage," which is coverage under a group health plan:

- that is made available to an employee by an employer, and

- that either

  o is actually excludable from gross income under Code Section 106, or

  o would be excludable if it were employer-provided coverage within the meaning of Code Section 106.[3]

The excise tax is imposed on the "excess benefit" provided to the employees.

There is no exception to the tax for grandfathered plans.

---

1. IRC Sec. 4980I(d)(1)(A).
2. IRC Sec. 4980I(d)(1)(E).
3. IRC Sec. 4980I(d)(1)(A).

Excess benefit is determined by comparing the cost of the actual coverage provided (calculated using rules similar to those for determining COBRA premiums) that exceeds annual limits. For 2018, the annual limit for employee-only coverage is $10,200 per year (as adjusted by a "health cost adjustment percentage" or HCAP) and $27,500 per year (as adjusted by the HCAP) for coverage other than employee-only.

The HCAP takes into account year-to-year increases in the cost of health care coverage, including increases attributable to age and gender differences.

400. What is the effect on the excise tax if the employee pays for all or part of the coverage?

Whether the employer or the employee pays for coverage does not impact the determination of whether it is "applicable employer-sponsored coverage."[1] However, it can affect the cost of that coverage when the amount of an employee's excess benefit is calculated, which affects the amount of excise tax payable.

401. What coverage is not subject to the excise tax on high-cost employer-sponsored coverage?

In determining whether the value of health coverage exceeds the threshold amount, the following items are not included.[2]

- The value of employer sponsored coverage for long term care and the following benefits described in Code Section 9832(c)(1) that are excepted benefits and exempt from the portability, access and renewability requirements of the Health Insurance Portability and Accountability Act (HIPAA), namely:

    o coverage only for accident or disability income insurance, or any combination of these coverages;

    o coverage issued as a supplement to liability insurance;

    o liability insurance, including general liability insurance and automobile liability insurance;

    o workers' compensation or similar insurance;

    o automobile medical payment insurance;

    o credit-only insurance; and

---

1. IRC Sec. 4980I(d)(1)(C).
2. IRC Sec. 4980I(d)(1).

- o other similar insurance coverage, specified in regulations, under which benefits for medical care are secondary or incidental to other insurance benefits.

- The value of independent, noncoordinated coverage described in Code Section 9832(c)(3) if that coverage is purchased exclusively by the employee with after-tax dollars (or, in the case of a self-employed individual, for which a deduction under Code Section 162(l) is not allowable). Such Code Section 9832(c)(3) coverage includes coverage only for a specified disease or illness, as well as hospital indemnity or other fixed indemnity insurance. Fixed indemnity health coverage pays fixed dollar amounts based on the occurrence of qualifying events, including but not limited to the diagnosis of a specific disease, an accidental injury or a hospitalization, and no coordination with other health coverage. The value of employer-sponsored health insurance coverage does include the value of such coverage if any portion of the coverage is employer-provided or, in the case of a self-employed individual, if a deduction is allowable for any portion of the payment for the coverage.

- Any coverage under a separate policy, certificate, or contract of insurance that provides benefits substantially all of which are for treatment of the mouth (including any organ or structure within the mouth) or for treatment of the eye.

402. Is there any relief in the Cadillac tax rules for people whose health coverage is expensive because their occupation is dangerous?

Yes. The annual limits noted in Q 399 are increased by $1,650 and $3,450, respectively, for employees in high-risk professions (e.g., law enforcement, EMT/paramedics, construction, mining, longshoremen, and so forth).

403. How is the tax calculated and paid?

Liability for the excise tax is determined on a monthly basis. Employers are required to calculate the amount of the excess benefit subject to the excise tax for each taxable period and to determine each coverage provider's "applicable share" of the excess benefit. A coverage provider's applicable share of an employee's excess benefit is determined by multiplying the aggregate excess benefit for the employee by the ratio obtained by comparing (i) the cost of the coverage provided to the employee by the coverage provider to (ii) the aggregate cost of all applicable coverage.[1]

The amount subject to the excise tax on high-cost employer-sponsored health insurance coverage for each employee is the sum of the aggregate premiums for health insurance coverage, the amount of any salary reduction contributions to a health flexible spending account (FSA) for the tax year, and the dollar amount of employer contributions to a health savings account

---

1. IRC Sec. 4980I(d).

(HSA) or an Archer medical savings account (MSA), minus the dollar amount of the threshold. The aggregate premiums for health insurance coverage include all employer sponsored health insurance coverage including coverage for any supplementary health insurance coverage. The applicable premium for health coverage provided through health reimbursement account (HRA) is also included in this aggregate amount.[1]

The tax is equal to 40 percent of the aggregate value of the health insurance coverage that exceeds:

(1)   the threshold dollar amount[2],

(2)   multiplied by the health cost adjustment percentage, and

(3)   increased by the age and gender adjusted excess premium amount.[3]

For 2018, the threshold dollar amount is $10,200 for individual coverage and $27,500 for family coverage.[4] However, increased thresholds apply for certain classes of taxpayers. The threshold amounts are increased for an individual who has attained age 55, is not Medicare eligible, and is receiving employer-sponsored retiree health coverage, or is covered by a plan sponsored by an employer, the majority of whose employees covered by the plan are engaged in a high-risk profession[5] or employed to repair or install electrical and telecommunications lines. For these individuals, the threshold amount in 2018 is increased by:

(1) $1,650 for individual coverage or $3,450 for family coverage, and

(2)   the age and gender-adjusted excess premium amount.[6]

The basic thresholds are also adjusted by the health cost adjustment percentage for growth in the cost of U.S. healthcare between 2010 and 2018 that exceeds the projected growth for that period. The health cost adjustment percentage is equal to 100 percent plus the excess, if any, of

(1)   the percentage by which the per employee cost of coverage under the Blue Cross/Blue Shield standard benefit option under the Federal Employees Health Benefits Plan (standard FEHBP coverage) for plan year 2018 (as determined using the benefit package for standard FEHBP coverage for plan year 2010) exceeds the per employee cost of standard FEHBP coverage for plan year 2010; over

(2)   55 percent.[7]

---

1. IRC Sec. 4980I(d).
2. IRC Sec. 4980I(b)(3)(C).
3. IRC Sec. 4980I(b)(3).
4. IRC Sec. 4980I(b)(3)(C).
5. Law enforcement officers; those engaged in fire protection activities; providers of out-of-hospital emergency medical care (e.g., emergency medical technicians); those whose primary work is longshore work; and those engaged in the construction, mining, agriculture (not including food processing), forestry, and fishing industries. A retiree with at least twenty years of employment in a high-risk profession is also eligible for the increased threshold. IRC Sec. 4980I 4980I(f).
6. IRC Sec. 4980I(b)(3)(C)(iii) and (iv).
7. IRC Sec. 4980I(b)(3)(C)(ii).

In 2019, the threshold amounts, after application of the health cost adjustment percentage in 2018, if any, are indexed to the Consumer Price Index for All Urban Consumers (CPI-U), as determined by the Department of Labor, plus one percentage point, rounded to the nearest $50. In 2020 and thereafter, the threshold amounts are indexed to the CPI-U as determined by the Department of Labor, rounded to the nearest $50. For each employee (other than for certain retirees and employees in high-risk professions, whose thresholds are adjusted under rules described below), the age and gender adjusted excess premium amount is equal to the excess, if any, of:

(1)   the premium cost of standard FEHBP coverage for the type of coverage provided to the individual if priced for the age and gender characteristics of all employees of the individual's employer, over

(2)   the premium cost, determined under procedures proscribed by IRS, for that coverage if priced for the age and gender characteristics of the national workforce.[1]

In 2019, the primary threshold amounts and additional $1,650 and $3,450 amounts are indexed to the CPI-U, plus one percentage point, rounded to the nearest $50. In 2020 and thereafter, the additional threshold amounts are indexed to the CPI-U, rounded to the nearest $50.[2]

404. Who pays the excise tax and how it is allocated?

The excise tax is imposed pro rata on the issuers of the insurance. Presumably, that cost will be passed along to the insureds. For a self-insured group health plan, a health FSA or an HRA, the excise tax is paid by the entity that administers benefits under the plan or arrangement (the "plan administrator"). The excise tax is paid by the employer if it acts as plan administrator to a self-insured group health plan, a health FSA or an HRA. Where an employer contributes to an HSA or an Archer MSA, the employer is responsible for payment of the excise tax, as the insurer.[3]

The excise tax is allocated pro rata among the insurers, with each insurer responsible for payment of the excise tax on an amount equal to the amount subject to the total excise tax multiplied by a fraction, having as the numerator the amount of employer-sponsored health insurance coverage provided by that insurer to the employee and having as the denominator the aggregate value of all employer-sponsored health insurance coverage provided to the employee.[4]

For a self-insured group health plan, a health FSA or an HRA, the excise tax is allocated to the plan administrator.[5]

The employer is responsible for calculating the amount subject to the excise tax allocable to each insurer and plan administrator and for reporting these amounts to each insurer, plan

---

1. IRC Sec. 4980I(b)(3)(C)(iii).
2. IRC Sec. 4980I(b)(3)(C)(v).
3. IRC Sec. 4980I(c)(1) and (2).
4. IRC Sec. 4980I(c)(3).
5. IRC Sec. 4980I(c)(2)(C).

administrator and IRS, in the form and at the time that IRS may set. Each insurer and plan administrator is then responsible for calculating, reporting, and paying the excise tax to IRS on such forms and at such time as IRS may set.[1]

> **Example:** In 2018, an employee elects family coverage under a fully insured healthcare policy covering major medical and dental with a value of $32,000. The health cost adjustment percentage for that year is 100 percent, and the age and gender adjusted excess premium amount for the employee is $600. On these facts, the amount subject to the excise tax is $3,900 ($32,000 less the threshold of $28,100, which is the $27,500 threshold multiplied by 100 percent and increased by $600.) The employer reports $3,900 as taxable to the insurer, which calculates and remits the excise tax of $1,560 (40 percent of 3900) to the IRS.

405. What is the sanction on the employer for underreporting liability for the tax?

A penalty applies to an employer that reports to insurers, plan administrators and IRS a lower amount of insurance cost subject to the excise tax than required. The penalty is the sum of any additional excise tax that each such insurer and administrator would have owed if the employer had reported correctly plus interest[2] attributable to that additional excise tax from the date that the tax was otherwise due to the date paid by the employer.[3]

The penalty does not apply if it is established to IRS's satisfaction that the employer neither knew, nor by exercising reasonable diligence would have known, that the failure existed. In addition, no penalty will be imposed on any failure corrected within the thirty-day period beginning on the first date that the employer knew, or exercising reasonable diligence, would have known, that the failure existed, so long as the failure is due to reasonable cause and not to willful neglect. All or part of the penalty may be waived by IRS in the case of any failure due to reasonable cause and not to willful neglect, to the extent that the payment of the penalty would be excessive or otherwise inequitable relative to the failure involved.[4]

Patient Centered Outcomes Research Institute (PCORI) and PCORI Fees

406. What is the Patient Centered Outcomes Research Institute?

The Patient-Centered Outcomes Research Institute (PCORI) is authorized by Congress to conduct research to provide information about the best available evidence to help patients and their health care providers make more informed decisions. PCORI's research is intended to give patients a better understanding of the prevention, treatment, and care options available, as well as the science that supports those options.

---

1. IRC Sec. 4980I(c)(4).
2. Calculated under IRC Sec. 6621.
3. IRC Sec. 4980I(e).
4. IRC Sec. 4980I(e).

407. What are PCORI fees?

The ACA imposes a Patient Centered Outcomes Research Institute (PCORI) fee on plan sponsors and issuers of individual and group policies. The "PCORI fee" or the "Section 4376[1] fee" is intended to fund partially the Patient-Centered Outcomes Research Institute created by healthcare reform.

The fee applies to certain "specified health insurance" policies and includes medical policies, retiree-only policies, and any accident or health insurance policy (including a policy under a group health benefit plan) issued to individuals residing in the United States. This does not include:

- "Excepted benefits," as defined under HIPAA, such as stand-alone vision or dental plans;

- Employee Assistance Programs (EAP) or wellness programs;

- FSA plans, when they meet the excepted benefits test; or

- HRA, when it meets the excepted benefits test;

    o Expatriate coverage (those working outside the United States and their spouses and dependents)

    o Stop loss, where the issuer is liable for all losses in excess of a specified amount and where the plan sponsor retains its liability for losses

    o Indemnity reinsurance policies, where the reinsuring company accepts all or part of the risk of loss under the policy and the issuing company retains its liability for covered lives

    o Medicare

    o Medicaid

    o CHIP

    o TRICARE

    o Non-insurance health programs for members (spouses or dependents) of the Armed Forces or veterans

---

1. PPACA § 4376.

    o   Federally recognized Indian Health Services and programs under the Indian Health Care Improvement Act

408. How are PCORI fees to be paid?

IRS Form 720, Part II, line 133, and its voucher are used to report and remit the Patient Centered Outcomes Research Institute Fee ("PCORI fee") to the IRS by July 31 for the preceding year. The fee must be paid no later than July 31 of the year following the last day of the plan year.[1] The fee is a tax deductible business expense.[2]

The PCORI fee for the second year will increase to $2.00 times the average number of covered lives in the group health plan and is indexed for increases in national health expenditures for the following years.

409. When are PCORI fees due?

The "PCORI fee" is intended to fund partially the Patient-Centered Outcomes Research Institute created by healthcare reform. The PCORI fee is applicable to plan years ending after Sept. 30, 2012, and extends through plan years ending before October 1, 2019. The fee must be paid no later than July 31 of the year following the last day of the plan year.[3] Therefore, the first PCORI fees are due for 2012 calendar year self-insured plans and certain fiscal year plans by July 31, 2013. So, for example, if the fiscal year end is March 31, 2013, the calendar year in which that plan year ends is 2013, and the tax and return would be due July 31, 2014.

PCORI fee for the first year for plan years ending on or after October 1, 2012, and before October 1, 2013 is equal to $1.00 multiplied by the average number of covered lives in the group health plan. The PCORI fee for the second year will increase to $2.00 times the average number of covered lives in the group health plan and is indexed for increases in national health expenditures for the following years.

410. Who pays the PCORI fees?

Insurers file and pay the fee for insured plans.[4] The PCORI fee must be paid by employers that sponsor self-insured health plans (including many employer funded health reimbursement accounts ("HRAs") and medical expense reimbursement plans ("MERPs") by July 31, 2013, and each year thereafter.[5] The fee paid by insurers applies to certain "specified health insurance" policies and includes medical policies, retiree-only policies, and any accident or health insurance policy (including a policy under a group health benefit plan) issued to individuals residing in the United States.

The self-insured plan that is taxed is the "self-insured health plan." This is not tied to the definition of and exemptions from the term "group health plan." However, the regulations

---

1. 26 CFR § 6071(a)-1.
2. IRS Chief Counsel Memo (June 7, 2013) available at http://www.irs.gov/pub/irs-utl/AM2013-002.pdf.
3. 26 CFR § 6071(a)-1.
4. 26 CFR § 4375-1.
5. IRC § 4376(b)(1) and Reg § 46.4376 provide that the fee imposed by section 4376(a) shall be paid by the plan sponsor.

provide an exemption for an employer self-funded plan that provides benefits substantially all of which are excepted benefits."[1] On the other hand, plans that are not ERISA plans (covering only partners, for example) or retiree-only plans are not exempted.

Health reimbursement arrangements (HRAs) and medical expense reimbursement plans ("MERPs") are self-funded group health plans and are subject to the PCORI fee unless the employer also sponsors a *self-insured* group health plan, and both plans have the same plan year. If the plan sponsor maintains a self-funded medical plan with the same plan year, the medical plan and HRA may be treated as one plan for purposes of the PCORI fee if all participants participate in both plans.

However, if the medical plan is fully insured, the medical plan and HRA must be treated as separate plans for purposes of the PCORI fee, with the insurer paying the fee for the medical plan and the employer/plan sponsor paying the fee for the HRA. Treas. Reg. §46.4376-1(b) (1) provides the definition of self-insured plans that are subject to the tax, and includes medical expense reimbursement plans. It only excludes only health FSAs that are excepted benefits. A rule allows counting only the covered employees for purposes of determining the number of covered lives.

411. Can plan sponsors delegate the PCORI filing and fee payment to third parties?

No. Plan sponsors[2] of self-insured health plans[3] must make arrangements to complete and file the Form and pay the annual PCORI fees to the IRS, as the PCORI regulations directly prohibit using "third-party reporting" arrangements with respect to the Form 720. Plan sponsors are also advised that the fee must be paid by the plan sponsor and cannot be paid by the plan or from plan assets.

412. Are any plans excluded from being subject to the PCORI fees?

Yes, a number of employee benefit plans are excluded. They are

- "Excepted benefits," as defined under HIPAA, such as stand-alone vision or stand-alone dental plans. If the benefits covered under the FSA are limited to "excepted benefits," that FSA is also exempt from the PCORI payment even if FSA participants have no other health plan or the payments exceed the dollar limits described above.[4] Excepted benefits include but are not limited to:

  - coverage for only accident or disability income insurance,

  - liability insurance and coverage issued as a supplement to liability insurance,

---

1. Reg § 46.4376-1(b)(ii).
2. PPACA § 4376(b)(2).
3. 26 CFR § 4375-2.
4. Treas. Reg. § 46.4376–1(b)(1)(ii); IRS, Patient-Centered Outcomes Research Trust Fund Fee (IRC 4375, 4376 and 4377), Q&A-9 at http:// www.irs.gov/uac/Patient-Centered-Outcomes-Research-Trust-Fund-Fee:-Questions-and-Answers.

  - workers' compensation or similar insurance,

  - automobile medical payment insurance, and

  - coverage for onsite medical clinics.

- Employee Assistance Programs (EAP) or wellness programs.

- Health FSA plans, when they meet the excepted benefits test. An excepted benefit FSA provides that the maximum benefit payable by the FSA to the participant for a year does not exceed the greater of:

  - two times the participant's salary reduction election under the FSA for the year, or

  - $500 plus the amount of the participant's salary reduction election, meaning a $3000 benefit from a $2500 salary reduction election and an employer paid flex credit of $500 is possible. Most FSAs also meet the second requirement.

- Excepted Benefit FSA. If the benefits covered under the FSA are limited to "excepted benefits," that FSA is also exempt from the PCORI payment even if FSA participants have no other health plan or the payments exceed the dollar limits described above. Excepted benefits include but are not limited to:

  - coverage for only accident or disability income insurance,

  - liability insurance and coverage issued as a supplement to liability insurance,

  - workers' compensation or similar insurance,

  - automobile medical payment insurance, and

  - coverage for onsite medical clinics.

- Employer funded HRA and MERP plans where employer's *self-insured* group health plan if both plans have the same plan year.

- Expatriate coverage (those working outside the United States and their spouses and dependents).

- Long-term care, home health care, and nursing home care.

- Stop loss, where the issuer is liable for all losses in excess of a specified amount and where the plan sponsor retains its liability for losses.

- Hospital and other indemnity insurance policies.

- Medicare.

- Medicaid.

- CHIP and TRICARE.

- Non-insurance health programs for members (spouses or dependents) of the Armed Forces or veterans.

- Federally recognized Indian Health Services and programs under the Indian Health Care Improvement Act.

413. How are the average number of lives determined and the fees calculated?

Fully Insured Plans

There are four optional methods for determining the average number of covered lives. Issuers must use the same method consistently for the duration of any year and the same method for all policies subject to the fee. (The insurance carrier is responsible for paying the required PCORI fee in the case of fully insured coverage.)

Actual Count – Count the total number of covered lives for each day of the policy year and divide by the number of days in a year.

Snapshot Method – Count the number of members on a single day (or days if consistent for each quarter) during a quarter and divide the total by the number of dates on which a count was made. The date used for each quarter must be the same (i.e., the first day, the last day).

NAIC Member Months Method – The issuer determines the average number of covered lives based on member months reported to the National Association of Insurance Commissioners (NAIC) on the Supplemental Health Care Exhibit for the calendar year. The average number of lives in effect for the calendar year equals member months divided by twelve.

State Form Method – This method is for issuers that are not required to file the NAIC Exhibit. These issuers may determine the number of covered lives using a form that is filed with the issuer's state of domicile, if the form reports the number of covered lives in the same manner as the NAIC Supplemental Exhibit.

Self-funded Plans

Self-funded plans may determine the average number of covered lives by using any of the following methods. Like fully insured plans, plan sponsors must use the same method consistently for the duration of any year and the same method for all policies subject to the fee.

Actual Count – Count the total covered lives for each day of the plan year and divide by the number of days in the plan year.

Snapshot Dates – Count the total number of covered lives on a single day in a quarter (or more than one day) and divide the total by the number of dates on which a count was made. (The date or dates must be consistent for each quarter.)

Snapshot Factor – In the case of self-only coverage, determine the sum of: (1) the number of participants with self-only coverage, and (2) the number of participants with other than self-only coverage multiplied by 2.35.

Form 5500 Method – For self-only coverage, determine the average number of participants by combining the total number of participants at the beginning of the plan year with the total number of participants at the end of the plan year as reported on the Form 5500 and divide by two. In the case of plans with self-only and other coverage, the average number of total lives is the sum of total participants covered at the beginning and the end of the plan year, as reported on the Form 5500.

414. How are multiple self-funded plans counted for purposes of the fee?

Under the final rule, if the plan sponsor of a self-funded plan has more than one self-funded plan (e.g., one for medical, another for pharmacy) it may treat them as a single self-funded plan for purposes of this fee to avoid double counting of the members. This special counting rule only applies to self-funded plans in the proposed rule.

415. How are the number of covered lives determined in the first year?

For the first year of the fee, plan years beginning before July 11, 2012, and ending on or after Oct. 1, 2012, a plan sponsor may determine the average number of covered lives using any reasonable method. In the first year, fully insured plans, for example, may report only 25 percent of the number of lives it reported on the NAIC form in 2012.

416. Are there special rules for health FSAs and HRAs?

If a plan sponsor only maintains a flexible spending account or a health reimbursement arrangement, the plan sponsor may treat each participant's account as covering a single life. (The plan sponsor is not required to count spouses or other dependents.)

If the FSA/HRA is sponsored by a plan sponsor that also has an applicable self-funded health plan (that is not a FSA or HRA), the two arrangements may be treated as one plan.

PART X: STATE INSURANCE EXCHANGES (MARKETPLACES)

State, State-federal Partnerships, and Federally Facilitated Exchanges (FFEs)

417. What are the state health insurance exchanges or marketplaces?

A centerpiece of healthcare reform is the state insurance exchanges, which the federal government more recently has labeled marketplaces. Healthcare reform requires states and certain other governmental entities[1] to create exchanges, a competitive marketplace for individuals and small businesses to purchase insurance. Exchanges, which must be operating in states by January 1, 2014, will be the main way that people gain insurance coverage when they do not receive it from their employer. (Initial enrollment begins Oct. 1, 2013.) While the exchanges will be a major avenue to health insurance, it is likely that the majority of people will continue to obtain coverage from their employers. As discussed elsewhere in this section, there are three types of state exchanges:

- those created by a state,

- state-federal partnership exchanges, and

- federally facilitated exchanges (FFEs) in those states that offer no assistance in creating or operating their own exchange.

Exchanges will provide individuals and small business owners with a "one stop shop" to compare and buy health insurance. The purpose is to provide consumers with more control and greater transparency for making choices about health insurance. People can also enroll in public programs, such as Medicaid and CHIP (for children), through exchanges. Exchanges are intended to use the power of a large insurance pool, made up of individuals and small businesses, to generate competition among insurers to offer better quality plans at a lower cost.

418. What is the relationship between the exchanges for individuals and small businesses?

Healthcare reform created two kinds of exchanges: health insurance exchanges for individuals and Small Business Health Options Program (SHOP) exchanges for small business owners.

The law delegates primary responsibility for governing and operating the exchanges to the states, with the federal government (primarily HHS) setting minimum standards. States have the option to merge the individual and SHOP exchanges, collaborate with other states to form multi-state regional exchanges, or to form multiple exchanges within their state if each one serves a geographically distinct area.

---

1. PPACA § 1311(b)(1) (2010). "State" means the 50 states of the U.S., the District of Columbia, Puerto Rico, the U.S. Virgin Islands, Guam, American Samoa, and the Northern Mariana Islands. PPACA § 1551; PHSA § 2791(d)(14).

Beginning in 2014, however, purchasing employer-provided health coverage for employees through a SHOP will be the only way for qualified employers to obtain a small business health care tax credit.

HHS will issue rules allowing a state that has already received conditional approval to operate a state-based exchange for 2014 to request permission to operate a SHOP-only Exchange instead while the individual market operates under an FFE.[1] For years after 2014, HHS will provide rules requiring states to request approval to operate a SHOP-only Exchange using a special application. The FAQs also clarify that a SHOP-only Exchange must have a state-run navigator program, but it may be limited to consumer outreach and education activities, while the FFE would operate its own navigator program in the individual market.[2]

419. What is the biggest loophole in the law as to exchange purchased health insurance?

This loophole is an intentional attempt to assist those who temporarily cannot afford the exchange health insurance they purchased. The result is that insureds receiving subsidies for their health insurance purchased on an exchange need only pay premiums for nine months for twelve months of health insurance coverage. As a result providers may inadvertently give uncompensated care for up to two months per year for such insureds. Under the law,[3] families who obtain subsidized health plan coverage through an exchange and fail to pay their premiums have a three-month grace period to pay the premiums[4] due before the policy is cancelled.[5]

Thus, doctors and hospitals who treat patients with such subsidized exchange health insurance could find themselves liable for uncompensated treatment costs due to the healthcare reform law. The three-month grace period was meant to ensure continuity of care for low-income families who might be between jobs and could not afford to pay their premiums for a few weeks. However, it also creates a loophole for insureds who want to game the system. Insurers are responsible only for paying claims during the first month of this three-month grace period. During months two and three, families are asked to pay their hospital and doctor's bills (or their delinquent insurance premium) if they seek health care services. However, if they do not pay either bill, providers will not be paid for the cost of the treatment.[6]

Providers might be unable to avoid treating exchange patients, even if they discover they will not be paid if the delinquent premiums are not paid. Contracts by providers with large health insurers often include an "all-products" clause, which requires that doctors treat any patients

1. Small Business Health Options Program (SHOP)-Only Marketplace FAQs, Q/A-1 at http://www.cms.gov/CCIIO/Resources/Fact-Sheets-and-FAQs/Downloads/shop-marketplace-5-10-2013.pdf.
2. Small Business Health Options Program (SHOP)-Only Marketplace FAQs, Q/A-4 at http://www.cms.gov/CCIIO/Resources/Fact-Sheets-and-FAQs/Downloads/shop-marketplace-5-10-2013.pdf.
3. PPACA § 1412(c)(2)(B)(iv)(II).
4. 45 CFR §§ 156.270(d).
5. 76 Fed. Reg. 41866; 45 CFR §§ 155.400, 155.430 & 156.270 available at https://www.federalregister.gov/articles/2012/03/27/2012-6125/patient-protection-and-affordable-care-act-establishment-of-exchanges-and-qualified-health-plans#h-165.
6. 45 CFR §§ 156.270(d)(3) provides that QHP issuers notify providers who submit claims for services rendered during the second and third months of the premium grace period that any such claims will be pended, and potentially not reimbursed by the QHP issuer if the individual does not settle outstanding premium payments.

covered under the health plan. Doctors have legal and ethical obligations not to abandon their patients during course of treatment.

In a notice published in the Federal Register,[1] HHS acknowledged that nonpayment of premiums for subsidized exchange policies would "increase uncertainty for providers and increase the burden of uncompensated care." HHS officials said that the agency will "monitor this issue moving forward and will continue to work on the development of policies to prevent misuse of the grace period."

Persons who have delinquent exchange insurance premiums would face tax penalties for any advance payment of premium tax credits paid on their behalf when the individual did not pay for coverage, but they would not receive a fine, a premium rate increase, or a repayment order. They could also enroll in another subsidized exchange policy the next year even if they never pay all or a part of the three months of missed premiums.

Here is how this three-month grace period works, according to examples #2 and 3 in the summary of the regulations[2]

Example #2: Individual misses $50 payment that is due February 28 for March coverage and misses $50 payment that is due March 31st for April coverage. Individual pays $150 on April 30 for March, April and May coverage.

- Issuer adjudicates claims for March

- Coverage continues for April and May (second and third months of the grace period), but:

  o Providers are notified of the potential for a denied claim.

  o Issuer pends claims for services performed in April and May until individual pays outstanding premiums.

  o Individual has paid full premium for March, April, and May as is eligible for premium tax credit for March, April, and May.

Example #3: Same facts as Example #1 except that individual does not pay enrollee's share of premium for March, April, or May.

- Coverage terminated retroactively to March 31

- Issuer can deny claims for services rendered during April and May. Providers could then seek payment directly from the individual for any services provided during that time.

---

1. Id.

2. Summary, Establishment of Exchanges and Qualified Health Plans; Exchange Standards for Employers, 77 Fed. Reg. 18310 at 18427 (March 27, 2012) et seq at https://www.federalregister.gov/articles/2012/03/27/2012-6125/patient-protection-and-affordable-care-act-establishment-of-exchanges-and-qualified-health-plans#h-166.

- Individual may have additional tax liability attributable to the $450 for the advance payment of the premium tax credit paid on his or her behalf for March's coverage. The exact amount of additional tax liability would be determined in accordance with the rules for tax credit reconciliation under section 36B of the Code.

420. What if a state elects not to create its own exchange?

If a state decides not to run its own exchange or does not meet minimum federal standards, HHS can create a federal exchange in that state or find a not-for-profit entity to run it. Sixteen states are setting up their own exchanges. Eight additional states are collaborating with HHS to set up exchanges. These are called state-federal exchanges. In the rest of the states, HHS is required to set up the state marketplaces, which are called federally facilitated exchanges (FFEs). In June 2013, GAO reported that it "cannot yet be determined" if the exchange marketplaces will be ready for enrollment in all states.

HHS has also provided for a federally facilitated SHOP (FF-SHOP) in states that do not establish a state-based Exchange.[1]

421. When can individuals and businesses purchase insurance on the exchanges?

HHS announced that the initial open enrollment period will run from October 1, 2013, through March 31, 2014.[2] The annual enrollment period for 2015 and subsequent years will begin October 15 and extend through December 7 of the preceding calendar year.[3]

Additionally, exchanges must offer special enrollment periods.[4] Under final exchange regulations, the exchanges must allow qualified individuals and enrollees to enroll in a QHP or change from one to another because of the following triggering events:[5]

- A qualified individual or dependent loses minimum essential coverage. Loss of minimum essential coverage does not include termination or loss due to failure to pay premiums on a timely basis (including COBRA premiums prior to expiration of COBRA coverage) or certain situations allowing for rescission.[6]

- A qualified individual gains a dependent or becomes a dependent through marriage, birth, adoption, or placement for adoption;

1. General Guidance on Federally-facilitated Exchanges (May 16, 2012); Fact Sheet: Affordable Insurance Exchanges (May 16, 2012) at http://www.cms.gov/CCIIO/Resources/Fact-Sheets-and-FAQs/Downloads/ffe-guidance-05-16-2012.pdf.
2. 45 CFR § 155.410(b).
3. 45 CFR § 155.410(e).
4. PPACA § 1311(c)(6) (2010). Special enrollment periods include those specified in Code § 9801, other special enrollments under circumstances similar to such periods under part D of title XVIII of the Social Security Act, and "special monthly enrollment periods for Indians (as defined in section 4 of the Indian Health Care Improvement Act)."
5. 45 CFR § 155.420(d).
6. 45 CFR § 155.420(e).

- An individual, who was not previously a citizen, national, or lawfully present individual gains such status;

- A qualified individual's enrollment or non-enrollment in a QHP is unintentional, inadvertent, or erroneous and is the result of the error, misrepresentation, or inaction of the exchange or HHS;

- An enrollee adequately demonstrates to the exchange that the QHP in which he or she is enrolled substantially violated a material provision of its contract in relation to the enrollee;

- An individual is determined newly eligible or newly ineligible for advance payments of the premium tax credit or has a change in eligibility for cost-sharing reductions, regardless of whether such individual is already enrolled in a QHP. (The exchange must permit individuals whose existing coverage through an eligible employer-sponsored plan will no longer be affordable or provide minimum value for his or her employer's upcoming plan year to access this special enrollment period prior to the end of his or her coverage through such eligible employer-sponsored plan);

- A qualified individual or enrollee gains access to new QHPs as a result of a permanent move;

- An individual may enroll in a QHP or change from one to another one time per month; and

- A qualified individual or enrollee demonstrates to the exchange that the individual meets other exceptional circumstances (as defined by the exchange).

The special enrollment period generally is 60 days from the date of the triggering event.[1] Coverage must be effective as of the first day of the following month for elections made by the 15th of the preceding month and on the first day of the second following month for elections made between the 16th and the last day of a month (but coverage must be effective on the date of birth, adoption, or placement for adoption, when that is the special enrollment triggering event).

422. What levels of health insurance are available on the exchanges?

There will be health insurance offerings at bronze, silver, gold, or platinum level coverage (benefits that are actuarially equivalent to 60 percent, 70 percent, 80 percent, or 90 percent of the full actuarial benefits provided under the plan[2] or a catastrophic plan (also known as "young invincibles" coverage).[3]

---

1. 45 CFR § 155.420(c).
2. PPACA § 1302(d).
3. PPACA § 1302(e).

Insurers can offer a catastrophic plan to two types of insureds on an exchange. A catastrophic plan is one that provides coverage for essential health benefits and provides no benefit for any plan year until the individual has incurred cost-sharing expenses equal to the overall cost-sharing limit ($5,000 deductible for single coverage and $10,000 deductible for family coverage) for the plan year.[1] The deductible cannot apply to at least three primary care visits. A catastrophic plan is permitted only in the individual market and only for (a) young adults who are under age thirty before the plan year begins (called the "young invincibles" because they are more likely not to purchase insurance), and (b) persons exempt from the individual mandate because affordable coverage is not available or they have an HHS hardship exemption.[2]

423. What subsidies are available for individuals purchasing health insurance on an exchange?

Subsidies are provided for individuals earning less than 400 percent of the federal poverty level. The lower a person's income, the greater the subsidy will be.

424. What consumer consumer-assistance tools must exchanges provide?

Each state health insurance exchange (marketplace) must provide a variety of consumer-assistance tool, including the following:

- Information on the certifying, recertifying, and decertifying of qualified health plans (QHPs);

- The assigning of relative quality and price ratings to each QHP offered through the exchange;

- Toll-free call centers to address the needs of those seeking assistance;

- Internet websites providing a variety of features, including comparative information on available QHPs, certain financial information, and information about the navigator and call center;

- An exchange calculator to facilitate comparisons of QHPs that takes into consideration the premium tax credit and any cost-sharing reductions;

- A consumer-assistance function, including the navigator program discussed subsequently in this Part; and

- Outreach and education activities.[3]

---

1. PPACA § 1302(c)(1) and (e); Code § 223(c)(2)(A)(ii).
2. PPACA § 1302(c)(1) and (e).
3. 45 CFR § 155.205.

425. What are some of the problems and complexities experienced in setting up and operating the exchanges?

Comparing the various offerings on the exchanges will not be simple, especially the first time one uses an exchange, and thus the need for the specially trained navigators. Americans insist on choice among insurance products, enabling them to find coverage they believe will fit their personal needs. That choice comes at a stiff price. First, it adds considerably to the costs of administrative functions, which in the United States run about twice per capita what they are in other countries. Making the choice of what policy to purchase will take significant time due to the complexity.

The health insurance exchanges or marketplaces must perform several tasks and coordinate with other government programs and organizations. The state-based exchanges must coordinate with the Internal Revenue Service to determine eligibility for subsidies and their magnitude. The exchanges must also work with small employers as well as the state-administered Medicaid programs to determine whether an applicant on the exchanges should be referred to Medicaid or other government programs, such as CHIP. Additionally, some exchanges will negotiate premiums with insurers. While the Affordable Care Act specifies the basic benefits that must be covered, which each state can translate into its own basic benchmark package, some variation of covered services around the state benchmark package is possible within the same policy actuarial value, adding some complexity.[1]

Exchange Navigators

426. What is the role of the exchange navigators?

Healthcare reform requires each state exchange to establish a navigator program, under which it awards grants to public or private entities to carry out certain navigator functions.[2] HHS regulations set forth the eligibility requirements for navigators and the duties they are expected to perform. To be eligible, an entity must demonstrate that it has existing relationships or could readily establish relationships with employers, employees, consumers, or self-employed individuals likely to be eligible for enrollment in a qualified health plan (QHP); must meet licensing, certification, or other standards imposed by the state or exchange; and must not have a conflict of interest.

Exchanges are required to include entities from at least two of a variety of categories, including community and consumer-focused not-for-profit groups; unions; trade, industry, and professional associations; and licensed agents and brokers. However, a navigator must not be a health insurer or receive any direct or indirect consideration from a health insurer.[3]

The five duties of a navigator are:

(1)   maintain expertise in eligibility, enrollment, and program specifications and conduct public education activities to raise awareness of the exchanges;

1. Uwe E. Reinhardt, What Makes U.S. Health Insurance Exchanges So Complicated (July 19, 2013), at http://economix.blogs.nytimes.com/2013/07/19/what-makes-u-s-health-insurance-exchanges-so-complicated/?ref=policy.
2. PPACA § 1311(i).
3. 45 CFR § 155.210.

(2)   provide information and services in a fair, accurate, and impartial manner;

(3)   facilitate enrollment in QHPs;

(4)   provide referrals to any applicable consumer-assistance program or ombudsman in the case of grievances, complaints, or questions about health plans or coverage; and

(5)   provide information in a culturally and linguistically appropriate manner for the needs of the population being served by the exchange.[1]

427. What standards must navigators and non-navigator assistance personnel meet?

HHS regulations create standards for navigators and non-navigator assistance personnel in federally facilitated exchanges (FFEs) (including state-federal partnership exchanges) and for federally funded non-navigator assistance personnel in state-based exchanges.[2] State-based exchanges may, but need not, also establish non-navigator consumer assistance programs, which are funded by exchange establishment grants rather than navigator grants, to help provide outreach, education, and assistance to consumers. FFEs, other than certain state-federal partnership exchanges, likely will not include non-navigator assistance programs.

Navigators must have expertise in eligibility and enrollment rules and procedures but may not actually make eligibility determinations and may not select qualified health plans (QHPs) for consumers or enroll applicants into QHPs.[3]

States and exchanges cannot prescribe licensing or certification standards for navigators that would conflict with healthcare reform; e.g., they cannot require navigators to be licensed agents or brokers or obtain errors and omissions insurance.[4] There are detailed conflict of interest standards applicable to navigator and non-navigator personnel.[5] State-based exchanges are not required to adopt these standards for their navigators or for non-navigator assistance personnel that are not federally funded, such as enrollment assisters, certified application counselors, and producers (insurance agents and brokers).

428. What is the role of health insurance agents and brokers on the exchanges?

States may allow health insurance agents or brokers to (1) enroll individuals and small employers in qualified health plans on an exchange and (2) assist individuals in applying for premium tax credits and cost-sharing reductions in exchanges.[6] In states where a federally-facilitated or state-federal partnership exchange marketplace is operating, all agents and brokers

---

1. 45 CFR § 155.210(e).
2. PPACA; exchange Functions: Standards for Navigators and Non-navigator Assistance Personnel, 45 CFR Part 155, 78 Fed. Reg. 20581 (Apr. 5, 2013).
3. Prop. HHS Reg. § 155.310(d); PPACA; exchange Functions: Standards for Navigators and Non-navigator Assistance Personnel, 45 CFR Part 155, 78 Fed. Reg. 20581, 20583 (Apr. 5, 2013).
4. Prop. HHS Reg. § 155.210(c)(2); PPACA; exchange Functions: Standards for Navigators and Non-navigator Assistance Personnel, 45 CFR Part 155, 78 Fed. Reg. 20581, 20585 (Apr. 5, 2013).
5. Prop. HHS Reg. § 155.215.
6. PPACA § 1312; 45 CFR § 155.220.

must register with CMS so that they may assist qualified individuals for individual marketplace coverage.[1]

Although agents and brokers may help qualified individuals enroll in a QHP through the exchange, they cannot perform eligibility determinations. Eligibility determinations must be made through the exchange, and the information collected cannot be accessed by insurers, agents, and brokers.[2] Agents and brokers are also permitted to assist individuals in applying for advance payments of the premium tax credit and cost-sharing reductions.[3]

Agent and Broker Roles

429. What additional guidance has HHS issued about health insurance agents and brokers as to their role vis-à-vis the exchanges?

HHS has issued a memo focusing on the role of agents and brokers in FFEs and state-federal partnership FFEs. It also addresses certain questions related to state-based Exchanges.[4] It addresses, among others, the following issues.

Registration. In states where a federally-facilitated or state-federal partnership marketplace is operating, all agents and brokers must register with CMS so that they may assist qualified individuals for individual marketplace coverage. Agents and brokers will continue to be appointed by insurers that will check licensure status and verify the agent's or broker's registration with exchanges. In states with an FFE or state-federal partnership FFE, all agents and brokers must register with HHS and complete an online training course to assist with individual coverage beginning in the summer of 2013.[5] Agents and brokers working exclusively with employers in federally facilitated SHOP (FF-SHOP) exchanges (which may be combined with the regular exchange for individuals) are encouraged, but not required, to register and complete the training.

Two Website Pathways. Agents and brokers in FFEs and state-federal partnership FFEs will be permitted to assist individuals and employers through two internet "pathways": (a) an insurer-based pathway that redirects to an exchange website; or (b) an exchange-based pathway that directly accesses an exchange website. Both pathways will allow agents and brokers to assist individuals and employers to receive eligibility determinations, compare plans, and enroll in coverage, and will transmit agent and broker identifying information to the appropriate insurer to facilitate payment.[6] The individual will create a username and password on the exchange website and should not disclose this information to anyone.

Disclosure of All Available QHPs. HHS does not require agents and brokers to display all QHPs or to facilitate enrollment in all QHPs, but state-based exchanges may require agents

---

1. HHS Memo: Role of Agents, Brokers, and Web-Brokers in Health Insurance Marketplaces, I.A (May 1, 2013) at http://www.cms.gov/CCIIO/ Resources/Regulations-and-Guidance/Downloads/agent-broker-5-1-2013.pdf.
2. PPACA; Establishment of Exchanges and Qualified Health Plans; Exchange Standards for Employers, 77 Fed. Reg. 18310, 18425 (Mar. 27, 2012).
3. 45 CFR § 155.220(a)(3).
4. HHS Memo: Role of Agents, Brokers, and Web-Brokers in Health Insurance Marketplaces (May 1, 2013) at http://www.cms.gov/CCIIO/ Resources/Regulations-and-Guidance/Downloads/agent-broker-5-1-2013.pdf.
5. Id.
6. Id. at I and its Appendix.

and brokers to do so. HHS expects agents or brokers using the FFE insurer-based pathway to inform individuals when they are providing information for QHPs with which they have a business relationship, and that other choices and information can be directly accessed through the exchange website. The FFE exchange-based pathway will display all QHPs.

Broker/Agent Compensation. State-based exchanges may establish their own rules for compensation of agents or brokers, including parameters for direct compensation from an exchange or through insurer-paid commissions. HHS also notes that, if insurers will be paying commissions to agents or broker, it has encouraged state-based exchanges to consider providing information to insurers (agent or broker identifying information) to facilitate these transactions. FFEs and state-federal partnership FFEs will not establish a commission schedule or pay commissions directly to agents or brokers. The amount and terms of commissions will be negotiated by the insurer and the agent or broker. The QHP certification standards require QHP insurers to pay the same agent and broker compensation for enrollment in similar health plans offered inside and outside of FFEs and state-partnership FFEs. However, agents and brokers acting as navigators may not receive compensation from insurers.[1]

Web-Brokers. This HHS memo also addresses the role of web-brokers (i.e., agents or brokers who enroll individuals through public websites). State-based exchanges are permitted to work with web-brokers and that, with respect to FFEs, HHS is developing the ability to support integration between a web-broker's website and the FFE website to allow individuals to start shopping on the web-broker's website, connect to the FFE website to complete eligibility applications, and return to the web-broker's site to shop for QHPs. The HHS memo also includes information on how QHPs may be displayed on a web-broker's website and certain other relevant issues.

430. What other existing organizations will assist individuals on the exchanges?

State Health Insurance Assistance Programs (often called SHIPs) help Medicare beneficiaries understand their Medicare plan options and enroll. Government agencies, such as those that administer the Medicaid and Children's Health Insurance Programs (CHIP), help people sign up for those benefits, and community-based organizations also assist with Medicaid and CHIP enrollment. These entities will also help applicants who don't qualify for Medicaid or CHIP get coverage and premium assistance through the exchange.

---

1. Id.

PART XI: THE EMPLOYER MANDATE

(a/k/a Shared Responsibility or Play or Pay Rules)

Overview

431. What do the IRS regulations tell us about the employer mandate?

The IRS proposed regulations on Shared Responsibilities for Employer Regarding Health Coverage as well as Q&As deal with the application of the employer mandate and its penalties for "applicable large employers."[1] In determining the fifty-employee threshold, an employer, whether domestic or foreign, counts only those employees employed in the United States.[2] While the statute requires the employer mandate to apply beginning in 2014, the IRS has postponed the deadline until 2015.[3] The penalties are calculated on a calendar year basis regardless of the employer's health plan year.

Employers may rely on these proposed regulations for guidance pending the issuance of additional regulations.

432. What topics are covered in the employer mandate regulations?

These proposed regulations are organized as follows:

- Definitions;[4]

- Status as an applicable large employer and applicable large employer member;[5]

- Full-time employees;[6]

- Assessable payments under § 4980H(a);[7]

- Whether an employer is subject to assessable payments under § 4980H(b);[8] and

- Rules relating to the administration and assessment of assessable payments under § 4980H.[9]

---

1. http://www.irs.gov/uac/Newsroom/Questions-and-Answers-on-Employer-Shared-Responsibility-Provisions-Under-the-Affordable-Care-Act.
2. Id. at Q&A 8 and 9.
3. IRS Notice 2013-45.
4. Prop. Reg. § 54.4980H-1.
5. Prop. Reg. § 54.4980H-2.
6. Prop. Reg. § 54.4980H-3.
7. Prop. Reg. § 54.4980H-4.
8. Prop. Reg. § 54.4980H-5.
9. Prop. Reg. § 54.4980H-6.

Definitions

433. What employers are subject to the employer mandate penalty?

For purposes of the mandate, employer includes all related employers, predecessors, and successors.

The controlled and affiliated service group rules apply in counting employees, as all members of such a group are treated as one employer.[1] An employer includes a predecessor and successor employer.[2] The regulations do provide specific rules for identifying a predecessor or successor employer. Rules for identifying successor employers have been developed in the employment tax context for determining when wages paid by a predecessor may be attributed to a successor employer.[3] Section 4980H does not incorporate the separate line of business (SLOB) rules that allow separate testing for retirement plans. All employers (again including controlled group and affiliated service group members) that employ at least fifty full-time employees or an equivalent combination of full-time and part-time employees are subject to the Employer Shared Responsibility provisions, including for-profit, not-for-profit, and government entity employers.[4] "Disregarded entities" are not disregarded for §4980H purposes. The tax is imposed on the disregarded entity and not its owner(s).[5]

434. Which workers qualify as employees?

Section 4980H(c)(2) defines an applicable large employer with respect to a calendar year as an employer that employed an average of at least fifty full-time employees (taking into account full-time equivalent employees or FTEs) on business days during the preceding calendar year. The proposed regulations adopt the position outlined in Notice 2011-36 that an employee is an individual who is an employee under the common law standard, and an employer is the person that is the employer under the common law standard.

The common law standard provides that an employment relationship exists when the person for whom the services are performed has the right to control and direct the individual who performs the services, not only as to the result to be accomplished by the work but also as to the details and means by which that result is accomplished. Under the common law standard, an employment relationship exists if an employee is subject to the will and control of the employer as to not only what shall be done but also how it shall be done. In this connection, it is not necessary that the employer actually direct or control the manner in which the services are performed; it is sufficient if the employer has the right to do so.[6]

---

1. IRC § 4980H(c)(2)(C)(i); Prop. Treas. Reg. § 54.4980H-1(a)(15).
2. Prop. Treas. Reg. § 54.4980H-1(a)(15).
3. Reg. § 31.3121(a)(1)-1(b).
4. http://www.irs.gov/uac/Newsroom/Questions-and-Answers-on-Employer-Shared-Responsibility-Provisions-Under-the-Affordable-Care-Act at Q&A 6.
5. Prop. Reg. §301.7701-2(c)(2)(v)(A)(5).
6. Reg. § 31.3121(d)-1(c), 31.3231(b)-1(a)(2), 31.3306(i)-1(b), and 31.3401(c)-1(b).

435. Which workers are not considered employees?

Various self-employed individuals do not fall within the definition of employee. These include sole proprietors and partners, leased employees, and independent contractors.

A sole proprietor, a partner in a partnership, or a 2-percent or more S corporation shareholder is not an employee. Thus, LLPs, LLCs (taxed as partnerships), and partnerships can design eligibility, coverage, and premium obligations for their members/partners however the LLC/partnership desires. An individual who provides services as both an employee and a non-employee (such as an individual serving as both an employee and a director) is an employee for hours of service as an employee.

The regulations provide that a leased employee as defined under § 414(n) is not an employee for these rules.[1] However, those rules will seldom be met. Additionally, in many if not most cases, the IRS views leased employees as common law employees of the firm that uses their services (the service recipient), not the business that pays them, if the service recipient has the right to control their working conditions.

Bona fide independent contractors, as opposed to employees that an employer treats as independent contractors, are not employees for this purpose.

Applicable Large Employers

436. Which "applicable large employers" are subject to the employer mandate penalties?

Generally speaking, employers with fifty or more full-time-equivalent U.S. employees in the prior year are subject to the employer mandate penalties.

Employers are not required to provide health coverage but employer mandate penalties, discussed later in this Part, may apply if they do not and the "employer" has fifty or more full-time equivalent employees on business days during the preceding calendar year.[2] While large employers need not provide health care coverage to part-time employees working less than thirty hours per week, these part-time employees are included in calculating the threshold number of fifty workers (including full-time equivalents) that would require employers to offer affordable coverage to full-time employees and their dependents (but not spouses) or pay a penalty.

Employees working outside the United States are not counted and are excluded.[3] The reference to business days is not explained or defined. It is not clear whether the threshold must be met on one business day, all business days, or some average. Most employers will use an alternate method, discussed subsequently, which allows a monthly counting of employees in the prior year.

---

1. Prop. Treas. Reg. § 54.4980H–1(a)(13).
2. Code § 4980H(c)(2)(A); Prop. Treas. Reg. § 54.4980H–1(a)(4).
3. Shared Responsibility for Employers Regarding Health Coverage, 26 CFR Parts 1, 54, and 301, 78 Fed. Reg. 217, 221 (Jan. 2, 2013).

437. Are related employers treated as one employer?

As discussed in Q 433, related employers under the controlled group or affiliated service group rules are treated as one employer.

438. What about new employers that do not have a prior year to which to refer?

An employer not in existence during an entire preceding calendar year is an applicable large employer for the current calendar year if it is reasonably expected to employ an average of at least fifty full-time employees (taking into account FTEs) on business days during the current calendar year.[1] It is not clear what happens if circumstances change during the current year so that the original determination is no longer reasonable.

Two Alternate Employer Mandate Penalties

439. In general, what are the two alternative employer mandate penalties?

There are two alternative penalties. The annual amounts are $2,000 [4908H(a) penalty] or $3,000 [4908H(b) penalty], but the actual amount is calculated monthly. Both the $2,000 and $3,000 penalty amounts will be adjusted for inflation.[2] Neither penalty is triggered unless an employee receives a tax credit for the purchase of health insurance on a state exchange. See Q 23.

The 4980H(a) penalty is assessed when an employee does not offer the required minimum essential coverage (MEC). See Q 441. The 4908H(b) penalty is assessed if the MEC is offered but is unaffordable or does not provide minimum value. See Q 442.

One of the employer mandate penalties applies in 2015 to applicable large employers unless they offer affordable and adequate coverage with essential health benefits for insured plans that are not grandfathered plans. No special rules are provided as to what proof is required for an employer to demonstrate an offer of coverage, but an offer must occur at least once each plan year.[3] An applicable large employer is one with at least fifty full-time equivalent employees. This includes all controlled group and affiliated service group members. The exchanges will police this. Status as an "applicable large employer" is determined based on employees' actual hours of service for the preceding calendar year – full year, no equivalencies. However, the Proposed Regulations include special transition relief so that employers may use a shorter 2013 look-back period to determine whether the employer is an "applicable large employer" for 2015.

Note that neither penalty is triggered unless at least one full-time employee enrolls in a qualified health plan through an exchange for that month and must receive an applicable premium tax credit for that month's coverage.[4]

---

1. Code § 4980H(c)(2)(C)(ii); Prop. Treas. Reg. § 54.4980H-2(b)(3).
2. IRC Sec. 4980H(c)(5).
3. Prop. Treas. Reg. § 54.4980H-4(b).
4. Code § 4980H(a)(2).

440. What is an employer offer of health coverage?

If an employee has not been offered an effective opportunity to accept coverage, the employee will not be treated as having been offered the coverage for purposes of the employer mandate. This offer must be made no less than once during each plan year.[1] If the employee does not pay for the employee's share of coverage within thirty days of when payment is due, the employer need not provide coverage.[2]

441. How does the 4980H(a) penalty work?

The applicable large employer offers at least once during each plan year no minimum essential coverage (MEC)[3] to "substantially all" (all but 5 percent or five employees, if greater)[4] of its full-time employees (and their dependent and adult children up to age 26,[5] but not spouses)[6] and one or more full-time employee is certified to the employer by a state health insurance exchange as having received an applicable premium tax credit or cost- sharing reduction [section 4980H(a) liability]. The penalty is the number of full-times employees less thirty times $2,000 per year. Thus, if an employer has thirty-four full-time employees and does not offer MEC, the penalty is (34 – 30) = 4 x $2,000 or $8,000 for that year. The penalty is calculated monthly.

The 4980H(a) employer mandate penalty applies to an employer that fails to offer "minimum essential coverage." Minimum essential coverage does not include excepted benefits, such as stand-alone vision or stand-alone dental benefits. Employers seeking to minimize or avoid the employer penalty must offer minimum essential coverage to 95 percent of their full-time employees and their dependents, including children under age twenty six. Minimum essential coverage is the coverage required to avoid the individual and employer mandates.[7] It is an "eligible employer-sponsored plan," a term that means any group health plan (other than for excepted benefits) offered by an employer to employees, coverage offered in a state's small or large group market, or a self-insured plan[8] meeting only the required Public Health Service Act requirements (discussed in Part VII).[9] It includes grandfathered plans.[10] In other words, any health insurance plan legally sold in a state and self-insured plans meeting PHSA requirements are an "eligible employer-sponsored plan."

442. How does the 4980H(b) alternative penalty work?

Even if an applicable large employer is not subject to the 4980H(a) penalty because the employer offers minimum essential coverage to 95 percent of its employees and their dependents, including children up to age twenty six, that employer can be subject to the alternative 4980H(b)

---

1. Prop. Treas. Reg. § 54.4980H-4(b).
2. Prop. Treas. Reg. § 54.4980H-3(f).
3. Minimum essential coverage includes coverage offered by a grandfathered group health plan.
4. Prop. Treas. Reg. § 54.4980H-4(a).
5. "Dependent" is defined as an employee's child under IRC§152(f)(1) who is under 26 years of age. Prop. Reg. §54.4980H-1(a)(11).
6. Prop. Reg. §54.4980H-1(a)(11).
7. PPACA § 1301.
8. Prop Reg. §1.5000A-2(c)(1).
9. IRC § 5000A(f)(2)(B); Prop. Reg.§1.5000A-2(a) and (c)(1)(ii).
10. Prop. Reg. §1.5000A-2(a)(c)(1)(iii).

penalty. The 95 percent margin of error rule for the (a) penalty does not apply to the (b) penalty. The (b) penalty applies if the employer offers 95 percent of its full-time employees (and their dependent and adult children up to age twenty six) the opportunity to enroll in MEC[1] under an employer sponsored plan and one or more full-time employees is certified to the employer as having received an applicable premium tax credit or cost-sharing reduction. The second 4980H(b) penalty applies if the coverage offered by the employer is (a) <u>unaffordable</u> under IRC § 36B(c)(2)(C)(i) or (b) does not provide <u>minimum value</u> under § 36B(c)(2)(C)(ii).

The 4908H(b) penalty applies to employers that offer coverage to at least 95 percent of their full-time employees (or all but five employees if greater) and dependents in 2015, but that have one or more full-time employee who receives a premium tax credit because the coverage is not affordable or does not offer minimum value. The 4980H(b) penalty employer mandate penalty payment is computed separately each month. The amount of the payment for the month equals the number of full-time employees who receive the premium tax credit for that month multiplied by 1/12 of $3,000. The liability cannot exceed the payment that the employer would owe if it did not offer any minimum essential coverage, i.e., $2,000 times the number of full-times employees less thirty each year. Except in the case of terminated employees, if an employer fails to offer coverage to an eligible full-time employee for any day of a calendar month during which the employee is employed by the employer, the employee is treated as not being offered coverage during that month. However, the employer is not penalized if the employee fails to pay the employee's share of the premium if the employee is afforded the opportunity to do so.

Employer group health plans are not required to provide a particular benefits package to avoid the employer mandate assessable penalties, as long as the plan meets the "affordability" and "minimum value" standards.

443. What does "affordable value" for a plan mean?

Affordable plans are those that cost an employee no more for employee-only coverage than 9.5 percent of the employee's household (or using the safe harbor, the employee's W-2) income.[2]

Employees with household incomes between 100 percent and 400 percent of the federal poverty level, if not eligible for Medicaid, are eligible for tax credits for exchange coverage if they do not have access to affordable employer-sponsored coverage that is of at least a minimum value. The state health insurance exchange makes the determination as to whether their income is below 400 percent of federal poverty, but the employer can determine if coverage is affordable by using the employee's Box 1, W-2 Income for the current year to determine if the cost to the employee for employee-only coverage exceeds 9.5 percent of the employee's household (or using the safe harbor, the employee's W-2) income. See Q 446.

---

1. Essential health benefits are subject to the lifetime and annual dollar limits and must include at least the following services: ambulatory patient services, emergency services, hospitalization, maternity and newborn care, mental health benefits and substance use disorder services, prescription drugs, rehabilitative and habilitative services and devices, laboratory services, preventive and wellness services and chronic disease managements, and pediatric services including oral and vision care.
2. IRS Notice 2012-58, The 9.5 percent can be adjusted after 2014 to reflect rates of premium growth relative to growth in income and after 2018 to reflect rates of premium growth relative to growth in the consumer price index. See Prop. Treas. Regs. §§ 1.36B-0 through 1.36B-5.

444. When does an employer health plan provide minimum value?

A plan fails to provide minimum value if the plan's share of the total allowed costs of benefits provided under the plan is less than 60 percent of those costs.[1] Employers will be able to enter information about the plan, such as deductibles and copays, into a calculator being developed to determine whether its plan provides minimum value by covering at least 60 percent of the total allowed cost of benefits expected to be incurred under the plan.[2] Employers may also obtain an actuarial certification to show minimum value by an actuary who is a member of the American Academy of Actuaries.[3]

Employer contributions to an HSA and amounts newly made available under integrated HRAs that may be used only for cost sharing can be taken into account in determining minimum value.[4] For example, a $1,000 HSA employer contribution is treated in the MV calculator as if a plan with a $1,000 deductible is reduced to zero. The $1,000 contribution is counted as the average dollar value it would cost to reduce a $1,000 deductible to zero.[5] Whether other types of integrated HRAs could count toward minimum value is not yet determined. The HRA rules leave important questions unanswered, such as the definition of "integrated" and the meaning of the "used only for cost sharing" condition.

445. When is employer coverage unaffordable?

An employer-sponsored plan is affordable if the employee's required contribution (within the meaning of § 5000A(e)(1)(B) for that employee's self-only coverage does not exceed 9.5 percent of the employee's household income for the taxable year.[6] Household income is the modified adjusted gross income of the employee and any members of the employee's family (including a spouse and dependents) who are required to file income tax returns.[7] Thus, the cost of dependent coverage is irrelevant in measuring affordability.

446. What safe harbors are available for an employer to determine if its health coverage is affordable?

Three safe harbors for affordability (and employer immunity for the penalty) are offered.

(1) Employer's W-2 Pay for Current Year. One is the employee's W-2 wages reported in Box 1 safe harbor (this does not count 401(k) and 125 plan elective deferrals) by that employer.

(2) Rate of Pay Safe Harbor. The employer (1) takes the hourly rate of pay for each hourly employee who is eligible to participate in the health plan as of the beginning of the plan year, (2) multiplies that rate by 130 hours per month, and (3) determines

---

1. See IRS Notice 2012-31.
2. http://www.irs.gov/uac/Newsroom/Questions-and-Answers-on-Employer-Shared-Responsibility-Provisions-Under-the-Affordable-Care-Act. at Q&A 12.
3. 45 CFR § 156.145(b)(1).
4. 45 CFR § 156.145(d).
5. Minimum Value Calculator Methodology at http://cciio.cms.gov/resources/regulations/index.html.
6. § 36B(c)(2)(C)(i) and Reg. § 1.36B-1(e).
7. § 36B(d)(2)(A).

affordability based on the resulting monthly wage amount. Specifically, the employee's monthly contribution amount (for the self-only premium of the employer's lowest cost coverage that provides minimum value) is affordable if it is equal to or lower than 9.5 percent of the computed monthly wages (that is, the employee's applicable hourly rate of pay x 130 hours). For salaried employees, monthly salary would be used instead of hourly salary multiplied by 130. An employer may use this safe harbor only if, with respect to the employees for whom the employer applies the safe harbor, the employer did not reduce the hourly wages of hourly employees or the monthly wages of salaried employees during the year. The rate of pay safe harbor is a design-based safe harbor that should be easy for employers to apply and allows them prospectively to satisfy affordability without the need to analyze every employee's wages and hours.

(3)   Federal Poverty Line (FPL) Safe Harbor. Employer provided coverage offered to an employee is affordable if the employee's cost for self-only coverage under the plan does not exceed 9.5 percent of the FPL for that employee, not the family. Employers use the most recently published poverty guidelines as of the first day of the plan year of the health plan.

HRA Reimbursement Arrangements and the Employer Penalty

447. Can an employer health reimbursement account (HRA) that pays or reimburses employees for exchange purchased health insurance qualify as employer-provided minimum essential coverage to avoid the 4980H(a) penalty?

No. The definition of eligible employer-sponsored plan is that of a "group health plan" and not individual policy arrangements.[1] FAQ guidance issued in January 2013 indicates that, for purposes of the application of the annual and lifetime limits, employer-sponsored health reimbursement accounts (HRAs) cannot satisfy the exception for integrated arrangements if they are integrated with individual market coverage or with an employer plan that provides coverage through individual policies.[2] Thus, even if an offer of HRA coverage constituted an offer of minimum essential coverage, the offer would violate the rule prohibiting annual and lifetime dollar limits.

Separate Assessment of Shared Responsibility Penalties within Controlled Group

448. Where there is an applicable large employer comprised of related employers, how is the employer mandate penalty, if applicable, calculated?

While determination of large employer status is made on a related group of employers basis, the assessment of the shared responsibility penalties is determined on a member-by-member

---

1. Prop. Treas. Reg. § 1.5000A-2(c).
2. See FAQs About the Affordable Care Act Implementation Part XI, Q/A-2, available at http://www.dol.gov/ebsa/faqs/faq-aca11.html (as visited Mar. 18, 2013).

basis within the employer group. Therefore, shared responsibility penalties are "computed and assessed separately for each applicable large employer, taking into account that member's offer of coverage and based on that member's number of full-time employees."

Thirty Full-Time Employee Subtraction Prorated. Within an employer group of related employers, only a single thirty full-time employee reduction in determining the penalty is allowed. It must be prorated among the employers in the employer group to prevent smaller members of the group from avoiding the penalty altogether.

449. Will the insured plan nondiscrimination requirements, when effective, impact health insurance offered by related employers?

Yes. While delayed indefinitely until the IRS issues regulations, the nondiscrimination requirements for insured plans (other than for grandfathered plans), when they are effective, will also apply to controlled and affiliated service group members. The nondiscrimination rules will limit an employer's ability to offer coverage to some members of an employer group, while not offering coverage to other members, unless done on a nondiscriminatory basis.

Determining Applicable Large Employer Status

450. How are those "applicable large employers" potentially subject to the employer mandate penalty determined?

Code § 4980H(c)(2) defines an applicable large employer on a calendar year basis and as an employer that employed an average of at least fifty full-time and full-time equivalent common law employees on business days during the preceding calendar year.

The rules discussed in this section allow the use of a measurement period and a subsequent stability period for counting employees. They apply for computing the employer mandate penalty under Code § 4980H but do not apply for purposes of determining whether an employer is an applicable large employer potentially subject to the penalty.

If the employer was not in existence during the preceding calendar year, the employer will qualify as an applicable large employer if the employer is reasonably expected to employ on average at least fifty full-time and full-time equivalent employees and actually employs an average of at least fifty fulltime and full-time equivalent employees. Any fractional full-time equivalent employee total is rounded down.

451. What if payroll periods begin after the calendar year starts or end after the calendar year ends?

Since payroll periods may not correspond to calendar months, employers using weekly, biweekly, or semi-monthly payroll periods can use those periods and exclude the portion of a payroll period otherwise falling within the measurement period, but only if the employer includes the portion of a payroll period otherwise falling outside the measurement period. For instance, an employer that uses a calendar-year measurement period can exclude the entire payroll period that includes January 1, Year 1, but only if it includes the entire payroll period that includes, and extends beyond, December 31, Year 1, into January of Year 2. An employer could exclude the payroll period that includes December 31, Year 2, but only if it includes the entire payroll period that includes January 1, Year 2 that includes a portion of December, Year 1.[1]

452. What if the employer only has fifty or more full time and full-time equivalent employees for four or fewer months?

If the employer only exceeds forty-nine employees for four or less calendar months (not necessarily consecutive) or 120 or fewer days (not necessarily consecutive) and the excess over forty-nine for those four months or 120 days are seasonal employees, then the employer is not an applicable large employer. Seasonal employees are defined by reference to a DOL regulation for seasonal agricultural workers[2] and also include retail workers employed exclusively during holiday seasons.[3] However, the preamble says that seasonal workers are not limited to agricultural or retail workers. Employers may apply a reasonable, good faith interpretation of the statutory definition of seasonal worker.[4]

Even if an employer is not an applicable large employer, it is subject to other healthcare reform rules, other than rules not applicable to grandfathered plans if it has a grandfathered plan, such as the health insurance reforms. For example, such employers are subject to the new wellness program rules and the ninety-day waiting period limitation, both of which go into effect for plan years beginning on or after January 1, 2014.

Counting U.S. Employees
Full-time and Part-time

453. How are employees' U.S. hours of service counted and determined?

Only hours of service in the United States are counted. The United States is the fifty states and the District of Columbia. "Hours of service" is defined as it is in ERISA, i.e., hours for which an employee is paid or entitled to be paid, including paid time off, such as vacation, holiday, illness, incapacity (including disability paid by a third party insurer), layoff, jury duty, military duty, or leave of absence.[5] This overturns the "hours worked" definition in IRS Notice 2012-58. However, special rules also result in counting unpaid FMLA or USERRA leave. Two options exist.[6] Hours of service worked outside of the U.S. are not counted, regardless of the residency or citizenship of the individual.

Hours of service calculations that result in a fraction are rounded up to the nearest whole number.

---

1. Prop. Treas. Reg. § 54.4980H-3(c)(1)(ii).
2. 29 CFR § 502.10(b)(3)(ii)(A) provides, "Labor is performed on a seasonal basis where, ordinarily, the employment pertains to or is of the kind exclusively performed at certain seasons or periods of the year and which, from its nature, may not be continuous or carried on throughout the year. A worker who moves from one seasonal activity to another, while employed in agriculture or performing agricultural labor, is employed on a seasonal basis even though he may continue to be employed during a major portion of the year."
3. IRC § 4980H(c)(2)(B)(ii).
4. 78 Fed. Reg. 217, 222 (Jan. 2, 2013).
5. Prop. Treas. Reg. § 54.4980H-1(a)(21). This definition borrows heavily from existing DOL regulations. 29 CFR § 2530.200b-2(a).
6. Prop. Reg. §54.4980H-3(e)(4)). Option #1: Determine the average hours of service per week for the employee during the measurement period, excluding the special unpaid leave period, and use that average as the average for the entire measurement period. Option #2: Treat employees as credited with hours of service for special unpaid leave at a rate equal to the average weekly rate at which the employee was credited with hours of service during the weeks in the measurement period that are not special unpaid leave.

454. How are hours of service counted for hourly workers?

For hourly paid employees, the employer is required to calculate actual hours of service from records of hours worked and for non-worked hours for which payment is made or due (vacation, holiday, illness, incapacity, etc., as described in Q 453).[1] .

455. How are salaried employees' hours of service counted?

For salaried employees, an employer has the option to count actual hours or service in each day or two equivalencies, i.e., eight hours per day worked or forty hours per week worked unless the equivalencies understate the hours. Thus, the daily equivalency cannot be used for someone who works three ten-hour days per week.[2] The employer is NOT required to use the same hours of service calculation method for all non-hourly employee as long as the classifications are reasonable and consistently applied.

456. Are there rules for employees with special work patterns?

Yes. Unless and until further guidance is issued, any reasonable method for calculating hours of service may be used for the following types of employees:

- Commissioned employees

- Adjunct faculty

- Transportation employees (e.g., airline pilots)

- Employees in similar positions

Hours of service for adjunct faculty must be based not only on time spent teaching classes, but also time preparing for classes. Hours of service for commissioned employees would also include business travel for a traveling salesperson compensated on a commission basis. An averaging method is provided for employees of education institutions that generally would result in an employee who works full-time during the active portions of the academic year being a full-time employee.

457. Can different counting methods be used by different controlled or affiliated group members?

Yes. An applicable large employer member is not required to apply the same methods as other applicable large employer members of the same applicable large employer group for the same or different classifications of non-hourly employees, provided that in each case the classifications are reasonable and consistently applied by the applicable large employer member.[3]

---

1. Prop. Treas. Reg. § 54.4980H-3(b)(1).
2. Prop. Treas. Reg. § 54.4980H-3(b)(2).
3. Prop. Treas. Reg. § 54.4980H-3(b)(2)(ii).

458. What is healthcare reform's definition of a full-time employee?

The statute defines full-time employees as those who, with respect to any month, have at least thirty hours of service per week or 130 hours of service in a calendar month, provided the employer applies the actual hour or equivalency rules (discussed subsequently) on a reasonable and consistent basis.[1] Hours of service worked outside of the U.S. are not counted, regardless of the residency or citizenship of the individual. Absent use of a look back period, employees must be counted monthly.

The employer mandate penalty must be paid monthly. It is not possible to know for certain whether coverage must be offered to any particular employee because of his or her full-time status until the end of a month because the excise tax payments are determined month-by-month. Since this monthly calculation would make determinations very difficult, the employer can use a look back period to determine if an employer is an "applicable large employer" potentially subject to the employer mandate penalty. If the employer is an applicable large employer during the look back period, then it must offer affordable minimum value coverage during the "stability period" to avoid the penalty.

459. What is the optional method for counting full-time employees in a prior year that eliminates the need to count for the current month?

The regulations provide a method for calculating the number of full-time employees during the preceding calendar year that does not differentiate between business days and non-business days.[2] Rather than looking at days, the method focuses on the number of full-time employees during each calendar month and then obtains an average number of full-time employees by dividing by twelve.

Specifically, the proposed method involves the following steps:

(1)   Calculate the number of full-time employees (including seasonal employees) for each calendar month in the preceding calendar year.

(2)   Calculate the number of full-time equivalents (including seasonal employees) for each calendar month in the preceding calendar year (using the method described above).

(3)   Add the number of full-time employees and full-time equivalents obtained in Steps 1 and 2 for each month of the preceding calendar year.

(4)   Add up the twelve monthly numbers from Step 3 and divide the sum by twelve. This is the average number of full-time employees for the preceding calendar year.[3]

(5)   If the number obtained in Step 4 is less than fifty, then the employer is not an applicable large employer for the current calendar year. If the number obtained in Step 4 is fifty or greater and the employer included seasonal employees in Step 1

---

1. Prop. Treas. Reg. § 54.4980H–1(a)(18).
2. Prop. Treas. Reg. § 54.4980H–2(b)(1).
3. Fractional amounts are ignored and the employer rounds down to the next-lowest whole number after dividing by 12 (i.e., 49.9 equals 49 full-time employees).

and/or Step 2, the employer may then apply the special rule for seasonal employees. This rule is described in Q 460.

460. How does one determine how part-time employees are converted into full-time equivalent employees?

The number of full-time equivalents the employer employed during the preceding calendar year are taken into account. All employees (including seasonal workers) who were not employed on an average of at least thirty hours of service per week for a calendar month in the preceding calendar year are included in calculating the number of full-time equivalents for that calendar month.[1] Hours of service worked outside of the U.S. are not counted, regardless of the residency or citizenship of the individual.

The approach for converting part-time employees to full-time equivalents is as follows:

- Calculate the aggregate hours of service in a month for employees who are not full-time employees, including seasonal employees, for that month. Do not include more than 120 hours of service for any employee.

- Divide the total hours of service from Step 1 by 120.[2]

Note that for part-time employees, unlike full-time employees, there is no 130-hour per month option. The number is 120 hours for this rule.

The result is the number of full-time equivalent employees for the month. This can result in a number and a fraction. The fraction is rounded down. For example, if for a calendar month employees who were not employed on average at least thirty hours of service per week have 1,260 hours of service taken together, there would be 10.5 FTEs for that month. Thus, 49.9 full-time employees (including FTEs) for the preceding calendar year would be rounded down to forty-nine full-time employees.

461. How are total U.S. employees for the preceding calendar year determined?

Calculate the number of full-time employees (including seasonal employees) for each calendar month in the preceding calendar year.

Calculate the number of full-time equivalents (including seasonal employees) for each calendar month in the preceding calendar year (using the method described above).

Add the number of full-time employees and full-time equivalents obtained in for each month of the preceding calendar year.

Add up the twelve monthly numbers from the preceding items and divide the sum by twelve. This is the average number of full-time employees for the preceding calendar year. Fractional amounts are disregarded.

---

1. Prop. Treas. Reg. § 54.4980H-2(c)(1).
2. Prop. Treas. Reg. § 54.4980H-2(c)(2).

If the number obtained is less than fifty, then the employer is not an applicable large employer for the current calendar year. If the number obtained is fifty or greater and the employer included seasonal employees in one or both of the first two steps, the employer may then apply the special rule for seasonal employees to see if they can be excluded, as discussed below

462. What if an employer's workforce exceeds fifty full-time employees for no more than 120 days?

The statute provides that an employer with fifty or more full-time employees can avoid applicable large employer status if

- the employer's workforce exceeds fifty full-time employees for no more than 120 days (or four calendar months) during the calendar year; and

- the employees in excess of fifty employed during such 120-day (or four calendar month) period were seasonal workers.[1]

The four-month or 120-day periods need not be consecutive.

Thus, large employer status does not exist where the employer's non-seasonal workforce (including full-time equivalents for part-time employees) is forty nine or fewer.

The 120-day period referred to in § 4980H(c)(2)(B)(ii) is not part of the definition of the term seasonal worker, and an employee would not necessarily be precluded from being treated as a seasonal worker merely because the employee works, for example, on a seasonal basis for five consecutive months. In addition, the 120-day period referred to in § 4980H(c)(2)(B)(ii) is relevant only for applying the seasonal worker exception for determining status as an applicable large employer. It is not relevant for determining whether an employee is a seasonal employee for purposes of the look-back measurement method (meaning that an employee who provides services for more than 120 days per year may nonetheless qualify as a seasonal employee).

An open question exists as to someone hired as a seasonal employee who is converted to a regular employee. Logic indicates that they should be immediately eligible for the employer's health plan if they were hired to work as seasonal help thirty-plus hours a week and remain employed beyond 120 days (or 4 months).

463. How is an employer with less than fifty employees except seasonal employees treated?

This question is addressed in a proposed treasury regulation's Example 3, as follows:[2]

During 2015, Employer has forty full-time employees for the entire calendar year, none of whom are seasonal workers. In addition, Employer has eighty seasonal full-time workers

---

1. Code § 4980H(c)(2)(B); Prop. Treas. Reg. § 54.4980H-2(b)(2).
2. Prop. Treas. Reg. § 54.4980H-2(d) Example 3.

who work from September through December 2015. Employer has no full-time equivalent employees during 2015.

Before applying the seasonal worker exception, Employer has forty full-time employees during each of eight calendar months of 2015, and 120 full-time employees during each of four calendar months of 2015, resulting in an average of 66.5 employees, namely, (40 × 8) plus (120 × 4) divided by twelve equals 66.66, rounded down to 66. However, Employer can apply the seasonal employees' exception because its workforce exceeded fifty full-time employees for only four calendar months (treated as 120 days) during 2015, and the number of full-time employees would be less than fifty during those months if seasonal workers were disregarded. Thus, Employer is not a large employer for 2016.

464. How are employees counted in the current year for the "applicable large employer" penalty calculation?

While the determination of whether a company is an applicable large employer is based on prior calendar year employment except for new employers, the shared responsibility penalties are calculated on a monthly basis in the current year. If an employer is not an applicable large employer based on the prior calendar year, then it need not worry how to determine if it is liable for any penalty and can ignore the following rules.

There are two ways to calculate the number of full-time employees.

One method, while difficult and burdensome, is the actual method. Under this method, full-time employee status is determined in the current year to calculate the penalty. There is no counting of full-time equivalent employees for calculating the penalty. The potential liability of a large employer for the "play or pay" penalty for a month is determined by the number of full-time employees it had during a calendar month, while the liability under the "play or pay" penalty is determined by the number of full-time employees who enrolled in Exchange coverage and received a premium tax credit or cost-sharing reduction during the calendar month.

The IRS acknowledged the difficulties employers may have with making monthly determinations of full-time status. Concerned that monthly determinations could result in employees moving in and out of employer versus Exchange coverage, the proposed regulations include an optional look-back measurement method to calculate the penalty that employers can use as an alternative to making a monthly determination.

465. Is there an alternate safe harbor option method for counting full-time employees?

Yes. Rather than using monthly calculations for the employer mandate penalty, employers can identify full-time employees by calculating employees' hours during a specified period selected by the employer of three to twelve months (lookback standard measurement period) and then locking in that status (full-time or not) for a subsequent specified period (stability period), which is the same length as the measurement period or six months, whichever is greater. If an employer wants to have an open enrollment during a period that is not part of a measurement or the subsequent stability period, it may do so by using an administrative period not to exceed ninety days between the stability and measurement periods. Thus, the rules require that

- the measurement and stability periods are no longer than twelve months,

- the stability period for ongoing employees who work full-time during the standard measurement period is not shorter than the standard measurement period,

- the stability period for ongoing employees who do not work full-time during the standard measurement period is no longer than the standard measurement period, and

- the administrative period is no longer than ninety days.

A "measurement period" is the look-back period over which hours are calculated to determine whether an employee has averaged at least thirty hours per week. There are two types of measurement periods: standard and initial measurement periods.

These alternative guidelines set out criteria that can help applicable large employers make determinations about the full-time status of employees, including following concepts:

- Initial measurement period – The term initial measurement period means a time period selected by an applicable large employer member of at least three consecutive calendar months but not more than twelve consecutive calendar months.[1] Pay periods including the beginning and end dates of the measurement period may be used.[2] The period begins on the employee's hire date and ends at the end of the three to twelve month initial measurement period.[3]

- Standard measurement period – An annual designated period of not less than three months or more than twelve months used to determine whether an ongoing variable or seasonal employee is full-time.

- Optional administrative period – A optional period of up to ninety days for making full-time determinations and offering/implementing full-time employee coverage for the stability period.

- Stability period – An annual designated period of not less than six months (and not less than the corresponding measurement period) during which the employer must offer affordable minimum essential health coverage to all full-time employees, or face financial penalties for not doing so.

---

1. Prop. Treas. Reg. § 54.4980H-1(a)(22).
2. Prop. Treas. Reg. § 54.4980H-3(c)(1)(ii).
3. Prop. Treas. Reg. §54.4980H-3(c)(1)(ii).

- <u>Full-time employees</u> – Employees are full-time if they average thirty hours of service per week or 130 hours of service per month. If a new employee is reasonably expected to average at least thirty hours per week at the time of hire, the employee must automatically be treated as full-time and offered group health coverage within three months of hire, which must also meet the ninety-day maximum waiting period rule.

- <u>Variable hour and seasonal employees</u> – A variable hour employee is someone whom the employer cannot reasonably determine will average at least thirty hours per week at the time of hire. No definition is provided for a seasonal employee, but presumably it would include anyone who works on a seasonal basis. Employers may use the initial measurement period to determine whether a newly hired variable or seasonal employee actually averages at least thirty hours per week, and the standard measurement period to determine whether an ongoing variable or seasonable employee actually averages at least thirty hours per week. If the employee does average at least thirty hours per week during the initial measurement period or standard measurement period, the employer must offer affordable minimum essential health coverage during the stability period or face financial penalties for not doing so.

- <u>Transition from new to ongoing employee status</u> – Once a new employee has completed an initial measurement period and has been employed for a full standard measurement period, the employee must be tested for full-time status under the ongoing employee rules for that standard measurement period, regardless of whether the employee was full-time during the initial measurement period.

These concepts are discussed in more detail in the following questions and answers.

466. How are new non-seasonal full-time employees treated?

If an employee is reasonably expected at his or her start date to be a full-time employee and average thirty hours of service or more per week, and is not a seasonal employee, the look-back and stability period safe harbor rules do not apply.[1] Service to more than one member in the controlled or affiliated service group is aggregated for purpose of determining full-time status.[2] If an applicable large employer does not offer coverage to such employee at or before the end of the employee's initial three full calendar months of employment, the employer may be subject to a penalty for those first three months as well as for any subsequent months of employment for which coverage is not offered.[3] The maximum ninety-calendar-day waiting period rule, which applies to employers of all sizes, must also be met and can require that coverage be offered more

---

1. Prop. Treas. Reg. § 54.4980H-3(c)(2).
2. Prop. Treas. Reg. § 54.4980H-1(a)(21)(ii).
3. Prop. Treas. Reg. § 54.4980H-3(c)(2).

quickly than the complete three-month rule when an employee is hired mid-month.[1] Employers are apparently not subject to penalties for failing to offer coverage to such an employee if the employee is hired for less than three months. However, an employee who is hired for a period of less than three months and then later rehired may be a "continuous employee" under the break in service rules. See the following for a more detailed discussion of the break in service rules.

If the employer did not offer coverage to the employee by the end of the employee's initial three full calendar months of employment, the employer may be subject to a section 4980H assessable payment for those months as well as for any subsequent months for which coverage was not offered.[2]

467. How are ongoing employees tested during the safe harbor standard measurement period?[3]

An "ongoing employee" is an employee who has been employed for at least one complete standard measurement period.[4] If an employer's group health plan offers coverage only to full-time employees, the employer may use both a measurement period of between three and twelve consecutive months. The months are not required to be calendar months. Thus, a twelve-month measurement period could begin Oct. 15 and end the following Oct. 14, followed by an optional administrative period of up to ninety days for variable-hour and seasonal employees. An employer can choose the months when the standard measurement period starts and ends, such as the calendar year, plan year, or the period ending just before open enrollment begins. Previously determined full-time employees already enrolled in coverage continue to be offered coverage through the administrative period.[5]

468. Can payroll periods be used in lieu of calendar months?

Yes. Since hours are commonly counted during payroll periods and since payroll periods may not correspond to calendar months, a special rule to align calendar month measurement periods with payroll periods for employers using weekly, biweekly, or semi-monthly payroll periods. The employer can exclude the portion of the first, partial payroll period falling in the measurement period if the employer includes the portion of the last payroll period otherwise falling outside the measurement period. For example, if the employer uses a calendar-year measurement period, it can exclude the entire payroll period that starts before the calendar year and includes January 1, Year 1, but only if it includes the entire last payroll period that includes, and extends beyond, December 31, Year 1, into January of Year 2. Similarly, the employer could exclude the entire payroll period that includes December 31 if it includes the entire payroll period that includes January 1, (which will include a portion of the prior calendar year).[6]

1. PHSA § 2708, added by PPACA § 1201 (2010). The 90 days cannot be extended to the first day of the next month or by a weekend. Thus, an employer wanting to enroll people on the first day of a month could use a 60 day wait with enrollment coinciding with or next following end of the 60 days. Prop. Treas. Reg. § 54.9815-2708(d); Prop. DOL Reg. § 2590.715-2708(d); Prop. HHS Reg. § 147.116(d).
2. Prop. Treas. Reg. § 54.4980H-3(c)(2).
3. Prop. Treas. Reg. § 54.4980H-1(a)(40).
4. Prop. Treas. Reg. § 54.4980H-1(a)(27).
5. Prop. Treas. Reg. § 54.4980H-3(c)(1)(viii), Example (i).
6. Prop. Treas. Reg. § 54.4980H-3(c)(1)(ii).

469. What happens after an employee has completed an initial measurement period and has been employed for a full standard measurement period?

Once a new employee has completed an initial measurement period and has been employed for a full standard measurement period, the employee must be tested for full-time status under the ongoing employee rules for that standard measurement period, regardless of whether the employee was full-time during the initial measurement period.

The "stability period" is the look-forward period for which an employee's status determined during the measurement period is locked in, regardless of the employee's actual hours during this stability period as long as the employee remains employed. The stability period begins at the end of the measurement period and any administrative period, if the employer elects to have one.[1]

If an employee was employed an average of at least thirty hours of service per week, this stability period must be least six consecutive calendar months and up to twelve months. The stability period can be no shorter than the standard measurement period.[2] Even if employee's position or employment status changes during the stability period, it will not affect the employee's coverage, which must continue to the end of the stability period.[3]

If an employee was not employed an average at least thirty hours of service per week during the standard measurement period, the applicable large employer may treat the employee as not a full-time employee during the stability period that follows, but is not longer than, the standard measurement period. The stability period must begin immediately after the end of the measurement period and any applicable administrative period.[4]

Thus, combining these two rules, if there is a measurement period in which some employees are full-time and others are not, the stability period must be the same length as the standard measurement period, and the standard measurement period must be at least six months.

470. How does the optional administrative period work?

The "optional administrative period," if utilized, is a period after the end of a measurement period and before the beginning of the next stability period, not to exceed ninety days, during which the employer can perform administrative tasks, such as calculating the hours for the measurement period, determining eligibility for coverage, providing enrollment materials to eligible employees, and conducting open enrollment.[5] An example would be an employer with a calendar year plan that chooses a measurement period of Oct. 15 to Oct. 14, 2014, a 2 ½ month administrative period from Oct. 15 to Dec. 31 in advance of its 2015 calendar plan year, which is the stability period. The administrative period must overlap with the prior stability

---

1. Prop. Treas. Reg. § 54.4980H-1(a)(39).
2. Prop. Treas. Reg. § 54.4980H-3(c)(1)(iii).
3. Prop. Treas. Reg. § 54.4980H-3(c)(1).
4. Prop. Treas. Reg. § 54.4980H-3(c)(1)(iv).
5. Prop. Treas. Reg. § 54.4980H-1(c)(1)(vi).

period, i.e., full-time employees enrolled in coverage based on a prior measurement period must continue to be covered through the administrative period connected to a more recent measurement period to prevent a gap in health coverage.[1]

Applicable large employer members may use administrative periods that differ in length for the categories of employees. Those categories are discussed in Q 472.

471. Can an employer changing measurement and stability periods?

Yes. An employer may change its standard measurement and stability periods each year but cannot make a change for a given year once the standard measurement period has begun.

472. May different measurement and stability periods be used for different types of employees?

Yes. A ninety-day or less stability period may be used after the measurement period, but any stability period selected by the applicable large employer member must be uniform for all employees. An applicable large employer member may apply different measurement periods, stability periods, and administrative periods for the following categories of employees:

(1)   each group of collectively bargained employees covered by a separate collective bargaining agreement,

(2)   collectively bargained and non-collectively bargained employees,

(3)   salaried employees and hourly employees,

(4)   employees whose primary places of employment are in different states, and

(5)   employees employed by different employers in the related employer group.[2]

473. Does the optional lookback method apply to new variable hour and new seasonal employees?

Yes. The look-back method for determining full-time status applies only to new "variable hour" and "new seasonal" employees. A new employee who is hired into a position that is full-time, and who does not qualify as variable hour or seasonal, must be offered coverage within ninety days in order to avoid the prospect of a $100 per day excise tax, and the employer mandate excise tax will apply if the employee is not offered coverage by the deadline of the three-complete-months rule. For new variable hour employees and new seasonal employees, applicable large employer members are permitted to determine whether the new employee is a full-time employee using an initial measurement period of between three and twelve months selected by that applicable large employer member that begins on any date between the employee's start date and the first day of the first calendar month following the employee's start date.[3] Thus, new non-full-time employees will have initial measurement periods depending on their employment commencement date. The applicable large employer member measures the new

1. Prop. Treas. Reg. § 54.4980H-3(c)(1)(vi).
2. Prop. Treas. Reg. § 4980H- 3(c)(1)(v).
3. Prop. Treas. Reg. § 54.4980H-3(c)(3)(i).

employee's hours of service during the initial measurement period and determines whether the employee was employed on average at least thirty hours of service per week during this period.

The stability period for such employees must be the same length as the stability period for ongoing employees.[1] The stability period begins immediately after the end of the initial measurement period and any associated administrative period and is the longer of six consecutive calendar months or the length of the standard measurement period.[2]

If an employer's group health plan offers coverage only to full-time employees, the employer may use both a measurement period of between three and twelve months and an administrative period of up to ninety days. The stability period for such employees cannot be more than one month longer than the initial measurement period and must not exceed the remainder of the standard measurement period plus any associated administrative period in which the initial measurement period ends. Thus, an employer could use an eleven-month initial measurement period and still comply with the general rule that the initial measurement period and administrative period combined may not extend beyond the last day of the first calendar month beginning on or after the one-year anniversary of the employee's start date.

474. What is a new employee?

A "new employee" is an employee who has not been employed for at least one complete standard measurement period.[3]

To determine if the employees meet any minimum hour plan requirements, for determining the full-time employee status of new employees, the methods vary depending upon whether the new employees are (1) reasonably expected to work full-time (and are not seasonal) or (2) are variable hour employees or seasonal employees.[4] If a new variable-hour or seasonal employee is determined not to be a full-time employee during the initial measurement period, the employer may treat the employee as not a full-time employee during the stability period that follows the initial measurement period.

475. How are new variable hour employees treated?

New variable-hour employees must be treated as if they will work the entire initial measurement period.

An employer cannot take into account the likelihood that the employee may terminate employment before the end of the initial measurement period.[5] Therefore, an employer cannot classify an employee as a variable-hour employee based solely on the expectation that the employee will terminate employment at some point before the initial measurement period ends (and therefore will not average thirty hours per week over the entire initial measurement period).

---

1. Prop. Treas. Reg. § 54.4980H-1(c)(3).
2. Prop. Treas. Reg. § 54.4980H-3(c)(3)(ii).
3. Prop. Treas. Reg. § 54.4980H-1(a)(26).
4. IRS Notice 2012-58.
5. Prop. Treas. Reg. § 54.4980H-1(a)(43).

476. What happens if there is a change in status to full-time for new variable hour or seasonal employees?

A new variable hour employee or seasonal employee who has a change in employment status, such that the individual is reasonably expected to work thirty or more hours of service per week during the initial measurement period, must be treated as a full-time employee on the first day of the fourth month following the change in status. However, a change in employment status of an ongoing employee does not change the employee's status as a full-time or non-full-time employee. However, in both of these situations, an employer is always allowed to change the employee's status to full-time.

477. What happens after variable-hour and seasonal employees have been employed for at least one standard measurement period?

Once a new employee has been employed for an entire standard measurement period, the employee must be tested for full-time status, beginning with that standard measurement period, at the same time and under the same conditions as other "ongoing employees." Thus, an employer, for example, with a calendar-year standard measurement period that also uses a one-year initial measurement period beginning on the employee's start date would test a new variable-hour employee whose start date is February 12 for full-time status first based on the initial measurement period (February 12 through February 11 of the following year) and again based on the calendar-year standard measurement period (if the employee continues in employment for that entire standard measurement period) beginning on January 1 of the year after the start date.

An employee determined to be a full-time employee during an initial measurement period or standard measurement period must be treated as a full-time employee for the entire associated stability period. This is the case even if the employee is determined to be a full-time employee during the initial measurement period but determined not to be a full-time employee during the overlapping or immediately following standard measurement period. In that case, the employer may treat the employee as not a full-time employee only after the end of the stability period associated with the initial measurement period. Thereafter, the employee's full-time status would be determined in the same manner as that of the employer's other ongoing employees.

In contrast, if the employee is determined not to be a full-time employee during the initial measurement period, but is determined to be a full-time employee during the overlapping or immediately following standard measurement period, the employee must be treated as a full-time employee for the entire stability period that corresponds to that standard measurement period (even if that stability period begins before the end of the stability period associated with the initial measurement period). Thereafter, the employee's full-time status would be determined in the same manner as that of the employer's other ongoing employees.

478. Can you provide examples of how these rules work?

Examples – New Variable Hour Employees

The following examples, which are from the IRS regulations,[1] illustrate the look-back measurement methods described in the regulations.[2] In all examples the applicable large employer member offers all of its full-time employees and their dependents the opportunity to enroll in minimum essential coverage under an eligible employer-sponsored plan. The coverage is affordable[3] or is treated as affordable coverage under one of the affordability safe harbors[4] and provides minimum value.[5]

Example (1): Twelve-Month Initial Measurement Period Followed by One-Plus Partial Month Administrative Period. Facts. Employer B uses a twelve-month standard measurement period for ongoing employees of October 15 to October 14 of the following year and a twelve-month stability period associated with that standard measurement period starting the following January 1. During the administrative period from October 15 through December 31 of each calendar year, the employer continues to offer coverage to employees who qualified for coverage for that entire calendar year based upon working on average at least thirty hours per week during the prior standard measurement period.

For new variable hour employees, Employer B uses a twelve-month initial measurement period that begins on the start date and applies an administrative period from the end of the initial measurement period through the end of the first calendar month beginning on or after the end of the initial measurement period. Employer B hires Employee Y on May 10, 2015. Employee Y's initial measurement period runs from May 10, 2015, through May 9, 2016. Employee Y has an average of thirty hours of service per week during this initial measurement period ending May 9. The administrative period runs from June 1 to June 30. Employer B offers coverage to Employee Y for a stability period that runs from July 1, 2016, through June 30, 2017.

Conclusion. Employee Y has an average of thirty hours of service per week during his initial measurement period and Employer B uses an initial measurement period that does not exceed twelve months; an administrative period totaling not more than ninety days; and a combined initial measurement period and administrative period that does not last beyond the final day of the first calendar month beginning on or after the one-year anniversary of Employee Y's start date. Accordingly, from Employee Y's start date through June 30, 2017, Employer B is not subject to any employer mandate payment for Employee Y, because Employer B complies with the standards for the initial measurement period and stability periods for a new variable hour employee. Employer B must test Employee Y again based on Employer B's first standard measurement period that begins after Employee Y's start date, i.e., from October 15, 2015, through October 14, 2016.

---

1. Prop. Treas. Reg. § 54.4980H-3(c)(5).
2. Prop. Treas. Reg. § 54.4980H-3(c)(2) through (4).
3. IRC § 36B(c)(2)(C)(i).
4. Described in Prop. Treas. Reg. § 54.4980H-5.
5. IRC § 36B(c)(2)(C)(ii).

Example (2): Eleven-Month Initial Measurement Period Followed by Two-Plus Partial Month Administrative Period. Facts. Same as Example 1, except that Employer B uses an eleven-month initial measurement period that begins on the start date and applies an administrative period from the end of the initial measurement period until the end of the second calendar month beginning after the end of the initial measurement period. Employer B hires Employee Y on May 10, 2015. Employee Y's initial measurement period runs from May 10, 2015, through April 9, 2016. Employee Y has an average of thirty hours of service per week during this initial measurement period. The administrative period runs from May 1 to June 30. Employer B offers coverage to Employee Y for a stability period that runs from July 1, 2016, through June 30, 2017.

Conclusion. Same as Example 1.

Example (3): Eleven-Month Initial Measurement Period Preceded by Partial Month Administrative Period Followed by Two-Month Administrative Period. Facts. Same as Example 1, except that Employer B uses an eleven-month initial measurement period that begins on the first day of the first calendar month beginning after the start date and applies an administrative period that runs from the end of the initial measurement period through the end of the second calendar month beginning on or after the end of the initial measurement period. Employer B hires Employee Y on May 10, 2015. Employee Y's initial measurement period runs from June 1, 2015, through April 30, 2016. Employee Y has an average of thirty hours of service per week during this initial measurement period. The administrative period is June 1 to June 30. Employer B offers coverage to Employee Y for a stability period that runs from July 1, 2016, through June 30, 2017.

Conclusion. Same as Example 1.

Example (4): Twelve-Month Initial Measurement Period Preceded by Partial Month Administrative Period and Followed by Two-Month Administrative Period. Facts. For new variable hour employees, Employer B uses a twelve-month initial measurement period that begins on the first day of the first month following the start date and applies an administrative period that runs from the end of the initial measurement period through the end of the second calendar month beginning on or after the end of the initial measurement period. Employer B hires Employee Y on May 10, 2015. Employee Y's initial measurement period runs from June 1, 2015, through May 31, 2016. Employee Y has an average of thirty hours of service per week during this initial measurement period. The stability period is June 1 to July 31. Employer B offers coverage to Employee Y for a stability period that runs from August 1, 2016, through July 31, 2017.

Conclusion. Employer B does not satisfy the standards for the look-back measurement method[1] because the combination of the initial partial month delay, the twelve-month initial measurement period, and the two month administrative period means that the coverage offered to Employee Y does not become effective until after the first day of the second calendar

---

1. Prop. Treas. Reg. § 54.4980H-3(c)(4)(v).

month following the first anniversary of Employee Y's start date. Accordingly, Employer B is potentially subject to an employer mandate penalty payment.

Examples for Staffing Firm Employees; Full-Time Employees Can Have Variable Hour Status. The provision barring employer reliance on expected employee tenure in making variable hour decisions does not mean, as some commentators have suggested, that beginning in 2015, newly-hired temporary employees who are offered full-time assignments on their start date cannot be treated as variable hour employees and must be offered health benefits within ninety days. This ignores the specific examples provided in the proposed regulations for determining the variable hour status of temporary employees assigned by staffing firms. The examples make clear that, in 2014 and in the years following, staffing firms can use up to a full twelve-month look-back period for temporary employees as long as they are properly classified as variable hour employees based on those examples. The following is a brief summary of the relevant examples:[1]

- In one example, a staffing firm expects, on the employee's start date, that the employee will be offered "short-term" assignments with "several different clients" with "significant gaps" in between, that the assignments will differ in average weekly hours, and that the number and duration of assignments offered and accepted, the gaps between, and the weekly hours, are all uncertain.

- In the other example, an employee is hired on an hourly basis to "fill in for employees who are absent and to provide additional staffing at peak times." In that example, the employer expects the employee to work "full-time for the first few months of employment, while assigned to a specific project, but also reasonably expects that the assignments will be of unpredictable duration, that there will be gaps of unpredictable duration between assignments, that the hours per week required by subsequent assignments will vary, and that [the employee] will not necessarily be available for all assignments."

The examples don't specifically define "short-term" or "few months" but the preamble to the regulations refers to assignment lengths "each generally lasting no more than two or three months"[2] and, at another point, describes short-term as "4 or 5 months."[3]

The examples reflect Treasury and IRS's recognition that temporary employees, when they do work, generally work full-time work weeks. Hence, the mere fact that temporary employee assignments are full-time at the start does not preclude a determination of variable hour status.[4]

---

1. 78 Fed. Reg. at 248. Examples 12 and 13.
2. 78 Fed. Reg. at 230.
3. 78 Fed. Reg. at 229.
4. 78 Fed. Reg. at 227.

Continuous Full-Time Employee

Example (5): Continuous Full-Time Employee. Facts. Employer B uses a twelve-month initial measurement period that begins on the start date and applies an administrative period from the end of the initial measurement period through the end of the first calendar month beginning on or after the end of the initial measurement period. Employer B hires Employee Y on May 10, 2015, as a variable hour employee. Employee Y's initial measurement period runs from May 10, 2015, through May 9, 2016. Employee Y has an average of thirty hours of service per week during this initial measurement period. Employer B offers coverage to Employee Y for a stability period that runs from July 1, 2016, through June 30, 2017. Employer B tests Employee Y again based on Employee Y's hours of service from October 15, 2015, through October 14, 2016, Employer B's first standard measurement period that begins after Employee Y's start date, and determines that Employee Y has an average of thirty hours of service a week during that period. It offers Employee Y coverage for July 1, 2017, through December 31, 2017. Employee Y also had an offer of coverage for the period of January 1, 2017, through June 30, 2017, because that period is covered by the initial stability period following the initial measurement period, during which Employee Y was determined to be a full-time employee.

Conclusion. Employer B is not subject to any potential employer mandate penalty payment for Employee Y.

Initially Full-Time Employee, Becomes Non-Full-Time Employee

Example (6): Initially Full-Time Employee, Becomes Non-Full-Time Employee. Facts. Same as Example 1; in addition, Employer B tests Employee Y again based on Employee Y's hours of service from October 15, 2015, through October 14, 2016, Employer B's first standard measurement period that begins after Employee Y's start date, and determines that Employee Y has an average of twenty-eight hours of service a week during that period. Employer B continues to offer coverage to Employee Y through June 30, 2017, (the end of the stability period based on the initial measurement period during which Employee Y was determined to be a full-time employee) but does not offer coverage to Employee Y for the period of July 1, 2017, through December 31, 2017.

Conclusion. Employer B is not subject to any potential penalty payment for 2016 with respect to Employee Y, provided that it offers coverage to Employee Y from July 1, 2016, through June 30, 2017, the stability period associated with the initial measurement period.

Initially Non-Full-Time Employee

Example (7): Initially Non-Full-Time Employee. Facts. Same as Example 1, except that Employee Y has an average of twenty-eight hours of service per week during the period from May 10, 2015, through May 9, 2016, and Employer B does not offer coverage to Employee Y in 2016.

<u>Conclusion</u>. From Employee Y's start date through the end of 2016, Employer B is not subject to any employer mandate payment under Code § 4980H because Employer B complies with the standards for the measurement and stability periods for a new variable hour employee with respect to Employee Y.

<u>Example (8): Initially Non-Full-Time Employee, Becomes Full-Time Employee. Facts</u>. Same as Example 7; in addition, Employer B tests Employee Y again based on Employee Y's hours of service from October 15, 2015, through October 14, 2016, Employer B's first standard measurement period that begins after Employee Y's start date, and determines that Employee Y has an average of thirty hours of service per week during this standard measurement period, and offers coverage to Employee Y for calendar year 2017.

<u>Conclusion</u>. Employer B is not subject to any employer mandate payment for 2017 for Employee Y.

Six-Month Measurement and Stability Periods

In Examples 9 and 10, the new employee is a new variable hour employee, and the employer uses a six-month standard measurement period with six-month stability periods associated with those standard measurement periods. The author believes that most employers will use twelve month measurement and stability periods, but shorter periods are permitted, as shown by the following examples.

<u>Example (9): Initially Full-Time Employee. Facts</u>. For new variable hour employees, Employer C uses a six-month initial measurement period that begins on the start date and applies an administrative period that runs from the end of the initial measurement period through the end of the first full calendar month beginning after the end of the initial measurement period. Employer C hires Employee Z on May 10, 2015. Employee Z's initial measurement period runs from May 10, 2015, through November 9, 2015, during which Employee Z has an average of thirty hours of service per week. The administrative period is Nov. 10 to Dec. 31. Employer C offers coverage to Employee Z for a stability period that runs from January 1, 2016, through June 30, 2016.

<u>Conclusion</u>. Employer C uses an initial measurement period that does not exceed twelve months; an administrative period totaling not more than ninety days; and a combined initial measurement period and administrative period that does not last longer than the final day of the first calendar month beginning on or after the one-year anniversary of Employee Z's start date. From Employee Z's start date through June 30, 2016, the end of the period when coverage was offered, Employer C is not subject to any employer mandate payment because Employer C complies with the standards for the measurement and stability periods for a new variable hour employee with respect to Employee Z. Employer C must test Employee Z again based on Employee Z's hours of service during the period from November 15, 2015, through May 14, 2016, Employer C's first standard measurement period that begins after Employee Z's start date.

Example (10): Initially Full-Time Employee, Becomes Non-Full-Time Employee. Facts. Same as Example 9; in addition, Employer C tests Employee Z again based on Employee Z's hours of service during the period from November 15, 2015, through May 14, 2016, i.e., Employer C's first standard measurement period that begins after Employee Z's start date, during which period Employee Z has an average of twenty-eight hours of service per week. Employer C continues to offer coverage to Employee Z through June 30, 2016, (the end of the initial stability period based on the initial measurement period during which Employee Z has an average of thirty hours of service per week) but does not offer coverage to Employee Z from July 1, 2016, through December 31, 2016.

Conclusion. Employer C is not subject to any employer mandate penalty payment for Employee Z for 2016.

New Seasonal Employee

Example (11): Seasonal Employee, Twelve-Month Initial Measurement Period; One-Plus Partial Month Administrative Period. Facts. Employer D offers health plan coverage only to full-time employees and their dependents. Employer D uses a twelve-month initial measurement period for new variable hour employees and seasonal employees that begins on the start date and applies an administrative period from the end of the initial measurement period through the end of the first calendar month beginning after the end of the initial measurement period. Employer D hires Employee S, a ski instructor, on November 15, 2015, with an anticipated season during which Employee S will work running through March 15, 2016. Employer D determines that Employee S is a seasonal employee based upon a reasonable good faith interpretation of that term. Employee S's initial measurement period runs from November 15, 2015, through November 14, 2016. Employee S is expected to have fifty hours of service per week from November 15, 2015, through March 15, 2016, but is not reasonably expected to average thirty hours of service per week for the twelve-month initial measurement period.

Conclusion. Employer D cannot determine that Employee S is reasonably expected to average at least thirty hours of service per week for the twelve-month initial measurement period. Accordingly, Employer D may treat Employee S as a variable hour employee during the initial measurement period.

New Variable Hour Employee of Staffing Company

Example (12): Variable Hour Employee. Facts. Employer E is in the business of providing temporary workers to numerous clients that are unrelated to Employer E and to one another. Employer E is the common law employer of the temporary workers based on all of the facts and circumstances. Employer E offers health plan coverage only to full-time employees (including temporary workers who are full-time employees) and their dependents. Employer E uses a twelve-month initial measurement period for new variable hour employees and new seasonal employees that begins on the start date and applies an administrative period from the end of the initial measurement period through the end of the first calendar month beginning after the end of the initial measurement period. Employer E hires Employee T on January 1, 2015, and anticipates that it will assign Employee T to provide services for various clients. As of the beginning of the initial measurement period, Employer E reasonably expects that, over the initial measurement period, Employee T is likely to be offered short-term assignments with several different clients, with significant gaps between the assignments and that the assignments will differ in the average hours of service per week (meaning averaging both above and below thirty hours of service per week), all depending on client needs and Employee T's availability. The number of actual assignments that Employee T will be offered, the number that Employee T will accept, the duration of assignments, the length of the gaps between assignments, and whether various assignments will result in Employee T being employed on average at least thirty hours of service per week during the assignment are all uncertain.

Conclusion. Employer E cannot determine whether Employee T is reasonably expected to average at least thirty hours of service per week for the twelve-month initial measurement period. Accordingly, Employer E may treat Employee T as a variable hour employee during the initial measurement period.

New Variable Hour Employee Initially and Temporarily Expected to Work at Least Thirty Hours per Week

Example (13). Variable Hour Employee. Facts. Employee A is hired on an hourly basis by Employer Y to fill in for employees who are absent and to provide additional staffing at peak times. Employer Y expects that Employee A will average thirty hours of service per week or more for A's first few months of employment, while assigned to a specific project, but also reasonably expects that the assignments will be of unpredictable duration, that there will be gaps of unpredictable duration between assignments, that the hours per week required by subsequent assignments will vary, and that A will not necessarily be available for all assignments.

Conclusion. Employer Y cannot determine whether Employee A is reasonably expected to average at least thirty hours of service per week for the initial measurement period. Accordingly, Employer Y may treat Employee A as a variable hour employee.

Anti-abuse Rules and Staffing (Employee Leasing or Professional Employment Organization) Firms

479. Are any anti-abuse rules contemplated for employers who shift employees to staffing companies?

The proposed regulations preamble states that Treasury and IRS are aware of various structures being considered under which employers might use temporary staffing agencies (or other staffing agencies) purporting to be the common law employer to evade application of section 4980H. In one structure, the employer (referred to in this section as the "client") would purport to employ its employees for only part of a week, such as twenty hours, and then to hire those same individuals through a temporary staffing agency (or other staffing agency) for the remaining hours of the week, thereby resulting in neither the "client" employer nor the temporary staffing agency or other staffing agency appearing to employ the individual as a full-time employee. In another structure, one temporary staffing agency (or other staffing agency) would purport to employ an individual and supply the individual as a worker to a client for only part of a week, such as twenty hours, while a second temporary staffing agency or other staffing agency would purport to employ the same individual and supply that individual as a worker to the same client for the remainder of the week, thereby resulting in neither the temporary staffing agencies or the other staffing agencies, nor the client, appearing to employ the individual as a full-time employee.

The Treasury Department and the IRS anticipate that only in rare circumstances, if ever, would the "client" under these fact patterns not employ the individual under the common law standard as a full-time employee.

The final regulations will likely contain an anti-abuse rule to address the situations described in this section of the preamble. Under that anticipated rule, if an individual performs services as an employee of an employer and performs the same or similar services for that employer in the individual's purported employment at a temporary staffing agency or other staffing agency of which the employer is a client, then all the hours of service are attributed to the employer.

Planning to Minimize Impact of Employer Mandate Penalties

480. Since the employer mandate penalty is calculated solely based on full-time (thirty hours of service per week) employees, can an employer reduce or eliminate the mandate's impact by reducing hours of service to less than thirty hours per week?

Section 510 of the Employee Retirement Income Security Act (ERISA) bars discrimination for the purpose of interfering with the attainment of any right to employee benefits to which a worker may become entitled. An intentional reduction of hours from thirty or more to under thirty in order to prevent employees from getting benefits raises a potential ERISA § 510 claim. A violation can result in court ordered reinstatement of the worker, restitution, back pay, and the claimant's legal fees. For large companies, there is a potential for class actions to be filed. The best case for a plaintiff would be reducing the hours of an employee currently receiving health benefits to under thirty hours, resulting in a loss of those benefits.

However, adopting a policy allowing future workers to work no more than twenty-nine hours per week would likely be a safe move because no action was taken to deprive them of a benefit they otherwise would have received.

Additionally, healthcare reform provides whistleblower protection, which allows for recovery of damages and attorneys' fees. That section prohibits firing or discriminating against workers in retaliation for complaining to government authorities about noncompliance with healthcare reform's consumer protections or objecting to the employer about noncompliance.[1]

---

1. FLSA § 18C.

If a company fired workers to avoid the mandate, it might be permitted if it acted due to a legitimate need to save money. However, if it announced its intentions and then fired a worker who objected to the plan, it could be opening the door to a retaliation suit, even if that worker would have been fired regardless of the objections.

481. Is outsourcing work a solution to reduce the employee count?

The use of independent contractors to do work that would otherwise be done by employees is a way to reduce the workforce and the impact of the employer mandate penalties for applicable large employers. However, an employer that reclassifies existing employees as independent contractors takes a large risk in an audit challenging such reclassification. However, if the employees incorporate, with their corporations employing them and their corporation contracting with the employer, case law exists that would support such reclassification.[1]

482. How can an applicable large employer offer low cost health benefits and still avoid or reduce the impact of the employer mandate penalty?

The employer mandate penalty comes in two parts, the 4980H(a)[2] penalty and the 4980H(b)[3] penalty. The (b) penalty cannot be greater than the (a) penalty. The (a) penalty is easy to avoid. Whether the (b) penalty is a serious issue for an employer depends on the facts relating to an employer's workforce.

483. How does an employer avoid the 4980H(a) employer mandate penalty?

There are at least two ways to do so without an employer spending a lot on its health plan. One option to avoid the Code § 4980H(a) penalty is for an employer to offer its employees health coverage for which the employer pays nothing and employees pay for all of plan. Code § 4980H(a) merely requires that an employer make an offer of coverage. It does not require the employer to pay for any part of it. The affordability of the coverage is a concept involved in the 4980H((b) penalty only, as discussed in Q 484. This strategy to avoid the employer mandate would be premised on the employer's belief that most employees who refused the employer's offer of coverage would not purchase health insurance on an exchange, even if they qualified for a subsidy, because even with a subsidy, lower income healthy workers with no chronic medical condition would rather save the money and rely on hospital emergency room coverage if they need care.

Employers can also avoid the Code § 4980H(a) $2,000 employer mandate penalty (for every full time employee over thirty) by offering very limited (low benefit, skinny, or bare bones) health care plans that can lack key health benefits, such as hospital coverage. Such policies are low cost because they offer minimal benefits. Unlike the exchange plans, employer plans need not cover the ten categories of services for the healthcare law's essential health benefits. Thus, these low benefit plans are less expensive because they provide much lower benefits than an exchange plan. This technique will not work for employers in the small group insurance

---

1. *Idaho Ambucare Center Inc. v. U.S.*, 57 F.3d 752 (9th Cir. 1995); *Sargent v. CIR*, 929 F.2d 1252 (8th Cir. 1991).
2. IRC § 4980H(a).
3. IRC § 4980H(b).

market (generally employers with under 100 employees) because healthcare reform requires that insurance to cover all ten essential health benefits.[1]

Prior to healthcare reform, many employers, especially those with predominantly low wage employees, offered so-called "mini-med" health plans, which, as their name implies, had low cost and limited benefits. These low benefit plans may take their place. The law requires employers with fifty or more workers to offer coverage to 95 percent of their full-time employees and dependents or pay a penalty. Many persons understood the rules to require robust major medical insurance, covering a list of "essential" benefits such as mental-health services and a high percentage of workers' overall costs. However, that is not the way the law is written. Articles have reported that federal officials confirmed that this low benefit plan strategy works to avoid the 4980H(a) penalty.[2]

To comply with the law, the low benefit plan cannot have a lifetime or annual dollar limit on benefits that are provided and must cover preventive services like vaccines and cancer screenings without any cost-sharing, i.e., without any employee deductibles or copays. However, such plans may not cover surgery, imaging, or prenatal care. Alternatively, they could provide a very limited benefit for hospitalizations or surgeries. They might also limit the number of doctor visits or prescriptions available to participants. The cap would be on the number, not the dollar-value of the benefits so they would not have a concern about prohibited annual dollar limits. Anyone wanting better coverage could then opt out and go to an exchange. Such plans could be paired with other limited benefit packages, such as hospital indemnity plans paying specified dollar amounts per day and/or catastrophic coverage, a very high deductible insurance policy.

The 4980H(a) employer mandate penalty applies to an employer that fails to offer "minimum essential coverage." Minimum essential coverage does not include excepted benefits, such as stand-alone vision or stand-alone dental benefits. Employers seeking to minimize or avoid the employer penalty must offer minimum essential coverage to 95 percent of their full-time employees and their dependents, including children under age twenty six. Minimum essential coverage is the coverage required to avoid the individual and employer mandates.[3] It is an "eligible employer-sponsored plan," a term that means any group health plan (other than for excepted benefits) offered by an employer to employees or coverage offered in a state's small or large group market or a self-insured plan[4] meeting only the required Public Health Service

1. Beginning in 2014, a health insurance issuer that offers health insurance coverage in the individual or small group market must include essential health benefits package required under section 1302(a) of the Patient Protection and Affordable Care Act. A small employer is "an employer who employed an average of at least 1 but not more than 100 employees on business days during the preceding calendar year and who employs at least two employees on the first day of the plan year." For plan years beginning before January 1, 2016, a state may elect to define small employer as an employer who employed an average of at least 1 but not more than 50 employees on business days during the preceding calendar year, which likely will be appealing for states already using that definition. An employer not in existence throughout the preceding calendar year will determine whether it is a small or large employer "based on the average number of employees that it is reasonably expected such employer will employ on business days in the current calendar year." The control and affiliated service group aggregation rules set forth in Code §§ 414(b), (c), (m), and (o) apply to count employees of an "employer."
2. Employers Can Minimize Their Exposure To Obamacare's Penalties By Offering Low-Cost 'Skinny' Coverage, Forbes (June 21, 2013) at http://www.forbes.com/sites/theapothecary/2013/05/21/employers-can-minimize-their-exposure-to-obamacares-health-insurance-mandate-by-offering-low-cost-skinny-coverage, Kevin McCurdy, "Skinny" Plans Under PPACA: Are They a Solution?, at http://www.mondaq.com/unitedstates/x/252518/Employee+Benefits+Compensation/Skinny+Plans+Under+PPACA+Are+They+a+Solution&email access=on.
3. PPACA § 1301.
4. Prop Reg §1.5000A-2(c)(1)

Act requirements (discussed in Part VII).[1] It includes grandfathered plans.[2] In other words, any health insurance plan legally sold in a state and self-insured plans meeting PHSA requirements are an "eligible employer-sponsored plan." In many states, insurers market inexpensive plans that cover a limited range of services. Further, PHSA requirements only apply if the plan offers the benefit in question. None of the PHSA benefit mandates apply to plans that do not offer a particular benefit. Thus, for example, the protections for mothers and newborns do not apply where a plan does not offer maternity benefits.

Thus, minimum essential coverage includes coverage that need not include the ten types of "essential health benefits." Essential health benefits is the term used by health care reform to describe the benefits that qualified health plans (QHPs) sold on the state exchanges are required to cover.[3] HHS defines essential health benefits with reference to state benchmark plans offered on state exchanges (marketplaces).[4]

Also see Q 439 through Q 441.

484. How does an employer avoid or reduce the 4980H(b) employer mandate penalty?

Applicable large employers offering employee pay all coverage or a low benefit minimum essential coverage plan could still face the 4980H(b) penalty of $3,000 per year per full-time employee for workers who go to an exchange and qualify for subsidized coverage if the employer's coverage is either (1) not affordable[5] or (2) lacks minimum value.[6] (See Q 439 and Q 442 through Q 445.) Whether this will be a significant penalty depends on how many of an employer's employees qualify for and purchase subsidized health insurance on an exchange when the employer's policy is unaffordable or fails to provide minimum value. In many cases, the result could be much less expensive than the 4980H(a) penalty because it is likely that many employees, especially those with low incomes, will not go to the exchanges due to the relatively high cost of the coverage after the subsidy and the availability of care at hospital emergency rooms. Additionally, employees can get insurance later if they develop a chronic condition because, beginning in 2014, insurers cannot impose a preexisting condition limit on insureds. Thus, some believe that many if not most of those going to the exchange will likely be only those with existing medical conditions.

Limited benefit policies can cost an employer far less than the employer mandate penalty or the cost of providing benefits that are more comprehensive. Some low benefit plans cost

1. IRC § 5000A(f)(2)(B); Prop. Reg.§1.5000A-2(a) and (c)(1)(ii).
2. Prop. Reg.§1.5000A-2(a)(c)(1)(iii).
3. PPACA § 1302(b).
4. 45 CFR § 156.100.
5. Coverage is affordable for IRC § 4980H purposes if the cost to the employee of self-only coverage does not exceed 9.5% of the employee's "household income." This is true irrespective of whether he or she qualifies for some other level of coverage (e.g., self plus dependents, family). Thus, although family coverage might require a larger employee premium, affordability for IRC § 4980H purposes is determined based on the cost of self-only coverage. The Act defines "household income" to mean "modified adjusted gross income of the employee and any members of the employee's family (including a spouse and dependents) who are required to file an income tax return." Alternatively, employers may use one of three safe harbors as proxies: W-2, rate-of-pay, or Federal Line.
6. To provide minimum value, a plan must pay for at least 60% of plan costs. The remaining 40% are paid for by the covered individual in the form of co-pays, deductibles, co-insurance, and other cost sharing features.

employers $40 − $100 monthly per employee depending on the benefits offered. The low benefit insurance approach is an attractive option for companies with many low wage workers, such as retailers and restaurant operators, especially if workers will not want to pay the cost of the richer exchange coverage. Only full-time employees who qualify for and purchase subsidized exchange coverage trigger the employer $3,000 per full-time employee employer mandate penalty. A full-time worker earning $9 an hour would have to pay approximately $70 a month for a midlevel exchange plan after the subsidies. At $12 an hour, an employee's share of the premium would be approximately $140 per month due to a reduced federal subsidy. Of course, these figures are only examples, as every state exchange will have insurance costs that are based on local conditions.

As an example, San Antonio-based Bill Miller Bar-B-Q, a 4,200-worker chain, announced that it will implement a low benefit health plan in July 2013 and will aim to price the plan at less than $50 a month,. The new plan will have no dollar limits on benefits but will cover only preventive services, six annual doctors' visits, generic drugs. X-rays, and tests at a local urgent care chain. It will not cover surgeries or hospital stays.[1] The chain plans to pay the $3,000 penalty for each worker who gets an exchange-plan subsidy. The employer believes that those are going to be the people who will be ill and need a more robust plan. Insuring them directly with major medical coverage would cost more than the penalty.

Many more workers will continue to go without insurance, despite the exchanges and the limited plan. Only one-quarter of workers eligible for the current Miller Bar-B-Q mini-med plan elect to take it.[2] For these employees who purchase no employer or exchange coverage, the employer savings would be even greater, as there would be no cost for health insurance and no employer mandate penalty because the 4980H(b) penalty is only paid for those full-time employees qualifying for and purchasing subsidized health coverage on an exchange. Tex-Mex restaurant chain El Fenix also has announced that it will offer limited plans to its 1,200 workers, covering doctors' visits, preventive care, and drugs, but not hospital stays or surgery. "What our goal was all along was to make [offering coverage] financially palatable for the company as a whole, so we didn't do damage and have to let people go or slow down our growth," said Brian Livingston, chief financial officer of Dallas-based Firebird Restaurant Group LLC, owner of El Fenix.[3]

485. How does an applicable large employer utilize the 95 percent rule in planning for the employer mandate penalties?

On January 1, 2015, employers with fifty or more full-time and full-time equivalent employees will need to track their workforces' hours of service (usually based on the prior year employee data) in order to comply with the employer mandate. The 95 percent rule allows an employer to be treated as offering qualifying coverage to all of its full-time employees and their dependents for a calendar month, if the employer offers coverage to all but five percent

1. Employers Eye Bare-Bones Health Plans Under New Law, Wall Street Journal (May 20, 2013) at http://online.wsj.com/article/SB10001424
127887324787004578493274030598186.html.
2. Id.
3. Id.

(or, if greater, five full-time employees) of its full-time employees and their dependents. The preamble to the proposed regulations' preamble states that an employer can utilize the 95 percent rule even if the failure to offer coverage is intentional. The proposed regulations when explaining the 95 percent rule do not condition a full-time employee being included in the calculation on any additional factor besides being a full-time employee (averaging thirty or more hours of service per week during the month).

Full-Time Employees under the Age of Twenty Six Count. An individual is eligible for a premium tax credit (which is required to trigger the employer mandate penalty) if the individual is not eligible for minimum essential coverage through a different medium other than eligibility through coverage in the individual market. Not all employees under the age of twenty six will be eligible for coverage through their parents or some other means. If such an employee met the other conditions to receive a premium tax credit, the full-time under age twenty six employee could trigger a §4980H penalty unless the 95 percent test is met, taking into account under age twenty six full-time employees.

Medicare and Medicaid Eligible Employees Count. Employees who are sixty-five years of age or older will not be eligible for a premium tax credit as they will be eligible for Medicare. However, it appears all full-time employees are included when calculating the 95 percent rule. Consequently, if employees eligible for Medicare are not offered the opportunity to enroll in qualifying employer coverage, they will count against the employer when calculating the 95 percent rule. Likewise, if Medicaid employees are not offered the opportunity to enroll in qualifying employer coverage, they will count against the employer when calculating the 95 percent rule.

Employees with Household Income of More than 400 Percent of the Federal Poverty Line Count. While not eligible for a premium subsidy on an Exchange, these employees will count against the employer when calculating the 95 percent rule.

Who Does Not Count When Calculating the 95 Percent Rule.

- Leased Employees, Sole Proprietors, Partners, and 2-Percent S Corporation Shareholders: Do No Count.

- Part-Time Employees. Whether or not a part-time employee is offered qualifying health coverage, the employee is not included when calculating the 95 percent rule.

New Employees – Rules Not Clear. A new non-variable hour employee who the employer reasonably expects to accumulate more than thirty hours of service per week must be offered coverage by the conclusion of the employee's third full calendar month of employment. If a new employee (who the employer knows will work forty hours a week) is hired on March 15, 2014, that particular employee's initial three full calendar months will be April 2014, May 2014, and June 2014. If the employer does not offer the employee coverage by June 30, 2014, the employee would count as a full-time employee who did not have coverage made available to him/her for April 2014, May 2014, and June 2014 as well as any subsequent month until coverage is offered for the entire calendar month when calculating the 95 percent rule. The partial month of March 2014 would not be included in the calculation of the 95 percent rule.

It is unclear how a new non-variable hour employee would count for the 95 percent rule if the employer offers coverage to the employee by the three-month deadline. For example, suppose a new employee (who the employer knows will work forty hours a week) is hired on March 15, 2014. The employer makes coverage available to the new employee by June 30, 2014. As in the example in the previous paragraph, it appears the partial month of March 2014 would not be included in the calculation of the 95 percent rule. There are three possibilities for April, May, and June:

1. The first possibility is to include the employee as a full-time employee who was not offered coverage for the calendar months of April 2014, May 2014, and June 2014. The proposed regulations make no exceptions to the rule that 95 percent of full-time employees be offered coverage.

2. A second possibility would include the employee as a full-time employee who was timely offered coverage for the calendar months of April 2014, May 2014, and June 2014 when calculating the 95 percent rule.

3. The third possibility is the months of April 2014, May 2014, and June 2014 are not considered in the calculation of the 95 percent rule. The employee would begin to be included in the calculation of the 95 percent rule in July 2014.

New Variable Hour Employees. If an employer cannot determine if the employee is reasonably expected to average at least thirty hours of service per week, the proposed regulations allow an employer to use the safe harbor measurement method if an employee can be classified as a variable hour employee. The proposed regulations provide no guidance on how the periods associated with the safe harbor interact with calculating the 95 percent rule.

A reasonable interpretation is that all employees during the initial measurement period are excluded from the calculation of the 95 percent rule. If an employee is determined to be a full-time employee during the initial measurement period, the employee would be included in the calculation of the 95 percent rule during the entire corresponding stability period regardless of whether the employee was offered coverage during that period. However, if an employee is determined not to be a full-time employee during the initial measurement period, the employee would not be included in the calculation of the 95 percent rule during the entire corresponding stability period regardless of whether the employee was offered coverage during that period.

If an employee is determined to be a full-time employee during the standard measurement period, the employee would be included in the calculation of the 95 percent rule during the entire corresponding stability period regardless of whether the employee was offered coverage during that period. However, if an employee is determined not to be a full-time employee during the standard measurement period, the employee would not be included in the calculation of the 95 percent rule during the entire corresponding stability period regardless of whether the employee was offered coverage during that period.

In the case of overlapping stability periods, the employee being included as a full-time employee will always trump the employee not being included as a full-time employee for purposes of calculating the 95 percent rule. Overlapping stability periods should not result in a single employee being included twice when calculating the 95 percent rule.

APPENDIX A

Model SBC and Uniform Glossary

Following are copies of the corrected Summary of Benefits and Coverage (SBC) that was released April 23, 2013, and Uniform Glossary, which provide a uniform summary of important provisions to assist individuals in understanding their coverage.

The SBC and a Uniform Glossary of commonly used terms are to be distributed to all persons with essential health benefits in an individual policy or group plan. They provide the information needed to compare it to other available options on an "apples to apples" basis. A self-funded plan must prepare its own SBC.

Form language and formatting must be precisely reproduced, unless instructions allow or instruct otherwise. The SBC and Uniform Glossary that are reproduced here replicate the forms, although for purposes of this publication certain aspects of required formatting—such as the font size—has been altered to fit the page.

The SBC and Uniform Glossary are discussed in detail in Parts VII and VIII of this book.

Source: Center for Consumer Information and Insurance Oversight (CCIIO). The Summary of Benefits and Coverage is available at: www.cms.gov/CCIIO/Resources/.../sample-completed-sbc-accessible.pdf. The Uniform Glossary is available at: http://cciio.cms.gov/resources/files/Files2/02102012/uniform-glossary-final.pdf.

Insurance Company 1: Plan Option 1

Coverage Period: 01/01/2014 – 12/31/2014

Summary of Benefits and Coverage: What this Plan Covers & What it Costs

Coverage for: Individual + Spouse | Plan Type: PPO

⚠️ **This is only a summary.** If you want more detail about your coverage and costs, you can get the complete terms in the policy or plan document at www.-[insert] or by calling 1-800-[insert].

Important Questions	Answers	Why this Matters:
What is the overall deductible?	**$500** person / **$1,000** family Doesn't apply to preventive care	You must pay all the costs up to the **deductible** amount before this plan begins to pay for covered services you use. Check your policy or plan document to see when the **deductible** starts over (usually, but not always, January 1st). See the chart starting on page 2 for how much you pay for covered services after you meet the **deductible**.
Are there other deductibles for specific services?	Yes. **$300** for prescription drug coverage. There are no other specific **deductibles**.	You must pay all of the costs for these services up to the specific **deductible** amount before this plan begins to pay for these services.
Is there an out-of-pocket limit on my expenses?	Yes. For participating providers **$2,500** person / **$5,000** family For non-participating providers **$4,000** person / **$8,000** family	The **out-of-pocket limit** is the most you could pay during a coverage period (usually one year) for your share of the cost of covered services. This limit helps you plan for health care expenses.
What is not included in the out-of-pocket limit?	Premiums, balance-billed charges, and health care this plan doesn't cover.	Even though you pay these expenses, they don't count toward the **out-of-pocket limit**.
Is there an overall annual limit on what the plan pays?	No.	The chart starting on page 2 describes any limits on what the plan will pay for *specific* covered services, such as office visits.
Does this plan use a network of providers?	Yes. See www.[insert].com or call 1-800-[insert] for a list of participating providers.	If you use an in-network doctor or other health care **provider**, this plan will pay some or all of the costs of covered services. Be aware, your in-network doctor or hospital may use an out-of-network **provider** for some services. Plans use the term in-network, **preferred**, or participating for **providers** in their **network**. See the chart starting on page 2 for how this plan pays different kinds of **providers**.
Do I need a referral to see a specialist?	No. You don't need a referral to see a specialist.	You can see the **specialist** you choose without permission from this plan.
Are there services this plan doesn't cover?	Yes.	Some of the services this plan doesn't cover are listed on page 4. See your policy or plan document for additional information about **excluded services**.

Questions: Call 1-800-[insert] or visit us at www.[insert].
If you aren't clear about any of the underlined terms used in this form, see the Glossary. You can view the Glossary at www.[insert] or call 1-800-[insert] to request a copy.

OMB Control Numbers 1545-2229, 1210-0147, and 0938-1146

1 of 8

Released on April 23, 2013 (corrected)

Insurance Company 1: Plan Option 1

Summary of Benefits and Coverage: What this Plan Covers & What it Costs

Coverage Period: 01/01/2014 – 12/31/2014

Coverage for: Individual + Spouse | **Plan Type:** PPO

- **Copayments** are fixed dollar amounts (for example, $15) you pay for covered health care, usually when you receive the service.
- **Coinsurance** is *your* share of the costs of a covered service, calculated as a percent of the **allowed amount** for the service. For example, if the plan's **allowed amount** for an overnight hospital stay is $1,000, your **coinsurance** payment of 20% would be $200. This may change if you haven't met your **deductible.**
- The amount the plan pays for covered services is based on the **allowed amount.** If an out-of-network **provider** charges more than the **allowed amount,** you may have to pay the difference. For example, if an out-of-network hospital charges $1,500 for an overnight stay and the **allowed amount** is $1,000, you may have to pay the $500 difference. (This is called **balance billing.**)
- This plan may encourage you to use participating **providers** by charging you lower **deductibles, copayments** and **coinsurance** amounts.

Common Medical Event	Services You May Need	Your Cost If You Use a Participating Provider	Your Cost If You Use a Non-Participating Provider	Limitations & Exceptions
If you visit a health care provider's office or clinic	Primary care visit to treat an injury or illness	$35 copay/visit	40% coinsurance	—none—
	Specialist visit	$50 copay/visit	40% coinsurance	—none—
	Other practitioner office visit	20% coinsurance for chiropractor and acupuncture	40% coinsurance for chiropractor and acupuncture	—none—
	Preventive care/screening/immunization	No charge	40% coinsurance	
If you have a test	Diagnostic test (x-ray, blood work)	$10 copay/test	40% coinsurance	—none—
	Imaging (CT/PET scans, MRIs)	$50 copay/test	40% coinsurance	—none—

Questions: Call 1-800-[insert] or visit us at www.[insert].
If you aren't clear about any of the underlined terms used in this form, see the Glossary. You can view the Glossary at www.[insert] or call 1-800-[insert] to request a copy.

Insurance Company 1: Plan Option 1

Coverage Period: 01/01/2014 – 12/31/2014

Summary of Benefits and Coverage: What this Plan Covers & What it Costs

Coverage for: Individual + Spouse | **Plan Type:** PPO

Common Medical Event	Services You May Need	Your Cost If You Use a Participating Provider	Your Cost If You Use a Non-Participating Provider	Limitations & Exceptions
If you need drugs to treat your illness or condition	Generic drugs	$10 copay/ prescription (retail and mail order)	40% coinsurance	Covers up to a 30-day supply (retail prescription); 31-90 day supply (mail order prescription)
	Preferred brand drugs	20% coinsurance (retail and mail order)	40% coinsurance	———none———
More information about prescription drug coverage is available at www. [insert].	Non-preferred brand drugs	40% coinsurance (retail and mail order)	60% coinsurance	———none———
	Specialty drugs	50% coinsurance	70% coinsurance	———none———
If you have outpatient surgery	Facility fee (e.g., ambulatory surgery center)	20% coinsurance	40% coinsurance	———none———
	Physician/surgeon fees	20% coinsurance	40% coinsurance	———none———
If you need immediate medical attention	Emergency room services	20% coinsurance	20% coinsurance	———none———
	Emergency medical transportation	20% coinsurance	20% coinsurance	———none———
	Urgent care	20% coinsurance	40% coinsurance	———none———
If you have a hospital stay	Facility fee (e.g., hospital room)	20% coinsurance	40% coinsurance	———none———
	Physician/surgeon fee	20% coinsurance	40% coinsurance	———none———

Questions: Call 1-800-[insert] or visit us at www. [insert].
If you aren't clear about any of the underlined terms used in this form, see the Glossary. You can view the Glossary at www.[insert] or call 1-800-[insert] to request a copy.

Insurance Company 1: Plan Option 1

Coverage Period: 01/01/2014 – 12/31/2014

Summary of Benefits and Coverage: What this Plan Covers & What it Costs

Coverage for: Individual + Spouse | **Plan Type:** PPO

Common Medical Event	Services You May Need	Your Cost If You Use a Participating Provider	Your Cost If You Use a Non-Participating Provider	Limitations & Exceptions
If you have mental health, behavioral health, or substance abuse needs	Mental/Behavioral health outpatient services	$35 copay/office visit and 20% coinsurance other outpatient services	40% coinsurance	-none-
	Mental/Behavioral health inpatient services	20% coinsurance	40% coinsurance	-none-
	Substance use disorder outpatient services	$35 copay/office visit and 20% coinsurance other outpatient services	40% coinsurance	-none-
	Substance use disorder inpatient services	20% coinsurance	40% coinsurance	-none-
If you are pregnant	Prenatal and postnatal care	20% coinsurance	40% coinsurance	-none-
	Delivery and all inpatient services	20% coinsurance	40% coinsurance	-none-
If you need help recovering or have other special health needs	Home health care	20% coinsurance	40% coinsurance	-none-
	Rehabilitation services	20% coinsurance	40% coinsurance	-none-
	Habilitation services	20% coinsurance	40% coinsurance	-none-
	Skilled nursing care	20% coinsurance	40% coinsurance	-none-
	Durable medical equipment	20% coinsurance	40% coinsurance	-none-
	Hospice service	20% coinsurance	40% coinsurance	-none-
If your child needs dental or eye care	Eye exam	$35 copay/ visit	Not Covered	Limited to one exam per year
	Glasses	20% coinsurance	Not Covered	Limited to one pair of glasses per year
	Dental check-up	No Charge	Not Covered	Covers up to $50 per year

Questions: Call 1-800-[insert] or visit us at www.[insert].
If you aren't clear about any of the underlined terms used in this form, see the Glossary. You can view the Glossary at www.[insert] or call 1-800-[insert] to request a copy.

Insurance Company 1: Plan Option 1

Coverage Period: 01/01/2014 – 12/31/2014

Summary of Benefits and Coverage: What this Plan Covers & What it Costs   **Coverage for:** Individual + Spouse | **Plan Type:** PPO

Excluded Services & Other Covered Services:

Services Your Plan Does NOT Cover (This isn't a complete list. Check your policy or plan document for other excluded services.)

- Cosmetic surgery
- Dental care (Adult)
- Infertility treatment

- Long-term care
- Non-emergency care when traveling outside the U.S.
- Private-duty nursing

- Routine eye care (Adult)
- Routine foot care

Other Covered Services (This isn't a complete list. Check your policy or plan document for other covered services and your costs for these services.)

- Acupuncture (if prescribed for rehabilitation purposes)
- Bariatric surgery

- Chiropractic care
- Hearing aids

- Most coverage provided outside the United States. See www.[insert]
- Weight loss programs

Questions: Call 1-800-[insert] or visit us at www.[insert].
If you aren't clear about any of the underlined terms used in this form, see the Glossary. You can view the Glossary at www.[insert] or call 1-800-[insert] to request a copy.

5 of 8

Insurance Company 1: Plan Option 1

Coverage Period: 01/01/2014 – 12/31/2014

Summary of Benefits and Coverage: What this Plan Covers & What it Costs   Coverage for: Individual + Spouse | **Plan Type:** PPO

Your Rights to Continue Coverage:

** Individual health insurance sample –

Federal and State laws may provide protections that allow you to keep this health insurance coverage as long as you pay your **premium**. There are exceptions, however, such as if:

- You commit fraud

- The insurer stops offering services in the State

- You move outside the coverage area

For more information on your rights to continue coverage, contact the insurer at [contact number]. You may also contact your state insurance department at [insert applicable State Department of Insurance contact information].

OR

** Group health coverage sample –

If you lose coverage under the plan, then, depending upon the circumstances, Federal and State laws may provide protections that allow you to keep health coverage. Any such rights may be limited in duration and will require you to pay a **premium,** which may be significantly higher than the premium you pay while covered under the plan. Other limitations on your rights to continue coverage may also apply.

For more information on your rights to continue coverage, contact the plan at [contact number]. You may also contact your state insurance department, the U.S. Department of Labor, Employee Benefits Security Administration at 1-866-444-3272 or www.dol.gov/ebsa, or the U.S. Department of Health and Human Services at 1-877-267-2323 x61565 or www.cciio.cms.gov.

Your Grievance and Appeals Rights:

If you have a complaint or are dissatisfied with a denial of coverage for claims under your plan, you may be able to **appeal** or file a **grievance**. For questions about your rights, this notice, or assistance, you can contact: [insert applicable contact information from instructions].

Does this Coverage Provide Minimum Essential Coverage?

The Affordable Care Act requires most people to have health care coverage that qualifies as "minimum essential coverage." **This plan or policy [does/ does not] provide minimum essential coverage.**

Does this Coverage Meet the Minimum Value Standard?

The Affordable Care Act establishes a minimum value standard of benefits of a health plan. The minimum value standard is 60% (actuarial value). **This health coverage [does/does not] meet the minimum value standard for the benefits it provides.**

––––––– *To see examples of how this plan might cover costs for a sample medical situation, see the next page.* –––––––

Questions: Call 1-800-[insert] or visit us at www.[insert].
If you aren't clear about any of the underlined terms used in this form, see the Glossary. You can view the Glossary at www.[insert] or call 1-800-[insert] to request a copy.

6 of 8

Insurance Company 1: Plan Option 1

Coverage Examples

Coverage Period: 1/1/2014 – 12/31/2014

Coverage for: Individual + Spouse | Plan Type: PPO

About these Coverage Examples:

These examples show how this plan might cover medical care in given situations. Use these examples to see, in general, how much financial protection a sample patient might get if they are covered under different plans.

This is not a cost estimator.

Don't use these examples to estimate your actual costs under this plan. The actual care you receive will be different from these examples, and the cost of that care will also be different.

See the next page for important information about these examples.

Having a baby
(normal delivery)

- **Amount owed to providers: $7,540**
- **Plan pays $5,490**
- **Patient pays $2,050**

Sample care costs:

Hospital charges (mother)	$2,700
Routine obstetric care	$2,100
Hospital charges (baby)	$900
Anesthesia	$900
Laboratory tests	$500
Prescriptions	$200
Radiology	$200
Vaccines, other preventive	$40
Total	**$7,540**

Patient pays:

Deductibles	$700
Copays	$30
Coinsurance	$1320
Limits or exclusions	$0
Total	**$2,050**

Managing type 2 diabetes
(routine maintenance of a well-controlled condition)

- **Amount owed to providers: $5,400**
- **Plan pays $3,520**
- **Patient pays $1,880**

Sample care costs:

Prescriptions	$2,900
Medical Equipment and Supplies	$1,300
Office Visits and Procedures	$700
Education	$300
Laboratory tests	$100
Vaccines, other preventive	$100
Total	**$5,400**

Patient pays:

Deductibles	$800
Copays	$500
Coinsurance	$500
Limits or exclusions	$80
Total	**$1,880**

Note: These numbers assume the patient is participating in our diabetes wellness program. If you have diabetes and do not participate in the wellness program, your costs may be higher. For more information about the diabetes wellness program, please contact: [insert].

Questions: Call 1-800-[insert] or visit us at www.[insert].
If you aren't clear about any of the underlined terms used in this form, see the Glossary. You can view the Glossary at www.[insert] or call 1-800-[insert] to request a copy.

Insurance Company 1: Plan Option 1

Coverage Examples

Coverage Period: 1/1/2014 – 12/31/2014

Coverage for: Individual + Spouse | Plan Type: PPO

Questions and answers about the Coverage Examples:

What are some of the assumptions behind the Coverage Examples?

- Costs don't include **premiums**.
- **Sample care costs** are based on national **averages** supplied by the U.S. Department of Health and Human Services, and aren't specific to a particular geographic area or health plan.
- The patient's condition was not an excluded or preexisting condition.
- All services and treatments started and ended in the same coverage period.
- There are no other medical expenses for any member covered under this plan.
- Out-of-pocket expenses are based only on treating the condition in the example.
- The patient received all care from in-network **providers**. If the patient had received care from out-of-network **providers**, costs would have been higher.

What does a Coverage Example show?

For each treatment situation, the Coverage Example helps you see how **deductibles**, **copayments**, and **coinsurance** can add up. It also helps you see what expenses might be left up to you to pay because the service or treatment isn't covered or payment is limited.

Does the Coverage Example predict my own care needs?

✖ **No.** Treatments shown are just examples. The care you would receive for this condition could be different based on your doctor's advice, your age, how serious your condition is, and many other factors.

Does the Coverage Example predict my future expenses?

✖ **No.** Coverage Examples are **not** cost estimators. You can't use the examples to estimate costs for an actual condition. They are for comparative purposes only. Your own costs will be different depending on the care you receive, the prices your **providers** charge, and the reimbursement your health plan allows.

Can I use Coverage Examples to compare plans?

✓ **Yes.** When you look at the Summary of Benefits and Coverage for other plans, you'll find the same Coverage Examples. When you compare plans, check the "Patient Pays" box in each example. The smaller that number, the more coverage the plan provides.

Are there other costs I should consider when comparing plans?

✓ **Yes.** An important cost is the **premium** you pay. Generally, the lower your **premium**, the more you'll pay in out-of-pocket costs, such as **copayments**, **deductibles**, and **coinsurance**. You should also consider contributions to accounts such as health savings accounts (HSAs), flexible spending arrangements (FSAs) or health reimbursement accounts (HRAs) that help you pay out-of-pocket expenses.

Questions: Call 1-800-[insert] or visit us at www.[insert].
If you aren't clear about any of the underlined terms used in this form, see the Glossary. You can view the Glossary at www.[insert] or call 1-800-[insert] to request a copy.

8 of 8

Glossary of Health Coverage and Medical Terms

- This glossary has many commonly used terms, but isn't a full list. These glossary terms and definitions are intended to be educational and may be different from the terms and definitions in your plan. Some of these terms also might not have exactly the same meaning when used in your policy or plan, and in any such case, the policy or plan governs. (See your Summary of Benefits and Coverage for information on how to get a copy of your policy or plan document.)
- Bold blue text indicates a term defined in this Glossary.
- See page 4 for an example showing how deductibles, co-insurance and out-of-pocket limits work together in a real life situation.

Allowed Amount

Maximum amount on which payment is based for covered health care services. This may be called "eligible expense," "payment allowance" or "negotiated rate." If your provider charges more than the allowed amount, you may have to pay the difference. (See Balance Billing.)

Appeal

A request for your health insurer or plan to review a decision or a grievance again.

Balance Billing

When a provider bills you for the difference between the provider's charge and the allowed amount. For example, if the provider's charge is $100 and the allowed amount is $70, the provider may bill you for the remaining $30. A preferred provider may **not** balance bill you for covered services.

Co-insurance

Your share of the costs of a covered health care service, calculated as a percent (for example, 20%) of the allowed amount for the service. You pay co-insurance **plus** any deductibles you owe. For example, if the health insurance or plan's allowed amount for an office visit is $100 and you've met your deductible, your co-insurance payment of 20% would be $20. The health insurance or plan pays the rest of the allowed amount.

Jane pays 20% Her plan pays 80%
(See page 4 for a detailed example.)

Complications of Pregnancy

Conditions due to pregnancy, labor and delivery that require medical care to prevent serious harm to the health of the mother or the fetus. Morning sickness and a non-emergency caesarean section aren't complications of pregnancy.

Co-payment

A fixed amount (for example, $15) you pay for a covered health care service, usually when you receive the service. The amount can vary by the type of covered health care service.

Deductible

The amount you owe for health care services your health insurance or plan covers before your health insurance or plan begins to pay. For example, if your deductible is $1000, your plan won't pay anything until you've met your $1000 deductible for covered health care services subject to the deductible. The deductible may not apply to all services.

Jane pays 100% Her plan pays 0%
(See page 4 for a detailed example.)

Durable Medical Equipment (DME)

Equipment and supplies ordered by a health care provider for everyday or extended use. Coverage for DME may include: oxygen equipment, wheelchairs, crutches or blood testing strips for diabetics.

Emergency Medical Condition

An illness, injury, symptom or condition so serious that a reasonable person would seek care right away to avoid severe harm.

Emergency Medical Transportation

Ambulance services for an emergency medical condition.

Emergency Room Care

Emergency services you get in an emergency room.

Emergency Services

Evaluation of an emergency medical condition **and** treatment to keep the condition from getting **worse.**

Excluded Services
Health care services that your health insurance or plan doesn't pay for or cover.

Grievance
A complaint that you communicate to your health insurer or plan.

Habilitation Services
Health care services that help a person keep, learn or improve skills and functioning for daily living. Examples include therapy for a child who isn't walking or talking at the expected age. These services may include physical and occupational therapy, speech-language pathology and other services for people with disabilities in a variety of inpatient and/or outpatient settings.

Health Insurance
A contract that requires your health insurer to pay some or all of your health care costs in exchange for a premium.

Home Health Care
Health care services a person receives at home.

Hospice Services
Services to provide comfort and support for persons in the last stages of a terminal illness and their families.

Hospitalization
Care in a hospital that requires admission as an inpatient and usually requires an overnight stay. An overnight stay for observation could be outpatient care.

Hospital Outpatient Care
Care in a hospital that usually doesn't require an overnight stay.

In-network Co-insurance
The percent (for example, 20%) you pay of the allowed amount for covered health care services to providers who contract with your health insurance or plan. In-network co-insurance usually costs you less than out-of-network co-insurance.

In-network Co-payment
A fixed amount (for example, $15) you pay for covered health care services to providers who contract with your health insurance or plan. In-network co-payments usually are less than out-of-network co-payments.

Medically Necessary
Health care services or supplies needed to prevent, diagnose or treat an illness, injury, condition, disease or its symptoms and that meet accepted standards of medicine.

Network
The facilities, providers and suppliers your health insurer or plan has contracted with to provide health care services.

Non-Preferred Provider
A provider who doesn't have a contract with your health insurer or plan to provide services to you. You'll pay more to see a non-preferred provider. Check your policy to see if you can go to all providers who have contracted with your health insurance or plan, or if your health insurance or plan has a "tiered" network and you must pay extra to see some providers.

Out-of-network Co-insurance
The percent (for example, 40%) you pay of the allowed amount for covered health care services to providers who do *not* contract with your health insurance or plan. Out-of-network co-insurance usually costs you more than in-network co-insurance.

Out-of-network Co-payment
A fixed amount (for example, $30) you pay for covered health care services from providers who do *not* contract with your health insurance or plan. Out-of-network co-payments usually are more than in-network co-payments.

Out-of-Pocket Limit
The most you pay during a policy period (usually a year) before your health insurance or plan begins to pay 100% of the allowed amount. This limit never includes your premium, balance-billed charges or health care your health insurance or plan doesn't cover. Some health insurance or plans don't count all of your co-payments, deductibles, co-insurance payments, out-of-network payments or other expenses toward this limit.

Jane pays	Her plan pays
0%	100%

(See page 4 for a detailed example.)

Physician Services
Health care services a licensed medical physician (M.D. – Medical Doctor or D.O. – Doctor of Osteopathic Medicine) provides or coordinates.

Plan

A benefit your employer, union or other group sponsor provides to you to pay for your health care services.

Preauthorization

A decision by your health insurer or plan that a health care service, treatment plan, prescription drug or durable medical equipment is medically necessary. Sometimes called prior authorization, prior approval or precertification. Your health insurance or plan may require preauthorization for certain services before you receive them, except in an emergency. Preauthorization isn't a promise your health insurance or plan will cover the cost.

Preferred Provider

A provider who has a contract with your health insurer or plan to provide services to you at a discount. Check your policy to see if you can see all preferred providers or if your health insurance or plan has a "tiered" network and you must pay extra to see some providers. Your health insurance or plan may have preferred providers who are also "participating" providers. Participating providers also contract with your health insurer or plan, but the discount may not be as great, and you may have to pay more.

Premium

The amount that must be paid for your health insurance or plan. You and/or your employer usually pay it monthly, quarterly or yearly.

Prescription Drug Coverage

Health insurance or plan that helps pay for prescription drugs and medications.

Prescription Drugs

Drugs and medications that by law require a prescription.

Primary Care Physician

A physician (M.D. – Medical Doctor or D.O. – Doctor of Osteopathic Medicine) who directly provides or coordinates a range of health care services for a patient.

Primary Care Provider

A physician (M.D. – Medical Doctor or D.O. – Doctor of Osteopathic Medicine), nurse practitioner, clinical nurse specialist or physician assistant, as allowed under state law, who provides, coordinates or helps a patient access a range of health care services.

Provider

A physician (M.D. – Medical Doctor or D.O. – Doctor of Osteopathic Medicine), health care professional or health care facility licensed, certified or accredited as required by state law.

Reconstructive Surgery

Surgery and follow-up treatment needed to correct or improve a part of the body because of birth defects, accidents, injuries or medical conditions.

Rehabilitation Services

Health care services that help a person keep, get back or improve skills and functioning for daily living that have been lost or impaired because a person was sick, hurt or disabled. These services may include physical and occupational therapy, speech-language pathology and psychiatric rehabilitation services in a variety of inpatient and/or outpatient settings.

Skilled Nursing Care

Services from licensed nurses in your own home or in a nursing home. Skilled care services are from technicians and therapists in your own home or in a nursing home.

Specialist

A physician specialist focuses on a specific area of medicine or a group of patients to diagnose, manage, prevent or treat certain types of symptoms and conditions. A non-physician specialist is a provider who has more training in a specific area of health care.

UCR (Usual, Customary and Reasonable)

The amount paid for a medical service in a geographic area based on what providers in the area usually charge for the same or similar medical service. The UCR amount sometimes is used to determine the allowed amount.

Urgent Care

Care for an illness, injury or condition serious enough that a reasonable person would seek care right away, but not so severe as to require emergency room care.

How You and Your Insurer Share Costs - Example

Jane's Plan Deductible: $1,500   **Co-insurance:** 20%   **Out-of-Pocket Limit:** $5,000

January 1st
Beginning of Coverage Period

December 31st
End of Coverage Period

Jane pays
100%

Her plan pays
0%

Jane hasn't reached her $1,500 deductible yet

Her plan doesn't pay any of the costs.
Office visit costs: $125
Jane pays: $125
Her plan pays: $0

↑ more costs

Jane pays
20%

Her plan pays
80%

Jane reaches her $1,500 deductible, co-insurance begins

Jane has seen a doctor several times and paid $1,500 in total. Her plan pays some of the costs for her next visit.
Office visit costs: $75
Jane pays: 20% of $75 = $15
Her plan pays: 80% of $75 = $60

↑ more costs

Jane pays
0%

Her plan pays
100%

Jane reaches her $5,000 out-of-pocket limit

Jane has seen the doctor often and paid $5,000 in total. Her plan pays the full cost of her covered health care services for the rest of the year.
Office visit costs: $200
Jane pays: $0
Her plan pays: $200

APPENDIX B

U.S. Department of Labor Model Notices

Among the new PPACA Claims Regulations is a requirement that Notices be provided in a culturally and linguistically appropriate manner and must comply with certain content requirements. Details of the regulations are discussed in this book.

Nine model notices that have been issued by the Labor Department are reproduced in Appendix B.

Source: United States Department of Labor. The links to the three Claims Regulations Model Notices can be found at the bottom of the page at: http://www.dol.gov/ebsa/newsroom/tr11-02.html. The online locations of the other notices are noted at the bottom of each.

Model Notice of Final Internal Adverse Benefit Determination – Revised as of June 22, 2011

Date of Notice
Name of Plan   **Telephone/Fax**
Address   **Website/Email Address**

This document contains important information that you should retain for your records.

This document serves as notice of a final internal adverse benefit determination. We have declined to provide benefits, in whole or in part, for the requested treatment or service described below. If you think this determination was made in error, you may have the right to appeal (see the back of this page for information about your appeal rights).

Internal Appeal Case Details:

Patient Name:				ID Number:			
Address: (street, county, state, zip)							
Claim #:				**Date of Service:**			
Provider:							
Reason for Upholding Denial (in whole or in part):							
Amt. Charged	**Allowed Amt.**	**Other Insurance**	**Deductible**	**Co-pay**	**Coinsurance**	**Other Amts. Not Covered**	**Amt. Paid**
YTD Credit toward Deductible:				**YTD Credit toward Out-of-Pocket Maximum:**			
Description of Service:				**Denial Codes:**			

[If denial is not related to a specific claim, only name and ID number need to be included in the box. The reason for the denial would need to be clear in the narrative below.]

Background Information: *Describe facts of the case including type of appeal and date appeal filed.*

Final Internal Adverse Benefit Determination: *State that adverse benefit determination has been upheld. List all documents and statements that were reviewed to make this final internal adverse benefit determination.*

Findings: *Discuss the reason or reasons for the final internal adverse benefit determination.*

[Insert language assistance disclosure here, if applicable.

SPANISH (Español): Para obtener asistencia en Español, llame al [insert telephone number].
TAGALOG (Tagalog): Kung kailangan ninyo ang tulong sa Tagalog tumawag sa [insert telephone number].
CHINESE (中文): 如果需要中文的帮助，请拨打这个号码 [insert telephone number]。
NAVAJO (Dine): Dinek'ehgo shika at'ohwol ninisingo, kwiijigo holne' [insert telephone number].]

OMB Control Number 1210-0144 (expires 04/30/2014)

Model Notice of Final Internal Adverse Benefit Determination – Revised as of June 22, 2011

Important Information about Your Rights to External Review

What if I need help understanding this denial? Contact us [insert contact information] if you need assistance understanding this notice or our decision to deny you a service or coverage.

What if I don't agree with this decision? For certain types of claims, you are entitled to request an independent, external review of our decision. Contact [insert external review contact information] with any questions on your rights to external review. [For insured coverage, insert: If your claim is not eligible for independent external review but you still disagree with the denial, your state insurance regulator may be able to help to resolve the dispute.] See the "Other resources section" of this form for help filing a request for external review.

How do I file a request for external review? Complete the bottom of this page, make a copy, and send this document to {insert address}.] [or] [insert alternative instructions.] See also the "Other resources to help you" section of this form for assistance filing a request for external review.

What if my situation is urgent? If your situation meets the definition of urgent under the law, the external review of your claim will be conducted as expeditiously as possible. Generally, an urgent situation is one in which your health may be in serious jeopardy or, in the opinion of your physician, you may experience pain that cannot be adequately controlled while you wait for a decision on the external review of your claim. If you believe your situation is urgent, you may request an expedited external review by [insert instructions to begin the process (such as by phone, fax, electronic submission, etc.)].

Who may file a request for external review? You or someone you name to act for you (your authorized representative) may file a request for external review. [Insert information on how to designate an authorized representative.]

Can I provide additional information about my claim? Yes, once your external review is initiated, you will receive instructions on how to supply additional information.

Can I request copies of information relevant to my claim? Yes, you may request copies (free of charge) by contacting us at [insert contact information].

What happens next? If you request an external review, an independent organization will review our decision and provide you with a written determination. If this organization decides to overturn our decision, we will provide coverage or payment for your health care item or service.

Other resources to help you: For questions about your rights, this notice, or for assistance, you can contact: [if coverage is group health plan coverage, insert: the Employee Benefits Security Administration at 1-866-444-EBSA (3272)] [and/or] [if coverage is insured, insert State Department of Insurance contact information]. [Insert, if applicable in your state: Additionally, a consumer assistance program can help you file your appeal. Contact:[insert contact information].]

NAME OF PERSON FILING REQUEST FOR EXTERNAL REVIEW: _____

Circle one: Covered person   Patient   Authorized Representative

Contact information of person filing request for external review (if different from patient)

Address:_____**Daytime phone:**_____**Email:**_____

If person filing request for external review is other than patient, patient must indicate authorization by signing here:_____

Are you requesting an urgent review?   Yes   No

Briefly describe why you disagree with this decision (you may attach additional information, such as a physician's letter, bills, medical records, or other documents to support your claim):

_____

Send this form and your denial notice to: [Insert name and contact information]

Be certain to keep copies of this form, your denial notice, and all documents and correspondence related to this claim.

Model Notice of Adverse Benefit Determination – Revised as of June 22, 2011

Date of Notice
Name of Plan   **Telephone/Fax**
Address   **Website/Email Address**

This document contains important information that you should retain for your records.

This document serves as notice of an adverse benefit determination. We have declined to provide benefits, in whole or in part, for the requested treatment or service described below. If you think this determination was made in error, you have the right to appeal (see the back of this page for information about your appeal rights).

Case Details:

Patient Name:	ID Number:
Address: (street, county, state, zip)	
Claim #:	**Date of Service:**
Provider:	

Reason for Denial (in whole or in part):

Amt. Charged	Allowed Amt.	Other Insurance	Deductible	Co-pay	Coinsurance	Other Amts. Not Covered	Amt. Paid

YTD Credit toward Deductible:	YTD Credit toward Out-of-Pocket Maximum:	
Description of service:	**Denial Codes:**	

[If denial is not related to a specific claim, only name and ID number need to be included in the box. The reason for the denial would need to be clear in the narrative below.]

Explanation of Basis for Determination:

If the claim is denied (in whole or in part) and there is more explanation for the basis of the denial, such as the definition of a plan or policy term, include that information here.

[Insert language assistance disclosure here, if applicable.

SPANISH (Español): Para obtener asistencia en Español, llame al [insert telephone number].
TAGALOG (Tagalog): Kung kailangan ninyo ang tulong sa Tagalog tumawag sa [insert telephone number].
CHINESE (中文): 如果需要中文的帮助，请拨打这个号码 [insert telephone number]。
NAVAJO (Dine): Dinek'ehgo shika at'ohwol ninisingo, kwiijigo holne' [insert telephone number].]

OMB Control Number 1210-0144 (expires 04/30/2014)

Model Notice of Adverse Benefit Determination – Revised as of June 22, 2011

Important Information about Your Appeal Rights

What if I need help understanding this denial?
Contact us at [insert contact information] if you need
assistance understanding this notice or our decision to
deny you a service or coverage.

What if I don't agree with this decision? You have a
right to appeal any decision not to provide or pay for
an item or service (in whole or in part).

How do I file an appeal? [Complete the bottom of
this page, make a copy, and send this document to
{insert address}.] [or] [insert alternative instructions]
See also the "Other resources to help you" section of
this form for assistance filing a request for an appeal.

What if my situation is urgent? If your situation
meets the definition of urgent under the law, your
review will generally be conducted within 72 hours.
Generally, an urgent situation is one in which your
health may be in serious jeopardy or, in the opinion of
your physician, you may experience pain that cannot
be adequately controlled while you wait for a decision
on your appeal. If you believe your situation is urgent,
you may request an expedited appeal by following the
instructions above for filing an internal appeal and also
[insert instructions for filing request for simultaneous
external review)].

Who may file an appeal? You or someone you name
to act for you (your authorized representative) may file
an appeal. [Insert information on how to designate an
authorized representative.]

**Can I provide additional information about my
claim?** Yes, you may supply additional information.
[Insert any applicable procedures for submission of
additional information.]

**Can I request copies of information relevant to my
claim?** Yes, you may request copies (free of charge).
If you think a coding error may have caused this claim
to be denied, you have the right to have billing and
diagnosis codes sent to you, as well. You can request
copies of this information by contacting us at [insert
contact information].

What happens next? If you appeal, we will review
our decision and provide you with a written
determination. If we continue to deny the payment,
coverage, or service requested or you do not receive a
timely decision, you may be able to request an external
review of your claim by an independent third party,
who will review the denial and issue a final decision.

Other resources to help you: For questions about
your rights, this notice, or for assistance, you can
contact: [if coverage is group health plan coverage,
insert: the Employee Benefits Security Administration
at 1-866-444-EBSA (3272)] [and/or] [if coverage is
insured, insert State Department of Insurance contact
information]. [Insert, if applicable in your state:
Additionally, a consumer assistance program can help
you file your appeal. Contact [insert contact
information].]

Appeal Filing Form

NAME OF PERSON FILING APPEAL: _____
Circle one: Covered person   Patient   Authorized Representative
Contact information of person filing appeal (if different from patient)
Address:_____**Daytime phone:**_____**Email:**_____

If person filing appeal is other than patient, patient must indicate authorization by signing here:
_____

Are you requesting an urgent appeal?   Yes   No

Briefly describe why you disagree with this decision (you may attach additional information, such as a
physician's letter, bills, medical records, or other documents to support your claim)**:**
_____
_____

Send this form and your denial notice to: [Insert name and contact information]
**Be certain to keep copies of this form, your denial notice, and all documents and correspondence related
to this claim.**

Model Notice of Final External Review Decision – Revised June 22, 2011

Date of Notice
Name of Plan   **Telephone/Fax**
Address   **Website/Email Address**

This document contains important information that you should retain for your records.

This document serves as notice of a final external review decision. We have
[upheld/overturned/modified] the denial of your request for the provision of, or payment for, a
health care service or course of treatment.

Historical Case Details:

Patient Name:				ID Number:				
Address: (street, county, state, zip)								
Claim #:				Date of Service:				
Provider:								
Reason for Denial (in whole or in part):								
Amt. Charged	Allowed Amt.	Other Insurance	Deductible	Co-pay		Coinsurance	Other Amts. Not Covered	Amt. Paid
YTD Credit toward Deductible:				YTD Credit toward Out-of-Pocket Maximum:				
Description of Service:				Denial Codes:				

[If denial is not related to a specific claim, only name and ID number need to be included in the box. The reason for the denial would need to be clear in the narrative below.]

Background Information: *Describe facts of the case including type of appeal, date appeal filed, date appeal was received by IRO and date IRO decision was made.*

Final External Review Decision: *State decision. List all documents and statements that were reviewed to make this final external review decision.*

Findings: *Discuss the principal reason or reasons for IRO decision, including the rationale and any evidence-based standards or coverage provisions that were relied on in making this decision.*

OMB Control Number 1210-0144 (expires 04/30/2014)

Model Notice of Final External Review Decision – Revised June 22, 2011
Important Information about Your Appeal Rights

What if I need help understanding this decision?
Contact us [insert IRO contact information] if you need assistance understanding this notice.

What happens now? If we have overturned the denial, your plan or health insurance issuer will now provide service or payment.

If we have upheld the denial, there is no further review available under the appeals process. However, you may have other remedies available under State or Federal law, such as filing a lawsuit.

Other resources to help you: For questions about your appeal rights, this notice, or for assistance, you can contact [if coverage is group health plan coverage, insert: the Employee Benefits Security Administration at 1-866-444-EBSA (3272)] [and/or] [if coverage is insured, insert State Department of Insurance contact information]. [Insert, if applicable in your state: Additionally, you can contact your consumer assistance program at [insert contact information].]

New Health Insurance Marketplace Coverage
Options and Your Health Coverage

Form Approved
OMB No. 1210-0149
(expires 11-30-2013)

PART A: General Information

When key parts of the health care law take effect in 2014, there will be a new way to buy health insurance: the Health Insurance Marketplace. To assist you as you evaluate options for you and your family, this notice provides some basic information about the new Marketplace and employment-based health coverage offered by your employer.

What is the Health Insurance Marketplace?

The Marketplace is designed to help you find health insurance that meets your needs and fits your budget. The Marketplace offers "one-stop shopping" to find and compare private health insurance options. You may also be eligible for a new kind of tax credit that lowers your monthly premium right away. Open enrollment for health insurance coverage through the Marketplace begins in October 2013 for coverage starting as early as January 1, 2014.

Can I Save Money on my Health Insurance Premiums in the Marketplace?

You may qualify to save money and lower your monthly premium, but only if your employer does not offer coverage, or offers coverage that doesn't meet certain standards. The savings on your premium that you're eligible for depends on your household income.

Does Employer Health Coverage Affect Eligibility for Premium Savings through the Marketplace?

Yes. If you have an offer of health coverage from your employer that meets certain standards, you will not be eligible for a tax credit through the Marketplace and may wish to enroll in your employer's health plan. However, you may be eligible for a tax credit that lowers your monthly premium, or a reduction in certain cost-sharing if your employer does not offer coverage to you at all or does not offer coverage that meets certain standards. If the cost of a plan from your employer that would cover you (and not any other members of your family) is more than 9.5% of your household income for the year, or if the coverage your employer provides does not meet the "minimum value" standard set by the Affordable Care Act, you may be eligible for a tax credit.[1]

Note: If you purchase a health plan through the Marketplace instead of accepting health coverage offered by your employer, then you may lose the employer contribution (if any) to the employer-offered coverage. Also, this employer contribution -as well as your employee contribution to employer-offered coverage- is often excluded from income for Federal and State income tax purposes. Your payments for coverage through the Marketplace are made on an after-tax basis.

How Can I Get More Information?

For more information about your coverage offered by your employer, please check your summary plan description or contact _____ .

The Marketplace can help you evaluate your coverage options, including your eligibility for coverage through the Marketplace and its cost. Please visit HealthCare.gov for more information, including an online application for health insurance coverage and contact information for a Health Insurance Marketplace in your area.

---

[1] An employer-sponsored health plan meets the "minimum value standard" if the plan's share of the total allowed benefit costs covered by the plan is no less than 60 percent of such costs.

PART B: Information About Health Coverage Offered by Your Employer

This section contains information about any health coverage offered by your employer. If you decide to complete an application for coverage in the Marketplace, you will be asked to provide this information. This information is numbered to correspond to the Marketplace application.

3. Employer name		4. Employer Identification Number (EIN)	
5. Employer address		6. Employer phone number	
7. City		8. State	9. ZIP code
10. Who can we contact about employee health coverage at this job?			
11. Phone number (if different from above)	12. Email address		

Here is some basic information about health coverage offered by this employer:

- As your employer, we offer a health plan to:
  - ☐ All employees.

  - ☐ Some employees. Eligible employees are:

- With respect to dependents:
  - ☐ We do offer coverage. Eligible dependents are:

  - ☐ We do not offer coverage.

☐ If checked, this coverage meets the minimum value standard, and the cost of this coverage to you is intended to be affordable, based on employee wages.

  ** Even if your employer intends your coverage to be affordable, you may still be eligible for a premium discount through the Marketplace. The Marketplace will use your household income, along with other factors, to determine whether you may be eligible for a premium discount. If, for example, your wages vary from week to week (perhaps you are an hourly employee or you work on a commission basis), if you are newly employed mid-year, or if you have other income losses, you may still qualify for a premium discount.

If you decide to shop for coverage in the Marketplace, **HealthCare.gov** will guide you through the process. Here's the employer information you'll enter when you visit **HealthCare.gov** to find out if you can get a tax credit to lower your monthly premiums.

The information below corresponds to the Marketplace Employer Coverage Tool. Completing this section is optional for employers, but will help ensure employees understand their coverage choices.

---

13. Is the employee currently eligible for coverage offered by this employer, or will the employee be eligible in the next 3 months?

☐ **Yes** (Continue)

    13a. If the employee is not eligible today, including as a result of a waiting or probationary period, when is the

    employee eligible for coverage? _____ (mm/dd/yyyy) (Continue)

☐ **No** (STOP and return this form to employee)

---

14. Does the employer offer a health plan that meets the minimum value standard*?
    ☐ Yes (Go to question 15) ☐ No (STOP and return form to employee)

15. For the lowest-cost plan that meets the minimum value standard* offered **only to the employee** (don't include family plans): If the employer has wellness programs, provide the premium that the employee would pay if he/ she received the maximum discount for any tobacco cessation programs, and didn't receive any other discounts based on wellness programs.
    a. How much would the employee have to pay in premiums for this plan? $
    b. How often? ☐ Weekly ☐ Every 2 weeks ☐ Twice a month ☐ Monthly ☐ Quarterly ☐ Yearly

If the plan year will end soon and you know that the health plans offered will change, go to question 16. If you don't know, STOP and return form to employee.

---

16. What change will the employer make for the new plan year?
    ☐ Employer won't offer health coverage
    ☐ Employer will start offering health coverage to employees or change the premium for the lowest-cost plan available only to the employee that meets the minimum value standard.* (Premium should reflect the discount for wellness programs. See question 15.)
    a. How much will the employee have to pay in premiums for that plan? $
    b. How often? ☐ Weekly ☐ Every 2 weeks ☐ Twice a month ☐ Monthly ☐ Quarterly ☐ Yearly

    Date of change (mm/dd/yyyy):

---

* An employer–sponsored health plan meets the "minimum value standard" if the plan's share of the total allowed benefit costs covered by the plan is no less than 60 percent of such costs (Section 36B(c)(2)(C)(ii) of the Internal Revenue Code of 1986)

New Health Insurance Marketplace Coverage Options and Your Health Coverage

Form Approved
OMB No. 1210-0149
(expires 11-30-2013)

PART A: General Information

When key parts of the health care law take effect in 2014, there will be a new way to buy health insurance: the Health Insurance Marketplace. To assist you as you evaluate options for you and your family, this notice provides some basic information about the new Marketplace.

What is the Health Insurance Marketplace?

The Marketplace is designed to help you find health insurance that meets your needs and fits your budget. The Marketplace offers "one-stop shopping" to find and compare private health insurance options. You may also be eligible for a new kind of tax credit that lowers your monthly premium right away. Open enrollment for health insurance coverage through the Marketplace begins in October 2013 for coverage starting as early as January 1, 2014.

Can I Save Money on my Health Insurance Premiums in the Marketplace?

You may qualify to save money and lower your monthly premium, but only if your employer does not offer coverage, or offers coverage that doesn't meet certain standards. The savings on your premium that you're eligible for depends on your household income.

Does Employer Health Coverage Affect Eligibility for Premium Savings through the Marketplace?

Yes. If you have an offer of health coverage from your employer that meets certain standards, you will not be eligible for a tax credit through the Marketplace and may wish to enroll in your employer's health plan. However, you may be eligible for a tax credit that lowers your monthly premium, or a reduction in certain cost-sharing if your employer does not offer coverage to you at all or does not offer coverage that meets certain standards. If the cost of a plan from your employer that would cover you (and not any other members of your family) is more than 9.5% of your household income for the year, or if the coverage your employer provides does not meet the "minimum value" standard set by the Affordable Care Act, you may be eligible for a tax credit.[1]

Note: If you purchase a health plan through the Marketplace instead of accepting health coverage offered by your employer, then you may lose the employer contribution (if any) to the employer-offered coverage. Also, this employer contribution –as well as your employee contribution to employer-offered coverage– is often excluded from income for Federal and State income tax purposes. Your payments for coverage through the Marketplace are made on an after-tax basis.

How Can I Get More Information?

The Marketplace can help you evaluate your coverage options, including your eligibility for coverage through the Marketplace and its cost. Please visit HealthCare.gov for more information, including an online application for health insurance coverage and contact information for a Health Insurance Marketplace in your area.

---

[1] An employer-sponsored health plan meets the "minimum value standard" if the plan's share of the total allowed benefit costs covered by the plan is no less than 60 percent of such costs.

PART B: Information About Health Coverage Offered by Your Employer

This section contains information about any health coverage offered by your employer. If you decide to complete an application for coverage in the Marketplace, you will be asked to provide this information. This information is numbered to correspond to the Marketplace application.

3. Employer name	4. Employer Identification Number (EIN)	
5. Employer address	6. Employer phone number	
7. City	8. State	9. ZIP code
10. Who can we contact at this job?		
11. Phone number (if different from above)	12. Email address	

You are not eligible for health insurance coverage through this employer. You and your family may be able to obtain health coverage through the Marketplace, with a new kind of tax credit that lowers your monthly premiums and with assistance for out-of-pocket costs.

Model Notice – Opportunity To Enroll In Connection With Extension Of Dependent Coverage To Age 26

The interim final regulations extending dependent coverage to age 26 provide transitional relief for a child whose coverage ended, or who was denied coverage (or was not eligible for coverage) under a group health plan or health insurance coverage because, under the terms of the plan or coverage, the availability of dependent coverage of children ended before the attainment of age 26. The regulations require a plan or issuer to give such a child an opportunity to enroll that continues for at least 30 days (including written notice of the opportunity to enroll), regardless of whether the plan or coverage offers an open enrollment period and regardless of when any open enrollment period might otherwise occur. This enrollment opportunity (including the written notice) must be provided not later than the first day of the first plan year beginning on or after September 23, 2010. The notice may be included with other enrollment materials that a plan distributes, provided the statement is prominent. Enrollment must be effective as of the first day of the first plan year beginning on or after September 23, 2010.

The following model language can be used to satisfy the notice requirement:

Individuals whose coverage ended, or who were denied coverage (or were not eligible for coverage), because the availability of dependent coverage of children ended before attainment of age 26 are eligible to enroll in [Insert name of group health plan or health insurance coverage]. Individuals may request enrollment for such children for 30 days from the date of notice. Enrollment will be effective retroactively to [insert date that is the first day of the first plan year beginning on or after September 23, 2010.] For more information contact the [insert plan administrator or issuer] at [insert contact information].

Model Notice – Patient Protection; Right To Choose Pediatrician Or Ob/Gyn As Primary Provider

When applicable, it is important that individuals enrolled in a plan or health insurance coverage know of their rights to (1) choose a primary care provider or a pediatrician when a plan or issuer requires designation of a primary care physician; or (2) obtain obstetrical or gynecological care without prior authorization. Accordingly, the interim final regulations regarding patient protections under section 2719A of the Affordable Care Act require plans and issuers to provide notice to participants of these rights when applicable. The notice must be provided whenever the plan or issuer provides a participant with a summary plan description or other similar description of benefits under the plan or health insurance coverage. This notice must be provided no later than the first day of the first plan year beginning on or after September 23, 2010.

The following model language can be used to satisfy the notice requirement.

For plans and issuers that require or allow for the designation of primary care providers by participants or beneficiaries, insert:

> [Name of group health plan or health insurance issuer] generally [requires/allows] the designation of a primary care provider. You have the right to designate any primary care provider who participates in our network and who is available to accept you or your family members. [If the plan or health insurance coverage designates a primary care provider automatically, insert: Until you make this designation, [name of group health plan or health insurance issuer] designates one for you.] For information on how to select a primary care provider, and for a list of the participating primary care providers, contact the [plan administrator or issuer] at [insert contact information].

For plans and issuers that require or allow for the designation of a primary care provider for a child, add:

> For children, you may designate a pediatrician as the primary care provider.

For plans and issuers that provide coverage for obstetric or gynecological care and require the designation by a participant or beneficiary of a primary care provider, add:

> You do not need prior authorization from [name of group health plan or issuer] or from any other person (including a primary care provider) in order to obtain access to obstetrical or gynecological care from a health care professional in our network who specializes in obstetrics or gynecology. The health care professional, however, may be required to comply with certain procedures, including obtaining prior authorization for certain services, following a pre-approved treatment plan, or procedures for making referrals. For a list of participating health care professionals who specialize in obstetrics or gynecology, contact the [plan administrator or issuer] at [insert contact information].

Model Notice – Grandfathered Plan

This [group health plan or health insurance issuer] believes this [plan or coverage] is a "grandfathered health plan" under the Patient Protection and Affordable Care Act (the Affordable Care Act). As permitted by the Affordable Care Act, a grandfathered health plan can preserve certain basic health coverage that was already in effect when that law was enacted. Being a grandfathered health plan means that your [plan or policy] may not include certain consumer protections of the Affordable Care Act that apply to other plans, for example, the requirement for the provision of preventive health services without any cost sharing. However, grandfathered health plans must comply with certain other consumer protections in the Affordable Care Act, for example, the elimination of lifetime limits on benefits.

Questions regarding which protections apply and which protections do not apply to a grandfathered health plan and what might cause a plan to change from grandfathered health plan status can be directed to the plan administrator at [insert contact information]. [For ERISA plans, insert: You may also contact the Employee Benefits Security Administration, U.S. Department of Labor at 1-866-444-3272 or www.dol.gov/ebsa/healthreform. This website has a table summarizing which protections do and do not apply to grandfathered health plans.] [For individual market policies and nonfederal governmental plans, insert: You may also contact the U.S. Department of Health and Human Services at www.healthreform.gov.]

Model Notice – Lifetime Limit No Longer Applies & Health Plan Enrollment Opportunity

Plans and issuers are required to give written notice that the lifetime limit on the dollar value of all benefits no longer applies and that an individual, if covered, is once again eligible for benefits under the plan. Additionally, if the individual is not enrolled in the plan or health insurance coverage, or if an enrolled individual is eligible for but not enrolled in any benefit package under the plan or health insurance coverage, then the plan or issuer must also give such an individual an opportunity to enroll that continues for at least 30 days (including written notice of the opportunity to enroll). The notices and enrollment opportunity must be provided beginning not later than the first day of the first plan year beginning on or after September 23, 2010. For individuals who enroll under this opportunity, coverage must take effect not later than the first day of the first plan year beginning on or after September 23, 2010.

These notices may be provided to an employee on behalf of the employee's dependent. In addition, the notices may be included with other enrollment materials that a plan distributes to employees, provided the statement is prominent. For either notice, if a notice satisfying the requirements is provided to an individual, the obligation to provide the notice with respect to that individual is satisfied for both the plan and the issuer.

The following model language can be used to satisfy the notice requirement:

The lifetime limit on the dollar value of benefits under [Insert name of group health plan or health insurance issuer] no longer applies. Individuals whose coverage ended by reason of reaching a lifetime limit under the plan are eligible to enroll in the plan. Individuals have 30 days from the date of this notice to request enrollment. For more information contact the [insert plan administrator or issuer] at [insert contact information].

INDEX

References are to question numbers.

References are to question numbers.

References are to question numbers.

References are to question numbers.

References are to question numbers.

References are to question numbers.

References are to question numbers.